Upgrading To and Troubleshooting Windows Vista

Other Computer Titles

by

Robert Penfold

Upgrading To and Troubleshooting Windows Vista

Robert Penfold

Bernard Babani (publishing) Ltd
The Grampians
Shepherds Bush Road
London W6 7NF
England
www.babanibooks.com

Please note

Although every care has been taken with the production of this book to ensure that any projects, designs, modifications, and/or programs, etc., contained herewith, operate in a correct and safe manner and also that any components specified are normally available in Great Britain, the Publisher and Author do not accept responsibility in any way for the failure (including fault in design) of any projects, design, modification, or program to work correctly or to cause damage to any equipment that it may be connected to or used in conjunction with, or in respect of any other damage or injury that may be caused, nor do the Publishers accept responsibility in any way for the failure to obtain specified components.

Notice is also given that if any equipment that is still under warranty is modified in any way or used or connected with home-built equipment then that warranty may be void.

© 2007 BERNARD BABANI (publishing) LTD

First Published - April 2007

British Library Cataloguing in Publication Data
A catalogue record for this book is available from the British Library

ISBN   978 0 85934 579 8

Cover Design by Gregor Arthur
Printed and bound in Great Britain by Cox and Wyman

Preface

Although the Windows operating systems are widely regarded as having a lack of stability, this reputation is not entirely fair. Software as complex as any version of Windows is never likely to be fully debugged, but it is not really any built-in bugs that are the major problem with Windows. It is the alterations that are made to the operating system after the basic installation process has been completed. The operating system is added to and altered each time any hardware or major piece of software is added or removed. Windows can be used with an enormous range of software and hardware, but this leaves it vulnerable to problems that originate in hardware drivers, installation programs, and uninstallers. Applications programs can also introduce difficulties if they do not strictly abide by the rules involving memory management, file naming, etc.

Windows XP was more robust than earlier versions of the operating system such as Windows ME, and it was designed to do a good job of defending itself against incompatible drivers and applications software. Windows Vista does an even better job of guarding itself against damage, but Vista it is still not immune to problems. It is doubtful if an operating system can ever be made totally "bomb proof". In order to be usable an operating system must be flexible, but this flexibility inevitably leaves it vulnerable to problems.

Ideally the user would install Windows Vista and some applications programs, and then make no further changes to the system. For most users this is not practical though, and new hardware has to be added, software upgrades have to be installed from time to time, and so on. Most modern PCs tend to evolve over a period of time, and the operating system has to change to accommodate this evolution. If Windows Vista should cease working it is not usually too difficult to get it up and running again. Most faults introduced into the system are easily reversed, provided you know how. This book details some simple procedures that enable most Windows Vista faults to be quickly pinpointed and rectified. You do not have to be a computer expert in order to follow these procedures, but you do have to be familiar with the basics of using the Windows Vista user interface.

Where a Windows Vista installation becomes seriously damaged it may not be practical to repair it. Even if numerous files have been corrupted or deleted it is probably possible to repair the installation given enough time, but the more sensible approach is to reinstall the operating system.

Full instructions for reinstalling Windows are provided, including reinstallation over an existing version and the "from scratch" approach. Either option may seem to be a rather daunting prospect for those of limited experience at Windows troubleshooting, but reinstalling Windows Vista is not particularly difficult. It is the guaranteed method of curing Windows Vista problems and getting your PC back in full working order again.

In general, the contents of this book apply equally to all versions of Windows Vista. There are some sections that are only relevant to certain versions, but where applicable this is pointed out in the text. It should also be borne in mind that some PCs are supplied with Windows Vista preinstalled, and have some form of "Emergency" disc that can be used to reinstall Windows Vista. Such PCs do not always have the normal installation disc, which is needed to perform some of the tasks described in this book. The normal installation disc is often offered as an optional extra, and it is probably worth paying the extra in order to obtain the extra facilities it provides.

Robert Penfold

Trademarks

Microsoft, Windows, Windows Media Player, WMA, WMV, Windows Vista, Windows XP, Windows Me, Windows 98 and Windows 95 are either registered trademarks or trademarks of Microsoft Corporation.

All other brand and product names used in this book are recognised trademarks, or registered trademarks of their respective companies.

Contents

1

Upgrading problems 1

2

Prevention is................................. 69

3

Troubleshooting 147

4

Data rescue 197

5

Back up and restore 247

6

Reinstallation 297

Please note

Windows Vista includes security features that are designed to prevent malicious or accidental damage to the system. Many of the configuration adjustments, etc., described in this book produce a pop-up window requesting permission from the user. It is necessary for the user to provide the appropriate response each time this happens, and the changes to the system can not be implemented unless the user does provide permission. In order to avoid a great deal of unnecessary repetition, these pop-up Windows are not covered in the text and illustrations in this book. When the need arises, simply confirm that you wish to go ahead and run the program, change the configuration setting, or whatever. Also bear in mind that many changes can only be made when using an account that has administrator privileges. If there is only one account, this will have administrator status.

Upgrading problems

Out with the old...

Upgrading from Windows 3.1 to Windows 95 was a big step for those who made the change. A switch was being made from a 16-bit operating system to a 32-bit type. However, to some extent the original operating system was still there, albeit largely hidden away out of sight. Upgrading from Windows 95 to 98 or ME was a relatively minor step, since all three of these operating systems are firmly based on the same program code. Changing from Windows 95, 98, or ME to Windows XP is another big step, and many consider that it is actually a larger change than moving from 16-bit Windows to the 32-bit variety.

The reason for this is that the XP code is not based on a 16-bit version of Windows, and it was written "from scratch" as a 32-bit operating system. It would perhaps be more accurate to say that Windows NT was written purely as a 32-bit operating system, and that Windows 2000 and then XP were derived from this. Windows XP is therefore the successor to Windows NT/2000, and not Windows 9x. Upgrading from Windows 2000 to XP is a small change, but the change from 9x to XP is a major step.

Upgrading from Windows NT or 2000 to XP should therefore be relatively straightforward. This is not to say that it is possible to upgrade to XP using any PC that is currently running Windows NT 4 or 2000. The minimum hardware requirements for Windows XP are more stringent than for earlier versions. Most new PCs at the time XP was launched were up to the task of running the new operating system, but many earlier PCs were not. In fact many PCs less than a year old at the time XP was launched were not adequate to run this operating system properly, although in most cases a memory upgrade was all that was needed to rectify the problem.

Things are more straightforward for those upgrading to Windows Vista. Upgrading from anything other than Windows XP is not an option. I suppose it might be possible to upgrade a Windows ME installation to a Windows XP type, and then to a Windows Vista installation, but trying this is probably pointless. It would almost certainly be far easier to backup the data, install Windows Vista from scratch, reinstate the data, and install the application programs. This method would also have a far greater chance of being successful.

Although Windows Vista is in many ways similar to Windows XP, and upgrading from XP to Vista is not such a huge jump as some previous Windows upgrades, it is not safe to assume that any PC running Windows XP can be successfully upgraded to Vista. As with any operating system upgrade, there are two potential problems. The first of these is that some of the application programs and utilities installed on the PC will not run properly under Vista.

The other potential problem is that the hardware that was perfectly adequate for the earlier operating system might not be up to the task of running the new one. There are two aspects to this problem, and the more obvious one is that the hardware might lack sufficient computing power to run Vista. There can also be problems with the driver software needed to integrate items of hardware with Windows. In general, driver software for one version of Windows does not work well with other versions, and is quite likely to be completely unusable with anything other than its intended edition of the operating system.

Minimum specification

If you buy Windows Vista ready installed on a new PC there should be no problem, and it should have a specification that is high enough to run this operating system very well. The situation is very different when upgrading from any previous version of Windows, and it is essential to check that your PC is up to the task before buying the upgrade. Only proceed if there is a realistic chance of obtaining good results. This is the minimum specification needed to run Windows Vista:

A modern processor having a clock speed of 800MHz or more

512MB of memory

Video system capable of using DirectX 9.0 graphics

DVD drive

When looking at the minimum hardware requirements for any software it has to be borne in mind that the specification is the minimum required to run the software, and that a system of this specification might not give usable results. In fact, in most cases the quoted minimum hardware requirements do not represent the lowest specification that provides a usable system. A PC having the minimum requirements will run the software, but will usually perform so badly as to be of little or no practical use.

Memory

The amount of memory required is not governed by the operating system alone. Although 512 megabytes is sufficient to run Vista reasonably well, and should still be sufficient when running one or two "run of the mill" applications, it will not be adequate when running more demanding applications such as image and video editing software. A larger amount of memory is also required when running several application programs simultaneously.

Another point to bear in mind is that many computers have an integrated graphics system. In other words, the graphics circuits are on the main board rather than being provided by a separate graphics card. While it is not totally unknown for integrated graphics systems to have their own high-speed memory, it is more normal for them to share the system memory. With the integrated graphics system using (say) 128 megabytes of system memory, the available memory for the operating system and other software is reduced by 128 megabytes. Consequently, 640 or even 768 megabytes is a more realistic minimum for a PC that has an integrated graphics system.

Clock speed

The minimum processor clock speed can never be anything more than a rough guide, since a selection of PCs running at a certain clock speed will not provide the same level of performance. The overall speed of the PC is influenced by other factors, such as the type of processor in use, the chipset on the motherboard, the amount of memory, and performance of the video card. It is unlikely that any PC having an 800MHz processor will run Vista really well, and something closer to 2GHz is a more realistic minimum.

Any reasonably modern graphics card should be capable of running DirectX 9, but this ability can not be taken for granted with older graphics cards, or with integrated graphics systems. It should not be too difficult to check whether the graphics system in your PC can use DirectX 9. This information should be available from the manufacturer's web site.

Sound

In order to run Windows Vista it is not essential to have a particularly advanced sound system installed, but it is important to realise that some aspects of the more advanced versions of Vista can only be used with a computer that does have an upmarket soundcard. Actually, in order to fully utilise some aspects of Vista it is necessary to have other media equipment installed such as a television card and a remote control system. Using an advanced version of Vista will not turn a "run of the mill" PC into a top quality media type. The PC must have a suitably high specification, including any special hardware that is required by some functions.

Realistic minimum

In order to run Windows Vista reasonably really the minimum specification is therefore something like this:

Processor having a clock speed of 2GHz or more

1GB of memory

Large hard disc drive (40GB or more)

Modern video system capable of using DirectX 9.0 and a resolution of at least 1024 by 768 pixels

DVD drive

Mouse or other Windows compatible pointing device

Any reasonably modern soundcard

If required, additional media components such as a television card or an upmarket audio system

Do not be surprised if you obtain poor results using Windows Vista with a system that only just meets the absolute minimum requirements. Even with a somewhat higher specification it is possible that some aspects of performance might not be very good. On the other hand, your PC should run well enough under Vista when using most application software provided it has a reasonably fast processor and a reasonably large amount of memory installed.

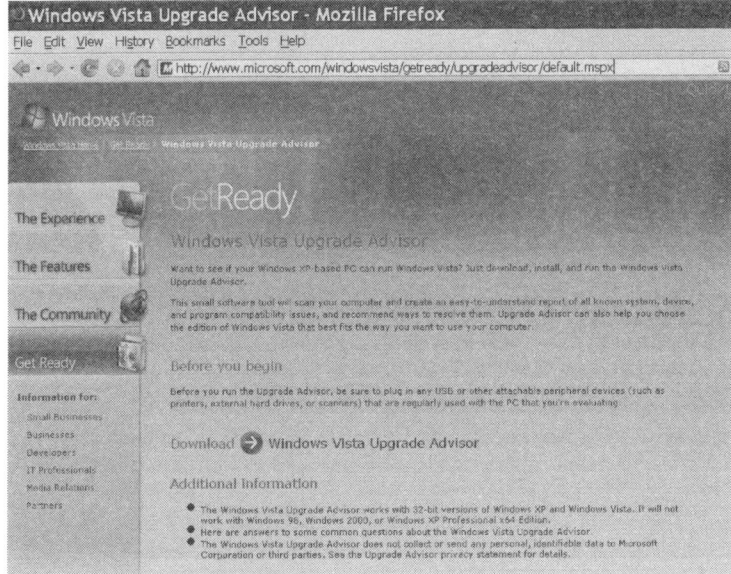

Fig.1.1 The Upgrade Advisor can be downloaded from Microsoft

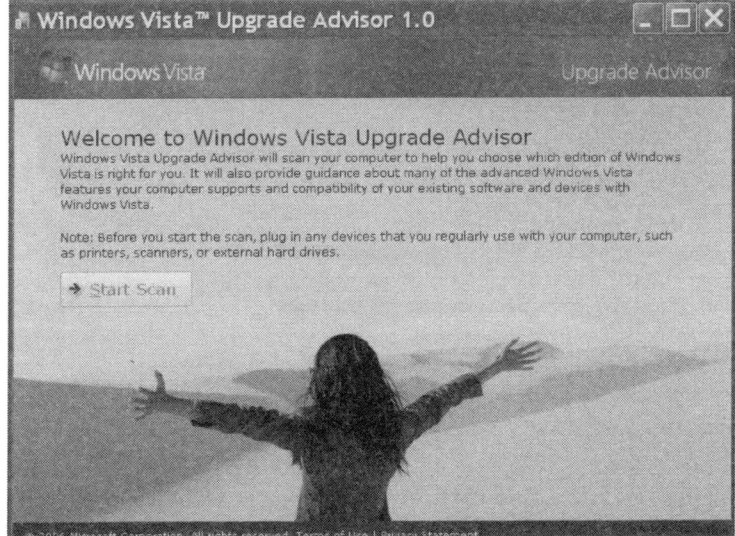

Fig.1.2 This is basically just an information screen

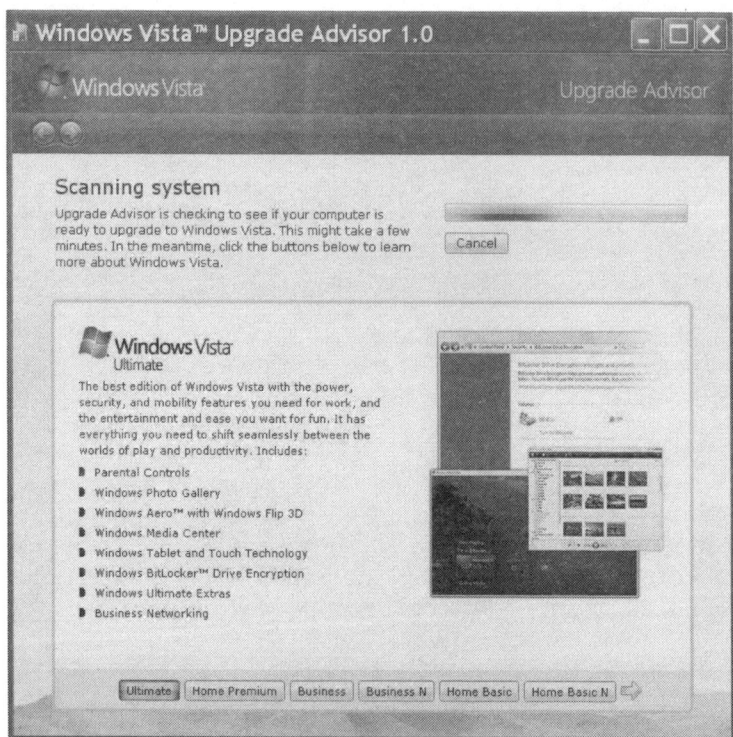

Fig.1.3 This screen appears while the scanning process is taking place

Checking

If in doubt, it is possible to run a program that will check whether your PC is suitable for an upgrade to Windows Vista. This program is actually part of the Windows Vista installation program. The suitability of the PC is checked as part of the normal upgrade process. The purpose of this routine is to warn you of any potential problems with the hardware and the installed software.

The standalone version of the advisor program is useful if you wish to upgrade, but would like to check the suitability of your PC before buying the upgrade software. It will probably be made available on a few of the "free" discs supplied with computer magazines, and it can be downloaded from the Microsoft web site at this address (Figure 1.1):

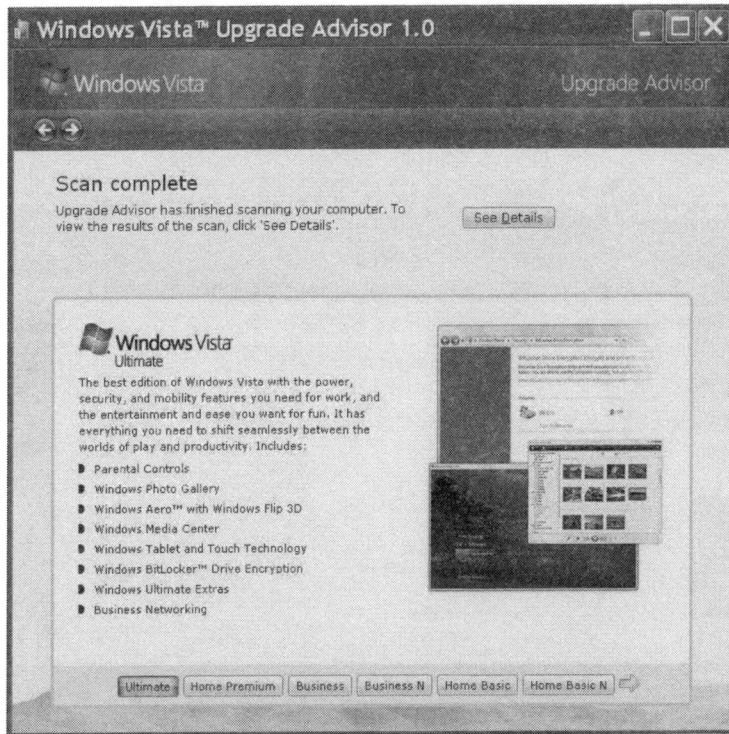

Fig.1.4 The scan has been completed successfully

**http://www.microsoft.com/windowsvista/getready/upgradeadvisor/
default.mspx**

A small information screen appears when the program is run, and this
indicates that the program is checking for updates. Of course, it will
only do so if the PC has an active Internet connection. Things then
move on to the initial screen of Figure 1.2. This explains what the program
will do, and it also points out that any USB devices used with the PC
should be connected to a USB port. The program can only scan and
check the suitability of USB hardware if it is accessible to the program,
so any USB devices not connected to the PC will not be checked.

Operating the Start Scan button starts the checking process, and the
window of Figure 1.3 then appears. An animated status bar indicates
that the checking process is underway, but it does not give any indication

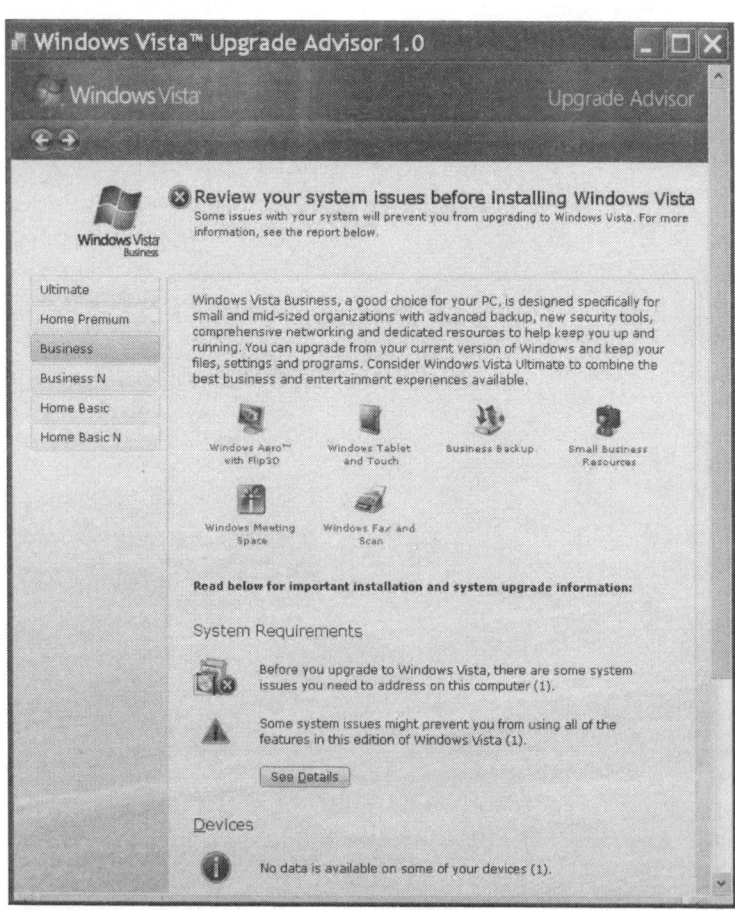

Fig.1.5 More information about incompatibility problems can be obtained

of the time required for completion. The text in the main panel gives basic details of the version of Vista selected using the buttons along the bottom of the window. This is intended to provide information that will help you to select the best version of Vista for your particular purposes. The scanning process is the same regardless of which button is operated.

The scanning process might take a few minutes, but eventually the window will change to look like Figure 1.4, confirming that the checking process has been completed. The PC used in this example has a fair

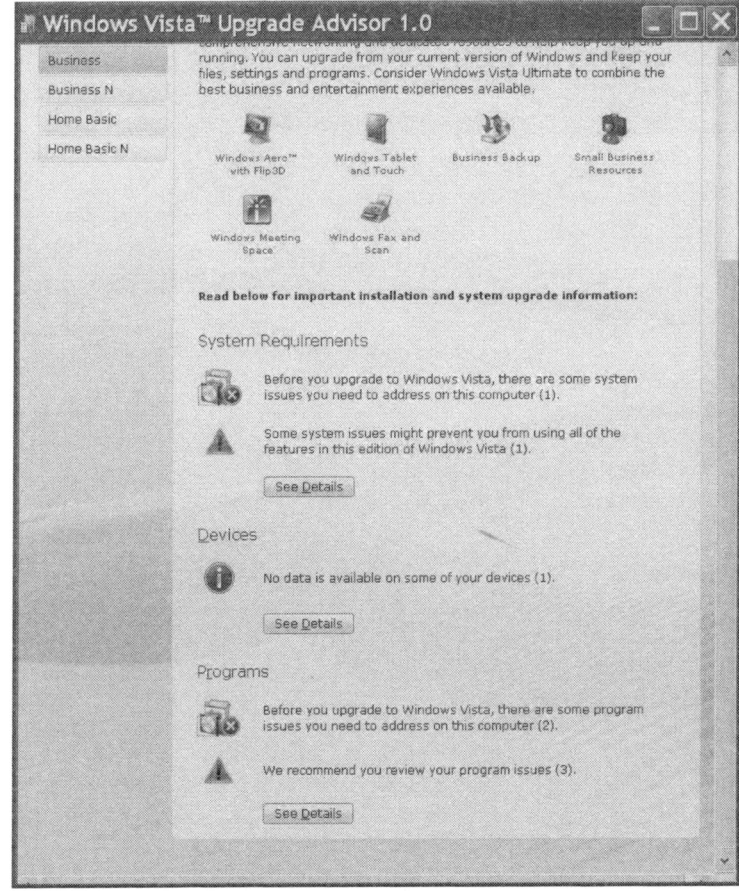

Fig.1.6 You may have to scroll down a long list of problems

amount of hardware and software installed, and it was virtually inevitable that at least one or two potential problems would be reported by the advisor program. Do not worry if your PC produces a list of compatibility issues, because it is possible that most or all of them will be minor problems. Operating the See Details button produces a window that gives more details about compatibility problems (Figure 1.5). You will probably have to scroll down the window in order to get the full list of problems (Figure 1.6).

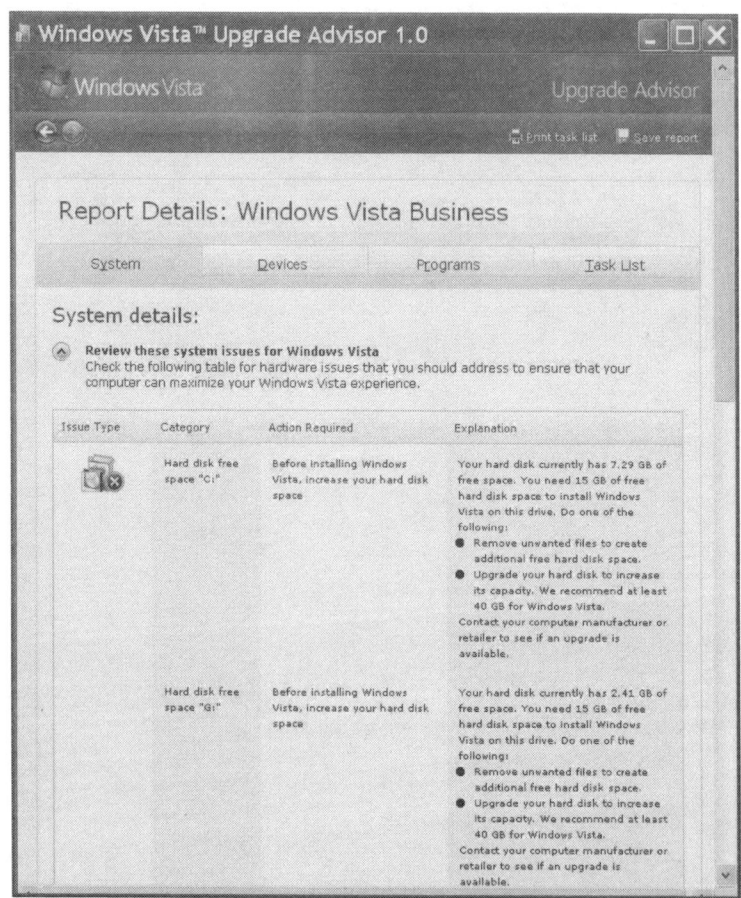

Fig.1.7 The main problem in this case seems to be a lack of hard disc space

For this example I operated the See Details button in the System Requirements section, and this produced the new window of Figure 1.7. Most of the problems are essentially the same one, which is a lack of hard disc space. The System Advisor program is indicating that some 15 gigabytes of hard disc space is needed in order to install the selected version of Windows Vista, but there is only about half this amount available on the main drive. None of the other hard disc drives have sufficient free space.

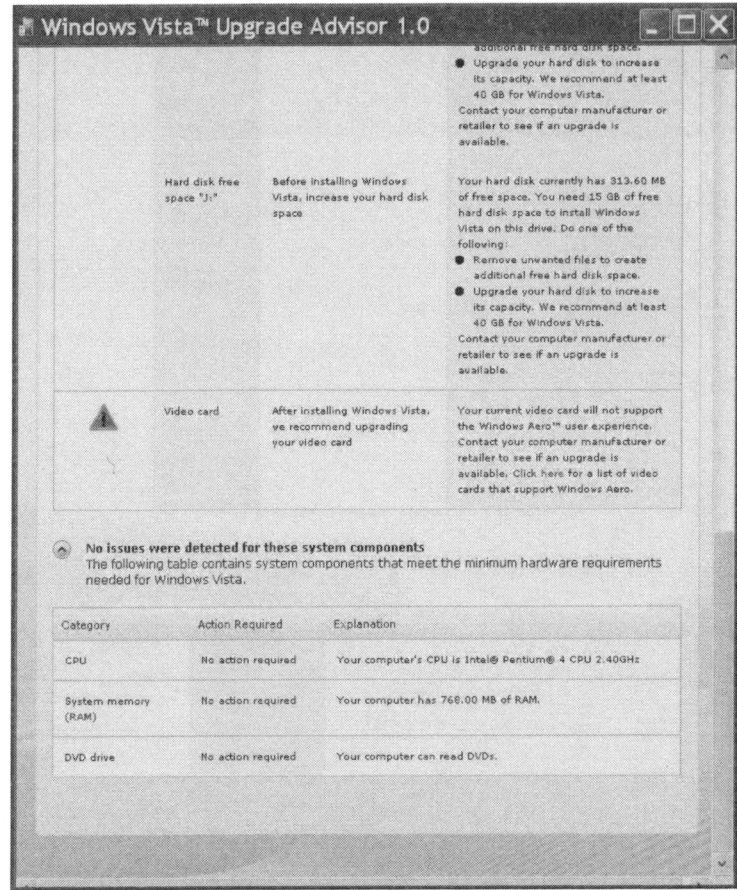

Fig.1.8 There is another problem, which is an inadequate video card

This is likely to be a common problem when upgrading to Windows Vista. The hard disc drives on computers from a few years ago tend to be much smaller than the monster drives that are fitted to most new computers these days. However, in most cases the main hard drive will have adequate capacity to accommodate Windows Vista, some application programs, and a substantial amount of data. Problem with a lack of hard disc space are usually caused by having too many old programs and old data files stored on the computer.

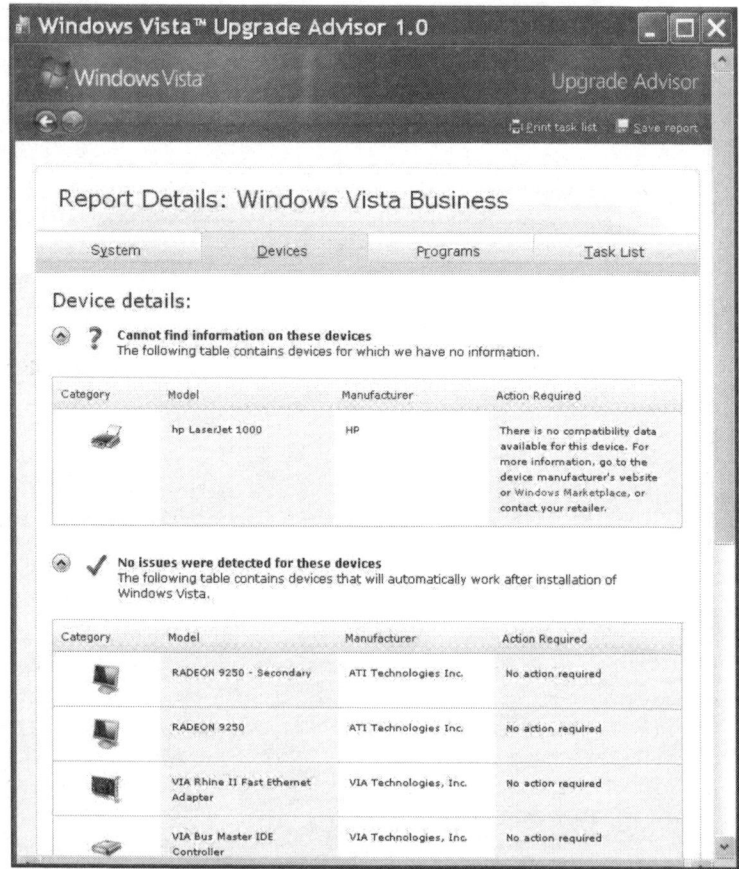

Fig.1.9 The Devices tab covers hardware problems

Uninstalling programs that are not used any more can free a significant amount of space, but is unlikely to increase the available capacity by the seven to eight gigabytes required in this case. Backing up and deleting large data files such as digital photographs and movies is more likely to free several gigabyte of disc space. The usual course of action when data starts to fill a hard disc drive is to copy the older data files onto CD-ROMs or DVDs, then make a second copy of the files to act as a backup of the archive copy. It is then safe to delete the original data files from the hard disc drive.

Scrolling down the list of problems revealed a second problem (Figure 1.8), which is an inadequate video card. The computer in question is intended for business applications, and it has a video card that is adequate for business applications. It has some 3D graphics capability, but even when new it was not exactly the "last word" in video technology. Many business PCs do not actually have a video card as such, but instead have the video circuits integrated with the main board and the PC's normal memory. This type of thing is fine for most business applications, but does not generally support clever graphics tricks.

On the face of it, a relatively simple graphics system should be capable of running an operating system such as Windows Vista. Indeed, such graphics systems have always been perfectly adequate when using earlier versions of Windows. The difference with Vista is that it can use fancy graphics (Windows Aero) that require an advanced graphics card. Windows Vista will actually run properly in most cases where the more advanced graphics effects are not supported by the hardware, but it obviously runs in a restricted and more conventional fashion. Whether it is worth upgrading to a newer graphics card is a subjective matter, but it is unlikely to be essential.

Devices tab

Near the top of the window there are four tabs, with each one covering a different type of compatibility issue. The Devices tab covers issues related to hardware problems (Figure 1.9), although any problems it indicates are unlikely to be genuine problems with the hardware. A genuine problem with hardware compatibility is where a device of some kind can not be physically connected to the PC, or it can not be connected in a fashion that gives satisfactory results. For example, if you buy a new PC and it does not have a serial port, then it is incompatible with any hardware you have that can only use a serial port. There is often a hardware solution to this type of problem. In the case of this example, a USB to serial converter will enable most serial port gadgets to be used with a PC via a USB port.

The hardware problems that the Update Advisor normally finds are more to do with driver incompatibility than true hardware issues. Practically every piece of hardware can only operate with Windows if it is integrated with the system via suitable driver software. Unfortunately, there is usually no single driver that will enable a piece of hardware to operate properly with practically every version of Windows. Virtually a complete new set of driver software is required each time a new version of Windows is launched.

Where the Update Advisor program indicates that there is a problem, it is not usually due to a true hardware problem, and it is more a matter of the existing driver software being unsuitable for use with Windows Vista. The new operating system has built-in driver programs for a wide range of hardware, but it is unlikely that it will be able to accommodate all the hardware in a complex computer system. If you are unlucky, it might not have suitable drivers for everything in a fairly modest computer system.

The fact that Upgrade Advisor indicates a problem does not necessarily mean that the item of hardware in question is not usable with Windows Vista. It just means that Upgrade Advisor has been unable to verify that suitable driver software is available. It is then a matter of visiting the hardware manufacturer's web site in search of suitable drivers for Windows Vista. Obviously, there is no guarantee that suitable device drivers will be available for every piece of hardware in your PC. Windows Vista device drivers have been produced for most hardware that is no more than a few years old, but support for older hardware is inevitably a bit patchier. No doubt some hardware is unusable with Windows Vista. If you are unlucky in this respect, you will have to use an older version of Windows in order to go on using any hardware that is not supported by Windows Vista, or upgrade the hardware.

It is unlikely that there will be any major hardware problems provided your PC uses "run of the mill" hardware that is reasonably up to date. As already pointed out, there will not always be Vista support for older hardware. It is unlikely that driver software for an earlier version of Windows will be usable with Vista, and it is even less likely that Vista would actually install and try to use old driver software. It is then a matter of "biting the bullet" and not going ahead with the upgrade to Windows Vista, or upgrading any unsupported hardware first.

If only one inexpensive item of hardware has to be replaced, it should certainly be worthwhile continuing with the upgrade. Obviously, the upgrade might not be feasible if the PC requires expensive changes in order to accommodate Windows Vista. This is a subjective matter and one where you have to weigh up the costs against the advantages and make your own decision. Bear in mind that older hardware is probably nearing the end of its useful life span and will probably have to be replaced before too long anyway.

So-called generic hardware is another likely cause of problems. This is either anonymous hardware that carries no manufacturer's name on the

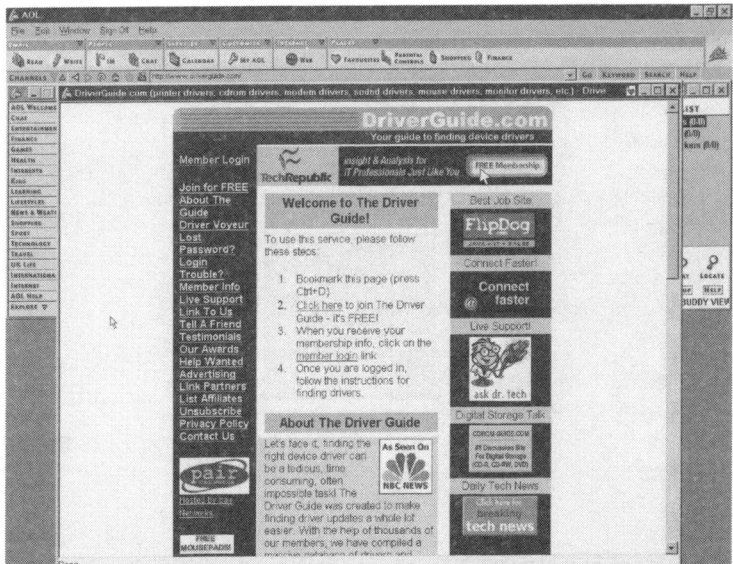

Fig.1.10 DriverGuide.com is one of many sites that deal with drivers

device itself or the documentation, or the name of the manufacturer is given but is one that no one has ever heard of. The problem with this type of hardware is that there is usually no support available from the manufacturer's web site. If you are lucky, a web address will be provided somewhere in the documentation or a search engine will help you locate one. In most cases though, the level of support provided by the big name manufacturers is not available for generic hardware. There is often no ongoing support at all for this type of hardware, which in part accounts for its low cost.

Finding drivers

The fact that a piece of generic hardware lacks a web address for support does not necessarily mean that there is no hope of finding Windows Vista drivers. However, it does mean that if the device drivers do exist, finding them will be much more difficult. With generic hardware that came as part of a PC, the Support section of the PC manufacturer's web site might have the drivers you need. A call to the PC manufacturer's help line might also produce some useful information. Provided the PC

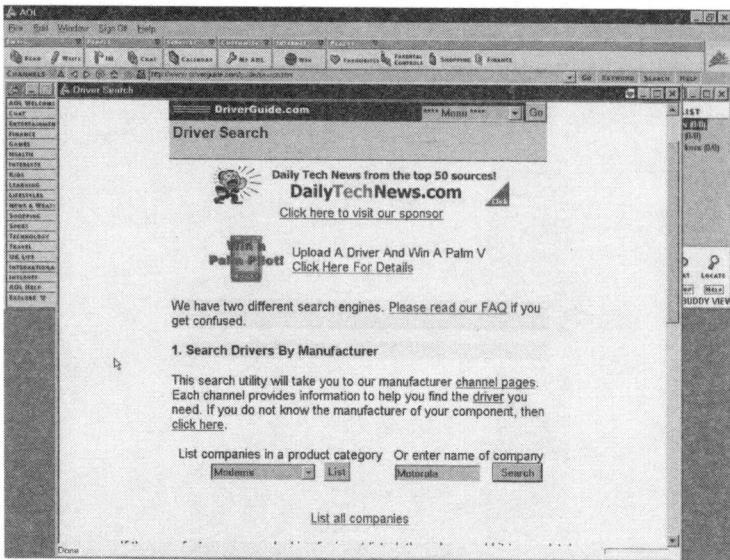

Fig.1.11 DriverGuide.com includes a search facility

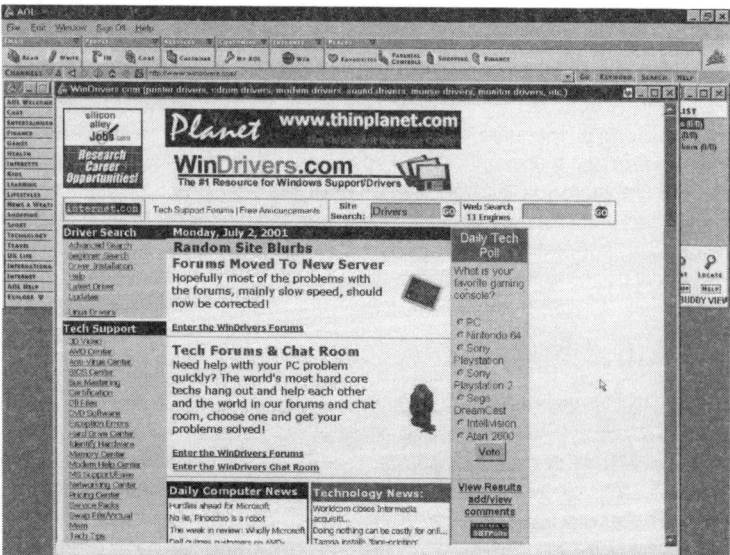

Fig.1.12 WinDrivers.com is one of the best known driver sites

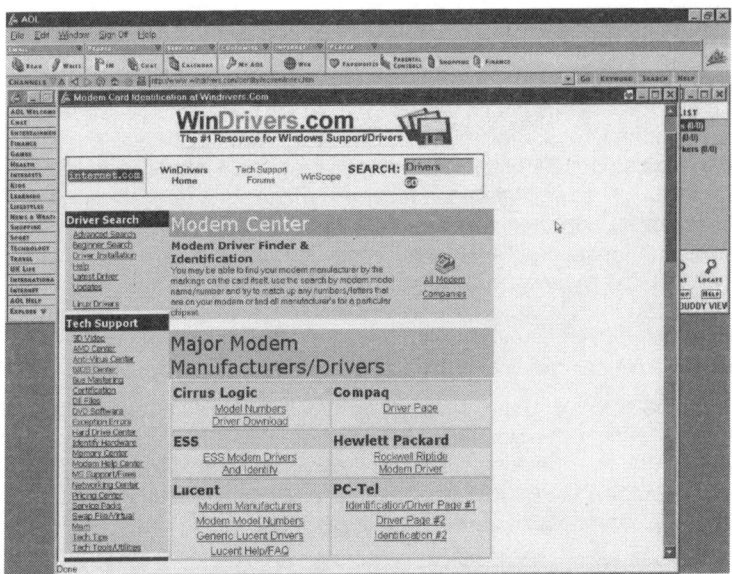

Fig.1.13 WinDrivers.com also includes a search facility

you are using is not in the "golden oldie" category, the maker should provide ongoing support for all the hardware, including any no-name hardware.

Computer chip manufacturers often produce generic driver software for their products. If your piece of problem hardware is a modem is based on (say) a Motorola chipset, the obvious starting point is the Motorola web site. Any search engine should soon locate the manufacturer's web site. This will not always produce a source of suitable drivers. Quite reasonably, the manufacturer of the chips might consider that it is the job of the equipment producer to supply support for their products. However, in practice the sites of chip makers often prove helpful, and it is certainly worthwhile looking to see if there is anything useful on offer.

If a search of the chip manufacturer's site proves to be fruitless, other avenues can be pursued. There are plenty of sites that offer help with device drivers, and using "device drivers" as the search string in the Yahoo search engine will produce a useful list of driver sites. These sites mostly offer a great deal of general information about software drivers, plus advice for beginners on installing them. In most cases there are also search facilities and advice on finding suitable driver programs.

One example of such a site is DriverGuide.com (Figure 1.10). You have to register in order to utilise this site, but registration is free. Amongst other things, it includes search facilities that enable the user to search for a certain manufacturer, drivers for a certain type of hardware, and so on (Figure 1.11). Probably the best know site for device drivers is WinDrivers.com (Figure 1.12). This site provides a lot of general advice together with useful search facilities (Figure 1.13). I have found HelpDrivers.com very useful when tracking down drivers. On one occasion I managed to find the device drivers I needed even though I had nothing more to go on than the markings on the main chip of a modem's circuit board. There is no guarantee that Windows Vista drivers will be available for any awkward pieces of hardware, but if they do exist they will almost certainly be available somewhere on the Internet.

Note that the new drivers must not be installed until after the upgrade to Windows Vista has been completed. Some installation programs will detect that the operating system is inappropriate to new device drivers and will refuse to install them. Other installation programs will go ahead anyway, regardless of the consequences.

If the new drivers are installed in the existing version of Windows, it is virtually certain that the relevant hardware will cease to work properly. It is also quite possible that the existing Windows installation will be damaged to the point where it fails to boot correctly. Never try to upgrade any Windows installation that has a serious fault. The upgrade program might detect the problem and refuse to continue. If an upgrade on a faulty Windows installation is allowed to go ahead, the most likely outcome is that things will come to an abrupt halt somewhere during the upgrade. It can then be very difficult indeed to sort things out. In most cases the hard disc has to be reformatted so that Windows can be installed from scratch. This process is described in a later chapter, and it is not something that should be taken lightly.

Integrated hardware

These days a fair percentage of the device drivers used by PCs are for hardware on the motherboard rather than hardware provided by expansion cards. In fact, the majority of the drivers are often for hardware on the main board. These days the sound system is usually built into the motherboard, and so is the graphics system with many business oriented PCs. There can be other integral hardware such as network adaptors and modems. Even if a PC lacks any built-in hardware of these types, there will still be ports and other hardware that requires device

Fig.1.14 Finding the maker's name and type number for the motherboard is not always straightforward

drivers. In addition to the serial and parallel ports, a modern PC has integral USB, hard disc, and floppy disc interfaces. These all require device drivers in order to work properly.

The ports are unlikely to be troublesome when upgrading, since the Windows Vista upgrade program will recognise the popular chipsets and load the appropriate device drivers. Problems are only likely to occur if the motherboard is very recent or very old. If the motherboard hardware is not recognised and the board is several years old, it is likely that the PC is unsuitable for use with Windows Vista. With a nearly new PC it is a matter of contacting the PC manufacturer's support centre. They should be able to supply the necessary device drivers or give a source for them.

The PC manufacturer's support centre should also be able to help with device drivers for integrated hardware such as sound systems and graphics adapters. Again, with an older PC there might be a lack of Windows Vista support for the motherboard's hardware, and the upgrade is not a practical proposition unless the necessary drivers can be found. If the PC manufacturer's support centre can not help, or the company has disappeared, it is worth removing the outer casing and looking at the motherboard. With luck, the name of the manufacturer and the model

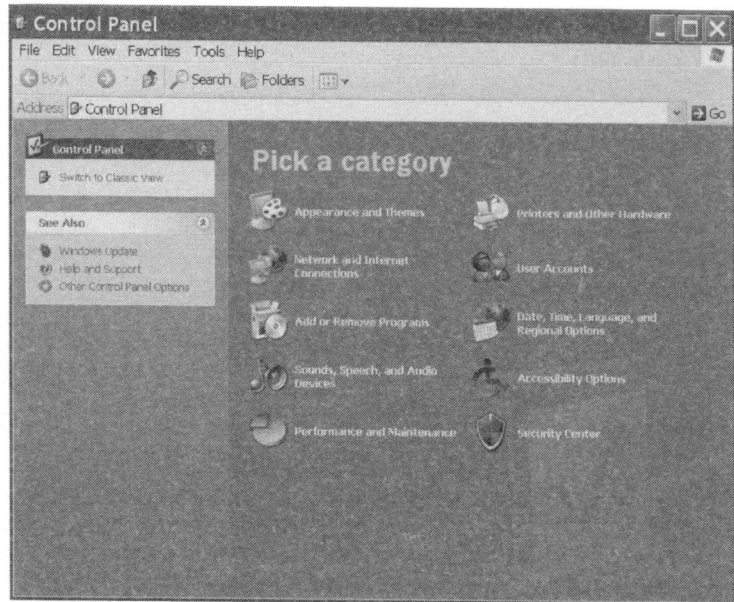

Fig.1.15 The XP version of the Windows Control Panel

number for the board will be shown somewhere on the board. Unfortunately, the labels can sometimes be rather cryptic, and there are often spurious labels mixed in with the important ones. The board shown in Figure 1.14 is a Chaintech 5TDM2. In this example the manufacturer's name is not included on the board, but their logo can be seen near the top right-hand corner of the photograph.

Provided you can identify the motherboard, it should be possible to find the latest device drivers on the manufacturer's web site. Failing that, it might be possible to identify the main support chip or chips on the motherboard. Unfortunately, on some boards one of the support chips is covered by a metal heatsink that obscures the manufacturer's name and type number. Provided the support chip or chips can be identified, the relevant web site can be searched for device drivers.

Uninstalling hardware

In general, there is no need to remove any hardware or device drivers before upgrading to Windows Vista. It is better to complete the upgrade

Fig.1.16 The Control Panel in Classic View

first and then install the new device drivers. Installing new drivers effectively removes the old ones, which should not adversely affect the new installation. It is not strictly necessary to remove any hardware that is not supported by Windows Vista, and will not be used once the PC has been upgraded. However, there is little point in leaving an expansion card in place if it will not be use any more, and uninstalling it ensures that it can not hinder the upgrade. It also makes sure that the card does not use any of the computer's resources.

It is advisable to uninstall the device drivers before physically removing an expansion card. First, go to the Windows Control Panel by selecting the Control Panel option from the Start menu. This produces a window like the one of Figure 1.15. Left-click the Switch to Class View link near the top left-hand corner of the window, which will change the window to look something like Figure 1.16. If necessary, scroll the window downward to reveal the System icon, and then double-click this icon. Note that the entries in Control Panel vary somewhat from one PC to another, but the System icon should always be present.

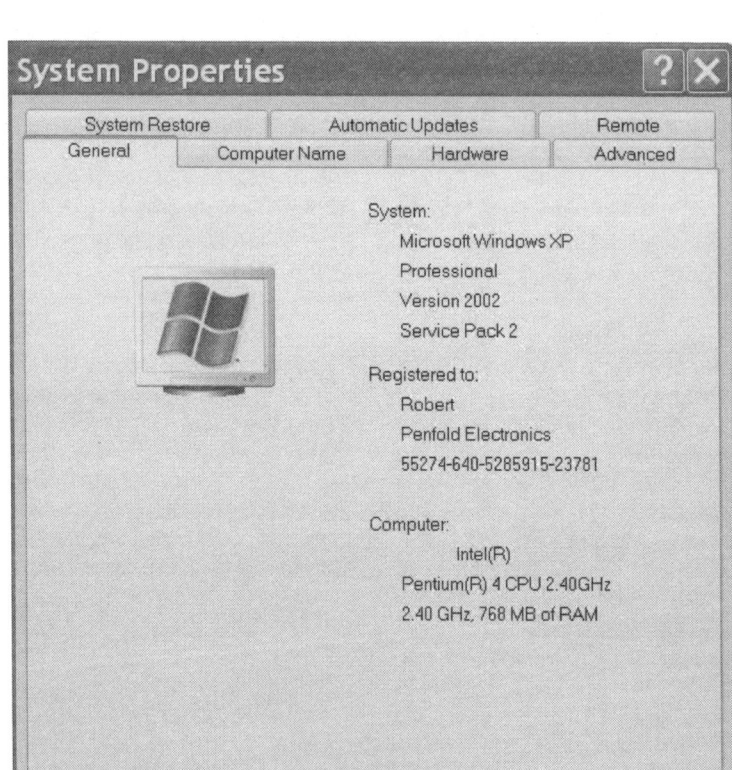

Fig.1.17 The General section of the System Properties window

Double-clicking the System icon produces a new window like the one of Figure 1.17. This is the System Properties window, and it defaults to the General section that gives some basic information about the PC. In this case it is the Hardware section that is required (Figure 1.18), and it is selected by left-clicking the appropriate tab at the top of the window. Then operate the Device Manager button, which launches the Device Manager program in a new window (Figure 1.19). The Device Manager window lists the various hardware categories that cover most of the PC's internal hardware, and it will probably include some external peripheral devices. One of these categories should contain the hardware you wish to uninstall, and double clicking the appropriate icon will expand that

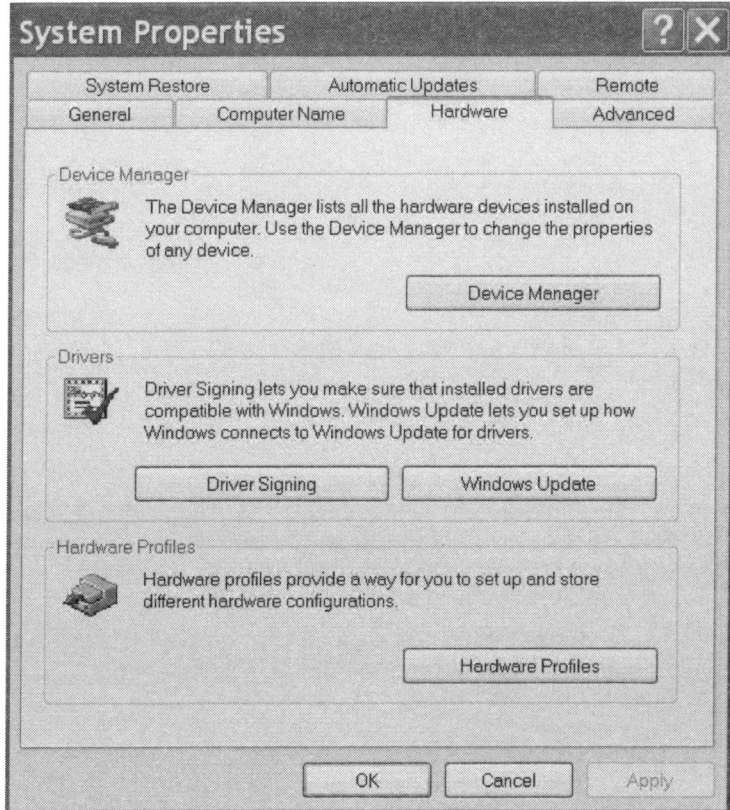

Fig.1.18 The Hardware section of the System Properties window

category to show the individual items it contains. In the example of Figure 1.20 the Display Adapters entry has been expanded, and it contains two items.

In order to uninstall an item of hardware, double-click its entry to launch its properties window (Figure 1.21), and then operate the Driver tab near the top of the window. The new version of the window (Figure 1.22) has an Uninstall button, and operating this produces a warning message like the one of Figure 1.23. Left-click the OK button to proceed and remove the drivers for the selected piece of hardware. The appropriate entry in Device Manager should then disappear. If the uninstalled hardware was the only device in its category, the entry for that category

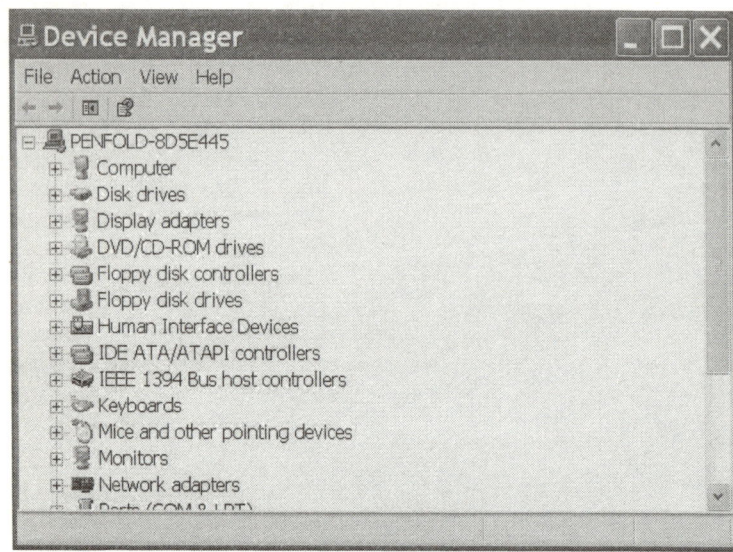

Fig.1.19 Device Manager lists the installed hardware

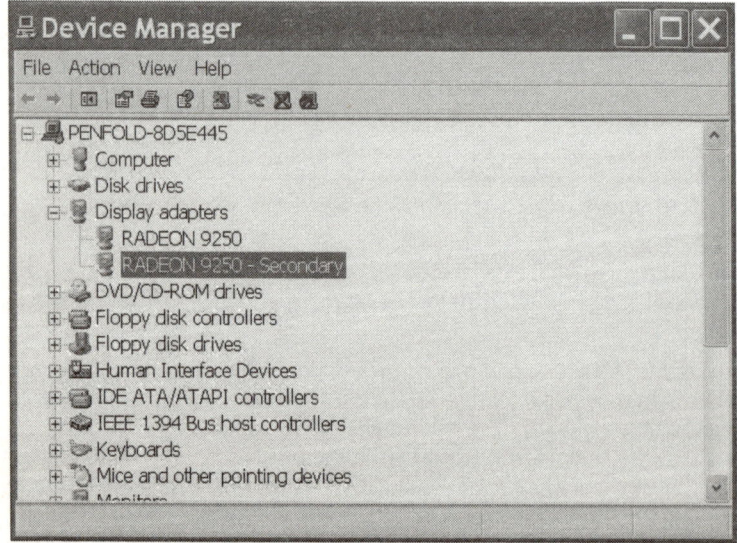

Fig.1.20 Entries can be expanded to show their contents

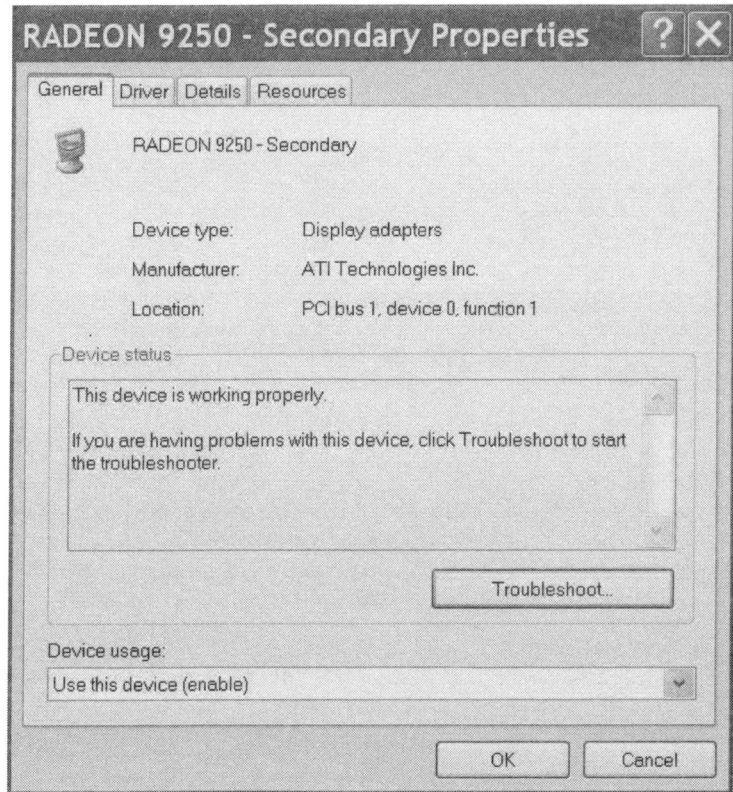

Fig.1.21 The properties window for an item of hardware

will also be removed. Note that it is not possible to select and then remove a category. The entry for a category can only be removed by individually uninstalling each piece of hardware it contains. If you get a message like the one in Figure 1.24, the hardware will not be uninstalled until the computer has been restarted.

Note that some pieces of hardware perform more than one function and therefore have multiple entries in Device Manager. An audio card for example, usually provides a MIDI interface and a game port in addition to various audio functions. Consequently, a typical audio card has three or four device drivers listed in Device Manager. I have encountered some that had five or six device drivers listed in Device Manager. All the relevant drivers should be removed when uninstalling any multifunction devices.

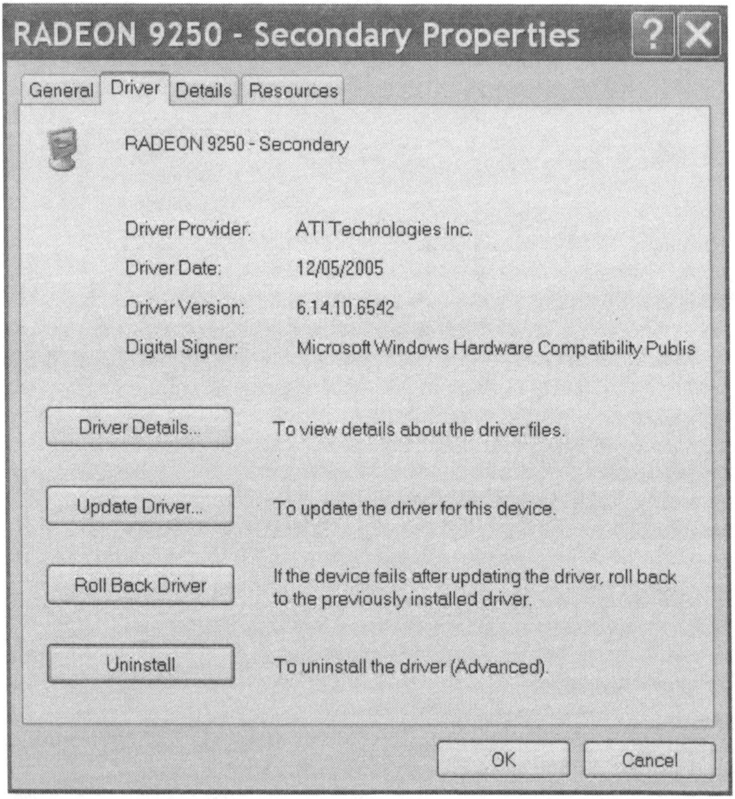

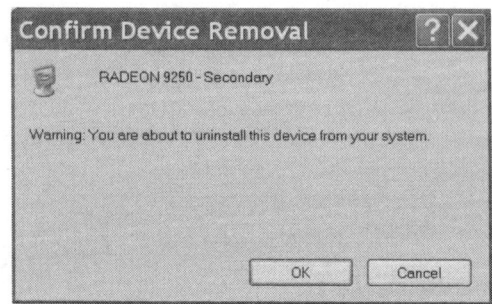

Fig.1.22 The Driver section of the properties window

Fig.1.23 Operate the OK button to proceed

Uninstalling hardware in Vista

If you do not uninstall any incompatible hardware before upgrading to Windows Vista, but subsequently feel it would be better to

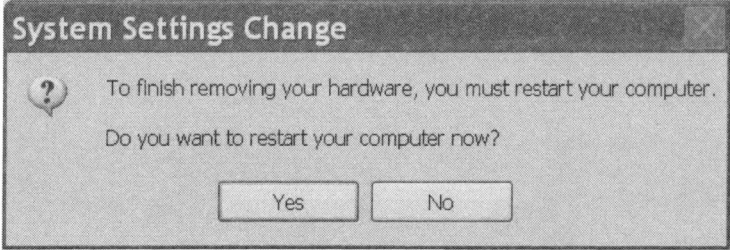

Fig.1.24 Operate the Yes button to restart the computer

remove it, essentially the same method is used to uninstall the device drivers in Windows Vista. However, Windows Vista is a classic case of things being "the same but different". As before, the Control Panel can be accessed direct from the Start menu. The Windows Vista version of the Control Panel is not identical to the Windows XP version, but it is very similar (Figure 1.25). Next, left-click the Classic View link in the top left-hand section of the window.

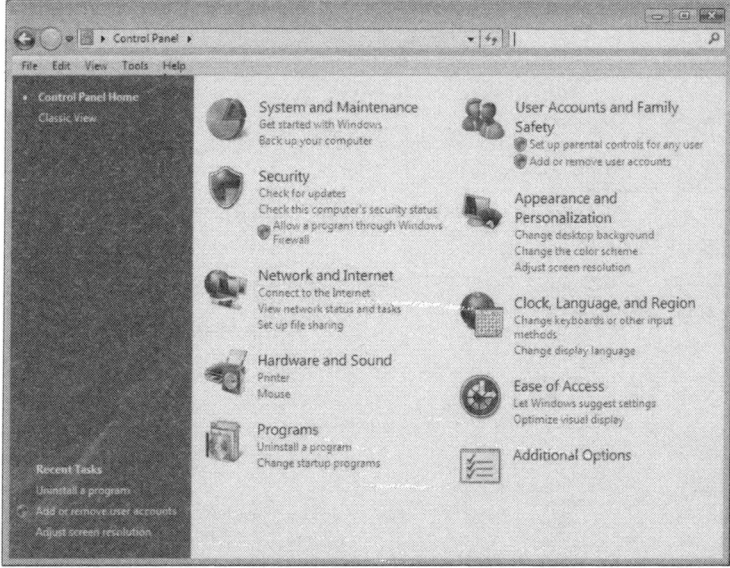

Fig.1.25 The Windows Vista version of the Control Panel

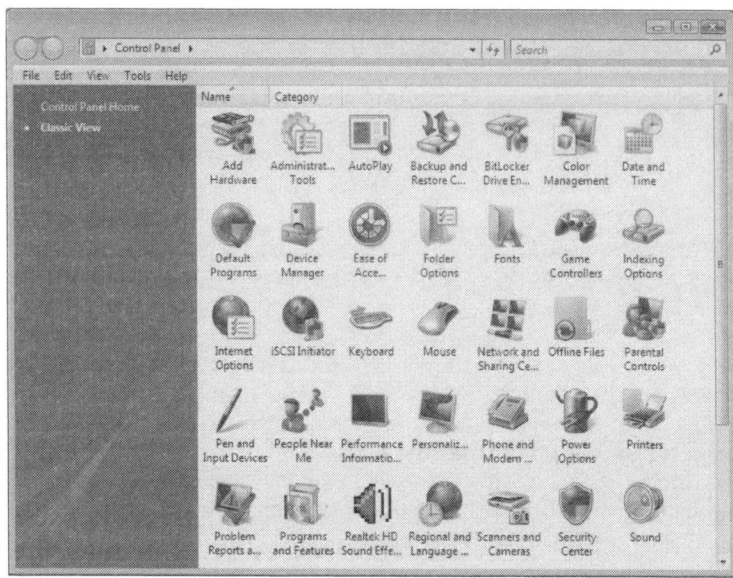

Fig.1.26 The Vista Control Panel in Classic View mode

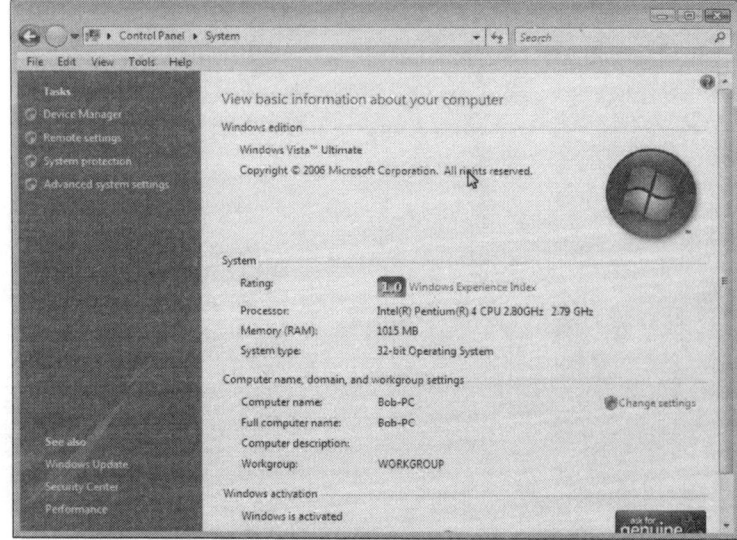

Fig.1.27 The System window has a link to Device Manager

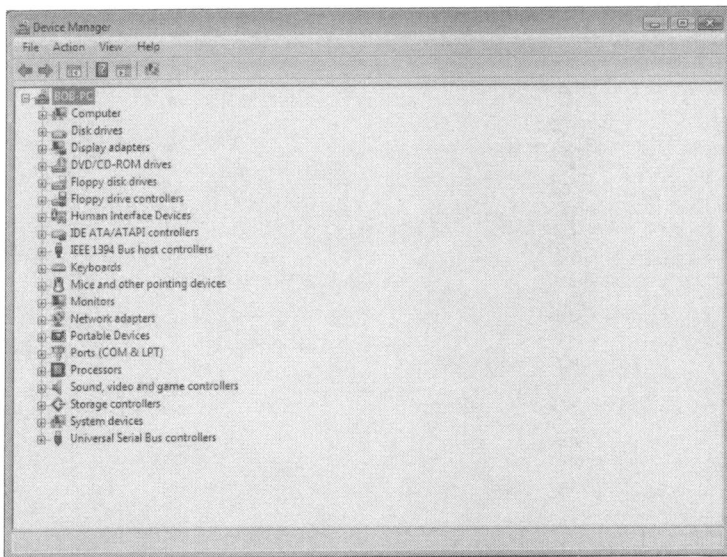

Fig.1.28 The Vista version of Device Manager lists installed devices

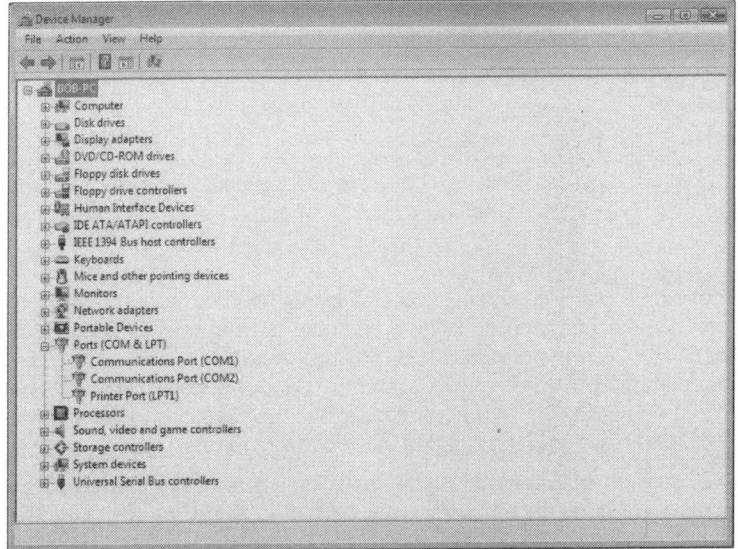

Fig.1.29 Categories can be expanded to show their contents

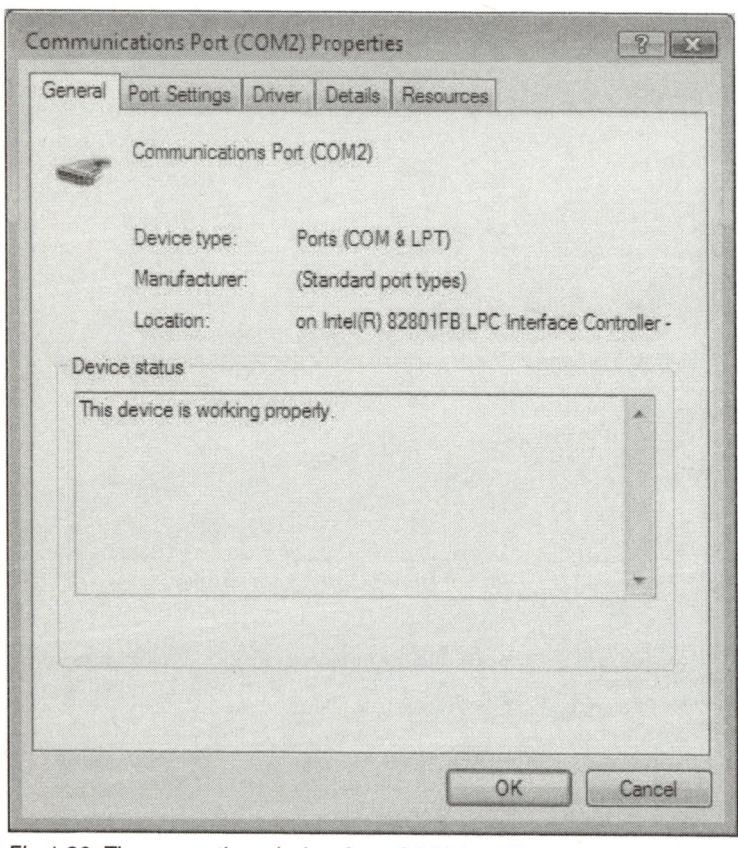

Fig.1.30 The properties window for a COM (serial) port

The usual icons should then appear (Figure 1.26), including the System icon somewhere near the bottom. Double-clicking this icon produces the System window (Figure 1.27). The initial window shows some basic information about the computer and the Windows installation. Device Manager is accessed via the link in the top left-hand section of the window, and operating this link produces the window of Figure 1.28.

This version of Device Manager permits unwanted hardware to be uninstalled in much the same way as it is in Windows XP. Like the Windows XP version, double-clicking on an entry expands it to show the individual pieces of hardware in that category (Figure 1.29). Right-clicking

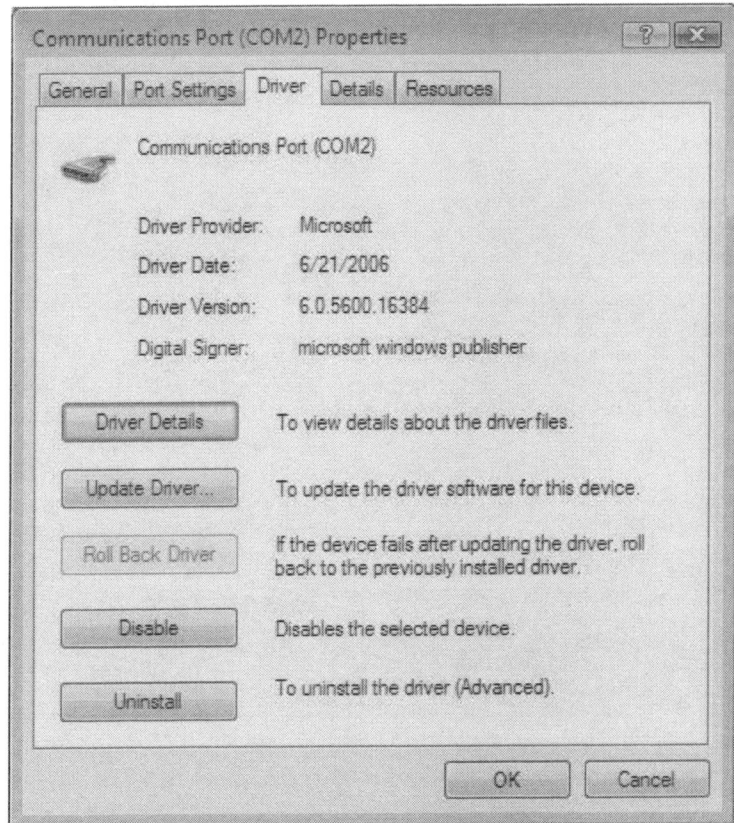

Fig.1.31 The Driver section of the properties window

on the entry for a piece of hardware produces a menu, and one of the menu options enables the device drivers to be uninstalled. There is also the option of disabling the device if you would like Windows to ignore it, but you do not wish to physically remove the hardware from the PC.

Double-clicking an entry or selecting Properties from the pop-up menu produces its properties window, as in the example of Figure 1.30. As before, the General section is shown by default, but it is the Driver section (Figure 1.31) that enables the device to be uninstalled or disabled.

Fig.1.32 *An expansion card has a metal bracket that is bolted to the*
rear of the chassis

Physically uninstalling

With the device drivers uninstalled, it is likely that the computer will try to reinstall the hardware the next time it is booted into Windows unless the hardware is removed from the PC. Shut down Windows and switch off the computer at the mains supply before doing any work on the computer. Modern desktop PC cases are mostly of the ATX variety, and with these it is only necessary to remove the left-hand side panel in order to gain access to the expansion cards. With ATX cases each panel is held in place by two or three screws, which are again situated at the rear of the unit.

There are usually other fixing screws at the rear of a PC, holding in place things like the power supply and subassemblies of the case. Look at the way everything fits together and be careful to remove the correct screws.

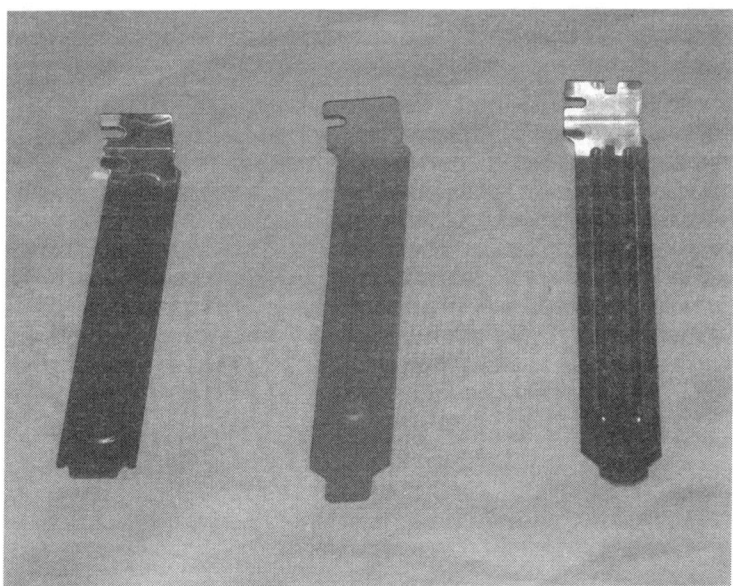

Fig.1.33 Three expansion slot blanking plates

Note that some PCs have fancy cases that can be difficult to open. However, if you study the problem for a while it should be possible to "crack" the case. The PC's instruction manual should give some guidance on gaining access to the interior of the case.

Each expansion card has a metal bracket that is bolted to the rear of the PC's chassis (Figure 1.32). With this bolt removed it not usually too difficult to pull the card free of its expansion slot, but it can require a fair amount of force to remove a card that has been in place for some time. Pull steadily on the card using no more force than is absolutely necessary to pull it free. Do not use brute force if the card is difficult to remove. A rocking action will usually loosen an awkward card so that it can be pulled free without having to use excessive force. If your PC was supplied with some spare blanking plates (Figure 1.33), one of these is bolted in the position formerly occupied by the mounting bracket of the expansion card. Some of these plates clip in place and do not require the mounting bolt. These are easy to spot, because the top section is not flat, but instead has a curved section that is used to clip it in place.

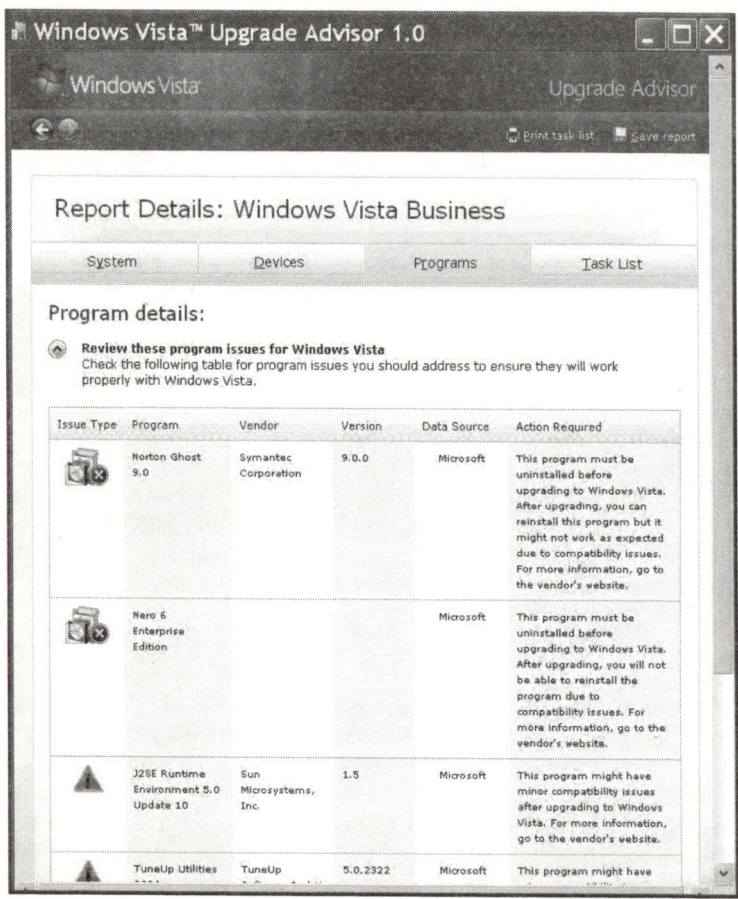

Fig.1.34 Known problems with installed software will be listed

With the card removed and the blanking plate in position, fit the outer casing and boot the computer into Windows. Once Windows has loaded, go to Device Manager and check that the entry for the deleted device driver has not reappeared. If necessary, remove the device driver's entry again, reboot Windows, and then look for the entry once more. You have probably deleted the wrong device driver if it keeps reappearing! The hardware for the driver is still present in the PC, so the Plug and Play system reinstalls the driver each time the computer is booted into

Windows. With the hardware removed from the computer, the entry for the correct driver should be easy to spot. It will probably be marked with a yellow exclamation mark.

Software problems

Returning to the Upgrade Advisor program; one of the tabs produces a list of problems with the installed software (Figure 1.34). There can be problems with software compatibility for a number of reasons. Some software directly controls parts of the computer's hardware rather than going via the operating system. This can give faster operation, but directly accessing the hardware is not permitted under Windows Vista, or Windows XP and 2000 come to that. These operating systems are designed to be more stable than Windows 9x, and but this stability is obtained by placing restrictions on the software. Permitting the applications programs to have a free for all with the hardware gives the potential for problems with two programs trying to simultaneously use the same piece of hardware. With the ports, etc., only accessed via the operating system, Windows can ensure that only one applications program uses each piece of hardware at any one time.

At one time it was possible to obtain some software in two versions. One version was for Windows 9x and the other was for a more recent version of Windows such as XP. Other programs were supplied in dual versions. The installation program installed one version if Windows 9x was detected on the hard disc, or an alternative version if Windows NT/2000/XP was detected. Software of this type should be usable when upgrading to Windows Vista, since software for Windows 2000/XP is mostly compatible with Windows Vista. Of course, with this type of thing there is no guarantee that the software will work with Windows Vista. It was probably designed for operation with an earlier version of Windows such as 2000 or XP and not Vista. However, software of this type will run perfectly well in the majority of cases.

Another cause of problems is software that you only have available in Windows 9x compatible form. This is a more serious problem because any software of this type is fundamentally incompatible with Windows Vista. This does not necessarily mean that you will be unable to use the software if you go ahead with the upgrade. Like Windows XP, Windows Vista has various compatibility modes that permit most Windows 9x software to be run successfully. Unfortunately, there is no "cast-iron" guarantee that one of the compatibility modes will render the software usable, although this feature is almost invariably successful. Using the compatibility modes is covered later in this chapter. It is probably worth checking with the manufacturer of incompatible software to see if an upgrade to a Windows Vista version is available. Using proper Windows Vista applications software is better than having to resort to a compatibility mode.

Software for use with CD-RW drives is a common cause of problems when upgrading. With Windows 9x it is necessary to have a program like Direct CD or In CD in order to use a CD-RW disc like a high capacity floppy disc. The situation changed slightly with Windows XP, which has software of this type built-in. As a result, existing CD-RW software often had to be removed in order to avoid conflicts. Windows Vista has more sophisticated built-in software for writing to CDs and DVDs, which can again give problems with burning software. Even burning software that ran perfectly well under Windows XP might not be fully compatible with Windows Vista.

In this example, the Upgrade Advisor program has indicated that a burning program must be uninstalled prior to upgrading to Widows Vista, and that it should not be installed again after the upgrade. In a situation such as this it is necessary to upgrade to a Windows Vista version of the troublesome software, find an alternative burning program that is Vista compatible, or just settle for Vista's built-in facilities.

Other types of program that are likely to cause problems are disc utilities, system tuning software, and backup software. Many of these programs do clever things that require the software to use equally clever programming tricks. These tricks work well with one version of Windows but are unlikely to work properly with any other version. In this example there is a backup program that must be installed prior to upgrading.

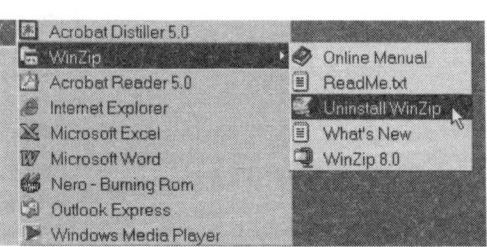

Fig.1.35 Some programs have an uninstall utility

Unlike the CD burning program, it can be reinstalled after the upgrade, but is not guaranteed to work perfectly. There are other programs where possible compatibility problems have been indicated by Upgrade Advisor, but it has stated that it is not essential to uninstall them prior to upgrading. With programs in this category you can test them once the upgrade has

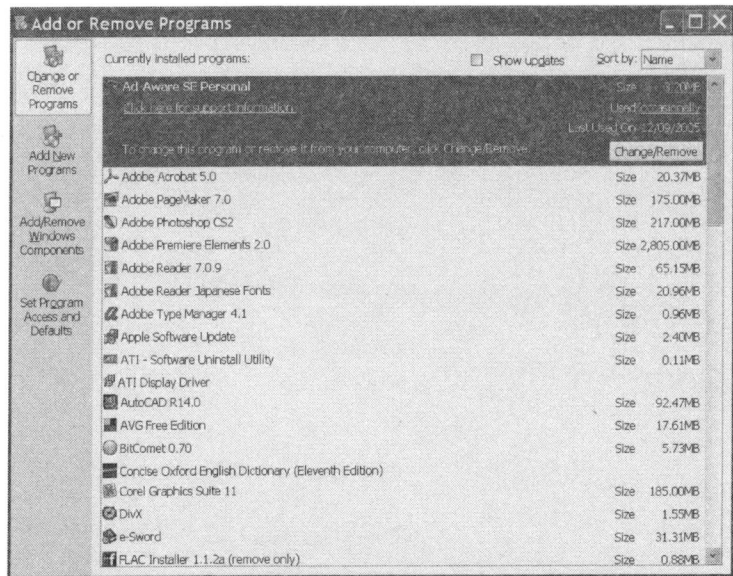

Fig.1.36 The Remove Programs window lists all installed programs

been completed. Depending on whether they perform satisfactorily or are not fully operational, they can then be left in place or uninstalled.

Uninstalling software

With Windows it is essential to uninstall software properly, rather than simply obliterating any folders that contain the files for the program that you wish to remove. Deleting folders that contain programs and support files is a good way to make Windows unstable, and can even prevent it from booting properly. Virtually all Windows programs are supplied with an uninstaller or they can be uninstalled using the built-in facilities of Windows. The only exceptions are old programs that were written for Windows 3.1. There are utility programs available that can help with the removal of this type of software. If an old Windows program is not doing any harm, the safest option is to leave it in place and ignore it. If reinstallation is needed, try reinstalling the program without removing the original installation first. In most cases this will get the program working properly again.

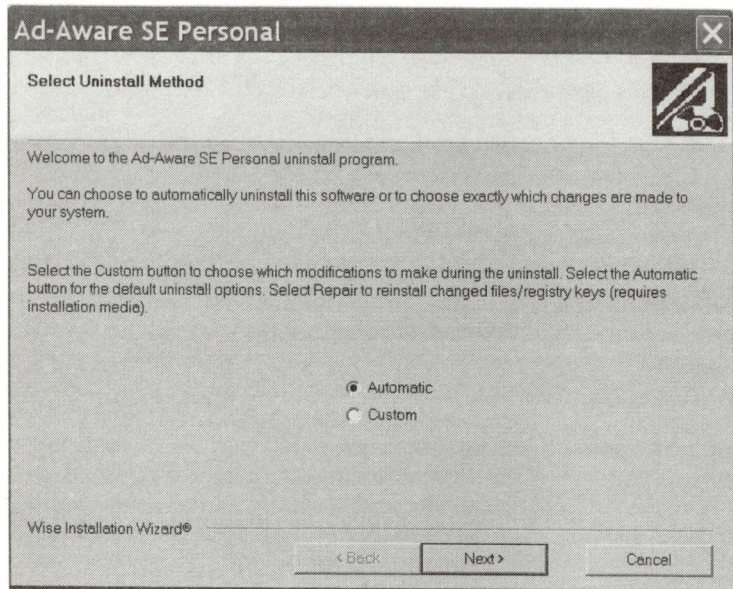

Fig.1.37 Automatic removal will usually suffice

Where a program has its own uninstaller, it will be listed in the appropriate section of the Program menu. Figure 1.35 shows the entry for the popular WinZip program, and this includes an option to uninstall the program. The way in which the software is removed using an uninstaller varies from one program to another, but the process is largely automated. In most cases the user has to do nothing more than confirm that they wish to uninstall the program.

Most programs are removed using the built-in facilities of Windows. To remove software via this route, go to the Windows Control Panel and double-click the icon labelled Add/Remove Programs. This produces the appropriate window (Figure 1.36), where the program you wish to remove should be listed. Left-click on its entry to select it, and then operate the Change/Remove button or the Remove button, as appropriate. The removal process is customised to suit the particular program being uninstalled, so there is some variation from one program to another.

Things are very straightforward, but operating the Remove button will usually require the user to provide some further input, even if it is only to

Fig.1.38 The computer may have to be restarted in order to complete the process

confirm that the uninstall process should be allowed to go ahead. In the example of Figure 1.37 the user is given the option of a fully automatic process or a customised removal of the software. Normally the customized version is only needed in cases where some parts of a suite of programs will be left in place while others must be uninstalled. In the current context it is only a complete removal of the program and the automatic option that will be needed. Some programs require the computer to be restarted in order to make the removal process take full effect (Figure 1.38). It is not essential to restart the computer immediately, but it is probably best to do so and check that software has been uninstalled correctly.

Uninstalling software in Vista

As pointed out previously, it is not essential to remove some potentially problematic programs prior to the upgrade to Windows Vista. They can be left in place, tested in Windows Vista, and then removed only if there is a significant problem of some kind. It is only fair to point out that difficulties can occur with programs that were not listed as potentially problematic by the upgrade advisor program. This can occur where

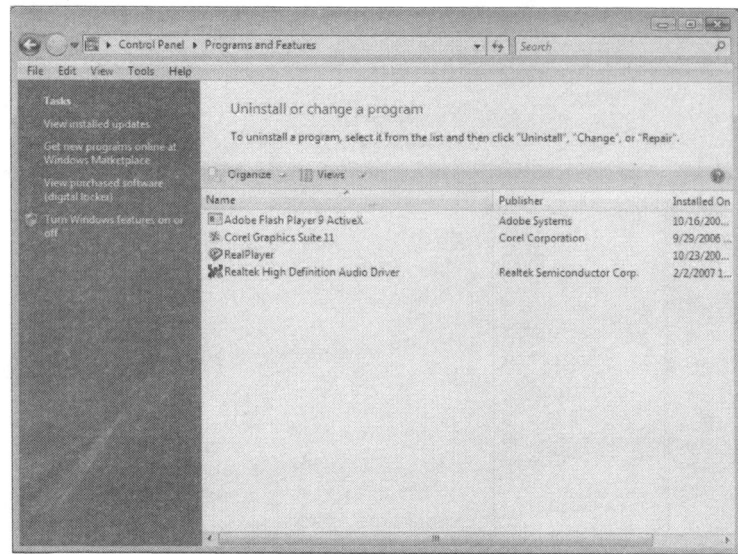

Fig.1.39 The Windows Vista program uninstaller

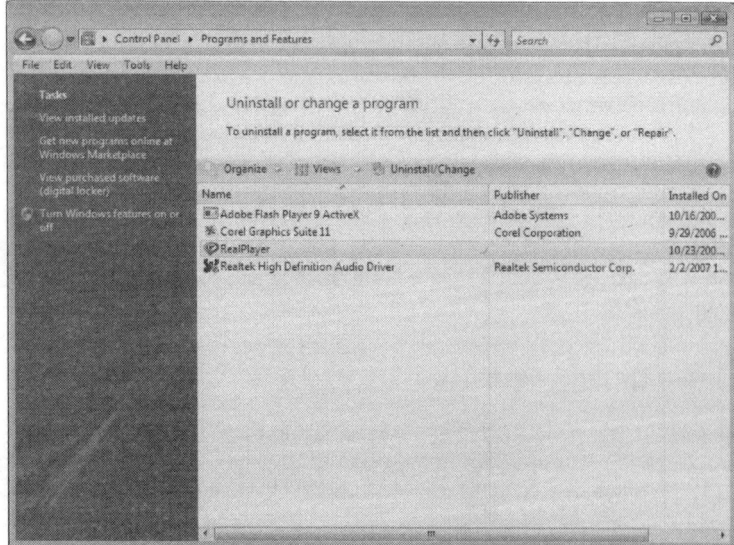

Fig.1.40 Operate the Uninstall or Change/Uninstall button

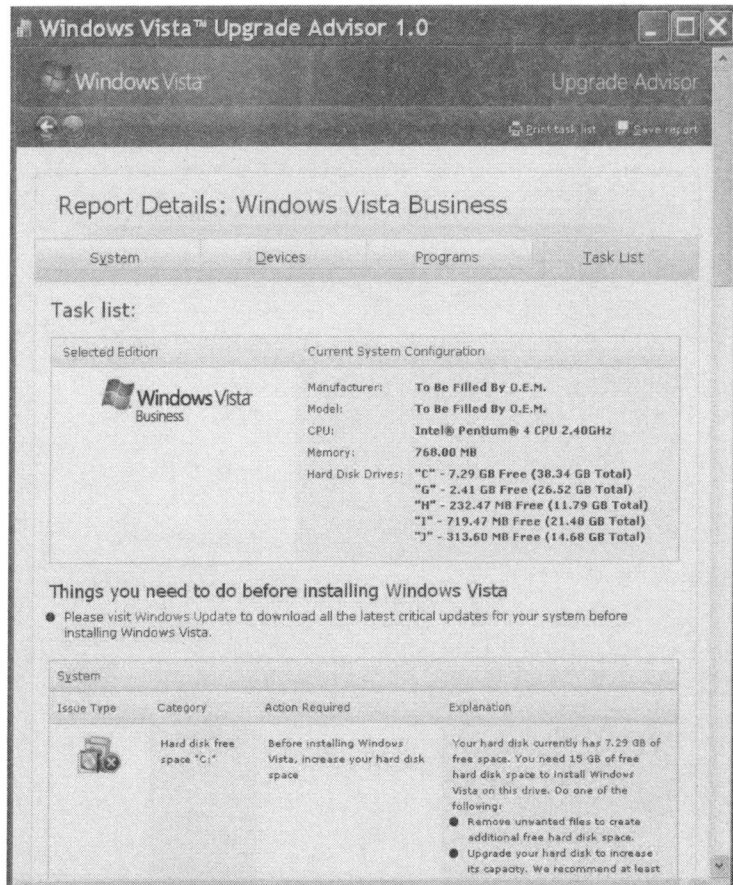

Fig.1.41 Upgrade Advisor provides a lists of tasks that must be completed before upgrading to Vista

there is no known issue for Upgrade Advisor to report, but there is a problem with the program when it operates in your particular setup. There can also be problems due to something going slightly awry during the upgrade process, rather than any compatibility issues. Problems can occur with any applications programs after an operating system upgrade. Uninstalling the problem software and reinstalling it will sometimes effect a cure.

If you need to remove a program from Windows Vista, either permanently or so that it can be reinstalled from scratch, the process is much the

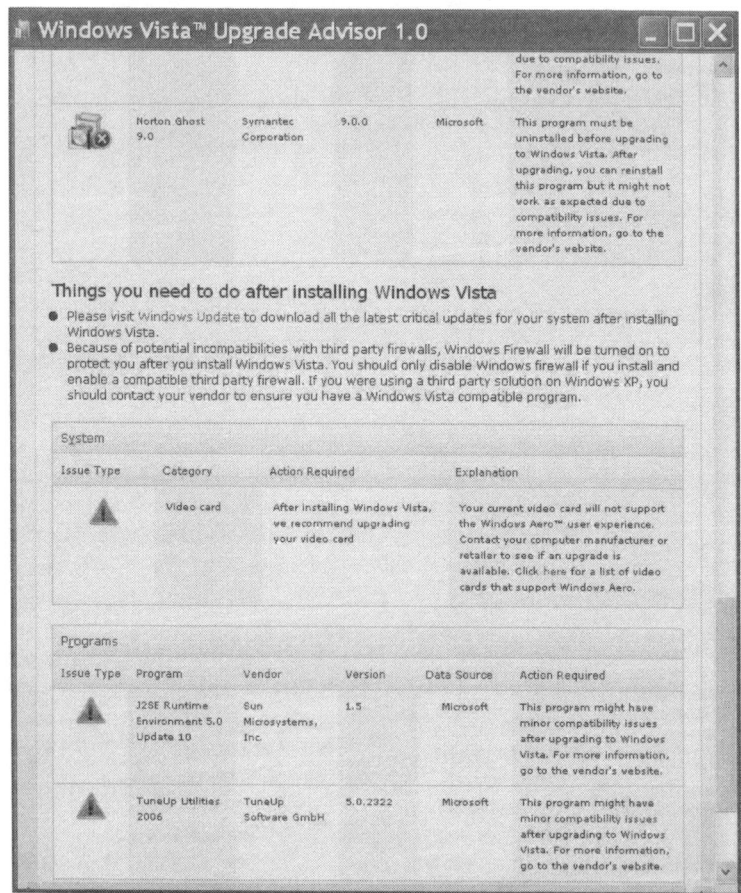

Fig.1.42 The will probably be a long (scrollable) list of tasks

same as under Windows XP. The route to Window's own uninstaller is slightly different though. Select Control Panel from the Start menu and in the Classic View double-click on the Programs and Features icon. This produces a window like the one shown in Figure 1.39. Left-click on the entry for the program that you wish to remove, and then operate the Uninstall or Uninstall/Change button in the bar immediately above the list of installed programs. Note that this button only appears when an entry in the program list has been selected (Figure 1.40). Things then proceed in much the same way as when using Windows XP.

Task List

The fourth tab of Upgrade Advisor provides a task list, which is simply a list of the things you need to do before and after upgrading to Windows Vista (Figures 1.41 and 1.42). This is really just a summary of the information provided in the other sections, and it places everything in one place for easy reference. Links at the top of the window give the options of printing the task list or saving it to disc. It is advisable to do one or other of these so that you can obtain a list of things to do without having to run Upgrade Advisor again.

Versions

There are, of course, several versions of Windows Vista, and the hardware requirements vary somewhat from one version to another. For example, some versions have facilities for using television cards and other multimedia hardware, but these facilities are only usable if suitable hardware is present in the system. Note that it is not just a matter of having hardware of an apposite type. Special items of hardware will only integrate fully with Windows Vista if they are also of a compatible type.

The initial windows of the Upgrade Advisor program have buttons that enable the appropriate version of Vista to be selected. You can go back to one of these windows and select a different version so that you can judge how well your PC will handle each version that is of interest. In general, the cheaper versions are less demanding than the more upmarket ones. However, the differences tend to be relatively minor as far as the basic specification is concerned.

Upgrade?

Whether an upgrade to Vista is worthwhile depends on the time and expense involved in making changes to the existing hardware and software. It is unlikely to be worthwhile where a lot of expense would be involved. Upgrading to Vista is unlikely to be a practical proposition in cases where the problem is primarily due to major inadequacies in the hardware. Simply buying a new budget PC with Vista as part of the bundled software is likely to be a more cost-effective solution. These days it is quite normal for the software to cost about the same or even more than the hardware that is being used to run it. The cost of upgrading to Vista is almost certain to be impractically high if it involves buying major pieces of software or a number of expensive upgrades.

It is important not to fall into the trap of upgrading any software just for the sake of it. The only valid reason for upgrading to a newer version of any program is that it brings some real benefits. Will Windows Vista genuinely provide new features that are of use to you, or is your current operating system providing all the facilities that you need? Windows Vista is an excellent operating system, but so is Windows XP. Windows XP has the advantage of being tried and tested, but it inevitably takes a while before a newly released program becomes reasonably trouble-free. Instead of upgrading to Vista now, would it be better to wait until you current PC is due for replacement and then buy a new one complete with a suitable version of Vista? These are subjective matters, and you have to reach you own conclusions.

Registering

Registering Windows was optional prior to Windows XP, but with XP and Vista it is not possible to use the program beyond a trial period unless you do so. Strictly speaking, it is not necessary to register Windows Vista in order to go on using it indefinitely. It is the Windows Product Activation (WPA) that is essential, but this is normally done as part of the registration process. In effect, the Windows Vista installation DVD contains a fully working 30-day demonstration version of the operating system. If you ignore the onscreen warning messages and do not go through the WPA/registration process, the operating system will refuse to boot properly. All is not lost if you reach this stage, because it is still possible to go through the WPA/registration process and get the operating system working again

Anti-piracy

Windows Product Activation was, to say the least, a bit controversial when it was introduced with Windows XP. The idea is to prevent casual piracy of the operating system. However, like most anti-piracy systems, it does not make life any easier for legitimate users of the product. It can make life very much more difficult for legitimate users, although it will not necessarily do so. As pointed out previously, the program on the disc when you buy Windows Vista is effectively just a 30-day demonstration version. Entering the product identification number during installation was sufficient to get earlier versions of Windows fully working, but with Windows XP and Vista it is only the first step in the activation process. You are locked out of the system if you do not activate Windows within 30 days of installing it, so you have to activate Windows or keep installing it from scratch!

Where possible, it is definitely advisable to opt for automatic activation via the Internet. The telephone alternative requires you to read a 50-digit code to a Microsoft representative. This code appears onscreen during the activation process. This is bad enough, but you then have to enter a 42-digit code supplied by the representative. This is clearly an awkward and time-consuming way of doing things, and there is plenty of scope for errors to occur. By contrast, activation over the Internet is quick and there is virtually no chance of errors occurring.

WPA problems

Having to go through the WPA process should be no more than a minor inconvenience, and it is not the necessity for activation that is the main "bone of contention". The activation key is derived from your Windows product identification number and the hardware installed in the PC. To be more precise, it is typically these items of hardware that are used to produce the number:

Microprocessor type

Microprocessor serial number

Display adapter

SCSI adapter (if fitted)

IDE adapter

Network adapter (if fitted)

RAM amount

Hard drive

Hard drive volume serial number

CD/DVD drives

When Windows Vista is booted, as part of the boot-up process the installed hardware is checked. The boot process is only completed if the installed hardware matches the full product key that is stored on the hard disc drive during the activation process. On the face of it, two computers having identical hardware could use the same activation key. In practice, this is not possible because the network adapter and processor serial numbers are unique. Two seemingly identical PCs would actually need different activation keys due to the processors and (where appropriate) the network card having different serial numbers.

There is a potential problem, in that any changes to the hardware will cause a mismatch during the checking process at boot-up. This problem is not as great as it might seem, because you are allowed a certain amount of leeway. Up to four of the items of hardware listed previously can be altered without the need to reactivate the operating system. If more than four items are changed, the activation mechanism will probably assume that the system has been copied to another computer, and it will halt the boot process.

This does not mean that you will have to buy Windows Vista again. It will be necessary to call the WPA clearing-house though, in order to obtain a new activation key. Frequent changes to the computer's hardware and calls to the WPA centre would presumably result in Microsoft refusing to provide further activation codes. You are permitted four changes to the hardware in 120 days or less. This suggests that you can make as many changes to the hardware as you like provided they are made slowly so that there are no more than four changes in each 120 day period. I have not tested this in practice though.

There is little likelihood of problems unless you undertake a massive hardware upgrade. A call to the WPA centre should then get things working again. However, it is best not to be too eager to activate a newly installed copy of Windows Vista. This is especially important when upgrading from an earlier version of Windows, if you are unsure about the compatibility of some pieces of hardware. You are given the opportunity to go through the activation process once the upgrade has been completed, but it is best not to do so at this stage.

First, load any new drivers that are required, and try out the new system. If necessary, upgrade some of the hardware, and only go through the activation process when everything is working properly. You have 30 days to get everything working properly, which should be more than ample. It is not necessary to wait for the 30 days to expire before activating Windows Vista. The activation process can be started at any time by going to the Start menu, selecting All Programs, followed by Accessories, System Tools, and Activate Windows.

Bundled Windows Vista

Product activation is always required when using a retail version of Windows Vista. In other words, activation is always needed if you buy a boxed version of Windows Vista from a computer shop, rather than getting it bundled with a PC. It makes no difference whether you use the full version or the upgrade, the activation rules are the same. It is also needed when using an OEM (original equipment manufacturer) version, which is essentially the same as the retail version, but it is supplied with a new PC.

The situation is different with some versions of Windows Vista that are supplied with PCs from one of the major PC manufacturers. These are special versions produced specifically for that particular manufacturer. Rather than using product activation, the program is licensed for use with one PC. That PC is the one with which the operating system was supplied. This system usually works by having the program read the serial number of the BIOS chip in the PC. The operating system will fail to work unless the correct serial number is found, making it unusable on any other PC. PCs covered by volume licences do not usually require product activation either.

NTFS or FAT32

Windows in general uses three file systems for hard disc drives. These are FAT (also known as FAT16), FAT32, and NTFS. Windows XP can use all three systems, but Windows Vista is less accommodating. With a few caveats it can use FAT system data discs, but it can not be installed on a FAT formatted disc. Neither can Vista be installed on a disc that is formatted using the FAT32 file system. This is not to say that Windows Vista is incompatible with FAT32 format discs. It will actually work perfectly well with FAT32 data discs, which can be in the form of additional hard discs, Flash cards in some form of adaptor, or any other form that the operating system recognises as a disc drive. Of course, any facilities that rely on the NTFS file system will not be available when using a FAT32 disc.

Windows Vista should have no difficulty in reading things like Flash cards from a digital camera or portable computing device, and it should be able to access all the discs in a dual boot system where there are one or more FAT32 partitions. It will not install on a FAT32 disc or partition, and it is not possible to upgrade a Windows installation on a FAT32 disc or partition. An error message will be obtained if you try to upgrade a Windows XP installation that is on a FAT32 drive.

A PC running Windows XP will almost certainly be using the NTFS format for the main (boot) drive. However, if you are in doubt about the file system of your PC, it is easy to find out which one is in use. Locate drive C: using Windows Explorer, right-click on its entry, and then choose Properties from the pop-down menu that appears. This will produce a window like the one shown in Figure 1.43. Details of the file system are given in the upper section of the window, and in this example the drive is a FAT32 type.

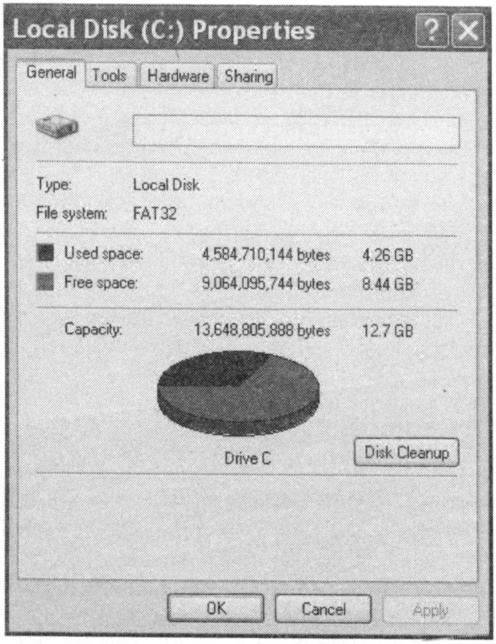

Fig.1.43 The disc in this example is a FAT32 type

Apart from a special case such as a dual boot system, it is better to use the NTFS file system for hard disc drives. This enables access to files and folders to be restricted using the permissions feature. Additionally, files can be encrypted. With the FAT and FAT32 file systems it is possible for anyone to access your files if they have possession of the disc drive. NTFS is more reliable than FAT or FAT32, due to its use of log files to monitor disc activity. This gives a much better chance of the system being able to automatically recover from hard disc problems. Another advantage of the NTFS file system is that disc drives having a capacity of more than 8 gigabytes are handled more efficiently.

Converting

Windows XP includes a conversion program that will convert FAT or FAT32 hard discs to NTFS operation, so it is possible to convert a FAT32 disc to NTFS operation before upgrading to Vista. Unfortunately, the conversion is made via a command line program and not a normal Windows application, but it is still reasonably easy to make the conversion. It can be run by first selecting the Run option from

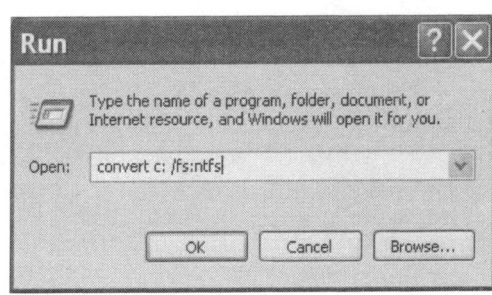

Fig.1.44 Running the conversion program

the Start menu. Then type this line into the textbox in the new Window that appears (Figure 1.44), making sure that it is exactly as shown here:

convert c: /fs:ntfs

It is assumed here that the disc to be converted is drive C:, and the drive letter given in this command must be changed if you wish to convert a different disc. The second part of the command indicates the file system that you wish to use for the disc, which is obvious NTFS in this example. Operate the OK button to run the program, which will result in a DOS box opening and a message like the one shown in Figure 1.45 appearing. The first part of the message simply indicates the current file system used on the disc, which should be FAT or (more probably) FAT32. The second part points out that the program can not run at this stage because the disc for conversion is currently in use.

This message might not appear if you are converting something other than the boot drive, and the conversion process with then go ahead instead. If you are trying to convert the boot disc, it will inevitably be used by Windows and probably numerous background tasks as well. You are given the opportunity to dismount the disc, but this option should not be taken. The only way to successfully use the conversion program on the boot disc is to have it run automatically at start-up. Presumably, the conversion program runs before Windows fully installs and the boot disc is properly utilised by Windows.

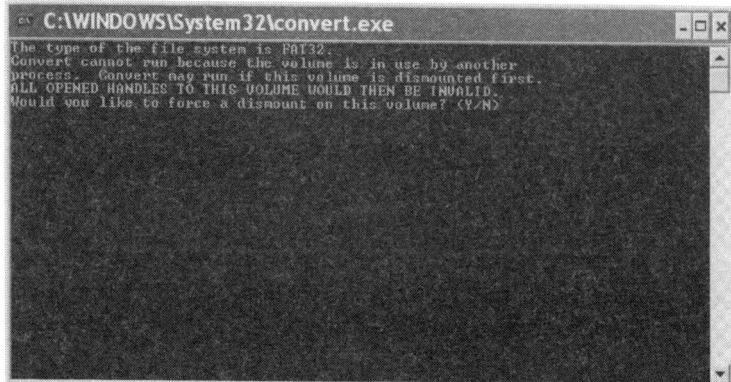

Fig.1.45 The conversion program is a command line utility

Programs are run automatically using the often-overlooked Scheduled Tasks facility. It is not difficult to set up this feature for yourself, and the first task is to go to the Control Panel and double-click the Scheduled

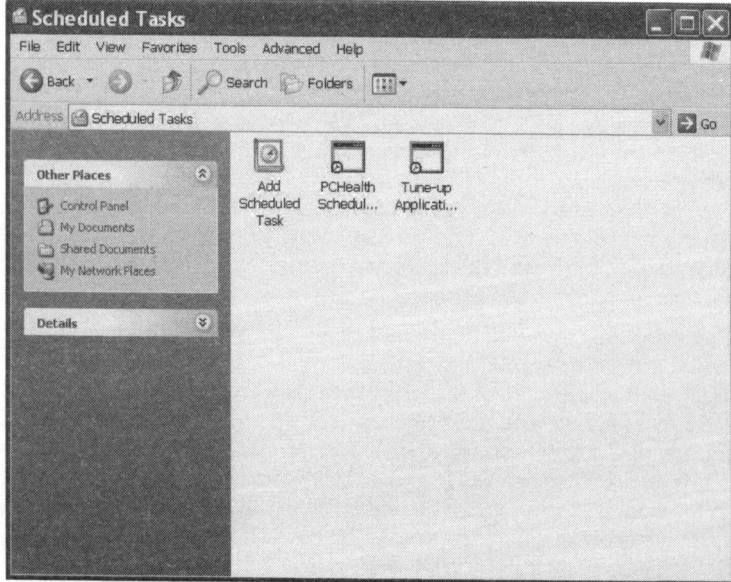

Fig.1.46 Windows XP includes a scheduled task facility

Tasks icon. This brings up a window like the one of Figure 1.46, and here the Add Scheduled Task icon is double-clicked. An information window like the one of Figure 1.47 then appears, and operating the Next button then moves things on to the window where the required program is selected (Figure 1.48). The program can be selected from the list or the program file can be selected using the standard browse feature. Having selected the appropriate program, operate the Next button to move on to the window where the schedule is selected (Figure 1.49). There are several options available via the radio buttons, including one that runs the program when the computer starts.

In this case it is probably best not to set things up manually, because the switches required by the program complicate matters. Also, Windows will arrange the scheduling for you if you try to run the program and answer "N" when asked if you would like to dismount the disc. Further information appears in the DOS box (Figure 1.50). This explains that the Convert program can not gain exclusive access to the disc, and it asks if you wish to run the program automatically next

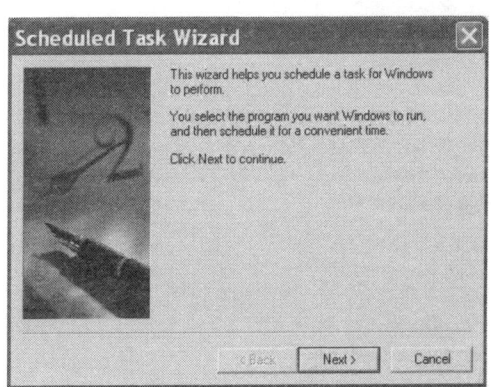

Fig.1.47 The first step in scheduling a task

time the computer is started. Answer "Y" to this question and then restart the computer.

During the boot-up process a screen like the one of Figure 1.51 will appear, explaining that the conversion program is about to run. You have 10 seconds to press any key and abort the process. Assuming that the program is allowed to run, it will start by checking the disc and reporting its results (Figure 1.52). If all is well, the conversion process will go ahead and eventually the program will report that its task has been completed successfully (Figure 1.53). At this stage the example system crashed and produced a standard error screen. However, Windows XP is very robust, and rebooting the computer resulted in it starting up correctly. After some frantic disc activity the process was

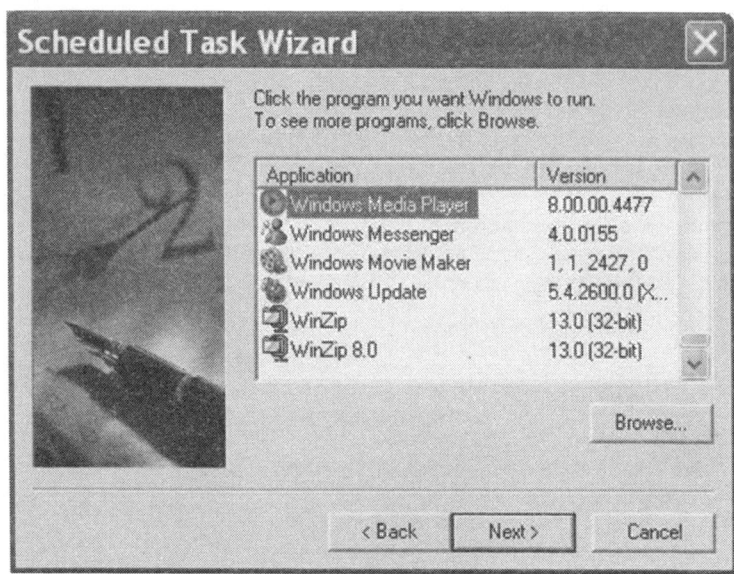

Fig.1.48 Selecting the program to be scheduled

complete and the disc was fully operational under the NTFS file system. It is as well to check that the conversion has been successful by bringing up the properties window for the disc. This should show that it uses the NTFS file system, as in Figure 1.54.

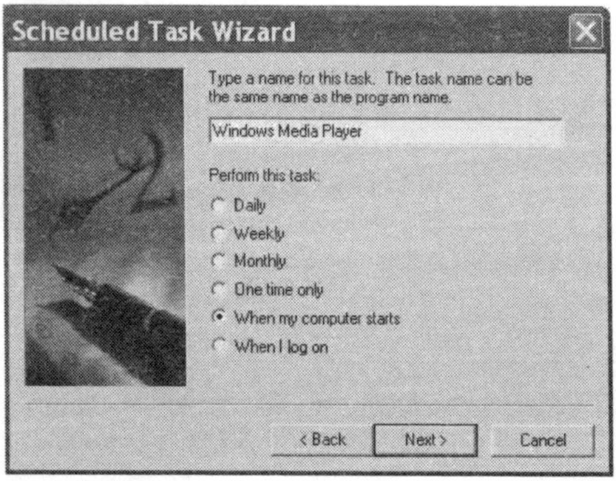

Some programs use files that are cleverly hidden away on the disc in order to store passwords. Using an image of a hard disc or changing its basic structure in some way will usually result in the disappearance of any passwords stored away in hidden files.

Fig.1.49 Selecting the schedule for the program

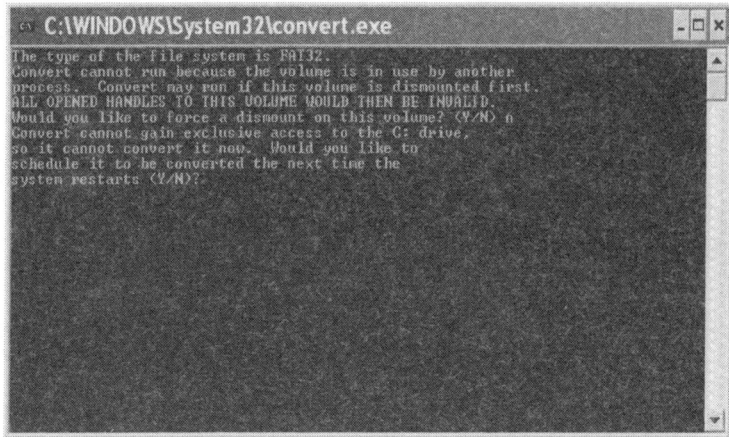

Fig.1.50 The conversion program can be scheduled automatically

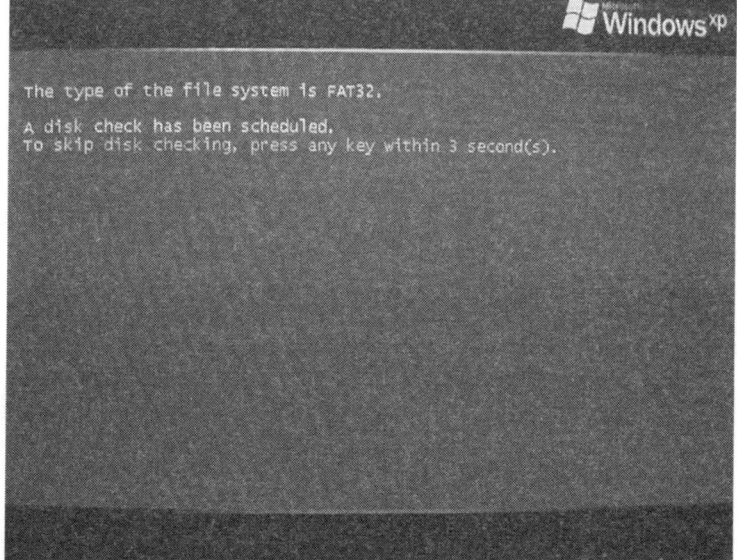

Fig.1.51 The program runs when the computer is restarted

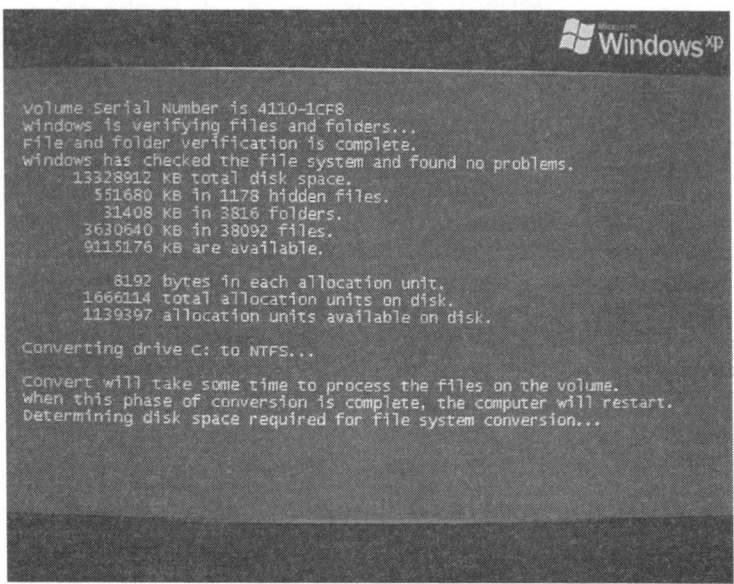

Fig.1.52 The program starts by checking the disc

Changing from one file system to another is almost certain to result in the disappearance of any concealed passwords, or any other concealed files. For example, if you have an AOL password stored on the disc,

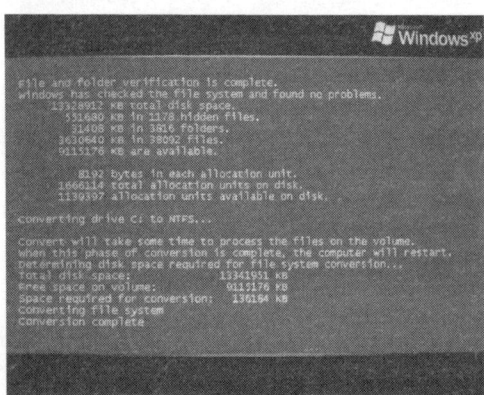

changing to the NTFS file system will result in its disappearance. Any loss of stored passwords should not cause any major problems. You will merely have to store them on the disc again in order to resume instant access to the protected files and programs.

Fig.1.53 The conversion has been completed successfully

Utilities

There is an unrivalled range of utility software available for the Windows operating system. Whether this software came into being because of numerous deficiencies and faults in these systems, or simply because the software houses wished to sell it to us is debatable. Something that is not debatable is that some of these programs are not compatible with Windows Vista. The fact that you have been using a utility

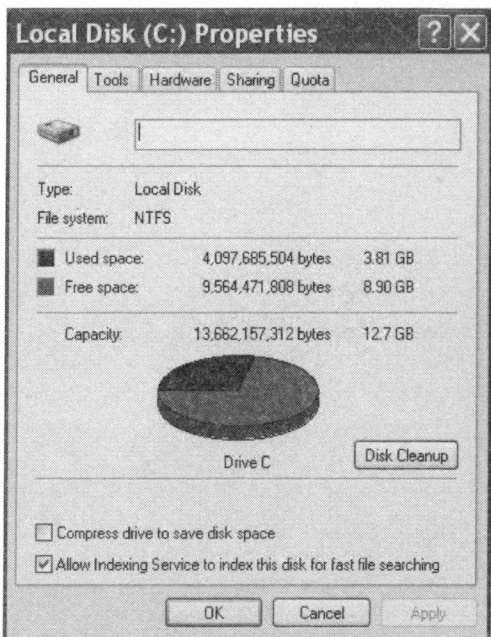

Fig.1.54 The disc is now an NTFS type

successfully for years with other Windows operating systems is no guarantee that it will work properly with Windows XP. Even if you have been using it with Windows XP or 2000, that is still no guarantee of compatibility with Windows Vista.

In some cases incompatible programs will just produce nonsense results or no data at all. With other programs there is a risk of the operating system being damaged rather than improved in some way. Particularly when using utility programs such as disc defragmenters and cleanup programs, check that they are suitable for use with Windows Vista before using them. The manufacturers' web sites should give up to date information on their utility programs, together with details of any upgrades to Vista compatible versions. Apart from the obvious risk of damaging the operating system, with some of these programs there is a danger of losing important data stored on the hard disc.

A warning message may well be produced if you try to install a popular program that has known issues when run on a PC that uses Windows

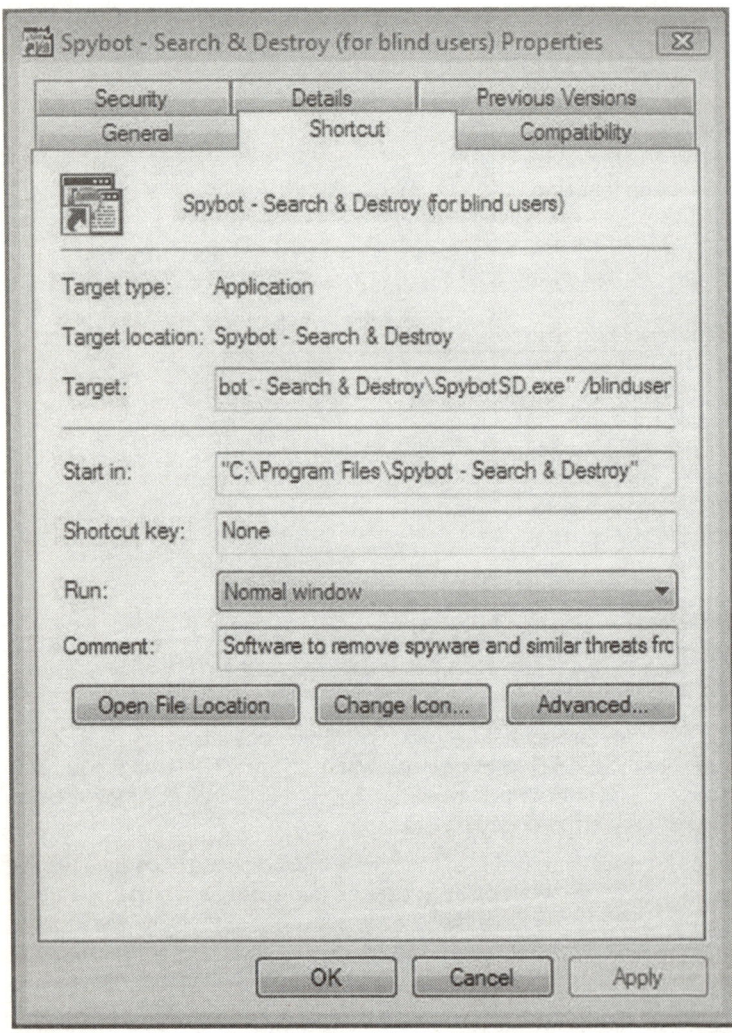

Fig.1.55 Left-click the Compatibilty tab

Vista. The fact that a warning appears does not necessarily mean that the program is totally incompatible with Vista. It might just be that there are minor problems when using certain screen resolutions, certain

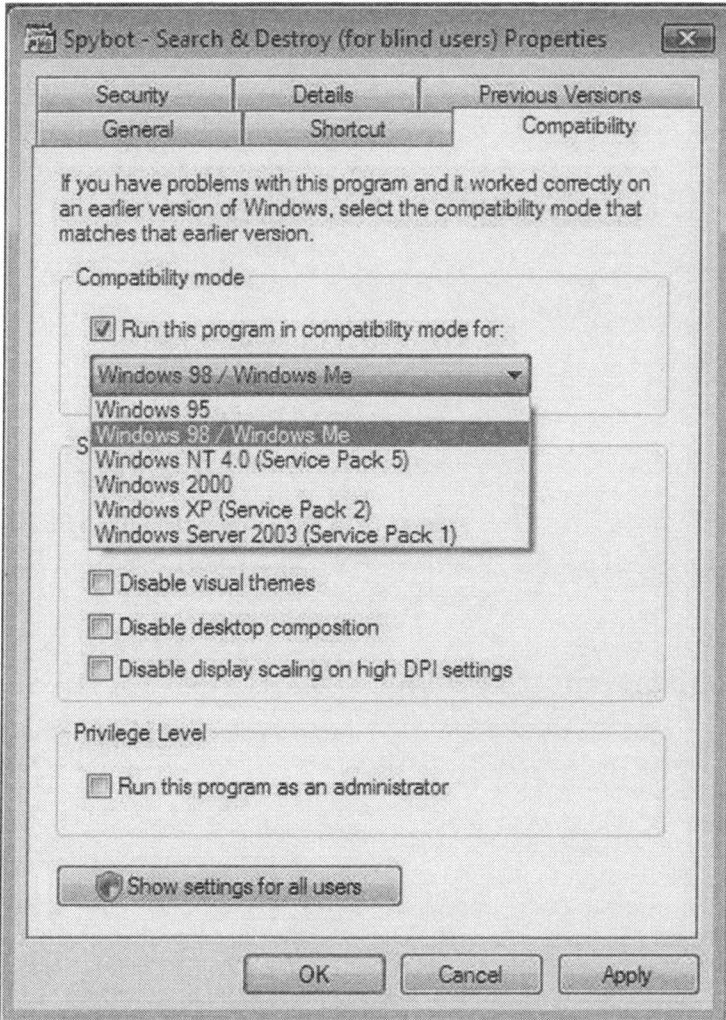

Fig.1.56 The menu offers compatibility with earlier versions of Windows

peripheral devices, or something of this type. However, it would definitely be advisable to investigate the matter further before deciding whether to go ahead with the installation.

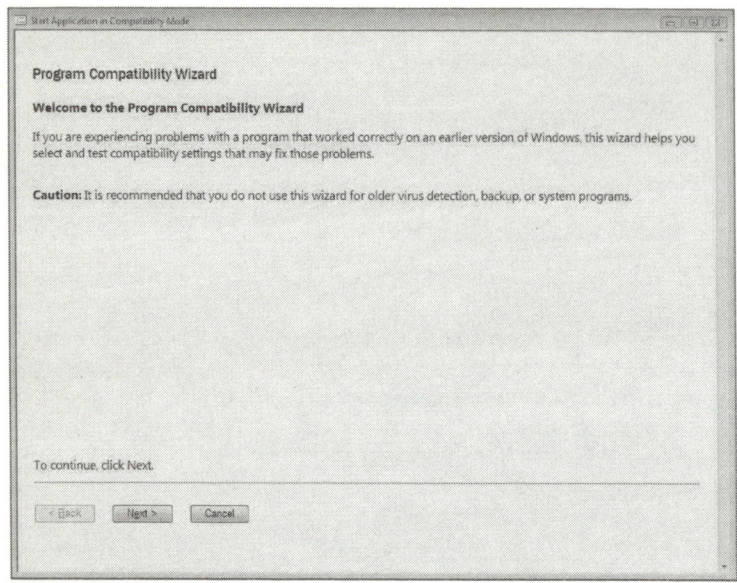

Fig.1.57 The first window of the Program Compatibility Wizard

Software compatibility

As pointed out previously, where an old program gives problems with Windows Vista it is possible to set the operating system to give a higher degree of compatibility. It has to be emphasised that this is not a good idea with utility software, or any programs that produce an incompatibility warning message from Windows Vista. Ignoring warnings is likely to cause damage to the operating system, and is unlikely to get the troublesome software working properly. If (say) a program uses a DLL file that gives problems with Windows Vista, and should not be used with this operating system, setting a greater level of compatibility will not stop it from causing problems. The idea of this facility is to make Windows Vista more accommodating to old programs that take shortcuts that are not normally permitted under this operating system.

The compatibility level can be adjusted manually by right-clicking on a shortcut to the program, or on the entry of the program file in Windows Explorer, and then selecting the Properties option. Using either method, a window similar to the one shown in Figure 1.55 should appear. The tabs at the top of the window vary somewhat depending on the exact

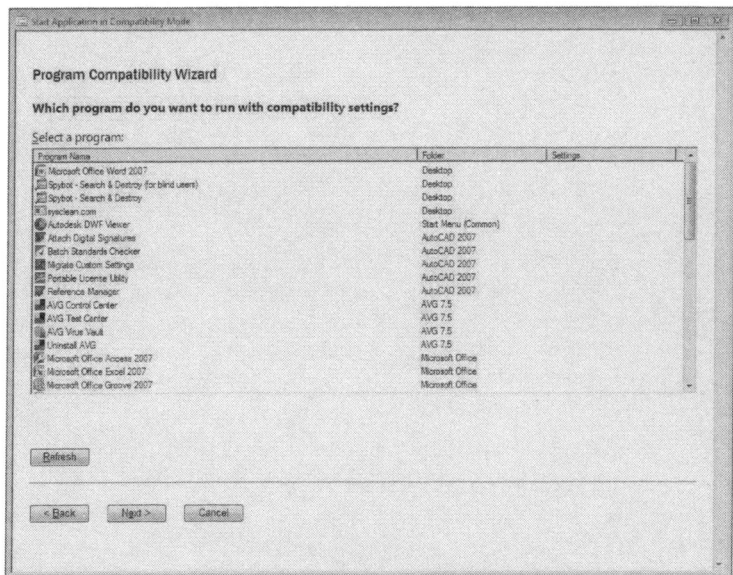

Fig.1.58 Use this window to select the right program

nature of the program file. Left-clicking the Compatibility tab produces a
window like the one shown in Figure 1.56. The middle section of the
window has checkboxes that can be used to limit the program to basic
video modes. In most cases it is the upper section that is needed, and
the first step is to tick the checkbox marked "Run this program in
compatibility mode for". This activates the menu that enables the program
to be run in modes that give compatibility with earlier 32-bit versions of
Windows. This menu can be seen in Figure 1.56. If the program had
previously worked perfectly under Windows ME for example, the Windows
98/ME option would be used. Note that it is only necessary to set the
level of compatibility once. The correct mode will then be used each
time the program is run.

Program compatibility can also be set using the Program Compatibility
Wizard. First go to the Start menu and launch the Help and Support
program. Use the search system to locate and launch the Program
Compatibility Wizard (Figure 1.57). I soon located it using "program
compatibility wizard" as the search string. It is then largely a matter of
answering questions by making the appropriate selections (Figure 1.58)
in standard Wizard fashion. The program should then be run in a suitable

Fig.1.59 The initial screen when upgrading to Vista

mode, but with both methods of mode selection there is no guarantee that the program will work properly under Windows Vista.

Upgrade method

Note that with Windows Vista you do not upgrade an XP installation by booting from the Vista installation disc. The only way to upgrade an XP system is to first go into Windows XP, which must be a legitimate installation, and then insert the Vista installation disc into a DVD drive. This should autorun, and the window shown in Figure 1.59 will then appear. Inevitably there are some differences between this method of installation and installing a fresh copy of Windows by booting from the installation disc, especially in the early stages.

A number of options are available from this window, including one to go online and check the compatibility of your PC. You should really have done this already, in addition to carrying out any recommendations. If no compatibility check has been made previously, then you should certainly go through this process now. Provided the necessary checks

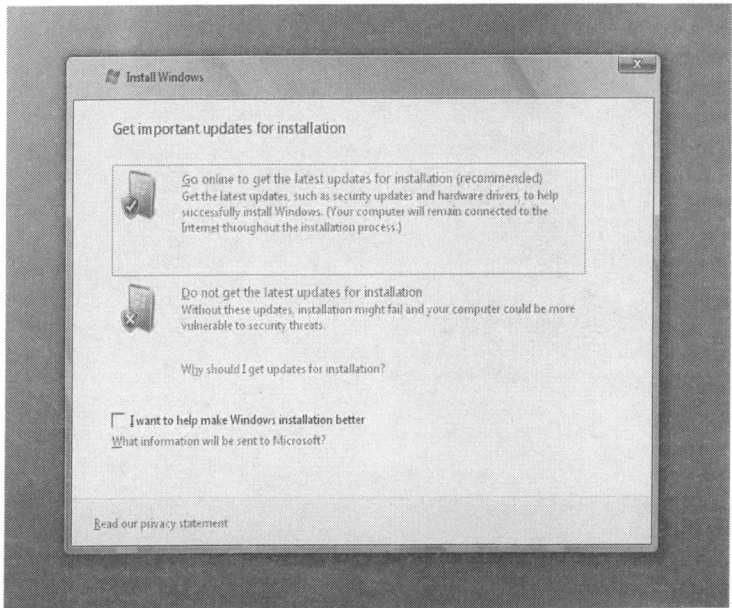

Fig.1.60 There is the option of checking for updates to Vista

and amendments to the system and hardware have been made, operate the Install Now button to proceed with the upgrade.

The next window (Figure 1.60) gives the options of installing Vista using the version on the DVD, or going online to get any available updates. It probably makes little difference whether you opt to install an updated version, or to install the original version and then update it later. The final installation is presumably the same either way. For this example I opted to install Vista without going online for the latest updates.

It is not mandatory to use your product key in order to install Windows Vista, but it is needed in order to activate the program and keep it working beyond the 30-day trial period. Therefore, it is probably best to enter it into the textbox at the next window (Figure 1.61). There is the option of automatically activating the program as part of the installation process. Tick the checkbox if you wish to use this method, which is the easiest way of handling product activation. However, it will obviously require the PC to have an active Internet connection. Also, it is probably best to get Vista installed and running to your satisfaction before activating your copy and tying it to a particular PC.

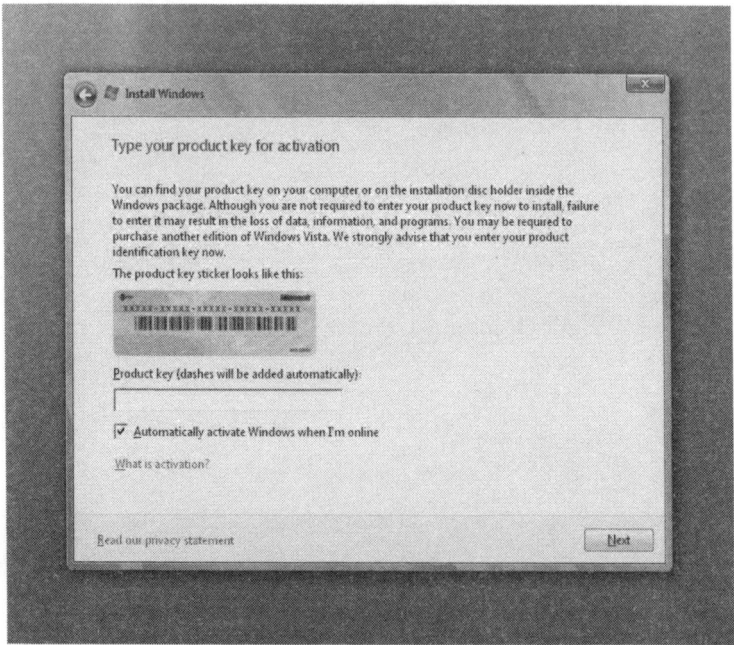

Fig.1.61 Your product key can be entered here

The OEM and retail versions of the Windows Vista installation disc have the wherewithal to install several different versions. You use the menu at the next window (Figure 1.62) to select the version you have purchased. Then tick the checkbox to confirm that you have selected the right one. It is essential to make the correct selection here, because it will not be possible to activate the product unless you do so. The product key supplied with your copy of Vista will only be usable with whatever version you actually bought. I think that I am correct is stating that the key will not even work with a cheaper version than the one you purchased. It will definitely not work with one of the more expensive versions. If you entered your product key at an earlier window, the installer will not proceed unless the right version is selected.

It is then necessary to agree to the licence conditions before proceeding further (Figure 1.63). You can not install Vista unless you agree to these conditions. A window offering the choice of upgrading or installing from

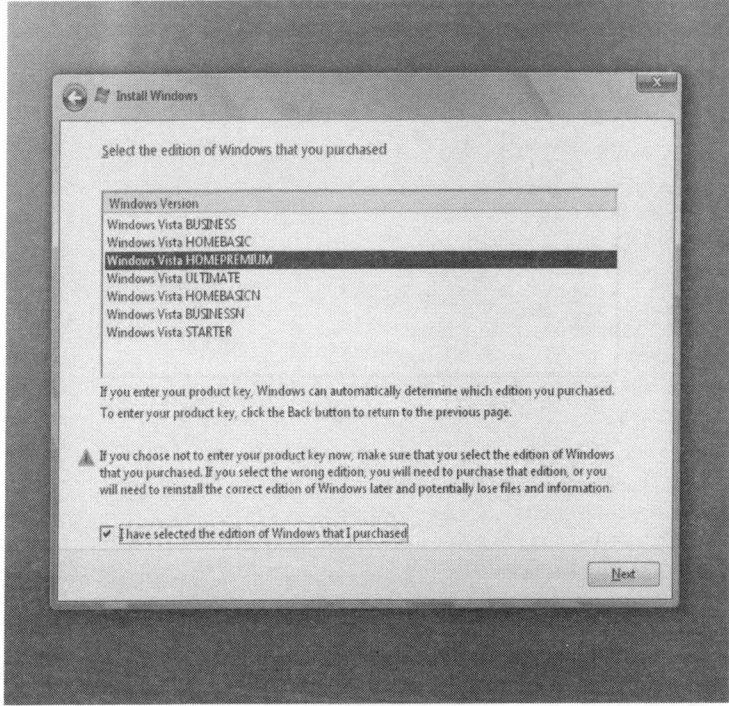

Fig.1.62 Make sure that you select the correct version of Vista

scratch should then appear (Figure 1.64). It is important to realise the difference between the two. With an upgrade, all your existing programs should run as before. It is assumed here that any incompatible programs will have already been dealt with.

Installing Vista from scratch, provided the existing Windows partition is used, seems to leave all your data files intact, together with all the programs files and much else. However, the programs will not be usable with Vista and will have to be reinstalled. This method is likely to leave vast numbers of duplicate and unused files on the hard disc drive, so it is advisable to opt for the upgrade path whenever this is possible.

It will not be possible to select the Upgrade option if the installer detects a problem. In this example I was not making a serious attempt at updating to Vista, and the lower part of the window lists two problems that prevent

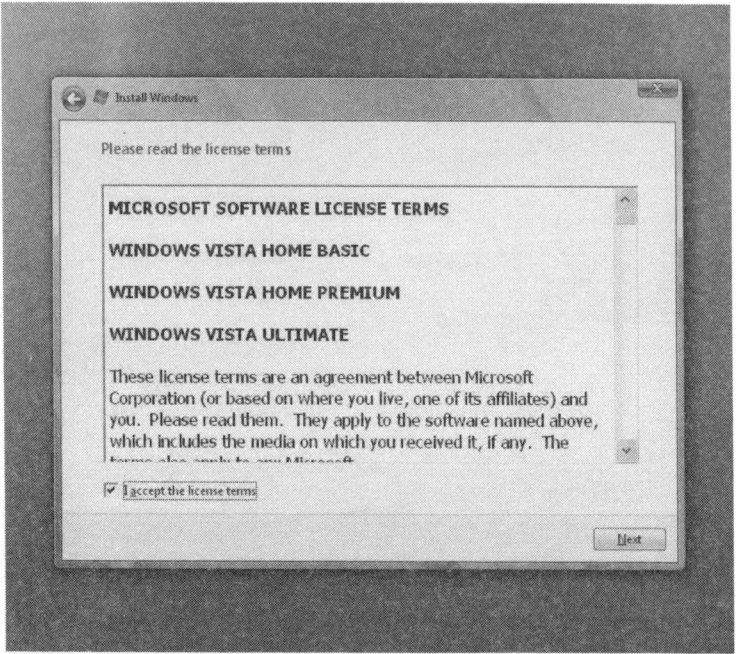

Fig.1.63 You must accept the licence conditions in order to proceed

the upgrade from proceeding. One is simply a lack of free hard disc space, and problems of this type can be detected by the Upgrade Advisor program. As pointed out previously, it is not possible to upgrade to Vista if the boot disc has the FAT32 format instead of the NTFS type. The disc has to be converted to NTFS format before upgrading.

The other problem is less obvious, and it is simply that I am trying to upgrade from Windows XP Professional to Windows Vista Home Premium. It is not possible to upgrade from any given version of XP to any desired version of Vista. There are some restrictions, and this particular upgrade path is not available. Strangely, this upgrade is not available in this instance, even though I am using the full retail version of Vista Home Premium, and not an upgrade disc. Consequently, installing Vista from scratch is possible and completely legitimate, but upgrading a Windows XP Professional installation is not. You clearly need to be very careful when buying a Vista upgrade product. Table 1 shows the upgrade paths that are and are not permitted.

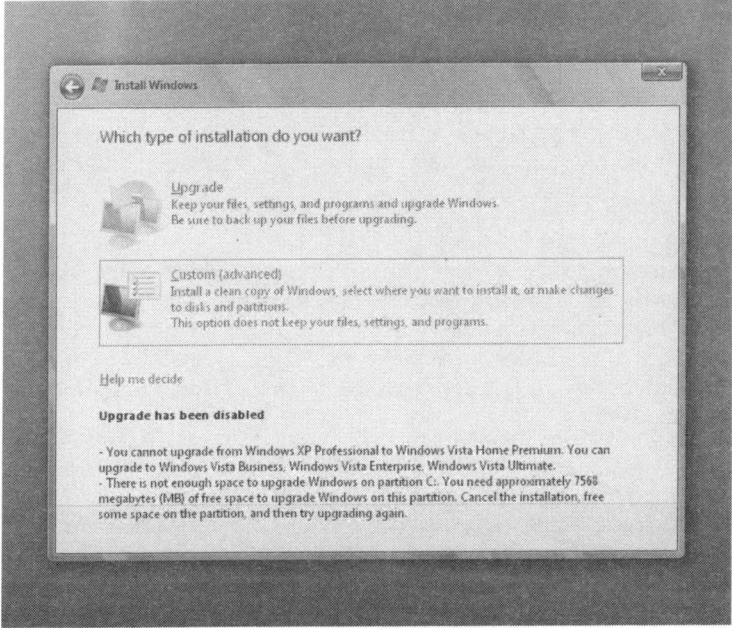

Fig.1.64 If there is a choice, select the Upgrade option

Table 1	WINDOWS VISTA EDITIONS			
	HB	HP	B	U
Windows XP Professional	N	N	Y	Y
Windows XP Home	Y	Y	Y	Y
Windows XP Media Center	N	Y	N	Y
Windows XP Tablet PC	N	N	Y	Y
Windows XP Pro x64	N	N	N	N
Windows 2000	N	N	N	N

Provided you can get the upgrade option active, it should then be "plain sailing" once this option has been selected. Things should then proceed in much the same way as when installing Vista from scratch.

Points to remember

The fact that your computer can run an earlier version of Windows does not mean that it will be able to handle Windows Vista. Something well beyond the minimum hardware requirement is needed in order to run Windows Vista really well.

The upgrade advisor program is useful for testing the hardware and software for incompatibility problems before upgrading to Windows Vista. A number of potential problems might be found by this program, but it is unlikely that any of them will make the upgrade impossible. In most cases some new device drivers will be needed, or software will have to be reinstalled.

It might be necessary to uninstall any incompatible software and hardware prior to the upgrade. Some software simply has to be uninstalled and then reinstalled in order to provide Windows Vista compatibility. It is possible that one or two programs will be totally incompatible with Vista.

The hardware manufacturer's web site is the first place to look if new device drivers are needed after the upgrade to Windows Vista has been completed. There are specialist web sites that can help with the location of device drivers. Where Windows Vista drivers have been produced, they will almost certainly be available somewhere on the Internet.

The video card might work with a full range of resolutions and colour depths after the upgrade, but it will almost certainly run very slowly until the proper Windows Vista device drivers are installed. If you are lucky, the correct drivers will be installed during the upgrade.

It is not necessary to register Windows Vista in order to use it, but it will stop working after 30 days unless it is activated. Reactivation will be needed if it is reinstalled, and might also be necessary if large changes are made to the hardware. Activation via the Internet is much easier than using the telephone method.

Windows Vista can not be installed on a hard disc that uses the FAT32 format. If the XP installation is on a FAT32 hard disc drive it will be necessary to convert the disc to NTFS format before upgrading. There is no need to convert data discs to NTFS types: it is only the boot disc that has to use this format.

If you are unable to get satisfactory results from Windows Vista it is possible to uninstall it and revert to the original operating system and set-up.

Troublesome software that worked with earlier versions of Windows can usually be made to work with Windows XP by running the software in a compatibility mode. Do not use a compatibility mode if Windows produces warring messages about incompatible DLL files, or something of this nature. Neither should a compatibility mode be used with utility programs such as disc defragmenters.

Do not use utility programs unless they are designed for operation with Windows Vista. If you use old software of this type there is a strong risk of major damage to the Windows installation and other files on the hard disc.

Note that it is not possible to upgrade from any given version of Windows XP to any version of Vista. Certain upgrade paths, such as from Windows XP Professional to Windows Vista Home Premium are not allowed. Make sure that your intended upgrade is actually possible before buying an upgrade version of Vista.

1   Upgrading problems

Prevention is...

Bugs

An installation of the Windows operating system coming to grief is not exactly a rare occurrence, but why should these problems happen at all? I suppose that the chances of removing every single bug from software as complex as this is virtually nil, but genuine bugs in Windows are almost certainly responsible for only a small percentage of the problems. Modern PC hardware is very reliable, and hardware glitches probably have nothing to do with the vast majority of problems either.

Most of the difficulties seem to be due to things that either the user or applications programs do to Windows. Unfortunately, quite minor things can prevent Windows from operating correctly, and it is easily "gummed up" by users making alterations to system settings or deleting essential files. Software that does not strictly abide by the rules can also generate problems. Windows Vista is much more robust than earlier versions such as Windows 95 and Windows ME, and it will hopefully be even more robust than Windows XP. However, the impression given by some that Windows XP was "bomb proof" certainly proved to be misleading, and it would be naïve to expect Windows Vista to be totally crash-proof either. Windows Vista places restrictions on software that largely prevent it from using the hardware in such a fashion that the computer will crash or operate unpredictably. It also protects important system files so that rogue software can not alter them.

In fact, there is a whole raft of measures that are designed to prevent accidental or malicious damage to the system. Compared with early versions, Windows Vista is also much better at recovering from major problems. Even so, problems can still occur and the computer can crash. In most cases, one program crashing will not bring down any others. Each program effectively has its own operating system. Crashing one program and system will leave the others working normally, and any data in the other systems will be safe. However, a catastrophic failure can still occur, and will usually produce a blue screen full of programming data and a suggestion that you contact the system administrator. Fortunately, this type of thing is quite rare.

Do not tweak

Probably the only sure-fire way of preventing Windows from getting into difficulties is to never install any applications programs at all, which is not exactly a practical proposition. However, you can certainly reduce the risk of problems occurring by following some simple rules. Experienced users fiddle around with the Windows configuration files and manage to customise the user interface in ways that are not normally possible. This is fine for those having suitable experience of Windows, because they know what they are doing. They can largely avoid problems and can soon backtrack to safety if something should go wrong.

Inexperienced users are almost certain to damage the operating system if they try this sort of tweaking, and will not have the expertise to quickly sort things out when problems arise. Just the opposite in fact and one thing can lead to another, with the operating system soon getting beyond redemption. If you are not an expert on the inner workings of Windows it is best not to delve into its configuration files. A great deal of customisation can be done using the normal Windows facilities, and there are applications programs that enable further customisation to be undertaken without having to directly alter files.

Even if you are familiar with earlier versions of Windows and their inner workings, it is not a good idea to start hacking into Windows Vista as if it was an earlier version of Windows. Although there are superficial similarities between the various versions of Windows, there are also major differences in their inner workings. Things that are acceptable with Windows ME or XP might not have the desired effect with Windows Vista, if they are permissible at all. If you really must tinker with Windows Vista, gain some experience with this operating system and learn as much about it as possible before you start altering things.

Careful deletion

In the days of MS/DOS it was perfectly acceptable to delete a program and any files associated with it if you no longer wished to use the program. Matters are very different with any version of Windows from Windows 95 onwards, where most software is installed into the operating system. There are actually some simple programs that have just one file, and

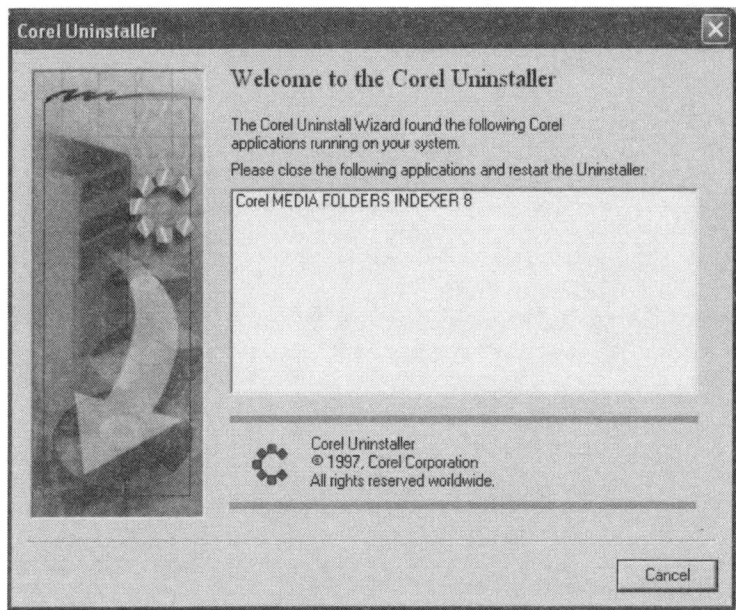

Fig.2.1 Background tasks can prevent an uninstaller from working

which do not require any installation. With others there is a program file and one or two support files, but again, no installation is required.

These standalone program files are quite rare these days, but they can be used much like old MS/DOS programs. To use the program you copy it, together with any support files, onto the hard disc. To run the program you use the Run option from the Start menu, or locate the file using Windows Explorer and double-click on it. No installation program is used, and it is perfectly all right to remove the program by deleting the program file.

Most programs are installed onto the computer using an installation program, and this program does not simply make folders on the hard disc and copy files into them from the CD-ROM. It will also make changes to the Windows configuration files so that the program is properly integrated with the operating system. In particular, it will make changes to the Windows Registry. If you simply delete the program's directory structure to get rid of it, Windows will not be aware that the program has been removed. During the boot-up process the operating system will

Fig.2.2 With Windows Vista, using the Control-Alt-Delete combination produces this screen

probably look for files associated with the deleted program, and will produce error messages when it fails to find them.

There is another potential problem in that Windows utilises shared files. This is where one file, such as a DLL type, is shared by two or more programs. In deleting a program and the other files in its directory structure you could also be deleting files needed by other programs. This could prevent other programs from working properly, or even from starting up at all. If a program is loaded onto the hard disc using an installation program, the only safe way of removing it is to use an uninstaller program. Uninstalling programs was covered to some extent in chapter one, but here we will consider the subject in more depth. There are three possible ways of uninstalling programs.

Custom uninstaller

Some programs load an uninstaller program onto the hard disc as part of the installation process. This program is then available via the Start

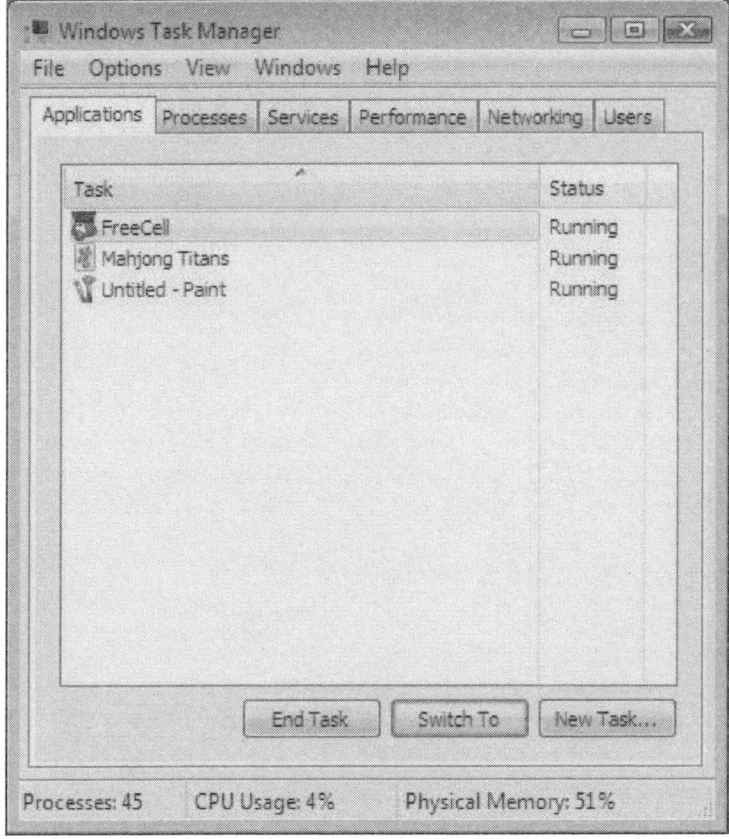

Fig.2.3 The Vista version of the Windows Task Manager

menu if you choose Programs, and then the name of the program concerned. When you choose this option there will be the program itself, plus at least one additional option in the sub-menu that appears. If there is no uninstall option here, no custom uninstaller has been installed for that program. Uninstaller programs of this type are almost invariably automatic in operation, so you have to do little more than instruct it to go ahead with the removal of the program.

Some uninstallers are quite complex, and these are used where a suite of software rather than just one program has been installed. The uninstaller is then more of a Setup program that permits more programs

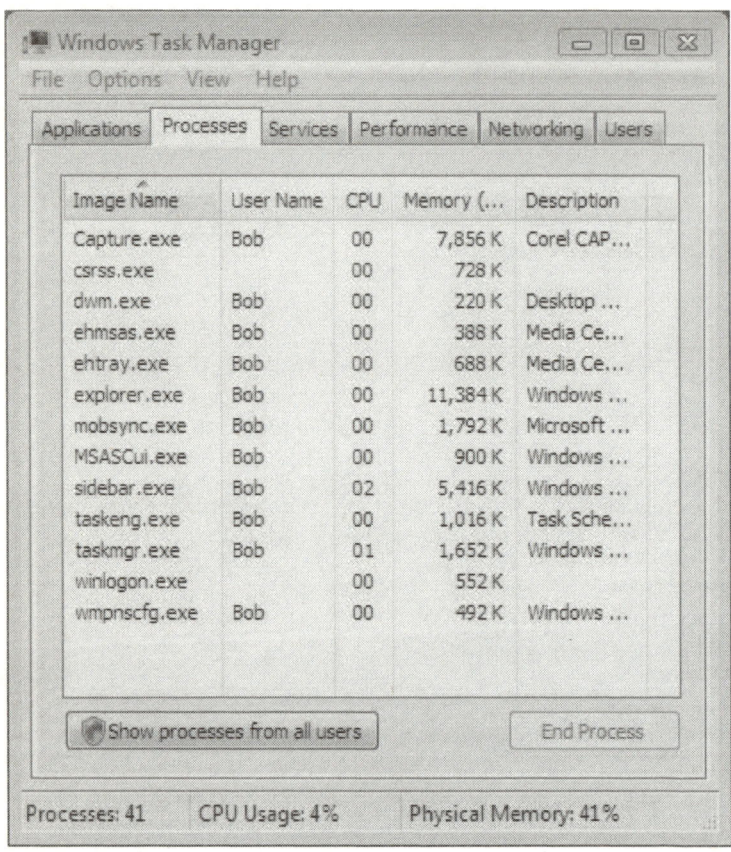

Fig.2.4 The Processes section of Task Manager

to be added in addition to allowing existing ones to be removed. These can be a little more difficult to use than basic uninstaller utilities. Figure 2.1 shows an error message produced by the Corel 8 uninstaller. This kind of error can occur when removing any software, but it is more common with software suites because they often have one or more utility programs running as background tasks. An uninstaller can not be used with software that is in use, so any software it can remove has to be switched off before running the installer.

The easy way of switching off background tasks is to launch the Windows Task Manager. Using the standard Control-Alt-Delete key combination

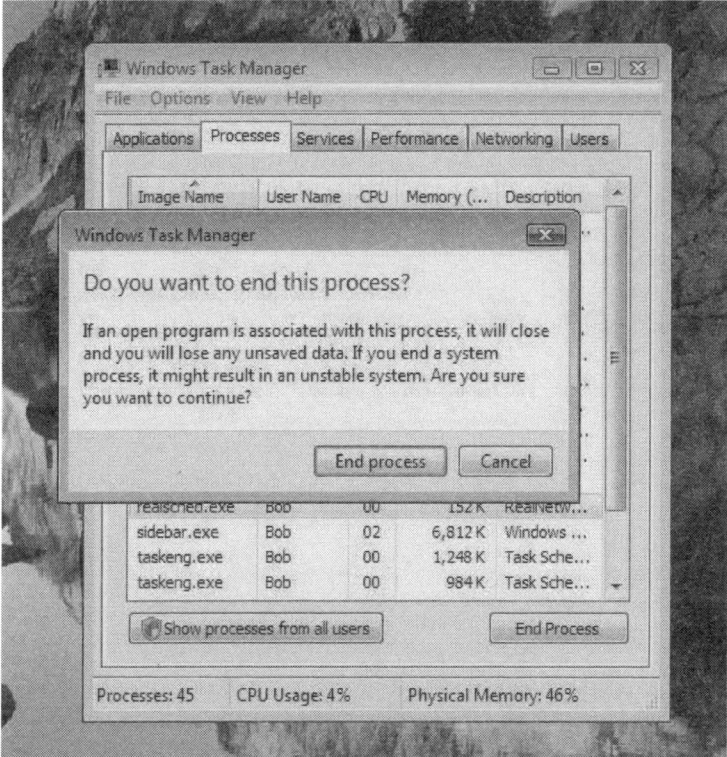

Fig.2.5 A warning is produced if you try to end a process

launches this utility, but in Windows Vista this feature is more complex than in earlier versions. Initially the screen changes to look like Figure 2.2, and a menu is provided in the middle section of the screen. Left-clicking the Start Task Manager option results in the normal desktop reappearing, complete with the Task Manager window (Figure 2.3). With Windows 9x a list of all the programs and tasks currently running is included. With the Windows XP and Vista versions only the main applications currently running are listed. In the example of Figure 2.3 there are three programs listed, but none of these is the one that has to be shut down.

In order to see all the tasks and applications that are running it is necessary to operate the Processes tab near the top of the window. This produces

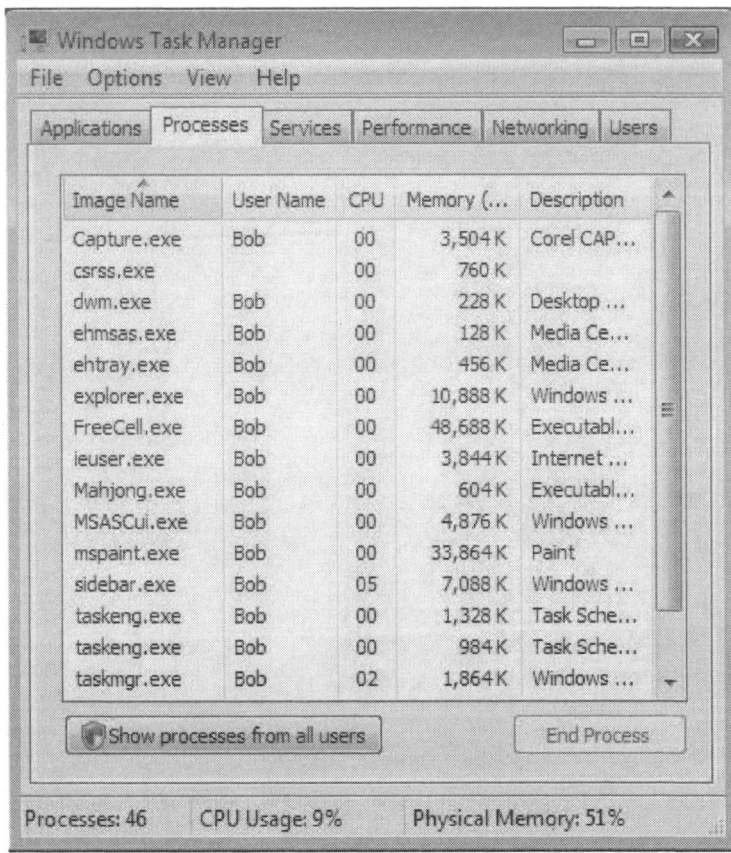

Fig.2.6 The halted process has disappeared from the list

what will usually be a very long list of programs, as in the Example of Figure 2.4. For the sake of this example a background task associate with the Real Player program will be shut down. In order to halt a process it is first selected by left-clicking on its entry, and then the End Process button is operated. This produces the warning message of Figure 2.5, but problems with lost data are unlikely when shutting down a background task. Left-click the Yes button in order to halt the process. The process should then disappear from the list (Figure 2.6). Returning to the Corel Uninstaller program, this time everything is fine (Figure 2.7), and there are no warning messages.

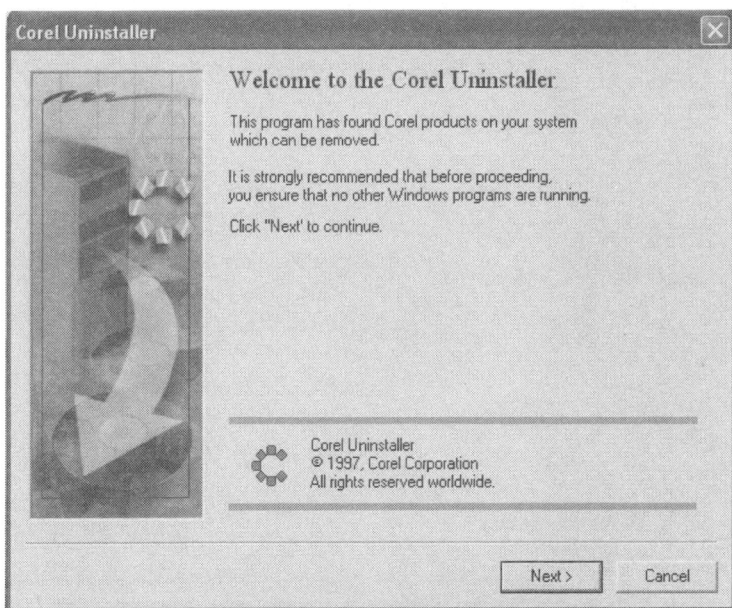

Fig.2.7 This time the uninstaller has worked correctly

With any uninstaller software you may be asked if certain files should be removed. This mostly occurs where the program finds shared files that no longer appear to be shared. This usually means files with a "DLL" extension, which are dynamic link library files. It should be safe to opt for removing any files that are no longer shared, but there is a slight danger that the uninstaller will overlook something and remove a file that is still in use elsewhere. This can produce problems with applications programs and can even produce boot problems. Many users prefer to take the safer option and leave the files in place, even if this results in files and possibly folders being left on the disc unnecessarily. If you are not very expert with Windows it is certainly best to play safe and operate the No button.

Windows uninstaller

Windows has a built-in uninstaller that can be accessed via the Control Panel. From the Start menu select Control Panel and then left-click the Uninstall Programs link in the Programs section of the Control Panel

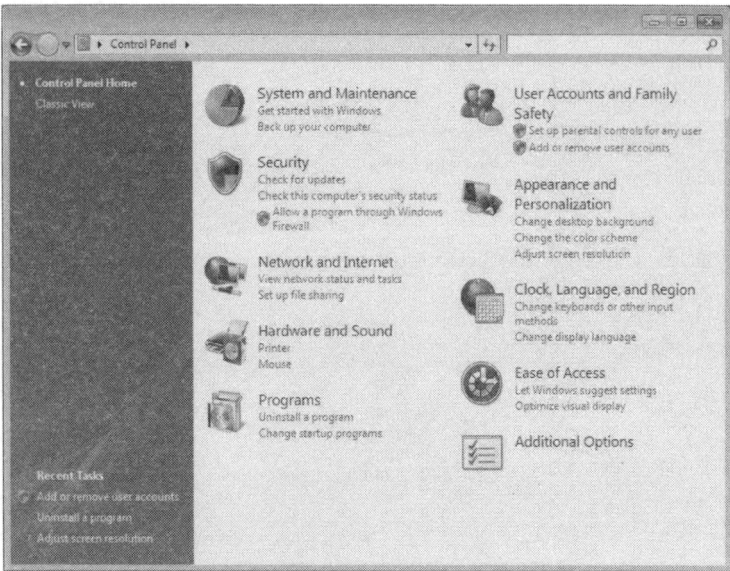

Fig.2.8 Activate the "Uninstall a program" link

(Figure 2.8). This takes you to the uninstaller, and the main section of the window shows a list of the programs that can be uninstalled via this route. In the example of Figure 2.9 there are only three entries because this is a new PC and only a few application programs have been added at this stage. With a PC that is a few years old it is quite normal for there to be two dozen or more entries.

In theory, the list should include all programs that have been added to the hard disc using an installation program. In practice, there are sometimes one or two that have not been installed "by the book" and can not be removed using this method. Some programs can only be removed using their own uninstaller program, while others have no means of removal at all.

It is mainly older software that falls into the non-removable category, particularly programs that were written for Windows 3.1 and not one of the 32-bit versions of Windows. 16-bit software written for Windows 3.1 is fundamentally incompatible with Windows Vista, but it can still be run under this operating system. However, it is run using what is termed a "virtual machine". This means that Windows Vista runs a program that

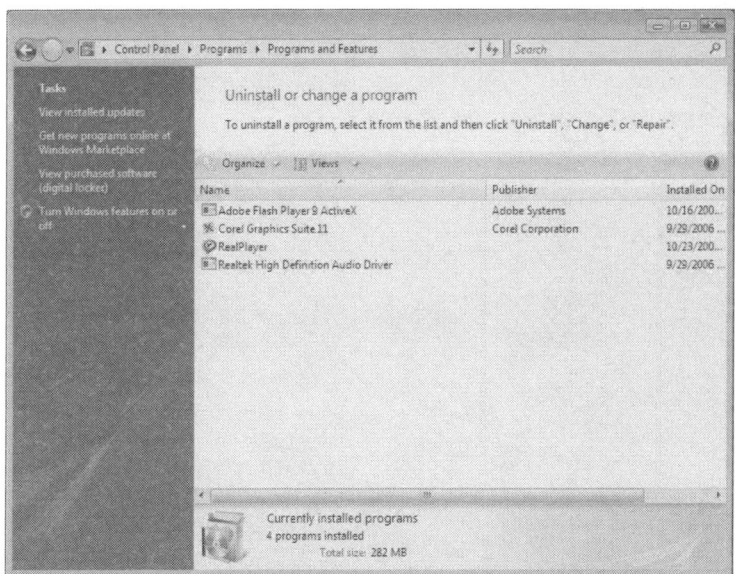

Fig.2.9 With this new installation there are only three programs installed

emulates the old Windows 3.1 operating system and the enhanced mode of the 80386 microprocessor. One consequence of this roundabout method is that 16-bit software may run more slowly than expected.

Windows 3.1 software does not necessarily conform to the current rules, and may try to directly control the hardware. Software of this type will only run under Windows Vista if special device drivers are installed. In general, it is best not to install 16-bit software unless you really do need to use it. If you have 16-bit software installed that you no longer need, third party uninstaller programs might help with its removal. However, the safer option is to simply leave it in place and ignore it. Most software of this type takes up little hard disc space by current standards.

Apart from some 16-bit applications, the only programs that will not be listed in the Add/Remove Programs window are basic standalone programs that did not use an installation process, and were simply copied onto the hard disc. As pointed out previously, these can be deleted manually without any risk of damaging the Windows installation. Where appropriate, the documentation supplied with the program should point out that it does not have to be uninstalled.

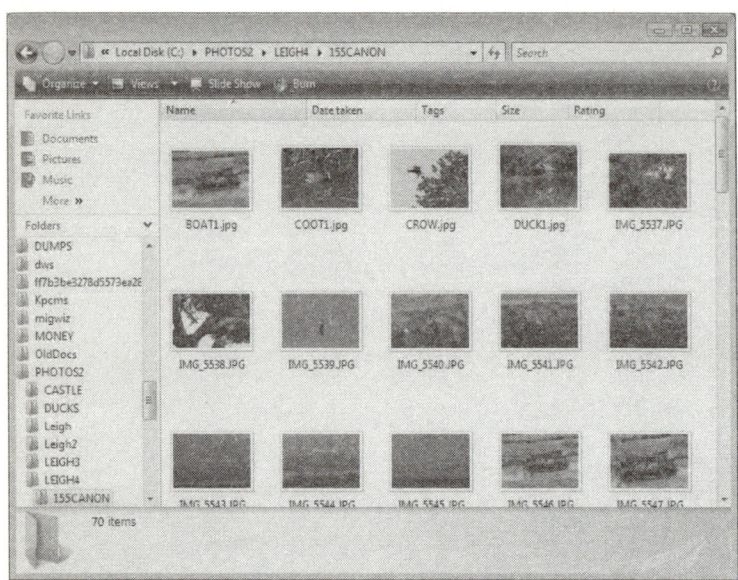

Fig.2.10 By default, large icons or thumbnail images are shown

Assuming the program you wish to remove is in the list, left-click on its entry to select it and then operate the Remove button. It is then a matter of going through the removal process, which is largely or totally automatic. Eventually you should end up back at the Add or Remove Programs window, with the entry for the program no longer listed.

Third party

As pointed out previously, there are third party uninstaller programs available. These can be used to monitor an installation and then uninstall the software at some later time. These programs are perhaps less useful than they once were, because this feature is built into Windows Vista and other versions since Windows 95. Also, the vast majority of applications programs now either utilise the built-in facility or have their own uninstaller software. Most uninstallers will also assist in the removal of programs that they have not been used to install, but this facility is of decreasing relevance to modern Windows computing.

Most of these programs will also help with the removal of things like unwanted entries in the Start menu and act as general cleanup software.

Although Windows itself provides means of clearing most of this software debris, these facilities are perhaps of more use to most users than the uninstaller routines. Inexperienced users will probably find this method easier than going through the official Windows channels.

Using utility software for "housekeeping" tasks should also involve less risk of damaging the system. It is worth repeating the warning that some Windows utility programs are not compatible with Windows Vista. Using incompatible utility software can seriously damage the system and other files on the hard disc. Always ensure that any utility programs are fully compatible with Windows Vista

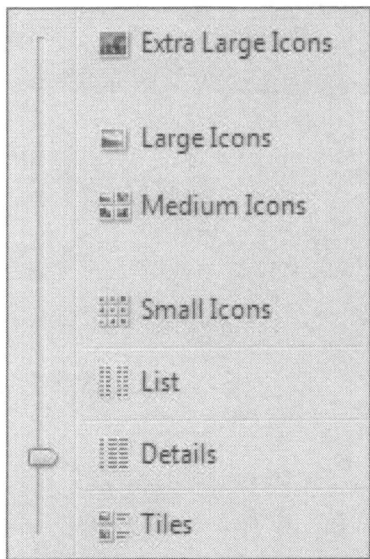

Fig.2.11 Use the Details setting

before trying to use them with this operating system. There is otherwise a strong risk that the program will do far more harm than good.

Leftovers

Having removed a program by whatever means, you will sometimes find that there are still some files and folders associated with the program remaining on the hard disc. In some cases the remaining files are simply data or configuration files that have been generated while you were trying out the program. If they are no longer of any use to you there should be no problems if they are deleted using Windows Explorer. In other cases the files could be system files that the uninstaller has decided not to remove because they are needed by other applications. Removing files of this type is very risky because the uninstaller was almost certainly correct. Manually deleting leftover files that are still in use is a common cause of problems with Windows, and files of this type should definitely be left in place.

Sometimes the folders may seem to be empty, but it is best to check carefully before removing them. An important point to bear in mind here

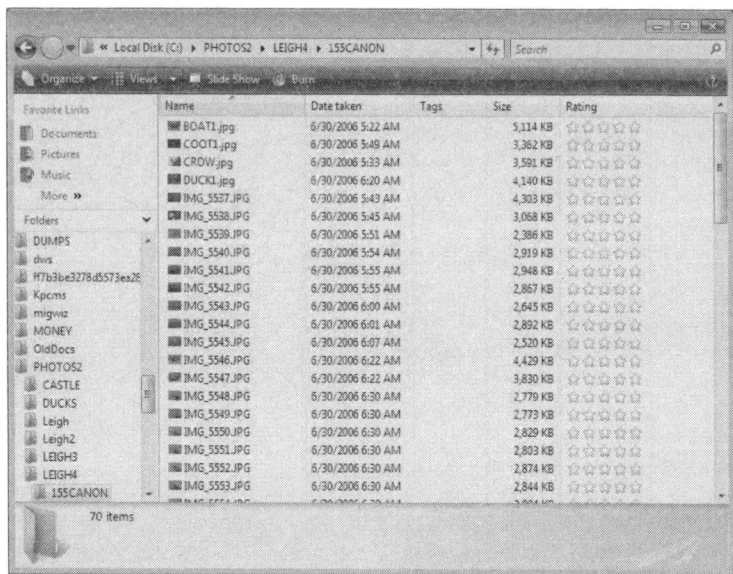

Fig.2.12 In the Details view each file is represented by a line of text that gives the file name, size, type, etc.

is that not all files are shown when using the default settings of Windows Explorer. Using the default settings hidden files will live up to their name, and files having certain extensions are not shown either. In normal use this can be helpful because it results in files that are likely to be of interest being shown, while those that are of no interest are hidden. This makes it much easier to find the files you require in a folder that contains large numbers of files. It is not helpful when Windows troubleshooting because it tends to have the opposite effect to normal. Things like data files that are of little interest are shown, while many of the system files that are of interest are hidden. Windows Explorer should be set to show as much detail about the files as possible.

By default, Windows Vista is set to show large icons or thumbnails (Figure 2.10), depending on the type of file concerned. This is fine in many situations, but in the current context it is often better to use the Details view. This is selected by going to the Views menu and selecting the Details option using the slider control (Figure 2.11). This will result in the icons being replaced with text that indicates the size, type, and date of each file (Figure 2.12).

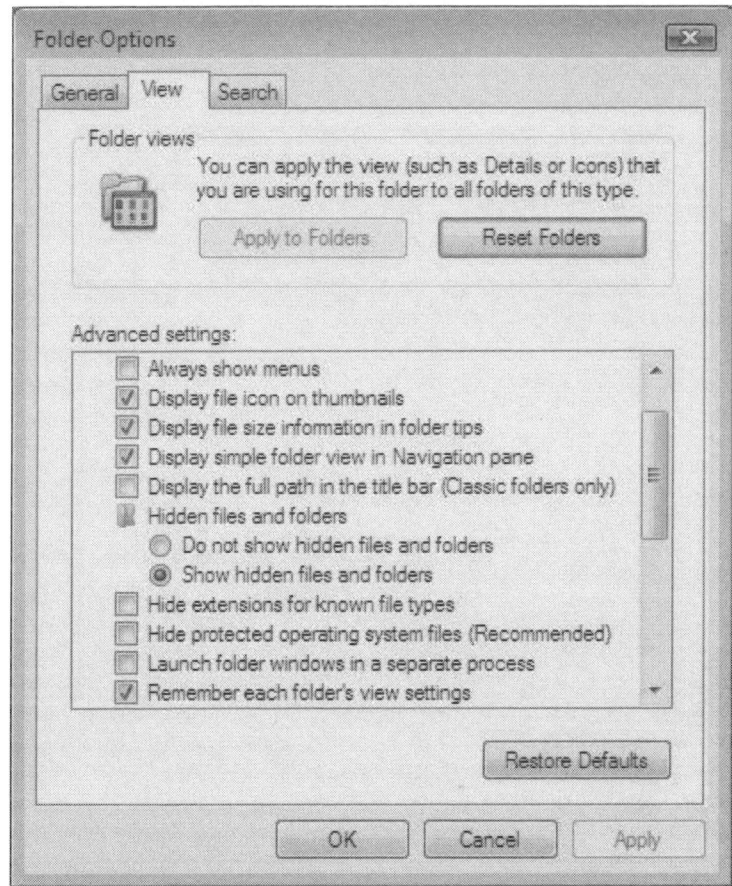

Fig.2.13 Select the View section of the Folder Options window

In order to reveal hidden files, go to the Organise menu and select Folder and Search Options, and then left-click on the View tab in the new Window that appears (Figure 2.13). Under the Hidden files and folders entry in the main section of the window, select the Show hidden files and folders option. The hidden files are certain critical system files, such as those associated with the Windows Registry, that are not normally displayed by Windows Explorer so that they can not be accidentally altered or erased by the user.

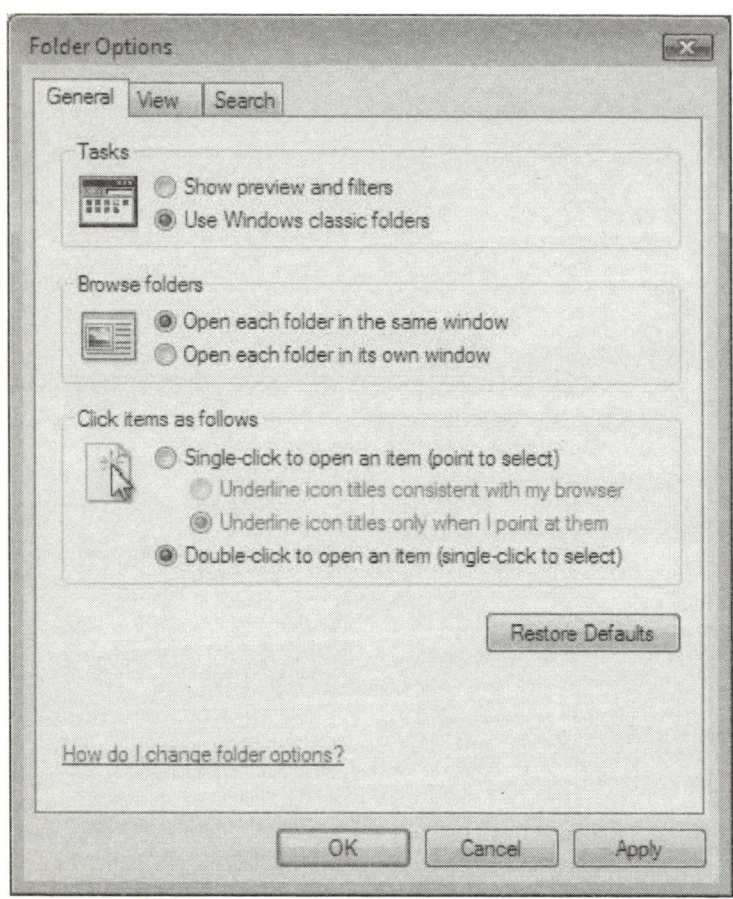

Fig.2.14 The General section of the Folder Options window

If you are using classic folders I would recommend ticking the checkbox for Display the full path in title bar (Classic folders only). This way you can always see exactly what folder you are investigating, even if it is one that is buried deep in a complex directory structure. In order to select the classic folders view it is just a matter of choosing Folders and Search Options from the Organize menu, and then selecting the General tab in the new window that appears. Then operate the Use Windows classic folders radio button in the top section of the window (Figure 2.14). Classic

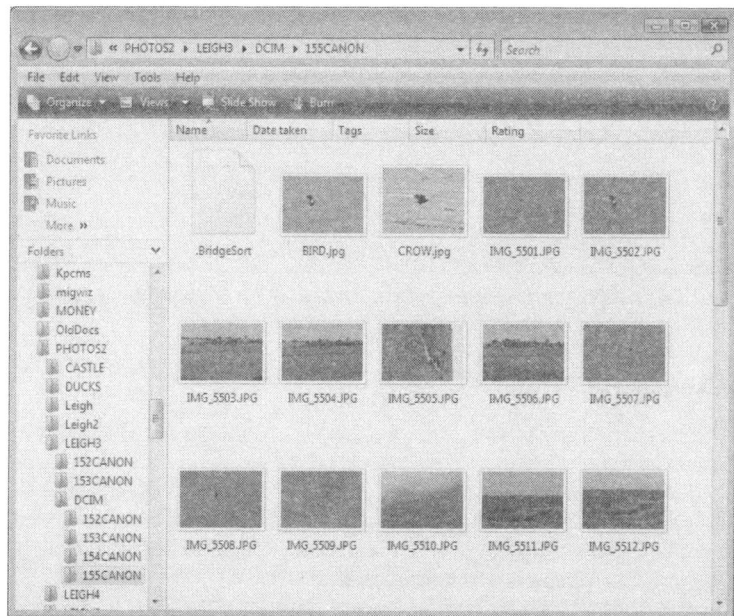

Fig.2.15 The old version of the menu bar is still available in Vista

folders are much the same as the standard Vista variety, but they have the old type of menu bar in addition to the Vista variety (Figure 2.15).

Back in the View section of the Folder Options window, it can be helpful to remove the tick in the checkbox next to Hide extensions for known file types. The extension should then be shown for all file types, which makes it easy to see which one is which when several files have the same main file name. When Windows troubleshooting you might need to view the contents of system folders, but by default these are blocked from view. Tick the "Display the contents of system folders" checkbox to make the system files viewable. In order to see all system files it is also necessary to remove the checkbox labelled "Hide protected operating system files (Recommended)". This will bring up the warning message of Figure 2.16, and it is a warning that should be heeded. By making the system files visible, it becomes easy to seriously damage the operating system, perhaps to the point where there is no option but to reinstall everything from scratch. Never move or delete files unless you know exactly what they are, but be especially careful if Windows Explorer is set to reveal the system files.

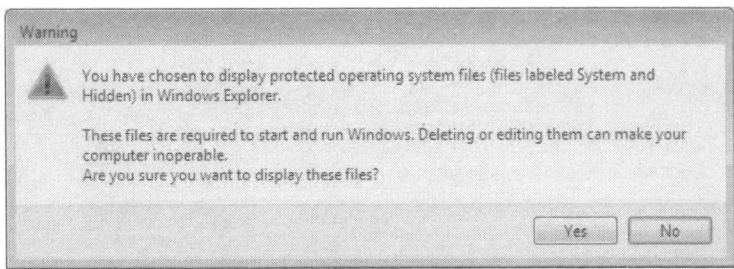

Fig.2.16 This warning appears if you opt to make hidden files visible

Attributes

When viewing the contents of directories you can use either the List or Details options under the View menu, but as explained previously, the Details option provides more information. It is also customisable, although the standard version will normally tell you everything you need to know. It is therefore the better option when Windows troubleshooting. One useful snippet of information that is missing is the file attribute. This can be added by using classic folders, going to the View menu, and then selecting Choose Details option. In Figure 2.17 the Attributes are shown in the extreme right-hand column. It can be useful to know the attribute of files, since some attributes place restrictions on what can be done with them. These are the letters used for each of the four attributes:

A   Archive

H   Hidden

R   Read-only

S   System

Thus a file that has "R" as its attribute letter it is a read-only type, and one that has "HA" in the attribute column is a hidden archive file.

Choose the List option if you prefer to have as many files as possible listed on the screen. Details of any file listed can be obtained by right-clicking on its entry in Windows Explorer and then choosing the Properties option from the pop-up menu. This will bring up a screen of the type shown in Figure 2.18, which shows the type of file, the creation date, when it was last modified, size, etc.

In the View section of the Folder Options window, make sure that the checkbox for "Remember each folder's view settings" is not ticked.

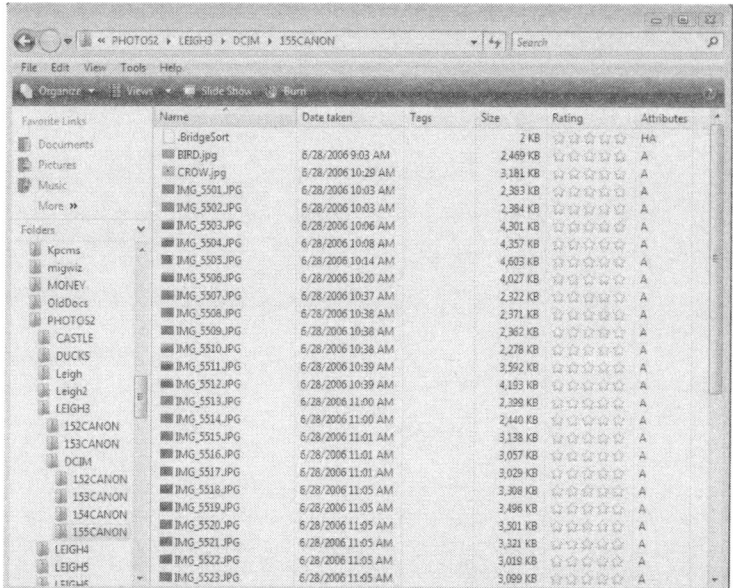

Fig.2.17 The attribute settings are shown in the extreme right-hand column

Placing a tick in this box gives each folder its own settings, making it necessary to alter the settings for individual folders rather than altering them globally. It is worth noting that there are buttons to permit the default settings to be restored, so you can easily go back to the original settings once a troubleshooting session has been completed, or if you mess things up when changing the settings. Reverting to the defaults will hide the system files again and remove the risk of accidentally damaging them.

Deleting files/folders

If any folders are definitely empty, there should be no problem if they are removed. The same is true of data and configuration files that are no longer needed. With other files it may not be clear what their exact purpose is, and it is a bit risky removing files of unknown function. Unfortunately, it seems to be quite common for uninstallers to leave large numbers of files on the hard disc. The uninstaller seems to go through its routine in standard fashion, and reports that the program has been

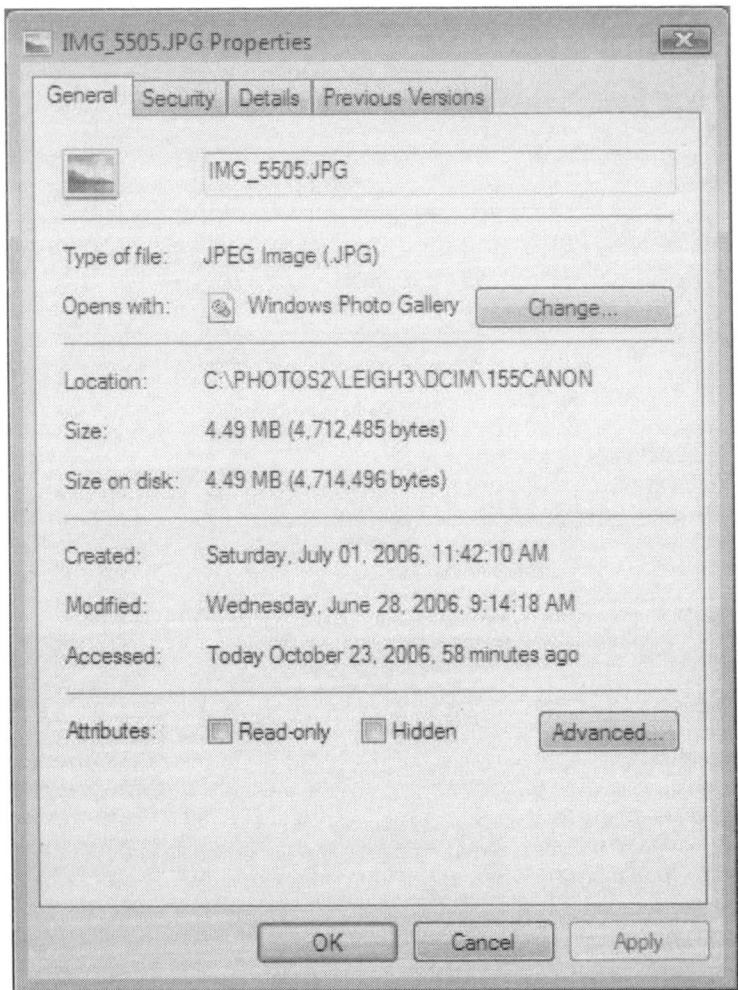

Fig.2.18 The properties window for a file

fully removed, but an inspection of the hard disc reveals that a vast directory structure remains. I have encountered uninstallers that have left more than 50 megabytes of files on the disc, removing only about 10% of those initially installed.

Other uninstallers report that some files and folders could not be removed, and that they must be dealt with manually. Some uninstallers seem to concentrate on extricating the program from the operating system by removing references to the program in the Windows registry, etc., rather than trying to remove all trace of it from the hard disc. With most modern computers having large hard disc drives, there would seem to be little point in removing files of unknown worth. Some extra hard disc space will be freed by removing them, but with gigabytes of free space already, this is of no real benefit. If the files do prove to be essential to the wellbeing of the computer, their removal could cause problems. It is best to adhere to the old adage "if in doubt do nowt".

Softly, softly

It might be best to do little or nothing when uninstalling a program leaves a hard disc containing vast numbers of unwanted files, but that is not necessarily the course most people follow. The temptation, and what many people actually do, is to simply drag the whole lot into the Recycle Bin. Sometimes this may be acceptable, but there is the risk that eventually Windows will look for some of the deleted files and start to produce error messages. If you are lucky, the deleted files will still be in the Recycle Bin, and they can then be restored to their original locations on the hard disc. If not, you may have problems sorting things out.

If you really must delete the leftover files, the safer way of handling things is to leave the directory structure and files intact, but change some file or folder names. If only a few files have been left behind, try adding a letter at the front of each filename. For example, a file called "drawprog.dll" could be renamed "zdrawprog.dll". This will prevent Windows from finding the file if it should be needed for some reason, but it is an easy matter for you to correct things by removing the "z" from the filename if problems occur.

Where there are numerous files in a complex directory structure to deal with it is not practical to rename all the individual files. Instead, the name of the highest folder in the directory structure should be renamed. This should make it impossible for Windows to find the file unless it does a complete search of the hard disc, and it is easily reversed if problems should occur. Ideally the complete directory structure should be copied to a mass storage device such as a CD writer, a backup hard disc drive, or another partition on the hard disc. The original structure can then be deleted. If problems occur and some of the files have been cleaned from the Recycle Bin, you can reinstate everything from the backup copy.

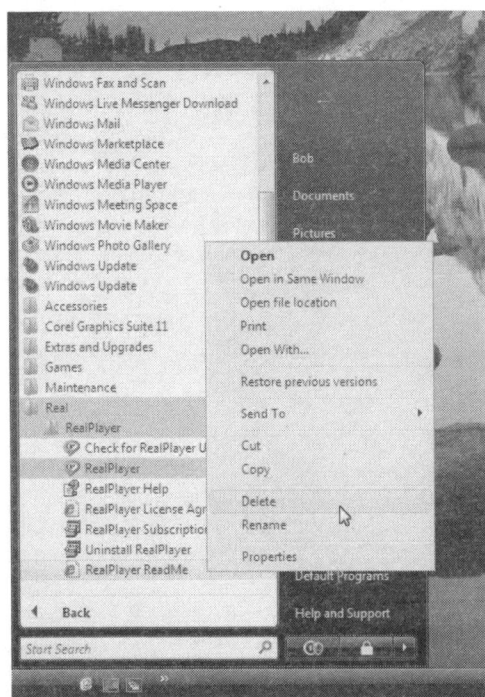

Fig.2.19 Select Delete from the pop-up menu

As already pointed out, modern hard disc drives have very high capacities so it is perhaps worthwhile considering whether it is really necessary to remove leftover files. In fact, do you really need to uninstall the program at all? The less installing and uninstalling you do the better the chances of avoiding problems. The downside of leaving programs on the hard disc is that eventually you will end up with a large number of installed programs, and this could generally slow the system down. In particular, the boot-up process can become a very long and drawn out process, and background tasks can use up the computer's resources.

However this can be overcome by occasionally wiping the hard disc clean and reinstalling the operating system and applications software from scratch. This is not a particularly quick and easy process, but it is the only totally reliable method of getting Windows back to a lean installation that operates at peak efficiency. Although it is a major undertaking, it should not be necessary to go through this process very often. Some power users routinely install everything from scratch so that their PC is kept at peak performance.

Icon and menu entries

After uninstalling a program you will often find that the shortcut icon is still present on the Windows desktop. If the installation program did not

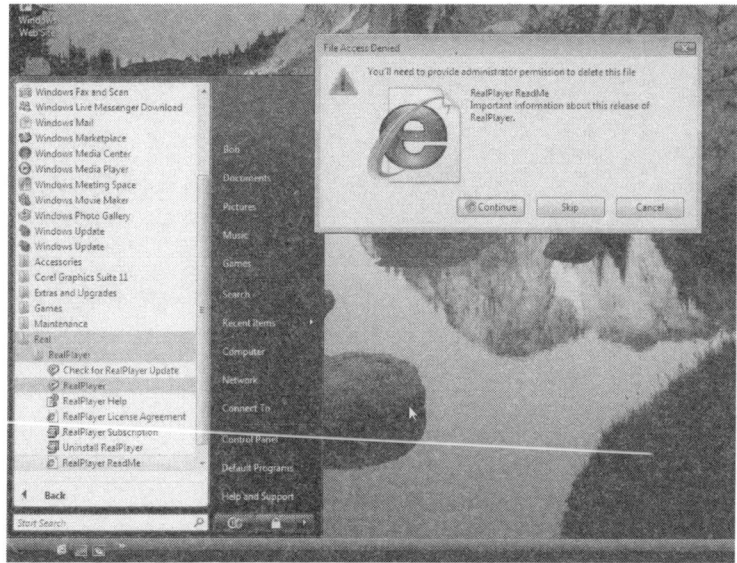

Fig.2.20 Administrator permission is needed in order to delete the file

put the icon there in the first place it is very unlikely that the uninstaller will remove it. Shortcut icons that are placed on the Windows desktop manually must be removed manually. This simply entails dragging the icon to the Recycle Bin. Alternatively, right-click on the icon and select Delete from the popup menu. A warning message will appear, explaining that deleting the icon does not uninstall the program. Left-click the Yes button to proceed and remove the icon from the desktop. Deleting a shortcut icon can not have an adverse effect on Windows operation, because the icon is all that is being removed. Any leftover files on the hard disc will remain intact.

An uninstaller should delete the entry in the Programs section of the Start menu when removing a program. Unfortunately, this item does sometimes seem to be overlooked, and after removing a number of programs there can be a growing band of orphan entries in the menu. Once again, removing these entries manually should not entail any risk of "gumming up" Windows. However, take care to avoid the complications that will arise if you remove the wrong entry.

To remove an entry, go to the Start menu, select the All Programs option, and then find the entry that you wish to remove. Next, right-click on the

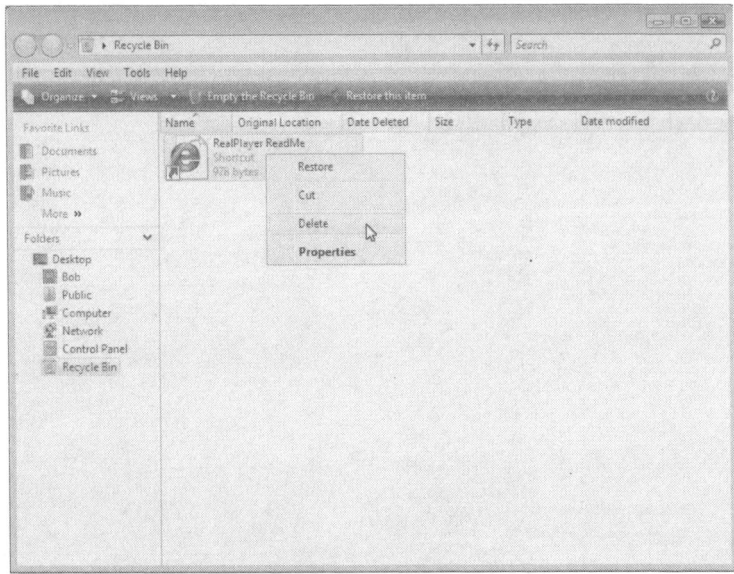

Fig.2.21 Select Restore from the pop-up menu

entry and select Delete from the pop-up menu (Figure 2.19), and a
warning message will probably appear on the screen (Figure 2.20). The
message points out that you will need to provide administrator permission
in order to delete the file. Operate the Continue button in order to proceed,
and then the Continue button again when the next window pops up. A
quick check of the Start menu should show that the offending entry has
been removed.

It is actually placed in the Recycle Bin, so it can be easily reinstated
provided you realise your mistake fairly quickly. To restore the entry,
launch the Recycle Bin, then locate and select the file you have just
deleted. Select Restore from the File menu (Figure 2.21), and the entry
in the All Programs menu should return to its original position.

Beta problems

Both old and brand new software are potential sources of problems with
Windows. As already pointed out, old programs can be problematic
because they do not adhere to the current rules for Windows software.

In the case of brand new software it is the Beta test versions or any other versions prior to the commercial release that are the main problem. These are not fully tried and tested, and can not be guaranteed to do things "by the book".

In all probability, some sections of the code will contain programming errors and simply will not work properly. People who make a living testing this type of software almost invariably use one PC for testing the software and a second PC for other purposes. That way there is no major loss if the test software runs amok and deletes half the files on the hard disc! If you do not have a second PC for use with dubious software it is best not to try it at all.

At one time the initial commercial releases of programs were not always reliable, and some software publishers seemed to be guilty of getting their customers to unwittingly do the final testing for them. This sort of thing may still go on in some niche markets, but it is thankfully something of a rarity these days. The cost of sending out replacement discs plus the loss of reputation makes it an unsustainable tactic. These days, new software whether it is totally new or an upgrade version, should be very reliable. In the past it was advisable to let new software mature before buying it, but this should no longer be necessary.

New software might contain a few minor bugs, but there should be nothing that will seriously damage your Windows installation. If new software should prove troublesome, there should be a help-line that can give advice on the problem. Software publishers' web sites often have software patches that can fix any obscure problems that have come to light after the final versions of the programs have been sent out to the shops.

Memory

In the early days of Windows 95 it was not unusual for the dreaded red exclamation marks to appear on the screen complete with a brief error message. In fact, there seemed to be one or two of these messages every time someone used a PC. Thankfully, this type of thing is relatively rare these days. There were probably two main reasons for these early problems, and one of them was a lack of memory in the PCs of the day. At that time memory was quite expensive. Eight megabytes of RAM was quite typical, and 16 megabytes was considered to be a large amount of memory. Software manufacturers were eager for their programs to appeal to as many people as possible, which often led them to be overoptimistic about the system requirements. If the requirements listed 8 megabytes of memory as the minimum and recommended at least 16 megabytes should be used, then 16 megabytes was probably the minimum that would really give trouble free and usable results.

These days memory is relatively cheap, and PCs are mostly well endowed in this respect. On the other hand, programs, including operating systems, seem to require ever more memory. Also, many users now have two or more programs running simultaneously, probably with several background tasks running as well. If you run memory hungry programs on a computer that has a modest amount of memory and error messages keep on appearing, it is worth investing in some extra memory. Even if it does not cure the problem, Windows and your programs will almost certainly run more quickly. If you wish to run a couple of major applications under Windows Vista there is a lot to be said for having at least 512 megabytes of RAM installed in your PC. With memory costing relatively little these days, many users now opt for a gigabyte.

Another problem when Windows 95 came along was that most of the Windows software available at the time was really intended for use with Windows 3.1. In theory, most of this software was fully compatible with Windows 95, but in practice there often seemed to be odd incompatibility problems. Most of this software is now long gone, but as already pointed out, it can usually be used with Windows XP. However, there is no guarantee that these old 16-bit programs will run properly under Windows XP. The only way to find out is to use the "suck it and see" method. It is advisable not to press on regardless if error or warning messages keep appearing on the screen.

Old Windows 3.1 software may be a rarity, but there is still plenty of Windows 9x software that is not recommended for use with Windows XP or Vista. There is also some software for Windows NT and 2000 that will not work properly with Windows XP or Vista. Even some Windows XP software is not compatible with Windows Vista. This includes many security programs and hard disc utilities. To avoid problems, check that software is Windows Vista compatible before installing it, and never use programs that are not compatible.

Windows Vista will do its best to intercept and disable incompatible files such as certain DLL types, but the best way of avoiding problems is to keep incompatible software off the system. As explained previously, it is necessary to take extra care with utility software such as disc defragmenters that have the potential to cause considerable damage to the Windows installation. Incompatible software of this type can and probably will do extensive damage to the files on the hard disc.

Windows problem?

Some users tend to jump to conclusions when there are problems with a PC running Windows. Probably most problems are the result of the operating system becoming damaged, but by no means all problems are caused in this way. I have often been asked to help with supposed Windows problems that turn out to be due to some other cause. A crucial consideration when locating the cause of a PC fault is where in the proceedings is it that things go awry? If the PC fails to start up at all, with no initial messages, etc., from the BIOS's POST (power-on self-test) program, the fault is clearly not a Windows problem. The fault is occurring long before the PC starts to boot into Windows, and there is certainly a hardware problem.

Matters are less clear cut if the PC gets through its initial checking, starts to boot into Windows, but rapidly comes to a halt. When this happens there will often be an error message along the lines that the boot disc is missing or has a corrupted boot sector, and you will be asked to insert a system disc and then press any key. This means that the computer has looked at the boot drives specified in the BIOS Setup program but has not found a bootable disc. An obvious first step is to check the BIOS settings by going into the Setup program.

The manual for your computer should give at least brief details of how to enter the BIOS and change the settings. This is also covered in more detail in a later chapter. Assuming the settings are suitable, the problem could be due to a hardware fault with the disc or the IDE interface on the motherboard, or it could be caused by corruption of the data in the boot sector of the disc.

Sometimes the PC will start booting, but it will stop almost immediately. When this happens there will not necessarily be an error message displayed on the screen. In fact there will probably be no message, with the computer instead "freezing". The Control-Alt-Del key combination might reset the computer so that it tries to boot again, but a hardware reset will probably be needed. In other words, operate the reset button on the computer if it has one, or switch off, wait a few seconds, and then switch the PC back on again. If the boot process almost instantly falters again it is possible that there is a hardware fault, but a corrupted boot sector on the disc is the most likely cause of the problem. If you are unlucky, the hard disc has failed and will have to be replaced.

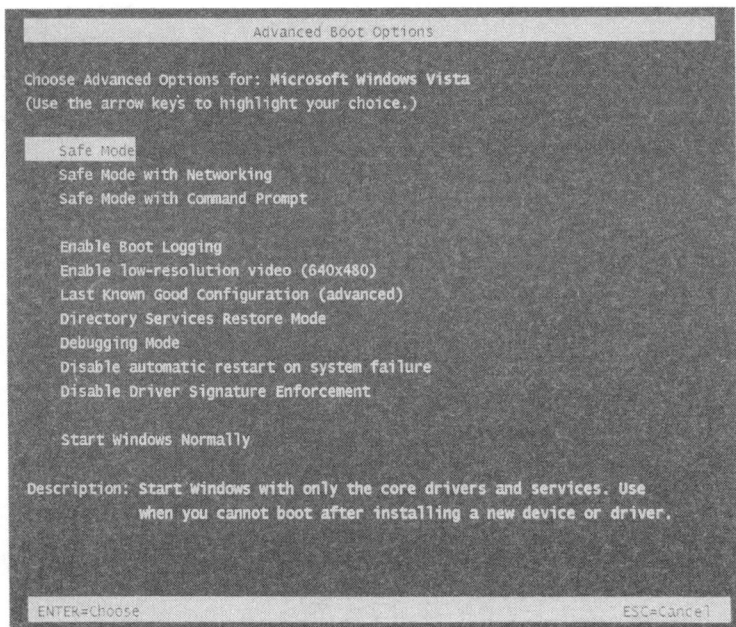

Fig.2.22 A number of boot options are available from this window

System files

If the system files in the boot sector of the disc have become damaged, the obvious first step is to replace them. In order to do this in Windows 9x the computer is booted using the Windows Startup disc in drive A:. Windows Vista does not rely on booting from a floppy disc in an emergency. It is possible to produce an MS-DOS boot disc using Windows Vista, but this is likely to be of little or no use when troubleshooting. In an emergency the normal approach is to first try to boot into Safe Mode, which is much like its equivalent in Windows 9x and XP.

The computer boots into Windows XP, but with a basic video driver and probably with some of the hardware not installed. Although the computer is something less than fully functioning, it should work well enough to permit some troubleshooting. If you can get the computer into Safe Mode it can probably be restored to full working order without too much difficulty.

Fig.2.23 Eventually a version of the logon screen appears

A menu giving a number of boot options can be obtained by pressing F8 as the computer starts to boot into Windows. This is essentially the same method that is used with Windows 9x, but the available options (Figure 2.22) are somewhat different. The various boot modes will not be considered at this stage, and the standard Safe Mode is all that is needed here. Use the up and down cursor keys to highlight the Safe Mode entry and then operate the Return key.

Initially the screen will fill with text that shows the drivers that have been loaded, and then the logon screen should appear (Figure 2.23). Log on in the normal way, and the Help window of Figure 2.24 will appear on the desktop. This explains that Windows is running in a basic diagnostic mode and that some devices will not be available.

It is virtually certain that the basic system files are intact if the PC manages to boot into Safe Mode. There is a good chance that these files are damaged if the boot process fails, especially if it fails quite early in the process. When the computer can not even boot into Safe Mode there are basically two choices. One is to simply abandon the current

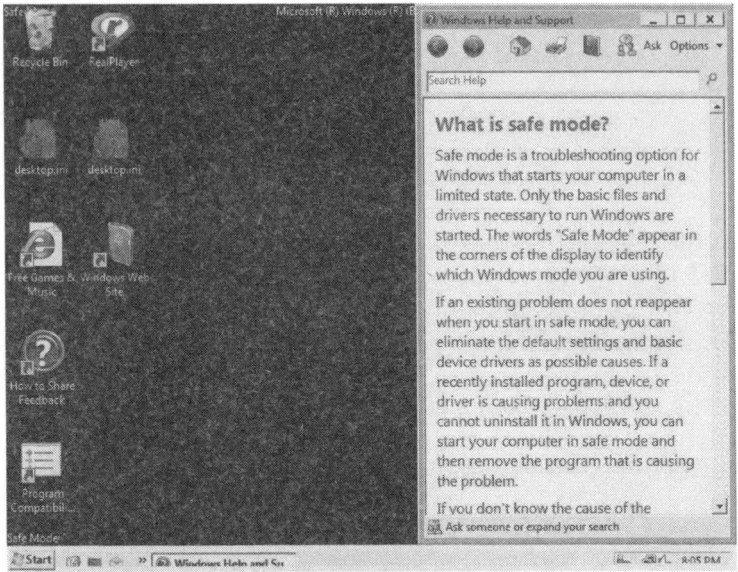

Fig.2.24 The initial screen once into Safe Mode

installation and reinstall everything from scratch. It is a bit early in the proceedings to consider this option, and the more normal course of action is to resort to the Windows Vista equivalent of the XP Recovery Console. This is a more sophisticated recovery set-up than the Startup floppy discs used with Windows 9x. In order to run the Recovery Console the computer must be booted from the Windows Vista installation disc.

Any modern PC should have no difficulty booting from a DVD drive, although it might be necessary to boot from the drive having the lowest letter if your PC has two or more DVD drives. In other words, if the DVDs are drives D: and E:, it will probably be necessary to boot from drive D:. A PC that has Windows Vista installed might be set to boot from the DVD drive first, and to then try the hard disc if no bootable DVD can be found. In this case, it is merely necessary to switch on the PC, put the Vista installation disc in the DVD drive, and wait for the system to boot from this drive.

If the computer is not set to boot from the DVD drive at all, it will be necessary to change some settings using the BIOS Setup program. The same is true if the computer is set to boot from the hard disc drive first.

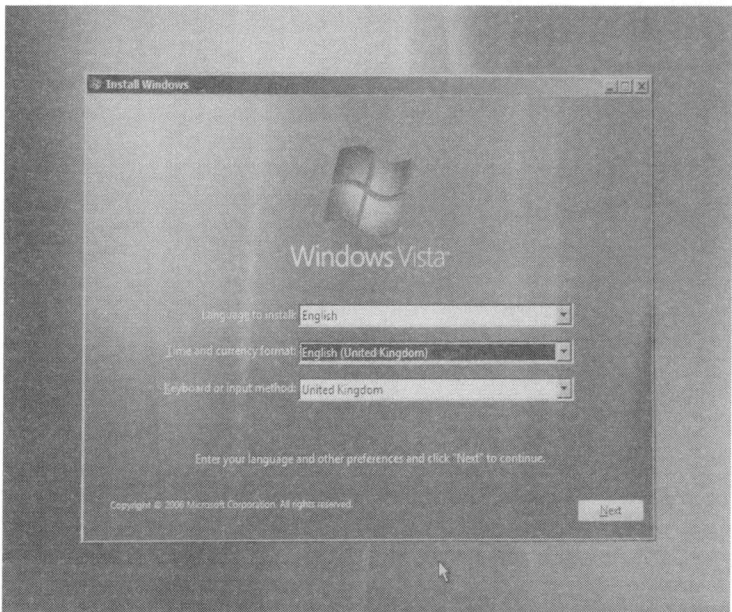

Fig.2.25 This screen is used to select the installation language

While it is possible that the BIOS will detect that it can not boot from the hard drive, and then move on to the DVD drive, this is unlikely. It is odds on that the BIOS will try to boot from the hard drive, and that things will grind to a halt somewhere during this process. The only way to tell whether it is possible to boot from the DVD drive is to use the "suck it and see" approach. It is clearly not possible without some adjustment to the CMOS settings if the computer ignores the DVD drive and tries to boot from the hard disc. Altering the settings stored in the CMOS RAM using the BIOS Setup program is covered in detail in a later chapter.

If everything is set up correctly, a message saying something like "Press any key to boot from CD/DVD" will appear on the screen. The message appears only briefly so you have to press a key almost immediately in order to boot from the DVD drive. The computer will try to boot from the hard disc if you are too late. It is then a matter of resetting or restarting the computer any trying again. An onscreen message will appear when the computer starts to boot from the DVD, and files are copied from the DVD. Eventually the boot process should finish and a screen like the one in Figure 2.25 will then appear. The problem is almost certainly a

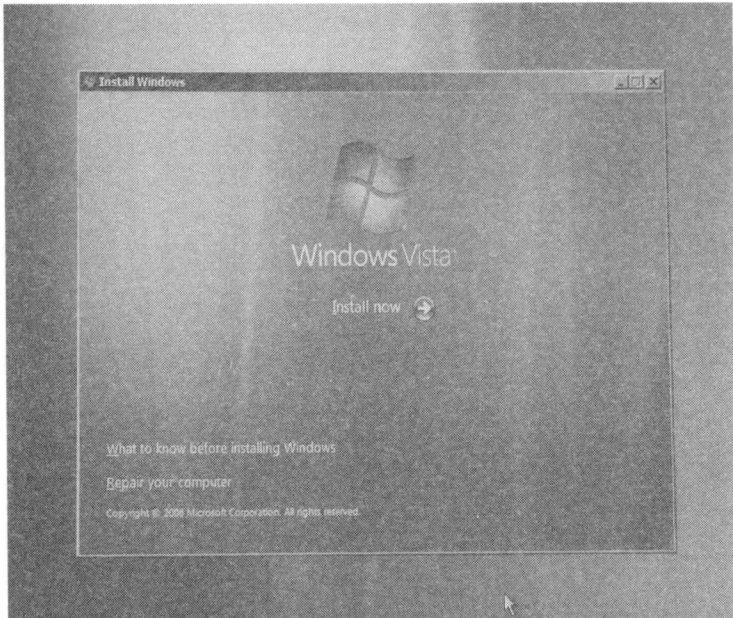

Fig.2.26 Use the "Repair your computer" link

hardware fault rather than a Windows problem if the PC will not boot from the hard disc or a CD-ROM.

The screen of Figure 2.25 is just a set of three drop-down menus where you select the appropriate installation language, date and currency format, and keyboard language. Having done this, operating the Next button moves things on to the screen of Figure 2.26 where there is the choice of Installing Windows Vista, accessing a Help system, or repairing the computer. In this case it is the "Repair your computer" link that is activated, and this moves things on to the screen of Figure 2.27.

Here you select the Windows installation that you wish to repair. In most cases, as in this example, there will only be one installation on offer. One of the buttons offers the option of loading any special drivers required by your PC. In most cases it will not be necessary to load any driver software, but where appropriate this option must be taken. You will need a disc containing the drivers, which is something that should have been supplied with your PC.

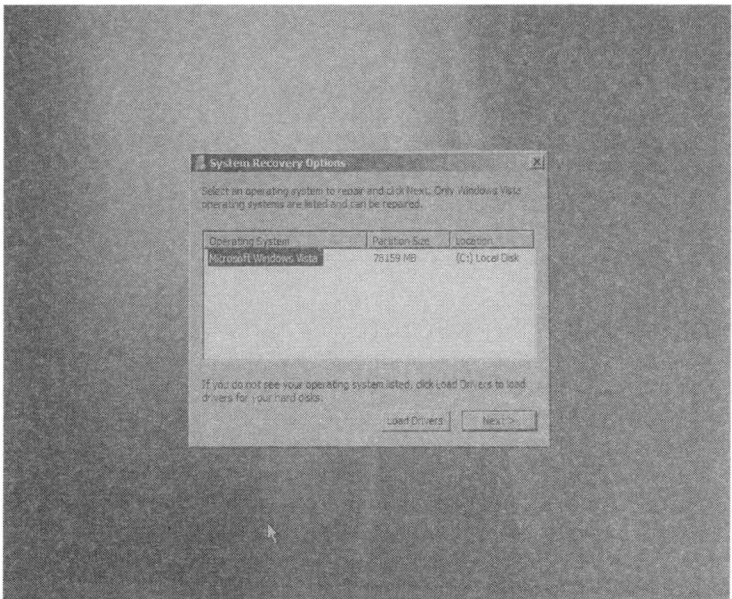

Fig.2.27 Usually there will be a choice of one operating system to repair

After operating the Next button the screen of Figure 2.28 appears. This offers several options that provide different ways of tackling the problem. Note that the Windows Boot Manager might run at boot-up, and the route to this screen is then slightly different. Operate the F8 key to obtain the Advanced Options, and then choose to boot the computer normally. This will boot the computer normally from the CD, and you then get to this screen using the method described previously.

Startup Repair

The Startup Repair option is the obvious starting point when it is proving to be impossible to boot into Windows. This utility is largely automatic, and the way it operates depends to some extent on the exact nature of any problems it detects. Initially the window of Figure 2.29 appears, and this simply explains that the program is searching for errors. With luck, the program will provide some possible solutions to the boot-up problem, although it could take some time.

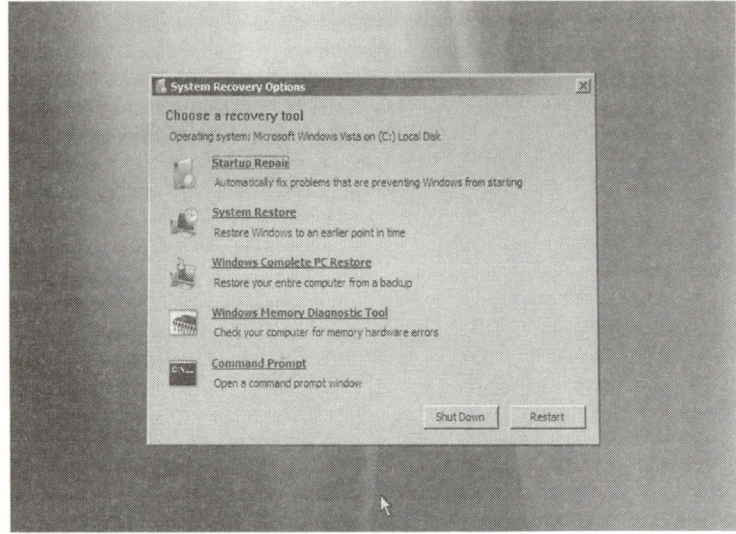

Fig.2.28 This window is a menu with five options

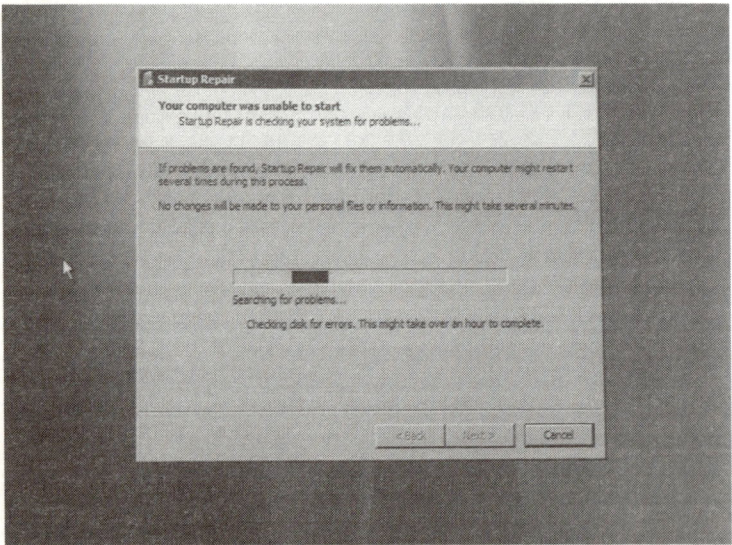

Fig.2.29 This window appears while Vista searches for errors

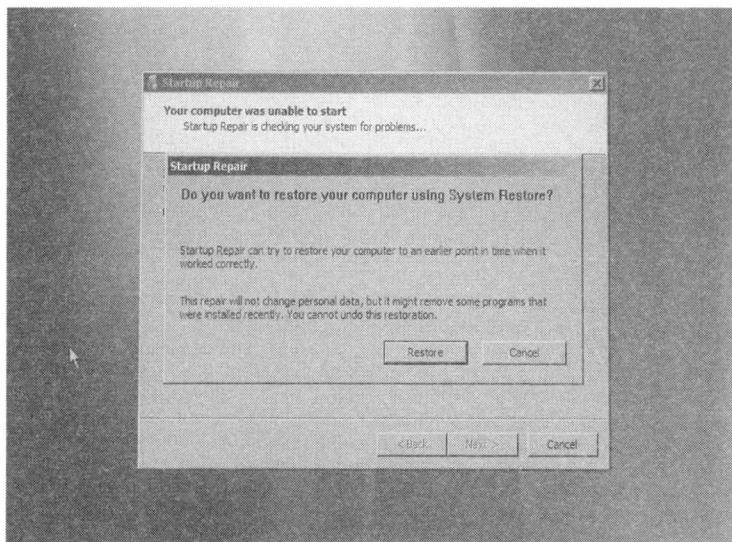

Fig.2.30 The option of using System Restore has been provided

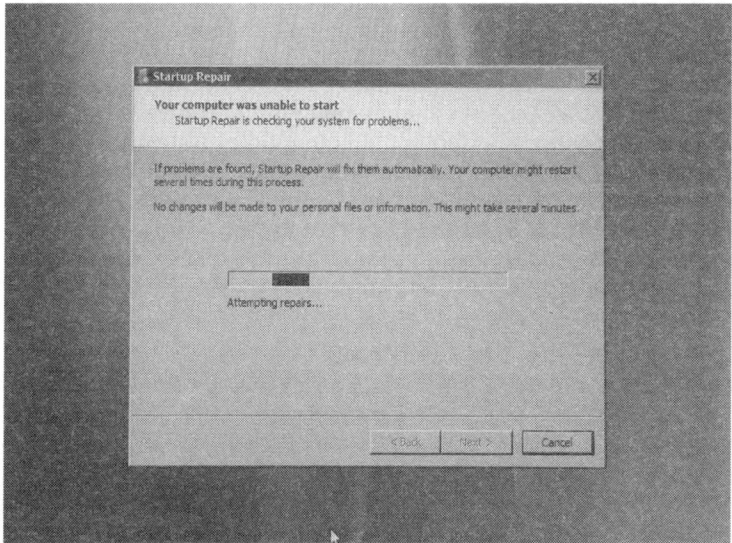

Fig.2.31 The program continues the search

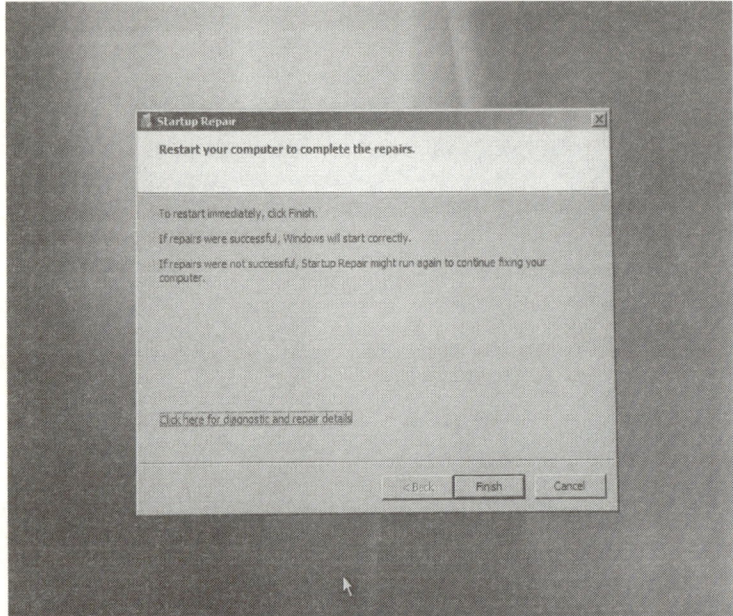

Fig.2.32 The program has completed its task, and it is now a matter of rebooting the PC to see if it will start

In this example the program gave the option of booting the PC using the System Restore function (Figure 2.30). The idea of System Restore is to take the operating system back to its state at an earlier date when the PC did boot into Windows properly. For the sake of this example I declined the offer and opted to have the program continue its attempts to repair the system (Figure 2.31). Eventually it completed its task (Figure 2.32), and it was then just a matter of operating the Finish button to see if the computer would boot correctly, which it did.

It would be unrealistic to expect the Startup Repair program to fix all boot problems, but it should cure a reasonable percentage of them. The message of Figure 2.33 appears in cases where no repairable problem can be found. It is certainly advisable to use this utility before trying any more drastic solutions. Its largely automatic operation makes Startup Repair a good choice for those with little experience at fixing Windows problems.

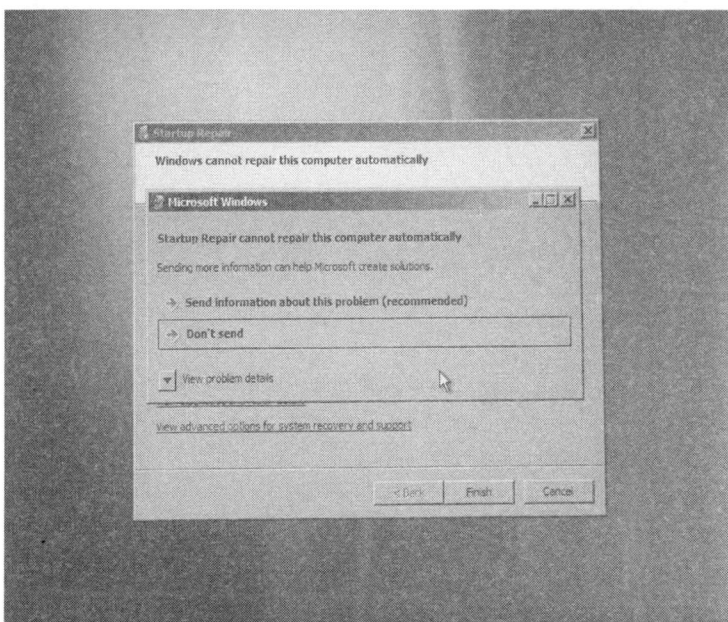

Fig.2.33 In this example the program could not find any errors

System Restore

There is a System Restore facility available from within Windows, but this is clearly of no use unless the computer can be booted into Windows. As already pointed out, the Startup Repair program might give the option of using a version of System Restore, but it is also available directly from the System Recovery Options window (refer back to Figure 2.28). You can therefore "cut to the chase" and run this utility straight away.

Although it is essentially the same utility as the one run from within Windows, using this version is very different to using the standard version. The first window (Figure 2.34) is simply an information screen. The next window (Figure 2.35) is used to select a restoration point, and only those for the last five days are shown by default. The checkbox enables more restoration points to be shown, but it is not normally necessary to go back more than a few days. If taking the system back to its state three or four days previously does not provide a cure, it is unlikely that taking the system back a few weeks will do any better.

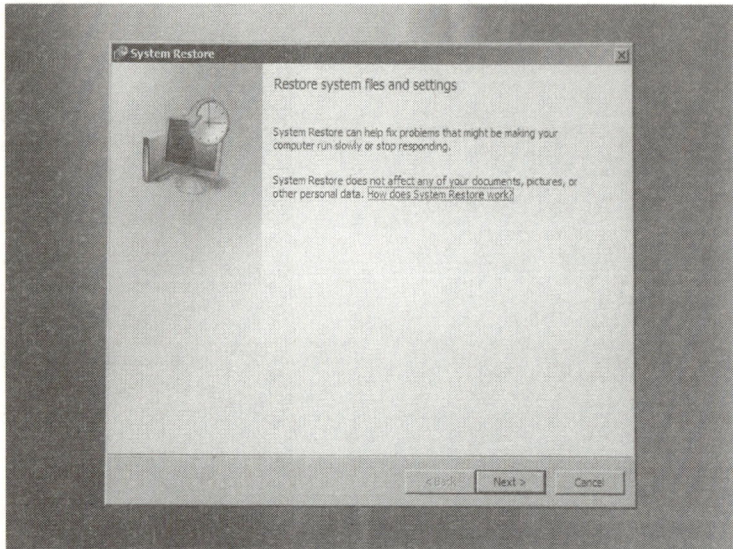

Fig.2.34 The first screen is simply an information type

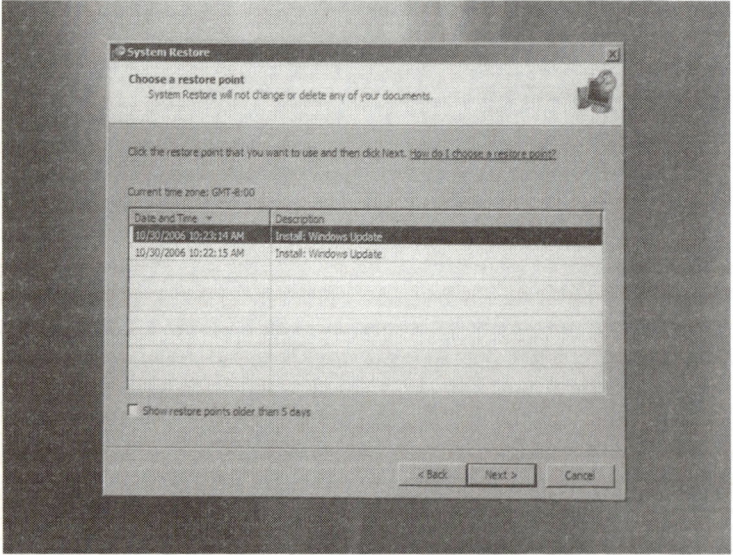

Fig.2.35 Use this window to select a restoration point

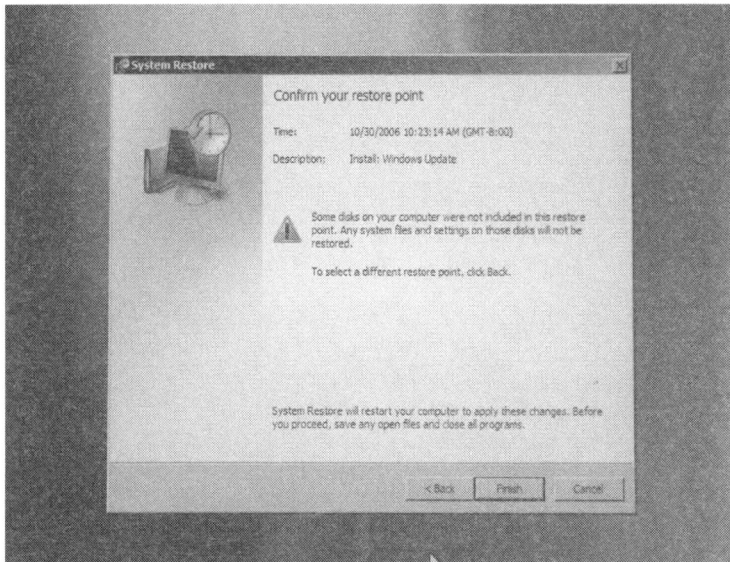

Fig.2.36 One or two warning messages might be displayed

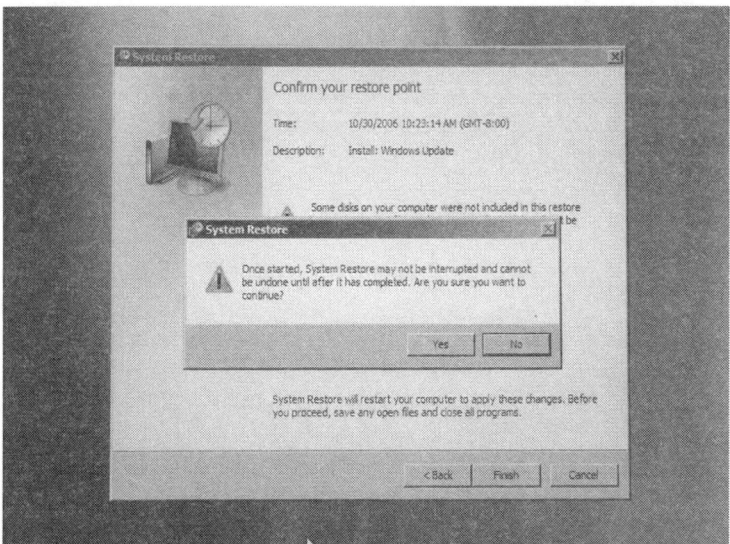

Fig.2.37 Once started, the restoration process must not be interrupted

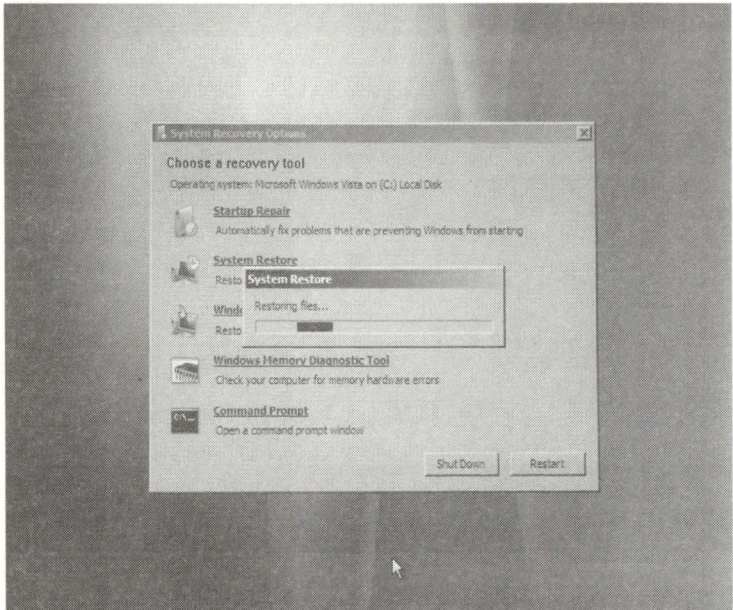

Fig.2.38 A small window appears while the changes are made

Depending on the hardware configuration and set-up of your PC, there might be one or two warning messages, such as the one shown in Figure 2.36. Opt to keep on going until the message of Figure 2.37 appears. This explains that the restoration process must not be interrupted once it has started, so you are committed to completing the process if you operate the Yes button. However, it should be possible to undo the process after it has been completed, so it is possible to take the system back to its original state if the System Restore facility makes things worse rather than better.

Assuming that you decide to go ahead with the restoration, a small window (Figure 2.38) will appear while the necessary changes are being made to the system files. Provided all goes well the small window will change to look like the one in Figure 2.39, and this simply explains that the restoration process has been completed successfully. Operating the Restart button reboots the computer, and with luck it will boot into Windows. In this case the computer did indeed boot into Windows correctly, and there was a small message window (Figure 2.40) explaining that System Restore had been run successfully.

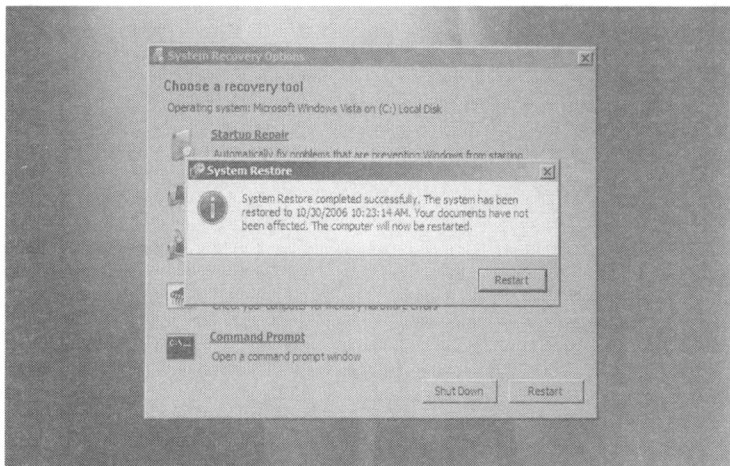

Fig.2.39 This message confirms that the restoration is finished

Fig.2.40 A message confirming the restoration point is displayed once the computer has booted into Vista

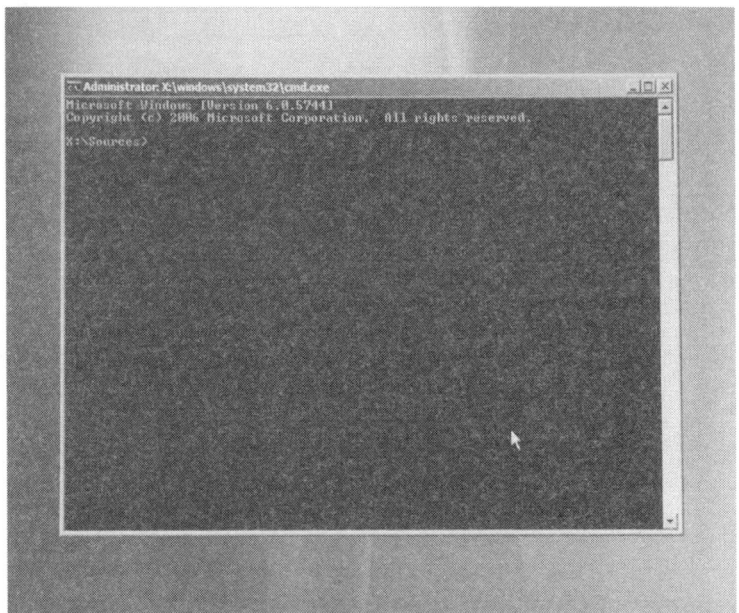

Fig.2.41 The Command Prompt utility provides a MS-DOS style text-only interface

Command Prompt

Windows Vista has no real equivalent of the Windows XP Recovery Console. The nearest function available from the System Recovery Options is the Command Prompt, which launches an MS-DOS style text-only user interface (Figure 2.41). This has the usual MS-DOS commands, so you can obtain a directory listing of a folder for example (Figure 2.42). It is also possible to copy files from one folder/drive to another, which could be useful if some valuable data files have to be rescued.

Although a reasonable range of MS-DOS commands are available from the command prompt, the additional commands of the Windows XP Recovery Console are absent. This is simply because there are now more sophisticated alternatives available, rendering things like the fixboot command unnecessary. The ability to use a command prompt could still be useful, but is something you are unlikely to need very much with Windows Vista.

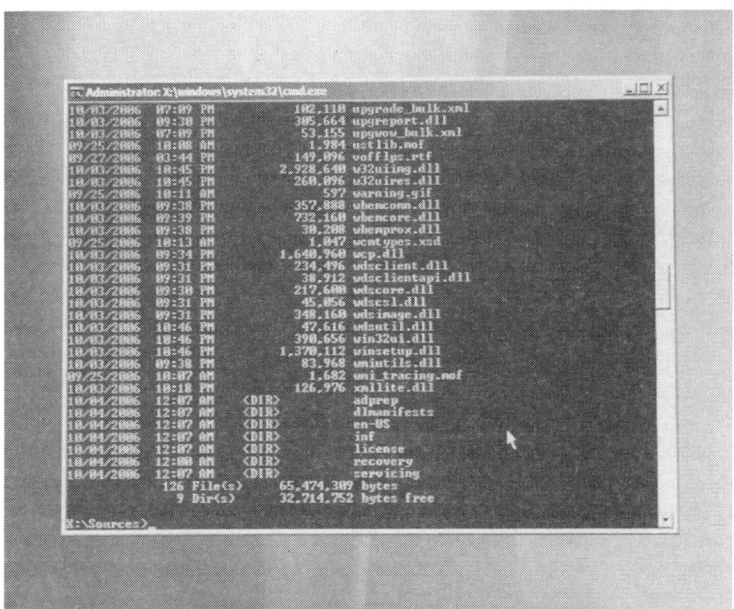

Fig.2.42 The usual MS-DOS commands are available, including the one to list the contents of a directory (folder)

Memory test

The memory test option is useful, because Windows boot failures can be caused by hardware problems as well as problems with the operating system. Faulty memory is probably the most common cause of hardware related boot problems. It can seem as though the problem is caused by a problem with the operating system, with the boot-up sequence always failing at the same point in the procedure. However, the problem can actually be due to a faulty area of memory being used when that point in the boot-up sequence is reached.

A small window (Figure 2.43) appears when this option is selected. This provides the choice of rebooting immediately and having the test performed, or having the test carried out next time the computer is booted into Windows. Probably in most cases you will wish to have the memory test performed at once, and using this option causes the computer to reboot after a short delay. Note that the computer should be allowed to reboot in the normal way rather than from the installation DVD. The

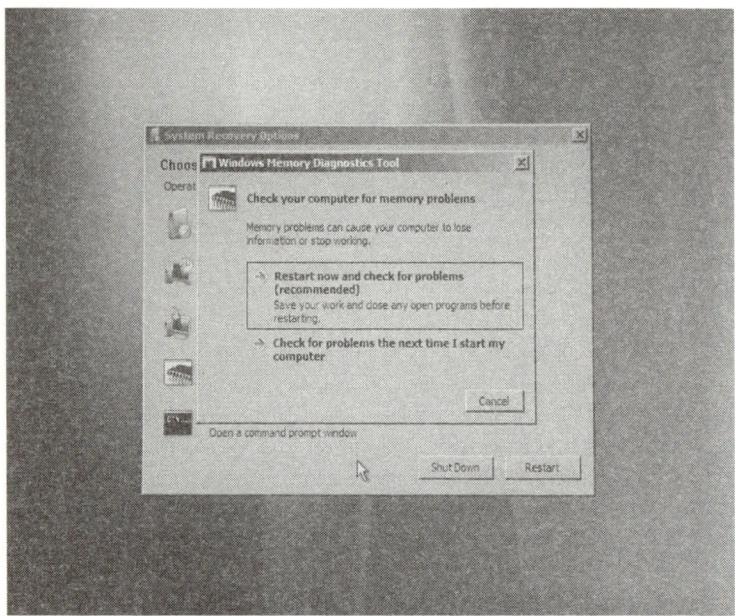

Fig.2.43 It is probably best to reboot and do the test immediately

same is also true if you opt to have the test performed next time the computer is booted into Windows.

The normal boot-up sequence will be interrupted and a screen like the one shown in Figure 2.44 will appear while the test is carried out. The computer's memory will actually be tested twice. Having completed the tests, the computer will be booted into Windows if no problems are found. A set of test results will be displayed if a memory fault is detected.

Emergency boot

In the past, it has been possible to use Windows to make a floppy disc that can be used to boot the PC when it is not possible to boot into Windows normally. It is doubtful whether it is worthwhile making an emergency boot disc when using Windows Vista. The obvious problem with an emergency boot disc is that many computers now lack a floppy disc drive. Another problem is that the low capacity of floppy discs makes it impossible to store anything more than a few essential files on the

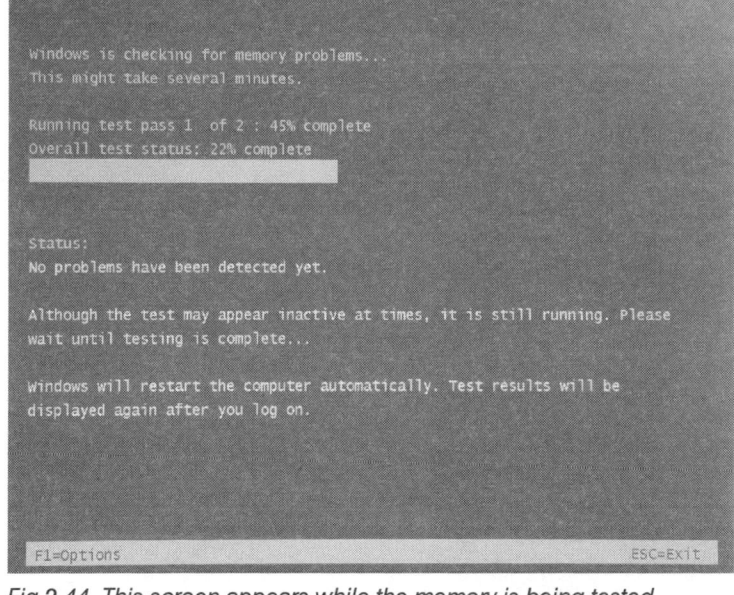

Fig.2.44 This screen appears while the memory is being tested

disc. These days the bootable DVD installation disc has usurped the emergency floppy disc.

It is still possible to make a bootable floppy disc. First locate the floppy drive in Windows Explorer, right-clicking on its entry, and then selecting the Format option. This brings up the window for the Format program, and the default options should be suitable, but tick the "Make an MS-DOS startup disk" checkbox. Operate the Start button, which will produce a warning message explaining that all data on the disc will be lost. Left-click the OK button if you wish to go ahead and format the disc.

Booting from an MS-DOS boot disc provides an environment that is essentially the same as the one provided by the Command Prompt option available when booting from the installation DVD. I suppose it could be worthwhile making a bootable floppy if you have an OEM version of Windows that does not include a conventional installation disc. Wherever possible it is advisable to obtain a full version of Windows that does include the full installation media, even if this does cost a little extra.

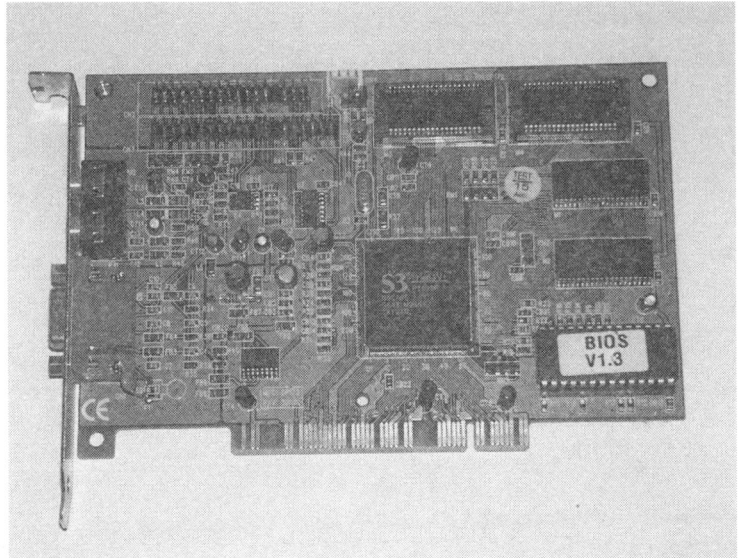

Fig.2.45 The fixing bracket is at the left end of the card

Late problems

Sometimes Windows seems to get 90 percent of the way through the boot-up process before it comes to a halt. When this happens it is likely that the problem is in the Windows installation and not due to a hardware fault. When things come to a halt with an error message stating that a certain file or files could not be found, this indicates that the problem is within Windows itself. Matters are less clear-cut if any error messages refer to an item of hardware, or Windows tries to reinstall an item of hardware that was previously installed correctly. It could be that the trouble is due to problems with a corrupted driver program, but it is also possible that a faulty item of hardware is giving the Windows Plug-N-Play facility some difficulties.

On the cards

Fixing hardware problems goes beyond the scope of this book, but it is covered in "Easy PC troubleshooting (BP484)" from the same publisher and author as this book. However, if the item of hardware that seems to be giving problems is an expansion card, it is probably worthwhile checking that it is properly seated in its expansion slot. To do this you will have to remove either the outer casing or a side panel, depending on the style of case used for your PC. An expansion card has a metal bracket that is used to secure it to the rear of the PC's chassis, and connections on the bottom edge that fit into the expansion slot. The metal bracket can be seen at the left end of the card shown in Figure 2.45, and the connections can be seen on the extended part of the card at the bottom.

Before the card can be removed, the fixing bolt for the mounting bracket must be fully unscrewed (Figure 2.46). The card can then be pulled free of its expansion slot. Many PC expansion cards are vulnerable to damage from static charges, even if those charges are of modest voltages. A certain amount of

Fig.2.46 Fully remove the fixing bolt before extracting an expansion card

care must therefore be exercised when pulling the card free of the expansion slot. In this case things are eased by the fact that the card does not need to be completely removed from the PC. It is just a matter of pulling the card free of the expansion slot and then pushing it firmly back into position again. This makes sure that the card is fully pushed down into place in its slot. Removing and replacing the card also tends to clean the connectors so that any connections that were previously a bit iffy make good contact once more.

In order to avoid damage from static charge it is advisable to leave the PC connected to the mains supply, but to switch it off at both the mains

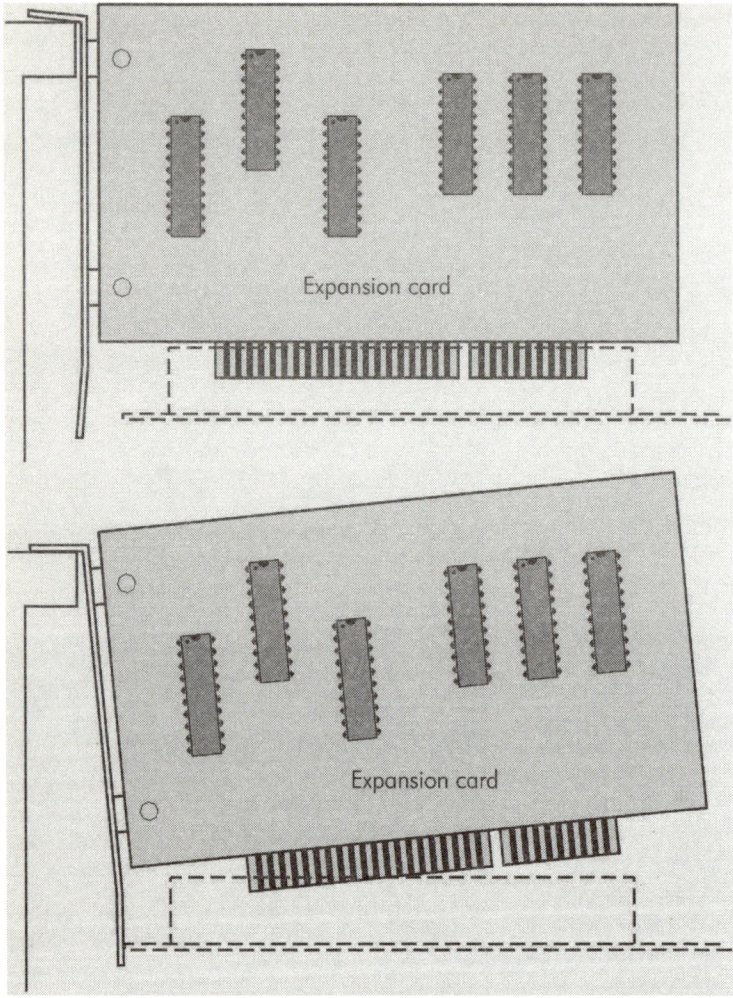

*Fig.2.47 An expansion card can cause problems its mounting bracket
does not have the correct right-angled bend*

socket and the PC's on/off switch. Although the PC is switched off, it will
be earthed to the mains earth connection. Touch the metal chassis of
the chassis before pulling the card from its slot. This will remove any
static charge in your body and should be sufficient to ensure that no

harm comes to any of the PC's hardware. Make sure that the card is parallel to the slot as in the upper view of Figure 2.47, and not at an angle to it as in the lower view. The bend at the top of the mounting bracket is often something less than a perfect right angle, which tends to skew the card slightly as the fixing bolt is screwed into place. Therefore, make quite sure that the card stays parallel to the expansion slot when the card is fixed in place. If necessary, remove the card again and carefully bend the top of bracket to produce a better approximation to a right angle.

Diagnostics software

Diagnostics software intended to help locate the source of hardware problems can be useful if you are unsure if a problem is due to an obscure Windows fault or an intermittent hardware problem. Suppose you have a PC that is largely working but seems to be a bit erratic or unreliable. Perhaps it sometimes boots into Windows all right but it hangs up on other occasions. Once into Windows, things may go perfectly well for a few minutes and then the computer suddenly crashes. This sort of thing can be caused by a software fault, but it is often due to something like a memory, processor, or disc problem.

If a problem only occurs when a certain applications program is run, it probably has its origins in that piece of software. Running hardware checks is then a little pointless, and it is matter of contacting the software publisher in search of a solution to the problem. Similarly, if the problem only occurs after a particular program has been used; it is very unlikely that either Windows or a hardware fault is the cause of the problem. It is again a matter of connecting the software publisher to see if there is a known problem with the applications program.

You may have some hardware diagnostics software, and if so it is certainly worthwhile running the software on a PC that is giving intermittent problems. In my experience, if a PC has a tendency to simply grind to a halt with the display freezing, the problem is more likely to be in the hardware than the software. This is also the case where things come to a halt with the screen going blank. The fault is more likely to be in the software if the dreaded Windows error messages ("This program has performed an illegal operation and will shut down", etc.) keep appearing. However, this is only a general rule and there are exceptions.

As explained previously, there is a program on the Windows installation disc that can be used to provide a memory check, even if it is not possible

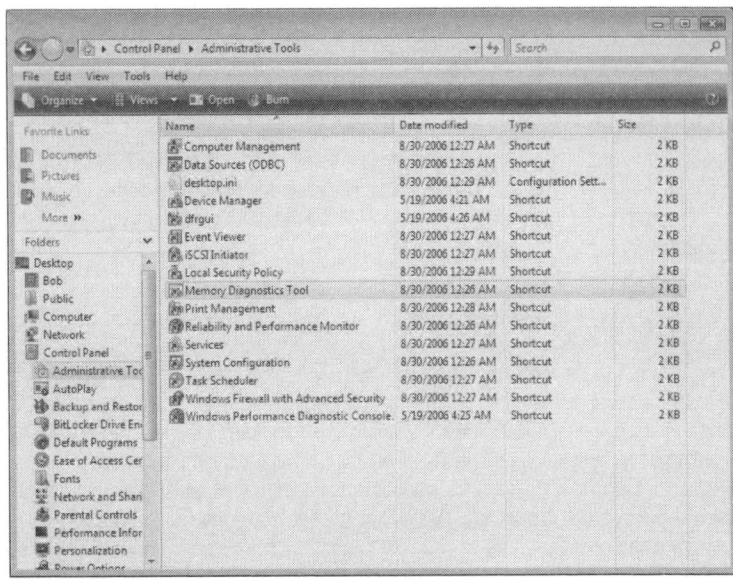

Fig.2.48 Double-click the Memory Diagnostic Tool entry

to boot into Windows. Windows will probably ask to run a memory test if it detects a possible memory problem during normal use. It is also possible to schedule the memory checking program from within Windows, but it will run until Windows is rebooted.

To schedule the memory checker it is a matter of going to the Windows Control Panel and double-clicking the Administrative Tools icon. The window will change to look line Figure 2.48, and here it is just a matter of double-clicking the Memory Diagnostic Tool in the main panel. This produces the small window of Figure 2.49, where you can opt to have the program run the next time the computer is booted, or to reboot the PC immediately and have the diagnostics program run.

The Windows memory checking utility is fine as far as it goes, but it only checks one aspect of the hardware. It is possible to obtain third-party diagnostics programs that will run tests on many parts of the system, including hard and floppy disc drives, the main memory, video memory, the processor, and the ports. Programs of this type sometimes operate under MS-DOS, or the software manufacturer's own MS-DOS style operating system. This is primarily so that they can take control of the memory when making memory tests.

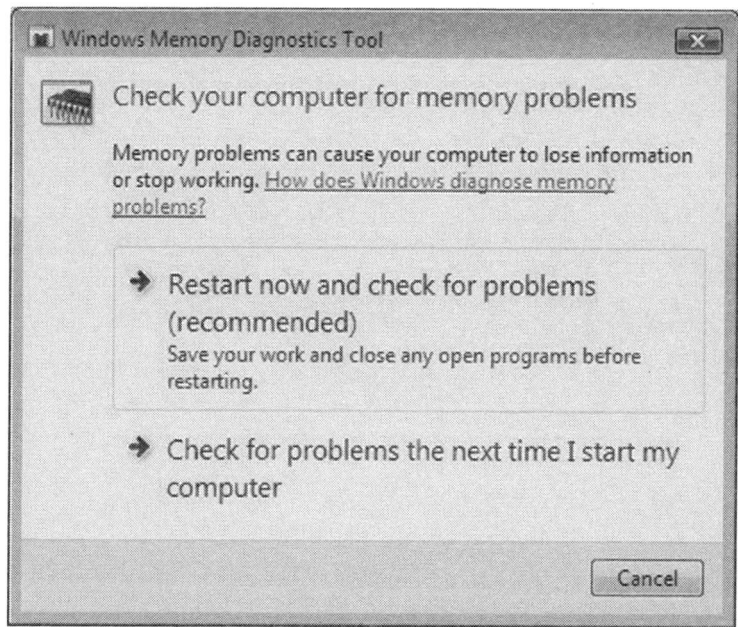

Fig.2.49 The computer can be rebooted immediately or the check can be carried out next time the computer is booted

Windows places restrictions on the way memory is allocated to programs, and would therefore place much of the memory beyond the reach of the diagnostics software. Note that it is no use trying to use this type of program by running it under any version of Windows using a DOS box. Windows would still be running and would not permit the program to function properly. Of course, another advantage of having the program run under its own operating system is that it will work with any PC regardless of the operating system it has installed.

Many diagnostics programs that run under Windows reboot into MS/DOS to perform some of the tests, and then go back into Windows to display the results. Programs of this type generally lack compatibility with Windows Vista, and are totally unusable with this operating system. In fact, at the time of writing this there is very little diagnostics software that is compatible with Windows Vista. No doubt this situation will soon change, but in the meantime there may be no alternative to using MS-DOS based programs. Do not be tempted to use diagnostics software under Windows Vista unless it is fully compatible with this operating

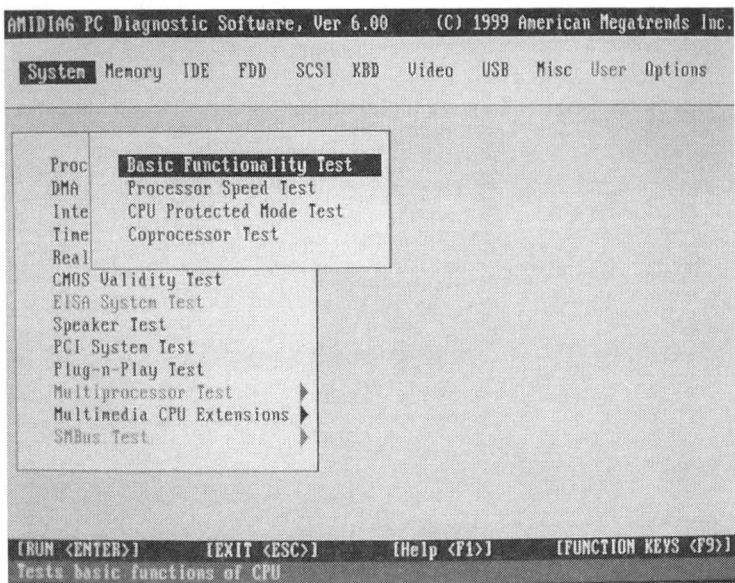

Fig.2.50 Amidiag 6.0 running under MS-DOS

system. Apart from the fact that it will not work properly with Windows Vista, if it works at all, incompatible software has the potential to damage the system further rather than help cure existing problems.

Making tests

When you manage to get some diagnostics software working with Windows Vista, what will it actually do? This obviously depends on the particular software in question, but there are a number of features that are common to most diagnostics programs. Most of these programs will perform a series of tests on the drives, the microprocessor, the memory, and most aspects of the hardware. Fig.2.50 shows Amidiag 6.00 in operation, and this program is being run using a floppy boot disc with the program files on a CD-R disc. It is therefore running in MS-DOS and it is completely independent of Windows Vista, or whatever operating system is installed on the PC's hard disc drive.

There are various hardware categories available from the menu bar across the top of the screen. The cursor and Return keys are used to select the

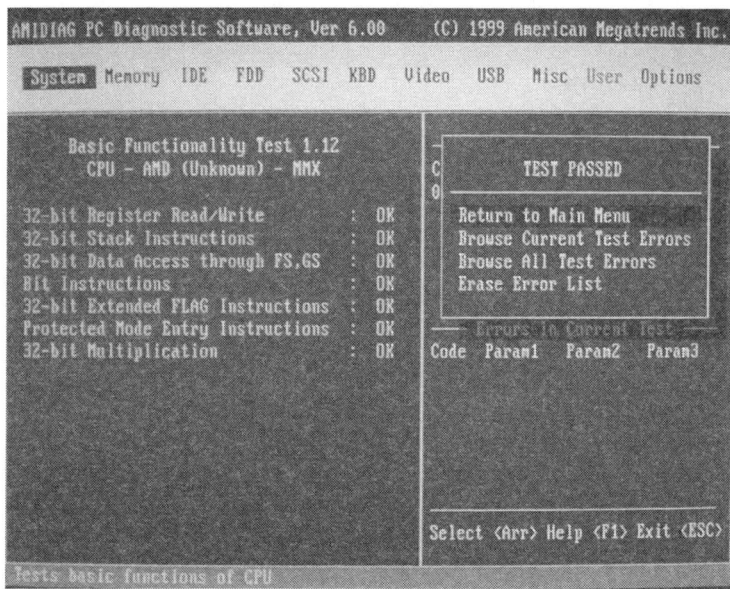

Fig.2.51 The processor has passed this test

required category, and items from the menus and submenus. In this example the processor is being tested for basic functionality, and Figure 2.51 shows the result of the test. No errors have been detected. Fig 2.52 shows a set of memory tests in progress, and again there have been no errors reported so far. Clearly, a wide range of tests can be performed using a diagnostics program such as Amidiag 6.00.

If a fault only occurs intermittently it might be necessary to repeat the test procedures a few times in order to coax the system into an error while the diagnostics software is running. Obviously you should try to concentrate on tests that are likely to bring results, and not bother too much about tests on parts of the system that are unlikely to be causing the problem. Faults associated with the ports and the floppy disc drive are unlikely to be responsible for bringing the system to a halt at times when none of these are in use. On the other hand, you may as well give every part of the system a "quick once over" while you are using the diagnostics software, just in case the problem does actually lie in an unlikely part of the system. If the system has a tendency to hang up periodically, the memory, processor and video card are probably the most likely sources of the problem.

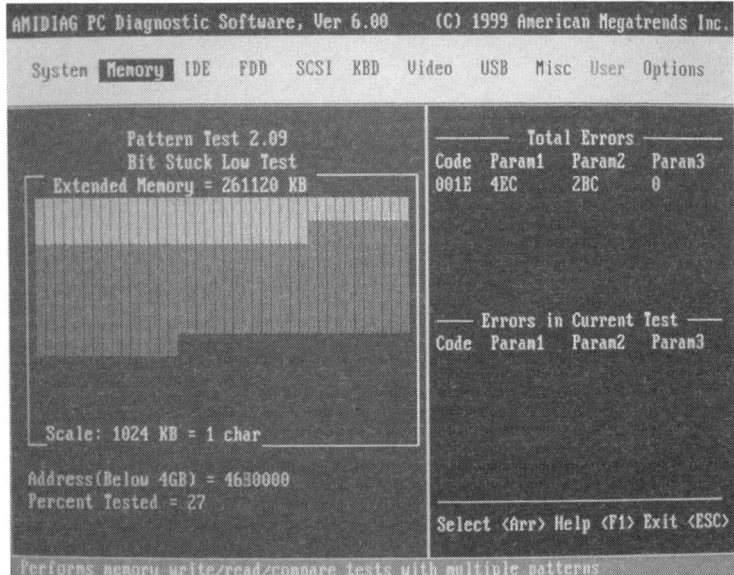

Fig.2.52 Memory testing in progress

What is a virus?

Do not overlook the possibility of problems being caused by a computer virus. There are actually several types of program that can attack a computer system and damage files on any accessible disc drive. These tend to be lumped together under the term "virus", but strictly speaking, a virus is a parasitic program that can reproduce itself and spread across a system or from one system to another. A virus attaches itself to other programs, but it is not immediately apparent to the user that anything has happened.

A virus can be benign, but usually it starts to do serious damage at some stage. It will often infect the boot sector of the hard disc, rendering the system unbootable. It can also affect the FAT (file allocation table) of a disc so that the computer can not find some of the files stored on the disc. The partition table can also be affected, so that the reported size of a disc does not match up with its true capacity. The disc might even be rendered totally inaccessible. The less subtle viruses take more direct action such as attempting to erase or overwrite everything on the hard disc, or erasing the system files while flashing an abusive message on the screen.

A virus can be spread from one computer to another via an infected file, which can enter the second computer via a disc, a modem, or over a network. In fact, any means of transferring a file from one computer to another is a potential route for spreading viruses. A program is really only a virus if it attaches itself to other programs or files and replicates itself. A program is not a virus if it is put forward as a useful application program but it actually starts damaging the system when it is run. This type of program is more correctly called a "Trojan Horse" or just a "Trojan". Either way, these programs can cause immense damage to the files on the disc, but there should be no risk of any hardware damage occurring.

Virus protection

This is a case where the old adage of "prevention is better than cure" certainly applies. There is probably a cure for every computer virus, but identifying and eradicating a virus can take a great deal of time. Also, having removed the virus there is no guarantee that your all your files will still be intact. Unfortunately, there is a good chance that some damage will have been done. Unless the virus is treated early in the proceedings there is a likelihood of massive damage to the files on the hard disc.

The ideal approach is to avoid doing anything that could introduce a virus into the system, but for most users this is not a practical proposition. These days, computing is increasingly about communications between PCs and any swapping of data between PCs provides a route for the spread of viruses. It used to be said that PC viruses could only be spread via discs that contained programs, and that data discs posed no major threat. It is in fact possible for a virus to infect a PC from a data disc, but only if the disc is left in the drive and the computer tries to boot from it at switch-on.

These days there is another method for viruses to spread from data discs, and this is via macros contained within the data files. Obviously not all applications software supports macros, but it is as well to regard data discs as potential virus carriers. Some of the most widespread and harmful viruses in recent times have been propagated via Emails containing macros infected with a virus, so this problem is one that needs to be taken very seriously.

Given that it is not practical for most users to avoid any possible contact with computer viruses, the alternative is to rely on anti-virus software to

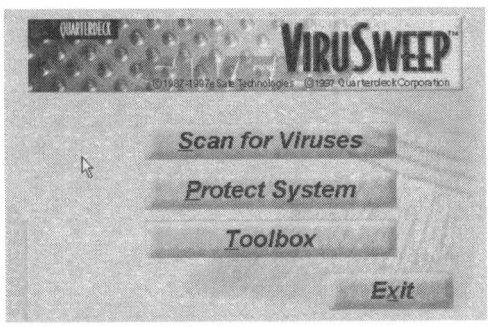

Fig.2.53 The ViruSweep startup screen

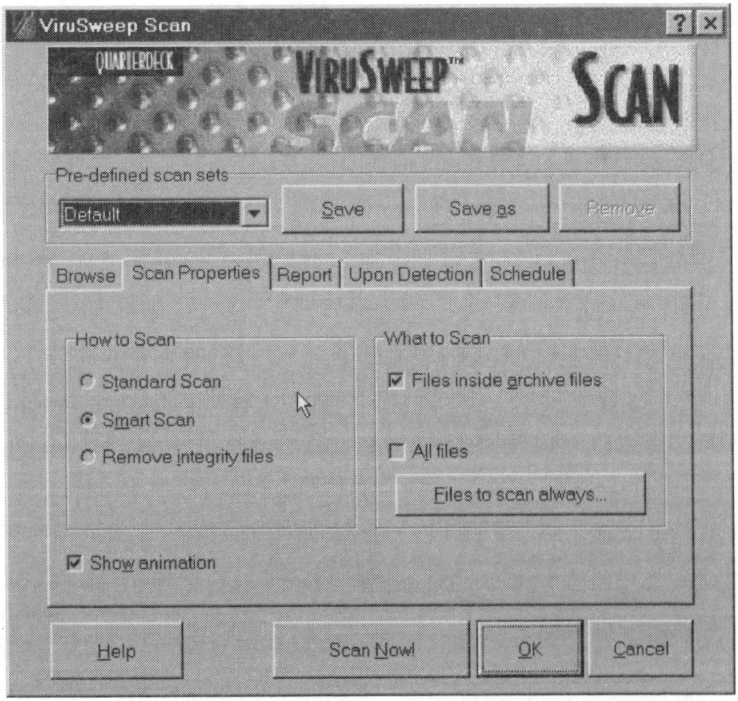

deal with any viruses that do come along. Ideally one of the "big name" anti-virus programs should be installed on the system and kept up to date. This should ensure that any infected disc is soon spotted and dealt with. Software of this type is designed for use before any problems occur, and it normally runs in the background, checking any potential sources of infection as they appear.

Fig.2.54 The first ViruSweep screen when scanning for viruses

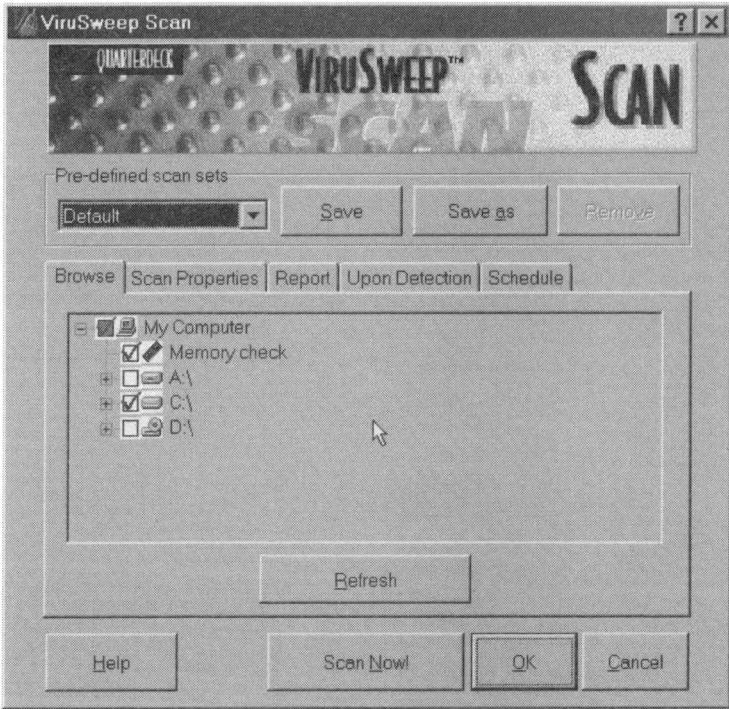

Fig.2.55 This screen enables the type of scan to be selected

There is usually a direct mode as well, which enables discs, memory, etc., to be checked for viruses. Figure 2.53 shows the startup screen for the Quarterdeck ViruSweep program, which is not running under Windows Vista incidentally, but it still demonstrates the basic method of using anti-virus programs. Selecting the "Scan For Viruses" option takes the user into further screens that permit various options to be selected. The first screen (Figure 2.54) permits the user to select the parts of the system that will be checked. Viruses can exist in memory as well as in disc files, so checking the memory is normally an option.

Response

Further screens enable the type of scan to be selected (Figure 2.55), and the action to be taken if a virus is detected (Figure 2.56). Most anti-virus software has the option of removing a virus rather than simply

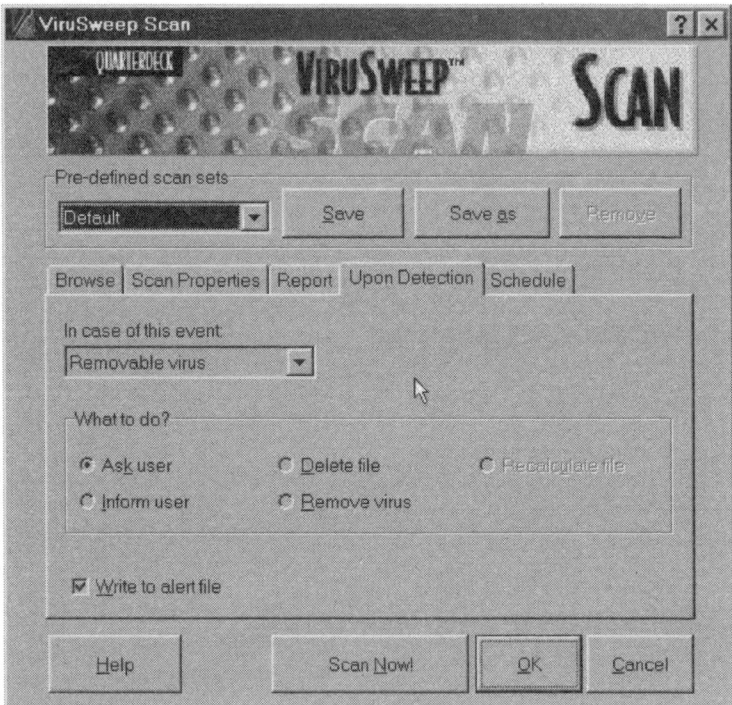

Fig.2.56 This screen gives control over the action taken when viruses are detected

indicating that it has been detected. Note though, that in some cases it might not be possible to automatically "kill" a virus. The program will then usually give details of how to manually remove the virus. Follow the removal instructions "to the letter", or you might make things worse rather than better.

Things are likely to be very difficult if you do not use anti-virus software and your PC becomes infected. On the face of it, you can simply load an anti-virus program onto the hard disc and then use it to remove the virus. In practice, it is definitely not advisable to try this method, and most software of this type will not load onto the hard disc if it detects that a virus is present. This may seem to greatly reduce the usefulness of the software, but there is a good reason for not loading any software onto an infected system. This is the risk of further spreading the virus by loading

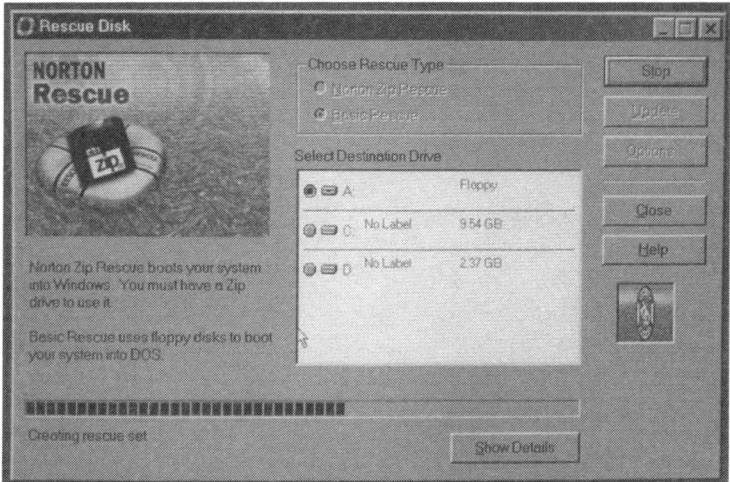

*Fig.2.57 Most antivurus programs can make recovery discs. This
version of Norton Antivirus makes a set of five recovery discs*

new software onto the computer. With a lot of new files loaded onto the
hard disc there is plenty of opportunity for the virus to spread.

Most viruses can actually be removed once they have infected a system,
but not usually by loading a major piece of anti-virus software onto the
hard disc and using it to remove the virus. The method offered by some
anti-virus suites is to boot from a special floppy disc that contains anti-
virus software. With this method there is no need to load any software
onto the hard disc, and consequently there is no risk of the anti-virus
software causing the virus to be spread further over the system.

With the Norton Anti-virus 2000 program a boot disc plus four support
discs are made during the installation process (Figure 2.57). If boot
problems occur at a later date, the PC can be booted using the Norton
boot disc, and with the aid of the support discs a comprehensive range
of virus scans can be undertaken (Figure 2.58). In some cases the virus
can be removed automatically, and it might also be possible to have any
damage to the system files repaired automatically as well.

It is increasingly common for antivirus software to be supplied on a
bootable CD-ROM or DVD. This avoids the need to make bootable discs.
It is just a matter of booting from the installation CD-ROM or DVD in
order to run the emergency antivirus software. This is clearly the only
way of running this type of software in cases where the PC lacks a floppy

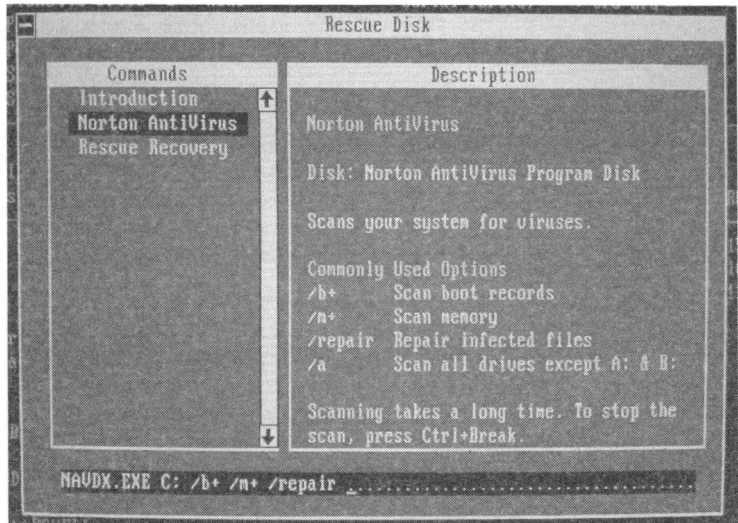

Fig.2.58 Virus scanning using the Norton recovery discs

drive. Few new laptop PCs have a floppy disc drive, and it is now a feature that is far from common with desktop PCs. It is therefore worthwhile using antivirus software that has the option of booting from the installation CD-ROM or DVD.

Firewall

Do not make the mistake of thinking that the built-in firewall of Windows Vista is a suitable alternative to anti-virus software. The purpose of a firewall is to stop hackers from gaining access to the files on your PC via a network connection, which usually means the Internet. A firewall does not provide protection against viruses, which are mainly spread by computer users unwittingly introducing them to their PCs, rather than someone hacking into their PCs and introducing the viruses. Ideally, both a firewall and anti-virus software should be used so that your PC is protected from both types of attack.

Bashful viruses

Often it soon becomes clear if a virus or similar program is the cause of Windows problems. The virus will proudly proclaim its presence with an onscreen message. In other cases it will not do so, making it difficult to determine whether the problem is due to a virus or a genuine problem with Windows. If there are repeated problems with the boot files becoming damaged or erased, it is very likely that a virus or similar program is responsible. A lot of inexplicable changes to the Windows Registry and other system or configuration files is also good grounds for suspicion.

There is plenty of anti-virus software available commercially, on the Internet at low cost or free, and it is often given away on the cover-mounted CD-ROMs supplied with computer magazines. If you suspect there may be a virus causing the problem it is best to use at least two and preferably three up to date anti-virus programs to check the PC's hard disc. Where applicable, download updates for the software so that you are using the most up to date versions. These should detect any new viruses. There is no guarantee that the problem is not due to a virus in the event that the programs fail to detect one. On the other hand, it becomes an outside chance and it is probably better to follow other avenues of investigation rather than pursue a virus that is probably not there.

It is only fair to point out that even if the anti-virus software does find a virus and kill it, you may still need to do some work in order to get the computer up and running again. The anti-virus program may be able to repair all the damage inflicted by the virus, but there is a fair chance that the damage will be too great for everything to be fixed. Anyway, with the virus killed off you are at least in a position to start repairing the damage and return things to normality.

Before continuing with this it is not a bad idea to give some thought to the way in which the virus found its way into your PC. There is otherwise a risk that it will soon return and undo the repairs you have made. If you had been using some discs from another computer prior to the problem occurring, check all those discs using the anti-virus programs. Bear in mind that many viruses have a sort of gestation period, and that there can be a substantial gap between the virus program finding its way into your PC and the program actually starting to do its worst. Ideally, you should check all discs that have been used with the PC in the previous few weeks or even months.

Closing notes

It helps to avoid problems if the PC is closed down in the approved fashion at the end of each session. Simply switching off with Windows Vista still running is unlikely to do any major harm, but is certainly not a good idea. Switching off with applications programs running is worse, and can lead to problems with Windows Vista or the applications programs. One potential cause of difficulties is that Windows Vista itself and many applications programs place temporary files on the hard disc drive. When Windows and the applications programs are shut down in the correct manner, these files are deleted. If you simply switch off with things still running, or the PC is suddenly switched off due to a power failure or hardware fault, these files are left on the disc. This may not matter, but there is a risk of the files confusing matters when the PC is switched on again.

Windows Vista is very good at dealing with the computer being shut down improperly, and the computer will probably appear to start up normally the next time it is used. There is no equivalent to the Scandisk startup routine of Windows 9x. Although there is no outward sign of anything out of the ordinary, Windows Vista is certainly dealing with the leftover files in the background. Do not rely on Windows Vista's expertise at dealing with problems to always get you out of trouble. Usually it will, but there is certainly no guarantee that it will always sort things out. Try to avoid problems by doing things properly. Always go through the logoff routine when you have finished using the computer.

Even if you do close down Windows correctly every time, it is still possible to run into difficulties with problem software. With earlier versions of Windows you soon encountered programs that just "froze" and would not respond to the mouse or keyboard. A more interesting but less common variation was the program that started to behave erratically with commands having the wrong effect, odd things happening on the screen, etc. Often when this occurred, the program failed to close down when the cross icon in the top right-hand corner of the screen was operated. Once an application program had gone seriously awry it was not uncommon for Windows itself to behave erratically, and it would often fail to close down properly.

Windows Vista is much better at spotting potentially risky programs and it often takes measures to avoid problems occurring. However, there is no guarantee that it will always head off problems, and it is best to avoid dodgy software in the first place. If you do run into problems with erratic or "frozen" programs, wherever possible applications and Windows itself should be shut down properly, or in a reasonably orderly fashion, rather than simply resorting to the on/off switch or Reset button.

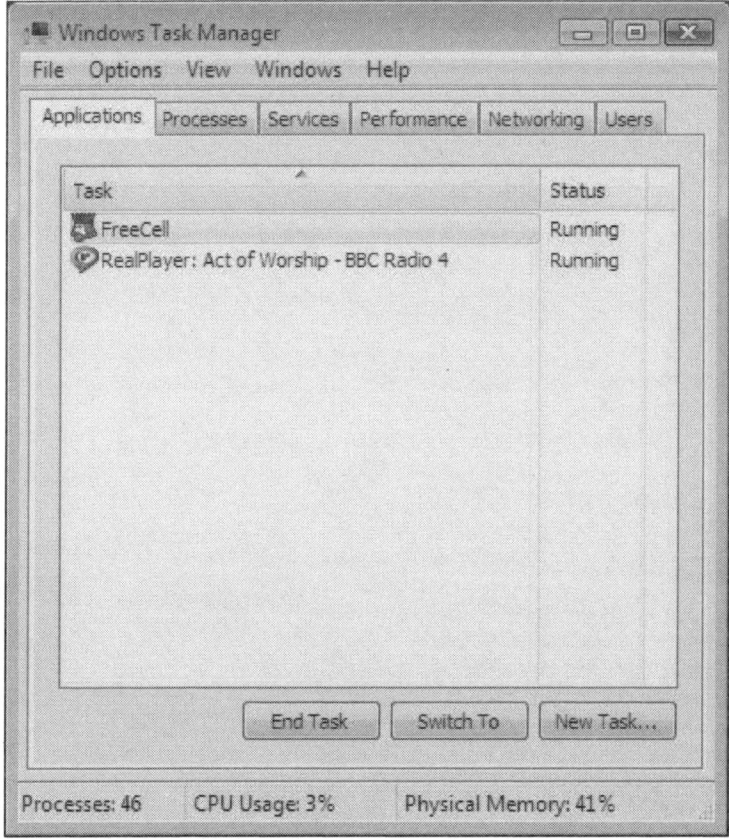

Fig.2.59 The Applications section of Windows Task Manager

Task Manager

Windows does provide an escape route that will usually do the trick if the PC becomes seriously "gummed up". As explained previously, the Control-Alt-Delete key combination gives access to the Windows Task Manager, but with Windows Vista it is not launched by this key combination. Instead you have to select it from a simple menu, and the Windows Vista version of the Task Manager will then appear. By default it lists the applications programs that are currently running (Figure 2.59). To be more precise, it lists programs that have taskbar buttons. If you

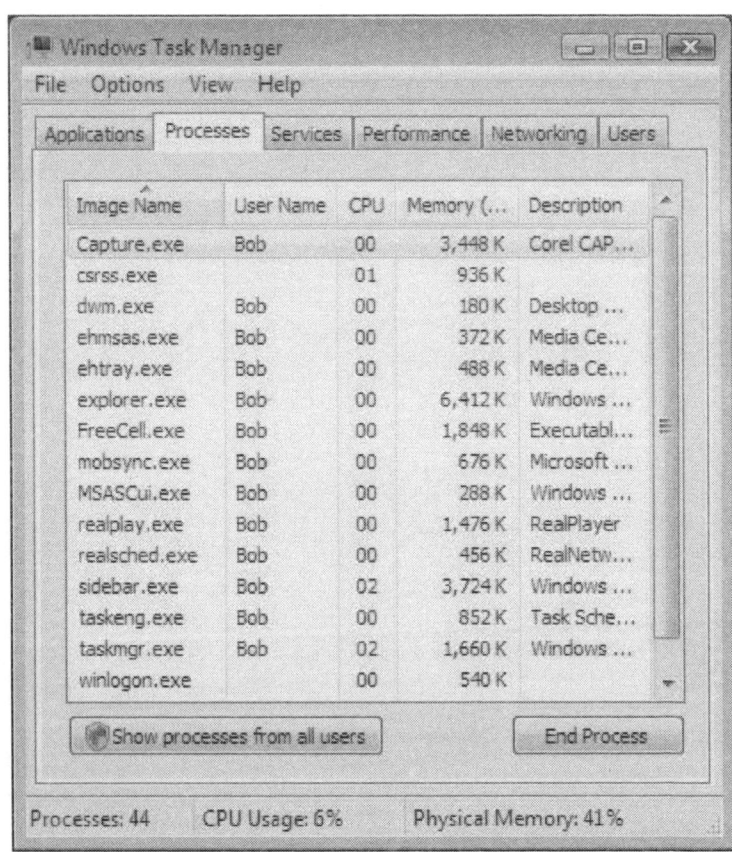

Fig.2.60 Expect to find a large number of processes running

launch something like a screen capture program that runs in the background and does not have a button on the taskbar, it will not be listed as an application by the Task Manager program.

A program can be shut down by left-clicking its entry in Task Manager to select it, and then operating the End Task button. Note that this is not intended to be a normal method of shutting down programs, and this method should only be used if the usual methods fail. In other words, where selecting Exit from the File menu or left-clicking the cross in the top right-hand corner of the window fails or is not possible for some reason.

When a program is in trouble there is usually a "(Not Responding)" message next to its entry in Task Manager. Bear in mind that a lack of response from a program does always mean that it has crashed. Similarly, the "(Not Responding)" message in Task Manager is not a cast-iron guarantee that something has gone wrong. The problem can simply be that the program is carrying out a complex task that is taking so much processing time that there are not enough resources left to permit periodic contact with the Task Manager program. It is therefore a good idea to wait a while before forcing a program to close down.

The waiting time depends on the type of task that the program is undertaking. If it is not doing anything particularly demanding there is probably no point in waiting more than a few seconds. If it is sorting the names of everyone in the world into alphabetical order it would probably be worthwhile waiting a few minutes. It is generally worth waiting a while if the program is still producing hard disc activity. This is not always a sign that everything is working properly but slowly, and some programs get stuck in a loop where the same disc activity is repeated ad infinitum. Therefore, if several minutes of waiting fail to resolve the problem it is probably time to force the program to close.

Using the End Task button in Task Manager is operationally much the same as closing a program via the usual routes. You should be presented with an opportunity to save any open files. It is possible that operating the End Task button will not have the desired effect, and it is then necessary to resort to the Processes section of Task Manager. In order to switch to this section it is merely necessary to operate the Processes tab near the top of the window. Most of the listed Processes are background tasks (Figure 2.60), but any applications that are running will also be included. For instance, in this example there is an entry for FreeCell game program.

A program can be forced to close by selecting its entry and operating the End Process button. Operate the End Process button when the warning message appears on the screen. This method is more or less guaranteed to end the program, but it will not give an opportunity to save any data that was in use by the program. Consequently, this method should only be used as a last resort. The applications program might rescue all or most of your data. It will then give the option of opening the saved data the next time the program is run. Failing that, you have to return to the last version you saved to disc. This will probably mean the loss of some work, but the loss should not be too great provided you save data at frequent intervals.

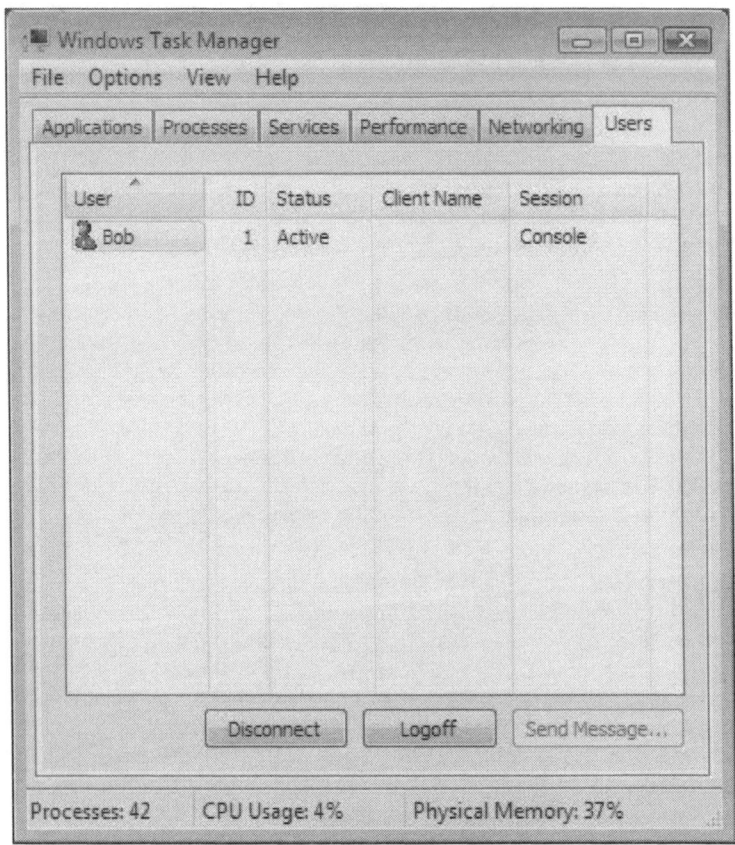

Fig.2.61 In this case there is just one user listed

When unstable applications software makes it impossible to sign off normally, Task Master can again provide a possible solution. Operating the Users tab brings up a list of the current users, and in the example of Figure 2.61 there is just one user logged on to the system. In order to log off, select the appropriate user and operate the Logoff button. Note that the Vista version of Task Manager does not have a Shut Down menu, and it therefore provides no way of shutting down the computer. This has to be done in the normal way via the Start menu.

If the system has well and truly hung-up and fails to respond to any user input, or you get an error screen explaining that Windows has been halted,

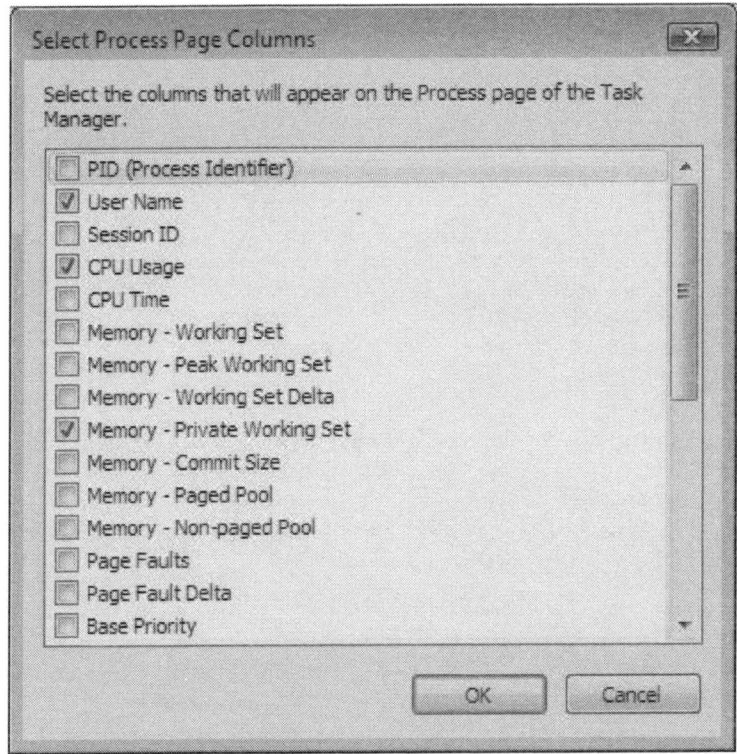

Fig.2.62 Tick the checkbox for each field you wish to include

there is no alternative to using a hardware reset. Operate the computer's reset button if it has one, or switch off the PC, wait a few seconds, and then switch it on again. Of course, any unsaved data will be lost if you have to exit the system in this way.

Where the system is showing signs of instability it is advisable to save your data to disc, using a new name rather than overwriting the existing file. This way, if anything should go wrong while saving the file, the existing version will not be damaged. If necessary, you can then resort to the existing version and salvage most of your data. Having saved the file, close all applications and shut down the system. Then restart it again, launch the applications, load the data files, and hope that everything then works more reliably.

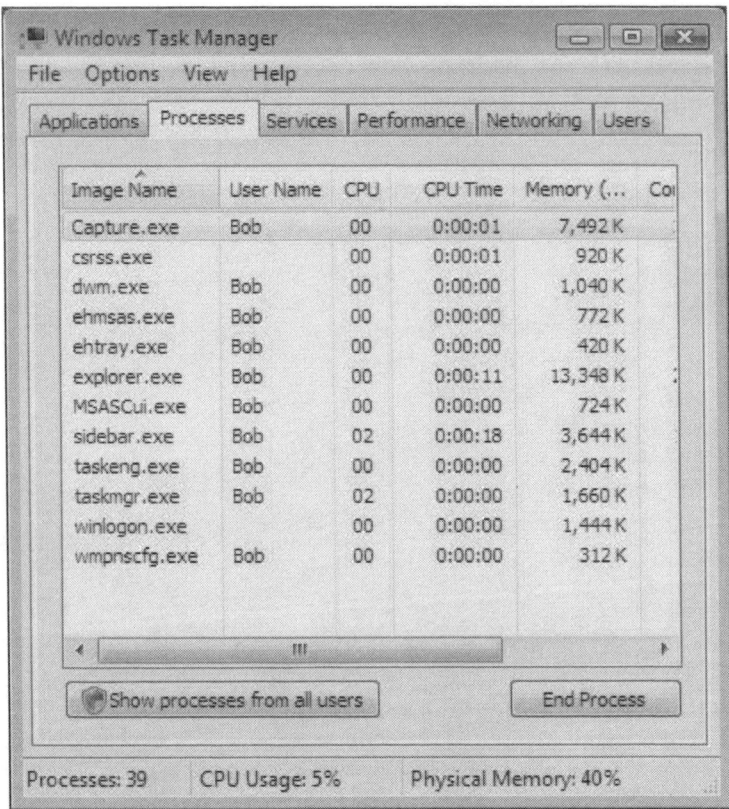

Fig.2.63 The changes will take immediate effect

It is definitely not a good idea to keep using an unstable system in the hope that things will get better. They might, but the more likely scenario is that the problem will get worse until things go seriously awry. Exiting the system and restarting is a much better strategy and it will often produce better results at the second attempt. Exiting at the first sign of trouble greatly reduces the risk of losing any data.

Customising

It is worth noting that the Processes section of Task Manager can be customised to show the required information fields. With the Processes

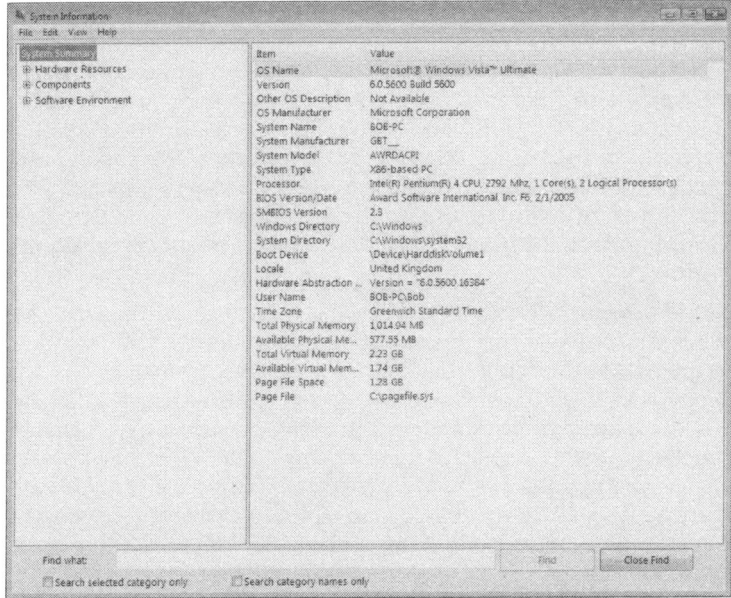

Fig.2.64 The Windows Vista version of System Information

tab selected, go to the View menu and choose the Select Columns option. This produces the window of Figure 2.62, where a tick is placed in the checkbox for each field you wish to include. Operate the OK button when you have finished, and the changes should then take immediate effect (Figure 2.63).

Background information

As pointed out previously, most modern PCs usually have a number of background tasks in operation, and not just Windows plus any applications you are running. If you use the Task Manager immediately after a PC has booted into Windows, you will probably find quite a long list of programs in the Processes section of the program. In fact a tally of about 20 to 30 is "par for the course" with a computer that has a reasonable range of software installed. Some of these programs are probably providing essential Windows functions, while others are media players, anti-virus monitoring routines, etc.

In theory, there should be no problem in having numerous background tasks provided the PC has enough memory to accommodate everything. In practice, the PC might not have sufficient memory to accommodate all the programs if there are a large number of them and you use memory hungry applications. Also, if your PC has only the minimum recommended amount of memory for the version of Windows in use, having large numbers of background tasks is inviting problems. The appearance of error messages mentioning illegal operations, fatal exception errors, and page faults is often indicative of faulty or inadequate memory.

With any version of Windows you can check the amount of free memory by running the System Information utility. From the Start menu select All programs, Accessories, System Tools, and then System Information. The Windows Vista version of this utility is shown in operation in Figure 2.64. The initial page provides some general information about the processor, operating system, amount of memory, and so on. The total physical memory is the amount of RAM installed in the computer, but obviously this is not all available for applications. A substantial amount is used by Windows itself, background tasks, and another section is set aside as temporary storage space. In some versions of Windows the amount of free system resources is given as a percentage, but with Windows Vista the available physical memory is quoted in megabytes instead. This is the important figure, and problems could result if this figure is very low.

Try running a couple of major applications, loading some data files into them, and then return to the System Information window. It does not automatically update the figures, so the amount of free physical memory should be the same as before. In order to update the figure go to the View menu and select the Refresh option. The information screen will go blank for a fraction of a second and it will then be updated with the new figures. These should include a reduced value for the amount of memory available. Incidentally, the figure for virtual memory includes hard disc space that can be used as a sort of slow alternative to RAM.

It is perhaps worth mentioning that a wide range of facts and figures can be obtained from the System Information program. Try double-clicking on one of the entries in the left-hand section of the window, and then select the subcategories one by one. Information on the running tasks, memory, and many other aspects of the PC can be obtained from this program. In Figure 2.65 the program is providing a list of the IRQ assignments.

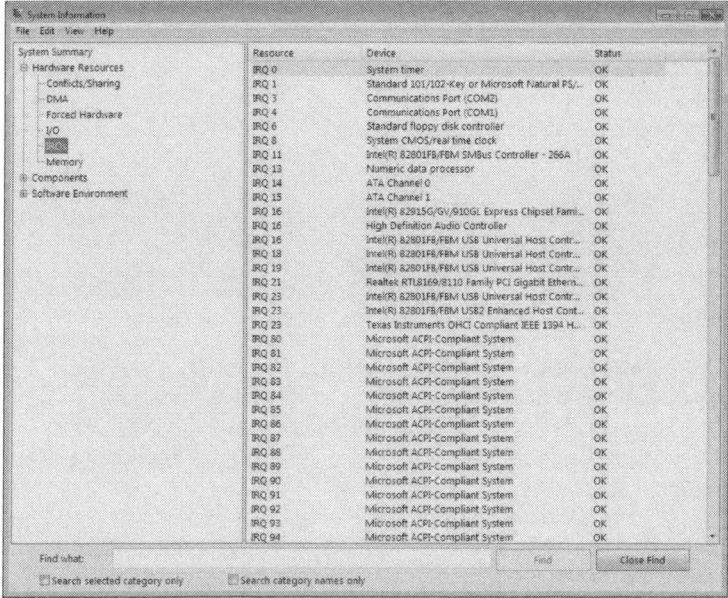

Fig.2.65 Here the program is providing a list of IRQ assignments

Dynamic information

As pointed out previously, the System Information utility does not automatically update the information, which can sometimes produce misleading results. The amount of memory used by a program can change massively from one instant to the next. The amount of memory used will often be relatively small while the program is idling and waiting for user input. A huge and almost instant increase in memory can occur if the program is then set a complex task. The same is true of microprocessor usage, which is generally minimal while a program is idle but can be very high when certain tasks are being undertaken.

The Processes section of the Windows Task Manager is usually a better source for information on memory and processor usage. This program does automatically update the information, and three refresh rates (high, normal, and low) are available from the View menu and the Update Speed submenu. There is also an option that permits the program to be paused. Remember that the information fields can be customised by way of the View menu and the Select Columns submenu.

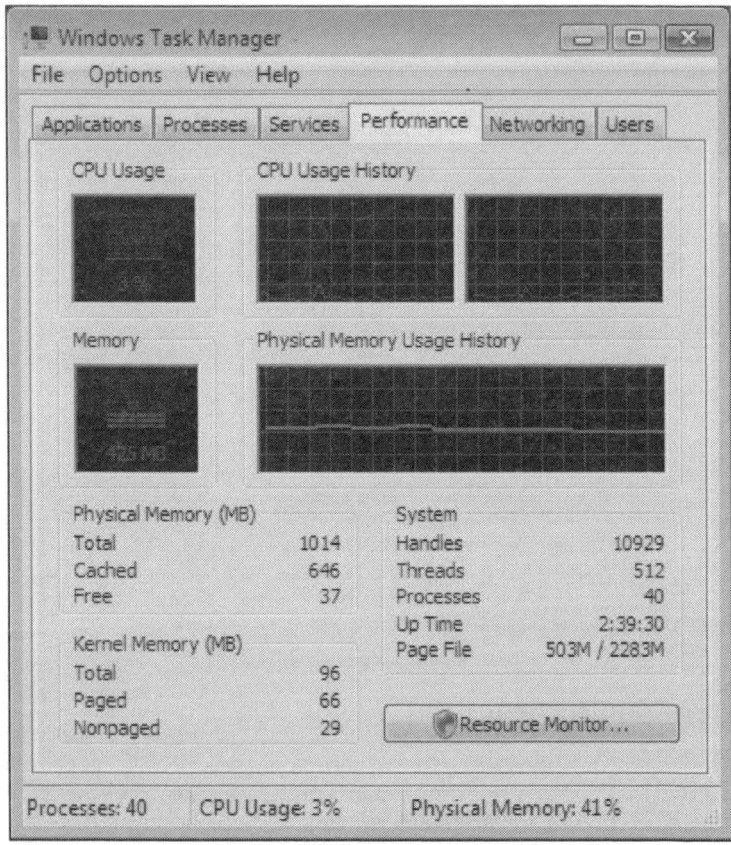

Fig.2.66 The performance section of Task Manager in operation

Memory – Peak Working Set is probably the most useful for checking the amount of memory used by applications. You can go through a typical session with a program and then check to determine the maximum amount of memory that it used. This is more practical than trying to manually monitor memory while using the program. The amount by which memory usage varies is often quite surprising. An image processing program for example, was found to use only about 15 megabytes of memory initially, but over 128 megabytes was used when processing a large bitmap.

In order to monitor processor usage it is best to operate the Performance tab in the Windows Task Manager, which produces a display like the one shown in Figure 2.66. The top section of the window includes a graph that shows how processor use varies over time. Note that by default the Task Manager will be displayed on top of other windows, so it is reasonably easy to monitor processor usage while using applications programs. If the Task Manager is minimised, its button appears towards the right-hand side of the Windows taskbar where it acts as a simple bargraph display that shows processor usage.

The lower graph in the Performance section of Task Manager shows the physical memory usage. Note that the Vista version of Task Manager differs from the Windows XP version in this respect. With the Windows XP version of Task Manager it is the page file usage that is displayed in the lower part of the window.

Solutions

It is usually pretty obvious when a computer is lacking in memory, because things slow very noticeably and the hard disc is accessed at practically every mouse click. A lack of processing power usually manifests itself by the computer seeming to hang-up when any major task is performed, although normal operation is restored when the processor eventually manages to complete the task. The Task Manager is useful in identifying the processes that use large amounts of memory or processing time.

Where a computer is lacking in speed, memory, or both, the only zero cost solution is to avoid running so many processes that it can not cope. Instead of running two or three major applications simultaneously, only run them one at a time. Memory is relatively cheap these days, so a memory upgrade is probably worthwhile in situations where a shortfall is seriously hampering performance. A processor upgrade is generally more expensive and difficult, where it is possible at all. The only solution to a serious lack of processing power might be to buy a new and much faster computer!

Reducing the number of background processes that are running can help to reduce both memory and processor usage, but do not expect this to have a dramatic effect on performance. Most background tasks do not use much memory or processor time, and switching off one or two of them will not produce a huge increase in performance. Also, bear in mind that many of these tasks are essential to the normal running of the computer. Switching off one of these essential tasks will probably

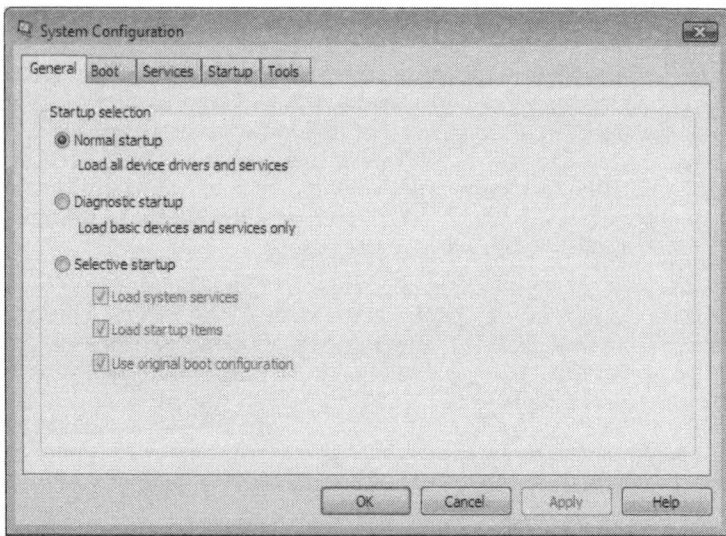

Fig.2.67 The General section of the Msconfig utility

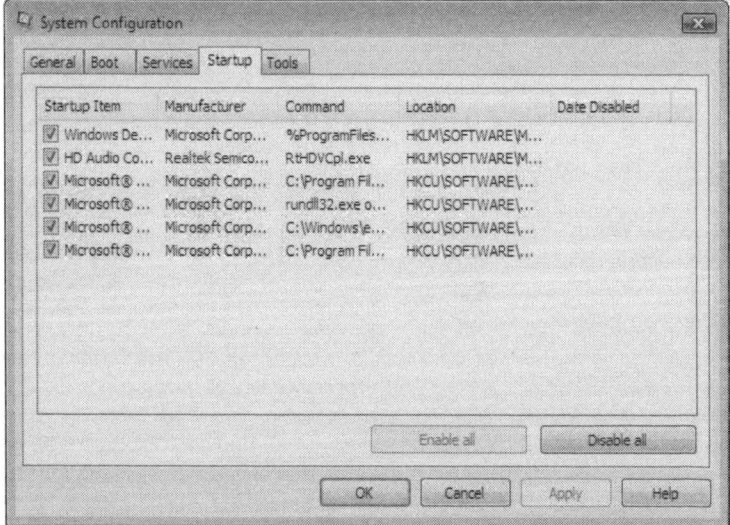

Fig.2.68 The Startup section will often list a number of programs

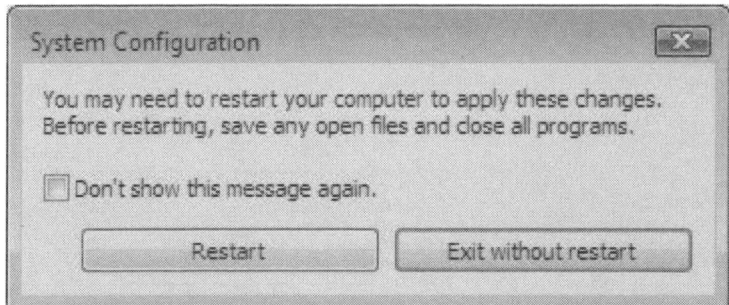

Fig.2.69 The programs will not stop running unless the computer is restarted

result in the computer rapidly coming to a halt. Only switch off tasks if you are sure that they are nonessential. Of course, where there are large numbers of these programs and the computer has a limited amount of memory, switching off several tasks could produce a very worthwhile boost in performance.

Non-starters

Rather than switching off non-essential tasks once the computer is under way, they can be prevented from starting up by removing their entries in the System Configuration utility. The programs can then be run when and if they are required. With Windows Vista it is not possible to start the System Configuration utility from the Run option in the Start menu. This

is for the very good reason that the Run option is no longer available from the Start menu. Instead, launch Windows Explorer and type "msconfig" (without the quotation marks) into the address

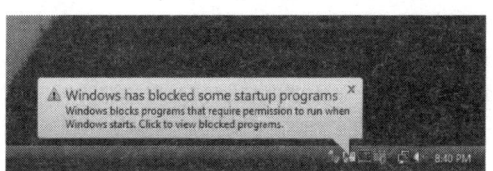

Fig.2.70 A message confirms that some programs have been blocked

textbox, and then operate the Return key. This will produce a window like the one shown in Figure 2.67. By default the General section is shown, and this is a useful diagnostics tool. In this case though, it is the Startup section that is required (Figure 2.68), and this is brought up by operating the appropriate tab.

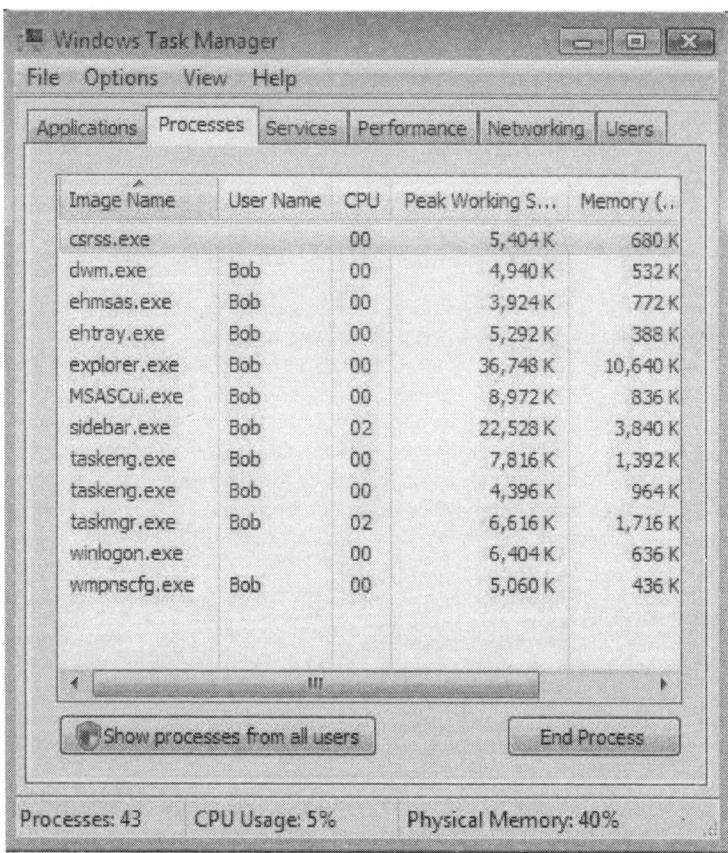

Fig.2.71 Blocked programs should not appear in Task Manager

A list of startup programs is shown, and each one has a checkbox. Removing the tick from a checkbox results in that program not being loaded at startup. By removing a tick you are not uninstalling that program and it can still be launched manually. In addition, a program can be reinstated by going back to the System Configuration utility and restoring the tick to its checkbox. For the sake of this example, the tick for the HD Audio program was removed. The Apply and Close buttons are operated once the required changes have been made.

The deselected program or programs will not be switched off by the System Configuration utility, and a warning message to this effect will be displayed on the screen (Figure 2.69). These programs will not be launched on subsequent occasions when the computer is booted. It is advisable to operate the Restart button so that you can check that the changes have taken effect.

Once back in Windows Vista, there will be a message indicating that Windows Vista has blocked some startup programs (Figure 2.70). To check that the program or programs have genuinely been suppressed, launch the Windows Task Manager and then operate the Processes tab to produce a list of running processes. This should not include any startup programs that have been suppressed. Figure 2.71 shows the list of running processes on the example system, and the HD Audio program is missing from the list.

Points to remember

Do not mess around with the Windows Registry, configuration files, or any part of the system unless you know exactly what you are doing.

Do not delete files manually unless you are sure it is safe to remove them. Where possible, programs should be removed using their own uninstall utility or the built-in facility of Windows.

Avoid using any form of beta or test software. If you wish to experiment with software of dubious stability, have a PC specifically for this purpose.

Do not blame Windows if things grind to a halt before the boot-up sequence starts. A failure this early in the start-up sequence is due to a hardware fault or an error in the BIOS settings.

A hardware fault can be responsible for the boot-up process failing almost as soon as it starts, or never actually starting. However, it could be due to damaged or missing boot files, so try repairing them using the software on the Windows installation disc.

If you have access to some diagnostics software, use it to check that the problem is not due to a hardware fault. Be careful to use Windows Vista compatible utilities, or MS-DOS programs run with the aid of an MS-DOS boot disc.

Make sure the expansion cards are fitted into their expansion slots correctly.

If the boot process stalls late in the boot sequence check that the hardware drivers are properly installed. One of the programs that runs at start-up could also be the cause of the problem.

The fact that a virus has not announced its presence does not mean it is not there. If there are inexplicable problems with the system, use anti-virus programs to scan the files on the hard disc, recently used floppy discs, etc. Ideally an anti-virus program should be installed on the PC and used to make regular checks of the system.

Do not switch off your PC while Windows is still running. Shutting down Windows should automatically switch off your PC. Even if the operating system or applications software is behaving abnormally, try to close down the system properly.

Do not get your computer to "bite off more than it can chew". There is a limit to the amount of software that a PC can have running at the same time. The operating system can be damaged if the computer keeps running out of resources and crashing. The Windows Task Manager is useful for monitoring running processes and their use of system resources.

Preventing unnecessary programs from running automatically at start-up can help to conserve system resources. Most start-up programs are easily blocked using the System Configuration utility.

Troubleshooting

Booting problems

Many users of MS/DOS were surprised at the ease with which the new operating system could be halted in its tracks when they moved to the new (at the time) Windows 95. A relatively simple operating system such as MS/DOS does not usually fail to boot unless there is damage to one of the boot files. Normally when things go wrong it will throw up a few error messages during the boot process, and some entries in the configuration files will be ignored. The operating system might not operate exactly as you would like once the system has booted, but the system will usually boot. Having booted, it will to a large extent be functioning and usable.

The situation is different with a complex operating systems such as Windows 95 and the subsequent Windows operating systems, including Windows Vista. These are all dependent on numerous files being present and correct on the hard disc. If any of these files is damaged or absent, or a configuration file erroneously specifies a file that is not present, the boot process will often stop about half-way through. When Windows does manage to boot successfully despite such problems, it is likely to be unstable or come to a halt later in the proceedings.

Windows XP was designed to be more robust than previous versions of Windows, and this philosophy has been carried on into Vista, but Vista does not operate under the "boot anyway" philosophy of MS/DOS. The cautious approach of Windows operating systems could be by accident rather than design, but it is probably a safety measure to ensure that the system only boots if it can do so reliably. With a complex operating system such as Windows Vista, the last thing you need is the system booting but then running amok.

Not all Windows faults centre on boot problems, but it is probably true to say that the vast majority of serious problems involve the boot process stalling at some point in the proceedings. Windows can boot normally and then give difficulties, but this is often the result of problems elsewhere

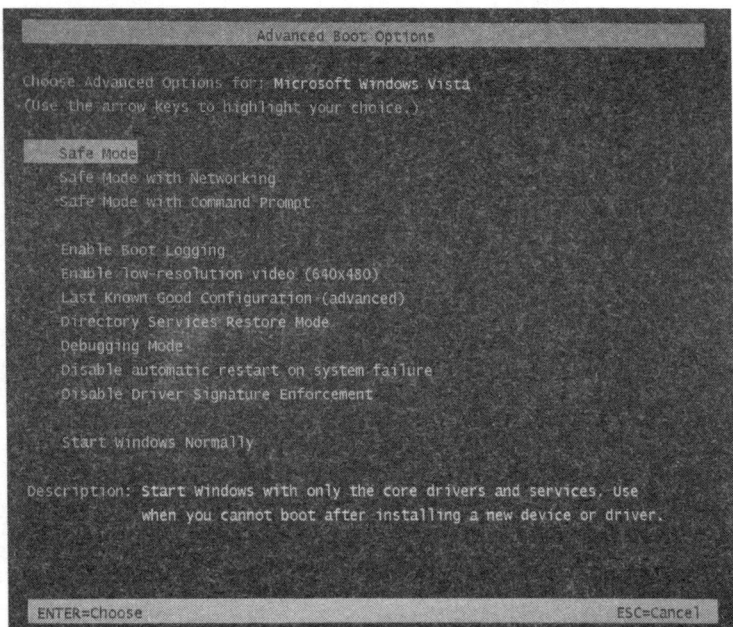

Fig.3.1 Safe Mode is available from the Advanced Boot Options menu

in the system. Hardware faults and bugs in applications software can both produce this kind of behaviour. Much of this chapter is therefore devoted to boot problems, and it is this topic that is covered first.

Safety first

Do not jump to the conclusion that the system has become unusable because Windows crashes during the boot-up sequence. There could be a major problem, but it is worth resetting the computer a couple of times to see if the problem clears itself. Also, try switching off, waiting a few seconds, and then turning the PC on again. There can be an occasional problem with a piece of hardware failing to reset properly at switch-on. Switching the PC off and on again will usually clear this sort of problem. If that fails, boot in Safe Mode (as described in detail in the next part of this chapter), shut down Windows in the usual way, and then try rebooting normally.

When repeated attempts to boot the system result in the boot process coming to a premature end, Windows should be booted in Safe Mode again. This is a sort of very basic "boot at all costs" mode that can be used when troubleshooting. There are other modes that can be useful when Windows troubleshooting. In order to boot into one of these modes the F8 function key must be pressed as soon as the BIOS start-up routine ends and the boot process begins. There is only a very brief gap between the BIOS finishing its start-up processes and the system starting to boot, so you must press F8 as soon as the BIOS has finished its routine. In fact with some systems the only reliable way of entering Safe mode is to repeatedly press F8 as the end of the start-up routine approaches. Pressing F8 when using Windows XP brings up the simple menu system shown in Figure 3.1. This is a summary of the options:

Start Windows Normally

Booting using the Normal option takes the PC through a normal Windows Vista boot-up process, but it is obviously of no use if the computer has a major boot problem. Selecting this option will simple result in the computer rebooting and hanging up again. Sometimes Windows "thinks" that it has detected an error during the boot sequence, and it might then go to the Advanced Boot Options screen. If you consider that all is actually well with the system, this option provides a means of trying to boot the computer normally.

Safe Mode

Safe Mode boots into Windows Vista, but only a minimalist version of the operating system. The display is a basic type that used to offer a minimum of 640 by 480 pixel resolution, often together with very limited colour depth. However, with Vista the resolution will be a minimum of 800 by 600 pixels, and the number of available colours is usually quite reasonable. This mode should be familiar to anyone familiar with troubleshooting on earlier versions of Windows, and it is much the same as the Windows 9x and XP equivalents. In general, the Windows Vista version of Safe Mode is better because less of the hardware is disabled. For example, drives such as CD-ROM and Flash card readers are usually available in the Vista version of Safe Mode, but are often ignored by this mode in earlier versions of Windows. Even with the basic 800 by 600 pixel resolution and the other limitations of this mode, it is often possible to use it to fix Windows problems.

Although more functional than the Windows 9x Safe Mode, or even the XP version, there are still some items of hardware that do not work in this mode. The soundcard will not be operational, and CD/DVD writers are likely to work as nothing more than simple CD-ROM (read-only) drives. Some hardware drivers are not loaded during the boot process in order to increase the chances of booting into Safe Mode. Any drives that require special drivers are unlikely to be operational in Windows Vista's Safe Mode. Peripherals connected to the USB ports do not normally function, but USB keyboards and mice will do so provided the computer's BIOS provides the necessary support. The same is true of most Flash card readers. Startup programs are not loaded when Safe Mode is used.

Many of the usual Windows fault-finding and configuration facilities are available from Safe Mode. In particular, Device Manager and the Registry Editor are both available. One notable omission is the Backup and Restore Center. However, it is not necessary to access these from within Windows, so it is still possible to go back to a restoration point or to restore a complete backup. These topics are fully covered in chapter 5 and will not be considered further here. Obviously in a minimalist Windows environment there can be some restrictions on services available, but those that are available work more or less normally. Boot problems are often caused by faults in the drivers for new hardware, and having access to Device Manager means that most problems of this type can be rapidly sorted out.

Safe Mode with Networking

This is essentially the same as the normal Safe Mode, but the drivers, etc., needed for Windows networking are loaded. It is possible that network access could be useful because it gives access to shared resources on other PCs, but it is mainly used where the PC is connected to the Internet via a router and some form of broadband connection. By enabling networking, and provided this does not prevent the computer from booting into Safe Mode, the computer will have access to the Internet.

Safe Mode with Command Prompt

Despite the name of this mode, it is nothing like the normal Safe Mode. The computer is booted using a basic set of drivers, but it is booted into an MS-DOS style environment, complete with a command prompt. In most cases it is much easier to undertake troubleshooting using the normal Safe Mode with its graphical user interface. However, the command line version of Safe Mode might be usable when it is impossible to boot into the standard version.

Enable Boot Logging

This mode boots the computer normally, but a log file showing the name and status of each driver is placed on the hard disc. The log file is updated as each driver is loaded, and the idea is that the last entry in the file will identify the driver that is causing the system to crash. In practice, things are not quite as simple as that, but it is nevertheless a useful feature if the problem is proving to be elusive.

Enable low-resolution video

The VGA mode is not a normal troubleshooting mode, and it is not intended as an aid to locating faults. It boots the computer normally, but into the standard VGA mode rather than the normal start-up mode of the video card. This is useful if there is a problem with the video settings, such as a refresh rate that is too high for the monitor. Boot in this mode and then adjust the video settings to restore proper operation.

Last Known Good Configuration

This mode is similar in concept to using the System Restore facility, but more limited in its scope. It effectively takes the computer back in time to the last settings that enabled it to boot successfully. Unlike the System Restore facility, this mode does not erase or restore files. The file structure remains unchanged, but an earlier version of the Registry is used when booting the computer. Obviously, this mode will only be successful when the cause of the problem is an error or errors in the Registry. The System Restore facility is more likely to restore normal operation.

Directory Services Restore Mode

This is the same as the equivalent mode of Windows XP Professional, and like its predecessor, it seems to be of very limited practical value.

Debugging Mode

This is another mode that you will probably never need to use. The computer is booted into Windows kernel mode, and the debugging is then achieved via another computer running a suitable debugger program, with a serial link used to provide communication between the two computers.

Disable automatic restart

Using this mode prevents Windows from automatically rebooting if a

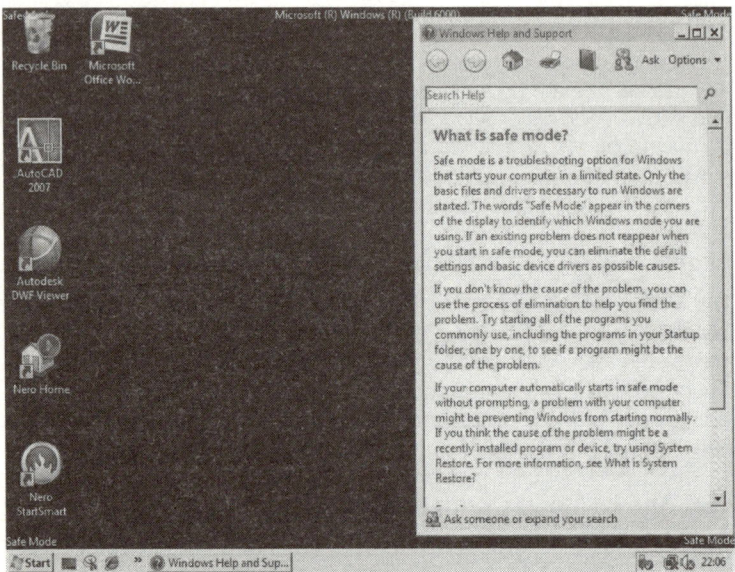

Fig.3.2 The Help system opens automatically on entering Safe Mode

system crash occurs. While this could conceivably aid fault diagnosis, leaving the system running in an unstable state could result in damage to system files, or probably any other files on the hard disc drive. This is not a mode that should be used unless you know exactly what you are doing.

Disable Driver Signature Enforcement

Drivers that contain an improper signature are loaded when using this mode. I presume that the point of this is to force the system to load a driver that it deems to be unsuitable, but the user considers to be fine, or would like to try anyway.

Using Safe Mode

Safe Mode is the usual starting point when boot problems occur. Use the cursor keys to highlight this option in the Windows Advanced Options menu, and then press enter to start the boot process. Where appropriate, select the correct operating system and then press the Return key to

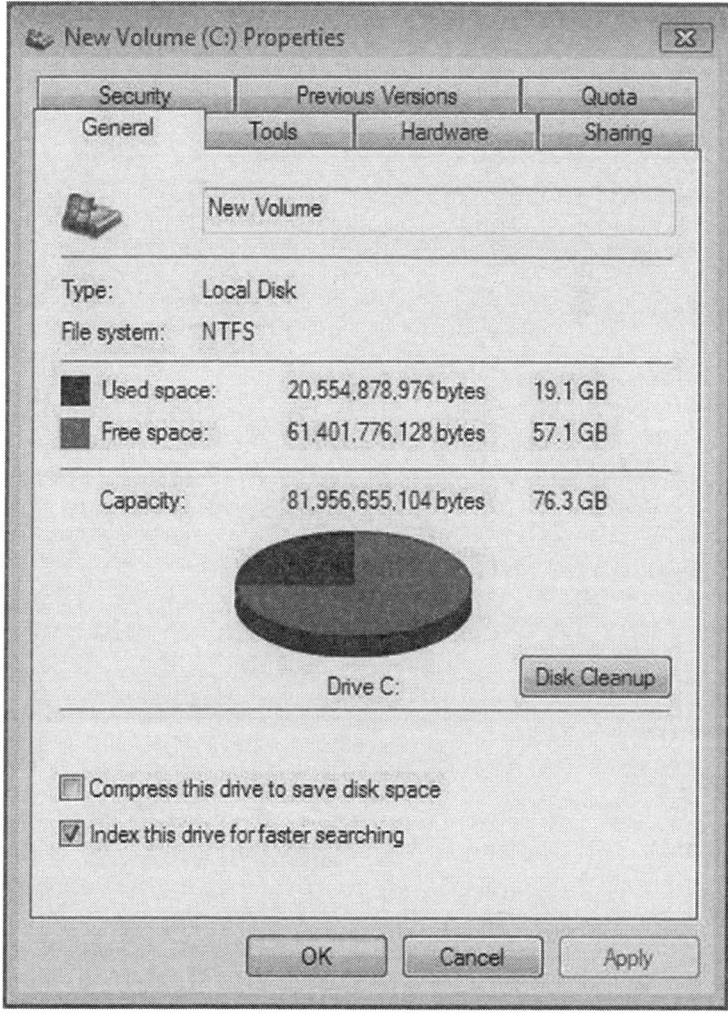

Fig.3.3 This window provides basic information for the drive

continue booting into Safe Mode. In most cases the computer will simply boot straight into Safe Mode from the initial screen. At the logon screen, sign in as the Administrator or use an account that has administrator status, so that you have maximum freedom to make adjustments to the

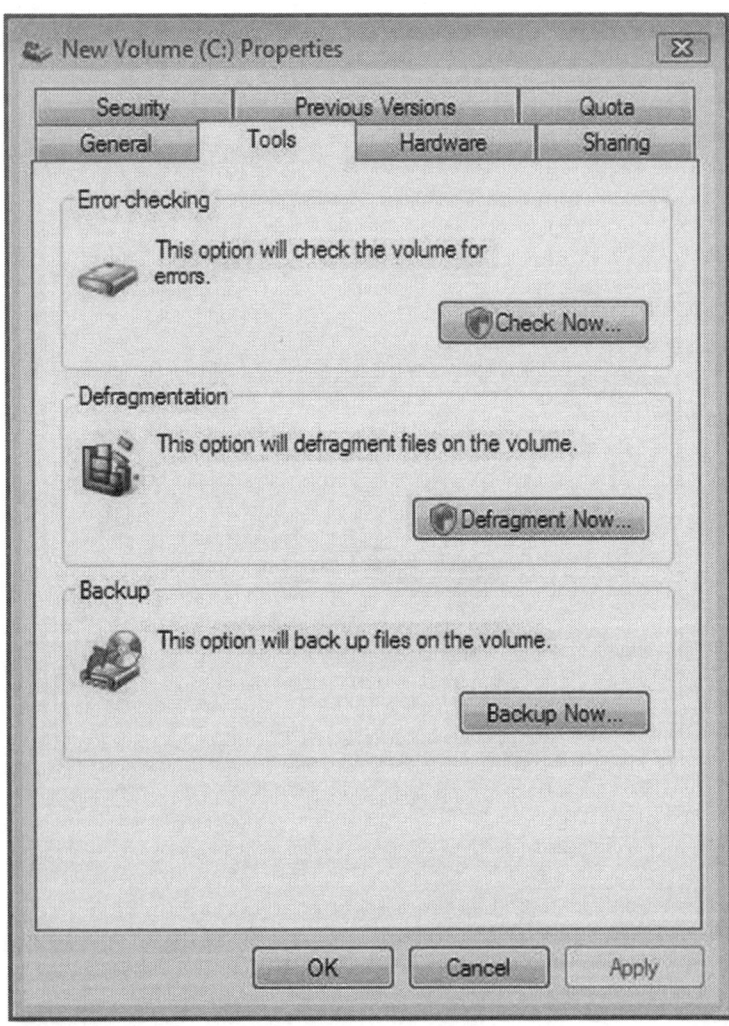

Fig.3.4 Error checking is available under the Tools tab

system. Once in Safe mode there will be "Safe Mode" legends in the comers of the screen to make it clear that the PC is not running in its normal mode. The Help system is opened automatically and it displays some information about using Safe Mode (Figure 3.2).

Once the PC is booted in Safe mode you can undertake some basic checks, and the usual starting point used to be the Windows Scandisk utility. However, this has not been included with Windows Vista, and was not included with Windows XP either. Both of these operating systems use the Check Disk program instead. This is supplied in two versions, which are a graphical user interface program and a command line utility (Chkdsk.exe). For most purposes the graphical user interface program will suffice, and this is easily accessed. In My Computer or

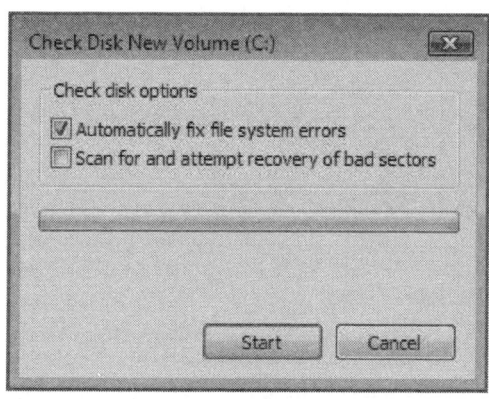

Fig.3.5 *This window provides two options*

Windows Explorer, right-click the entry for the drive you wish to check and then choose Properties from the pop-up menu. This produces a window like the one of Figure 3.3, which gives some basic information about the drive.

Operate the Tools tab to switch to a Window like the one in Figure 3.4, which includes an error checking facility. Left-clicking the Check Now button produces the small window of Figure 3.5, where two options are available via the checkboxes. Initially it is probably best to leave both checkboxes blank, and to go ahead with the checking process

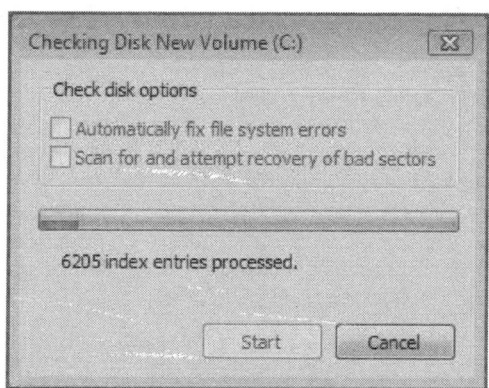

Fig.3.6 *The usual bargraph shows how far the process has progressed*

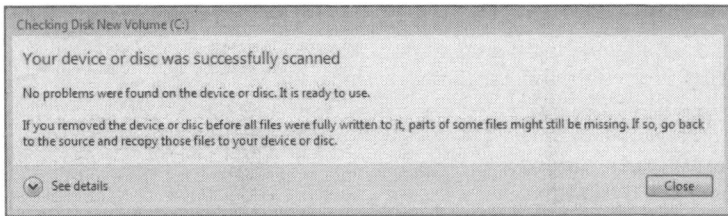

Fig.3.7 This scan did not detect any disc errors

by operating the Start button. The program will then check the disc for errors, showing its progress in the lower section of the Window (Figure 3.6). Once the process has been completed, the program will either report that there were no errors (Figure 3.7) or give a list of the problems that were detected.

If faults were detected it is advisable to run the program again, but using one or both of the options provided by the checkboxes. One option sets the program to automatically fix any errors that are detected. This is the quicker of the two options. The second option results in the program going through a very thorough checking process. It will try to recover located bad sectors in the disc and recover any data contained by those sectors. Using this option helps to minimise the damage caused by disc errors, but with large drives it can take many hours for the task to be completed. Once under way there is no way out of the program other than switching off the computer, which has the potential to increase the number of disc errors and is definitely not a good idea.

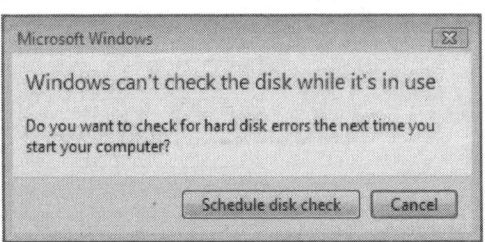

Fig.3.8 Windows can not check a disc that is in use

The program is unable to fix errors in a disc that is currently in use, which means that it can not check the boot drive while Windows is running. Trying to check a disc that is in use produces the error message of Figure 3.8. To go ahead with the checking and fixing process, operate the "Schedule disk check" button and restart the computer. The checking

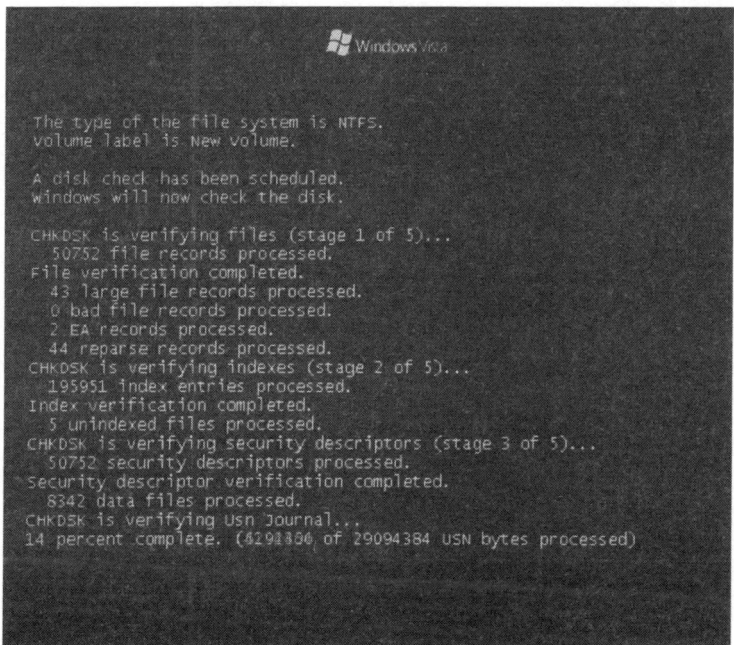

Fig.3.9 The checking is well under way. The computer will boot normally once the checking has been completed

program will be launched during the boot process, before the boot drive is left with any open files. The screen will show how things are progressing (Figure 3.9), and the boot process will continue once the disc checker has completed its task.

Users of Windows 9x operating systems soon became used to Scandisk running automatically during the boot routine if the computer has not been shut down properly. Check Disk is likely to run automatically at boot-up if a Windows XP system having a FAT32 boot disc is shut down abnormally, but it is unlikely to run automatically in systems that have a NTFS boot disc, which includes all PCs running Vista. This is because the NTFS system is better able to recover from abnormal disc activity, making it unnecessary to run Check Disk at the slightest excuse. There is probably no point in running Check Disk manually if the computer was not shut down properly, because it is unlikely that any disc writing errors would have been produced.

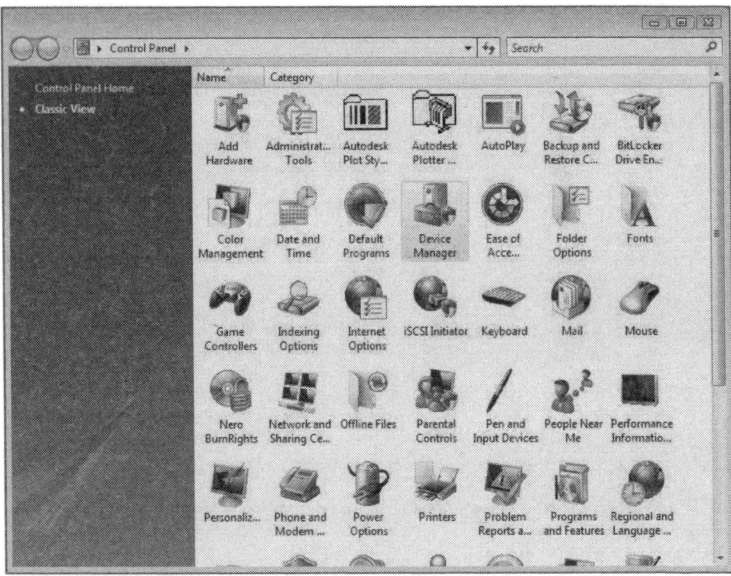

Fig.3.10 There might be a Device Manager icon, as in this case

Hardware drivers

Devices such as soundcards, video cards, and even the built-in interfaces of the PC such as the parallel and USB ports require drivers to integrate them with the Windows operating system. Problems with Windows drivers are not exactly a rarity, and it is best to check for driver faults sooner rather than later. The normal way of doing this is to go into Device Manager. In Windows Vista it can be launched from the Start menu by first selecting the Control Panel and left-clicking the Classic View link near the top left-hand corner of the window. Depending on the set-up of your PC, there might be a Device Manager icon (Figure 3.10). If so, double-clicking it will launch Device Manager. If this icon is not present, double-click the System icon, which launches a new window (Figure 3.11) where the Device Manager link is operated. You will then have a screen something like Figure 3.12.

Normally there will be a yellow exclamation mark (!) against an entry if the program has detected a problem with the item of hardware in that category. Double-clicking on an entry in the table expands it to show all the drivers in that category, and where appropriate there will be an

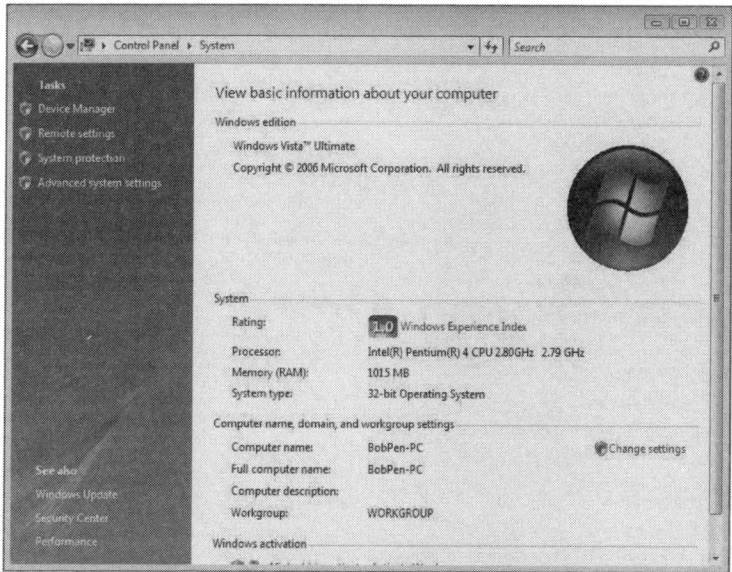

Fig.3.11 This window has a link for Device Manager

exclamation mark against an entry. In fact Windows will usually expand a category for you if it contains an item of hardware that seems to have a problem. In the example of Figure 3.12, the section for "Sound, video and games controllers" has been automatically expanded because a problem has been found. It is possible to double-click on an entry that has a question or exclamation mark in order to get further details on the problem.

Unfortunately, in Safe Mode Device Manager is not fully operational, and its diagnostic abilities are rather limited. No device drivers are loaded for several items of hardware, so no errors will be reported for these devices. If you try to get status information in Safe Mode you simply get a message of the type shown in Figure 3.13, explaining that status information is not available in Safe Mode. Note that Device Manager should provide status information for any hardware that is fully available in Safe Mode, such as the keyboard and floppy disc drive. For example, Figure 3.14 shows the properties window for the floppy disc drive, and it is being reported as working properly.

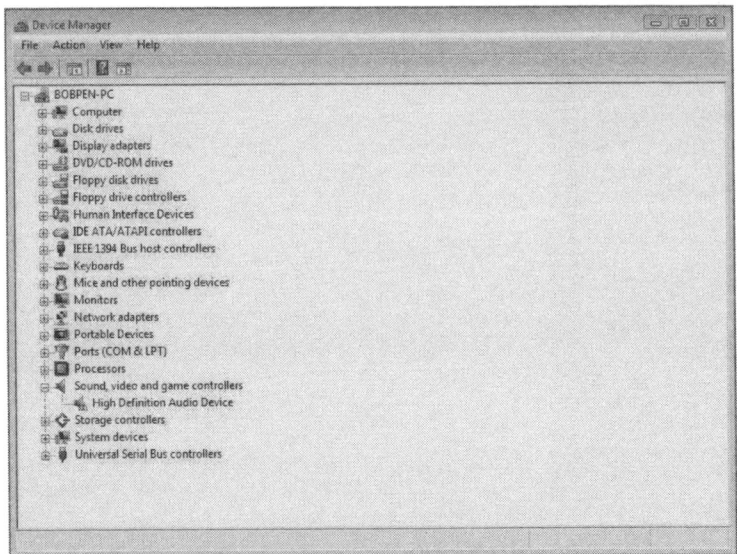

Fig.3.12 Device Manager lists all the installed hardware

With Windows XP there is a Troubleshoot button in the General section of a device's properties window, and operating this produces a wizard that offers various suggestions for curing the problem. While this built-in assistance was by no means guaranteed to solve any given problem, it could provide some useful advice for beginners. Unfortunately, it is a feature that seems to have been dropped from Windows Vista, although help is still available on a wide range of topics if you use "troubleshoot" as the search string in the Vista Help system.

Despite its limitations in Safe Mode, Device Manager can still be useful. It might indicate a problem with an item of hardware that is supported in Safe Mode. Often boot problems occur when a new piece of hardware has been added to a computer. It is not a foregone conclusion that the new hardware is the cause of the boot failure, but it is very likely that it is the culprit. Using Device Manager the device drivers for the new hardware can be removed, and with luck the computer will boot normally again. You are then in a better position to deal with the troublesome hardware. Going through the installation process again might produce better results, but in most cases an updated device driver will have to be obtained from the hardware manufacturer.

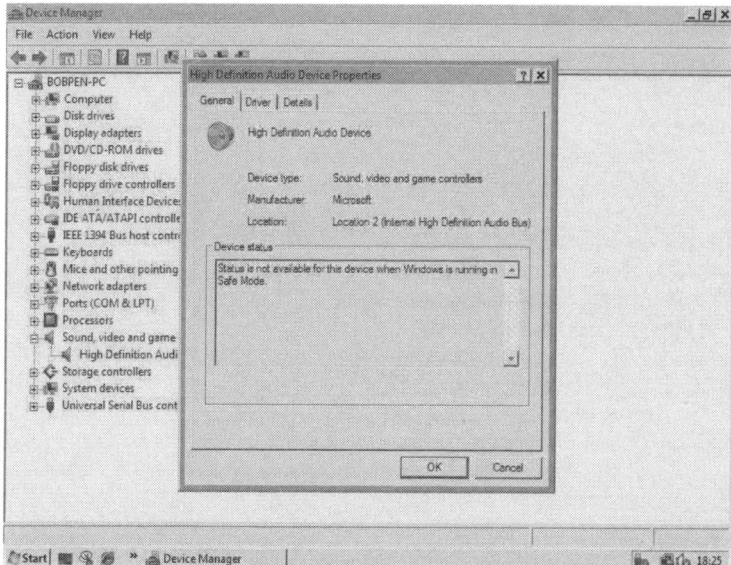

Fig.3.13 Status information is not available for some devices when in
Safe Mode

Old hardware

It is best not to jump to conclusions where the PC is one that has been in use for some time and it has undergone some changes to the hardware over the years. Is the "faulty" hardware actually something that was removed when you upgraded the computer a year ago? Is it something that is no longer in use because it ceased working when you upgraded the computer to Windows Vista? Windows Vista is good at automatically adjusting to changes in the hardware, but it might not always get it right.

Problems with hardware will not necessarily prevent Windows from booting, so the computer might have been working properly for some time although there was a perceived problem. With things such as mice and soundcards the PC will often boot up even if there is a problem, but the hardware concerned will not work properly. If the hardware is no longer in use or has actually been removed from the system, you will probably remain blissfully unaware of the problem reported in Device Manager. The drivers for more crucial items of hardware such as the hard disc drive and the video card are more likely to bring the boot process to a halt. Although they might not be doing any harm, it is a

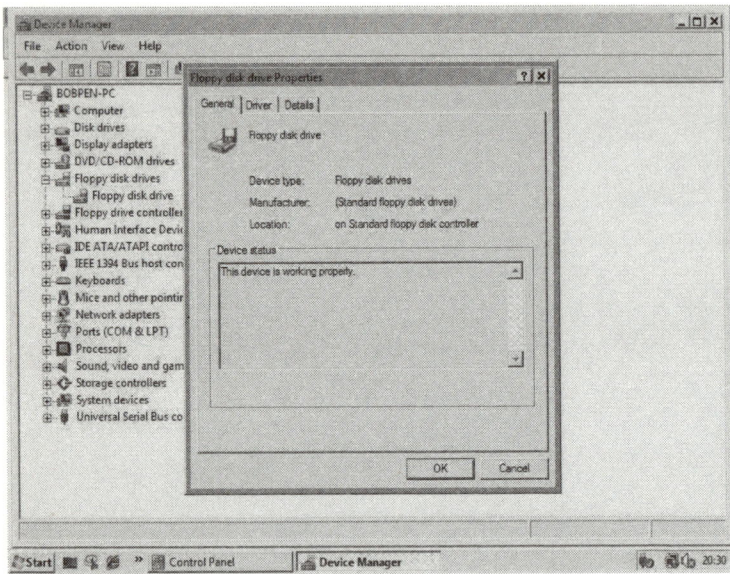

Fig.3.14 Status information is available for some devices

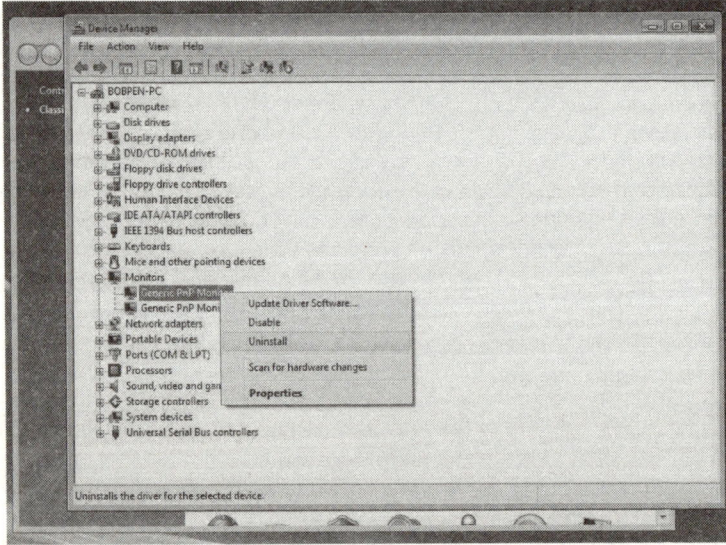

Fig.3.15 The pop-up menu has Disable and Uninstall options

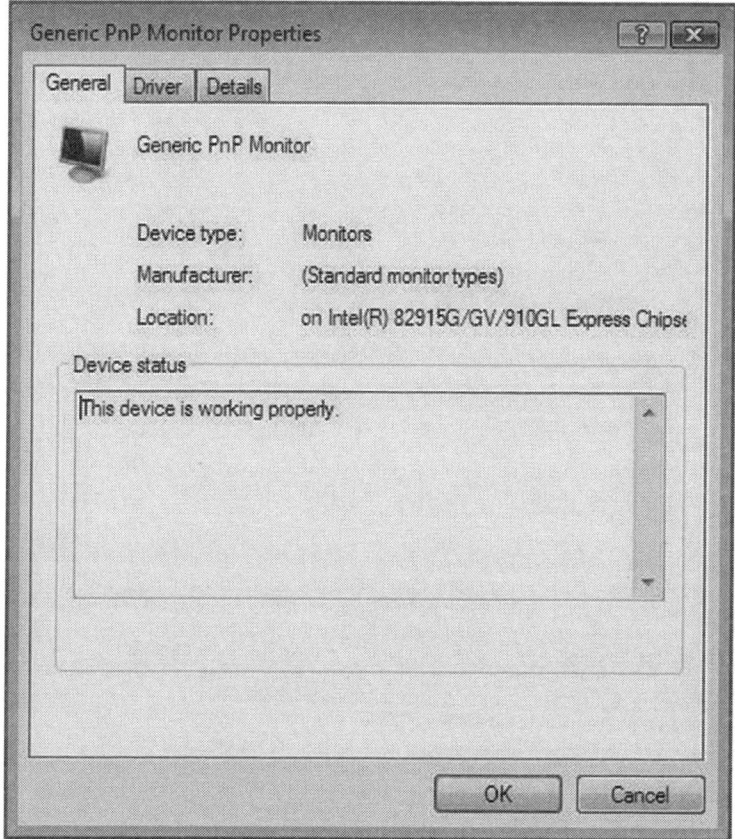

Fig.3.16 The properties window for an item of hardware (a monitor)

good idea to remove or disable any drivers for hardware that is no longer in use. This makes sure that the unnecessary drivers can not cause any problems.

Where hardware problems are found in Device Manager it certainly makes sense to sort them out before trying to proceed further. This might get the system working properly again or there could still be boot problems, but it at least clears away some potential causes of the problem. Reinstalling drivers can be problematic with the old drivers still in place. Even though there is a suspected problem with the existing ones, Windows can be reluctant to replace them with drivers that do not have

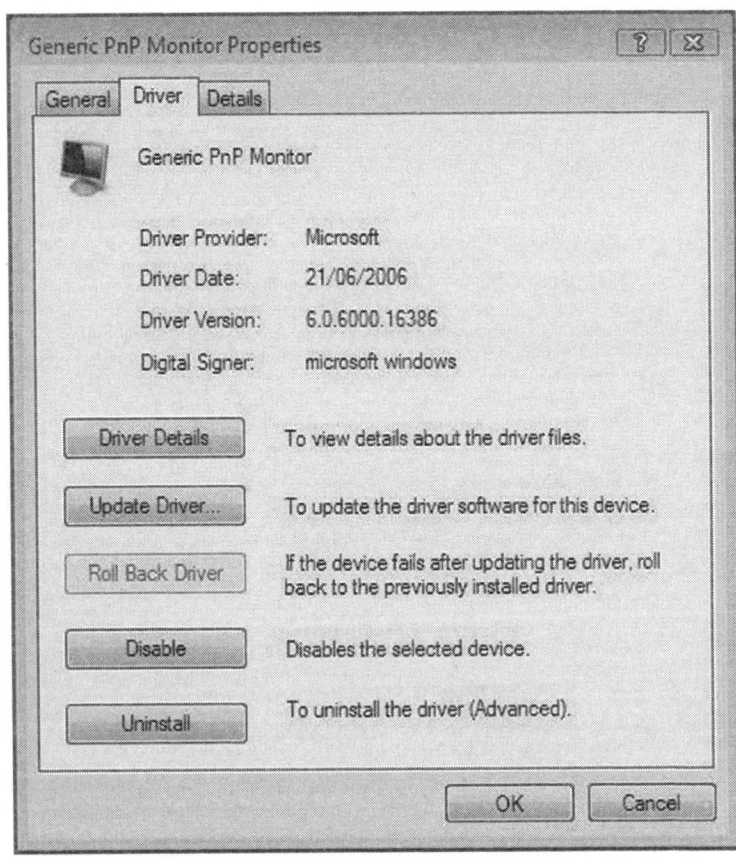

Fig.3.17 The Driver section offers several options

a later date. It is best to remove the existing drivers and then shut down Windows and reboot the system.

Removing drivers

Device drivers are easily removed using the Windows Vista. The method used is essentially the same as the one used in the XP version of Device Manager, but you will notice some differences if you are used to the Windows 9x version. Left-clicking on the relevant entry to highlight it and then operating the Remove button is not possible due to the lack of a Remove button! Instead, right-click on the relevant entry to produce a pop-up menu (Figure 3.15). The options available from the menu depend on the type of hardware concerned, but there are Disable and Uninstall options for normal hardware such as modems and game ports.

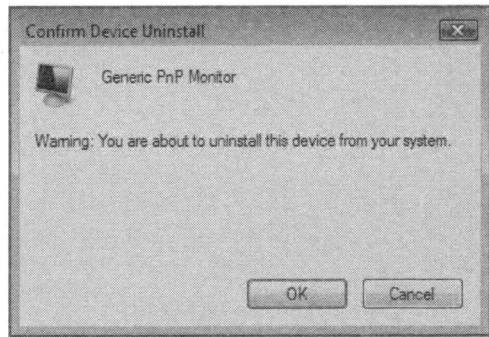

Fig.3.18 *This warning message appears when Uninstall is selected*

Essentially the same facilities can be obtained by double-clicking on an entry in Device Manager. This produces the property window for the device (Figure 3.16), and selecting the Driver tab switches the window to look something like Figure 3.17. Note that with Plug and Play devices the drivers can only be uninstalled if the hardware is present in the PC and active. With the hardware absent or disabled, it will not have an entry in Device Manager. A warning message like the one in Figure 3.18 appears when the Uninstall button is operated. Left-click the OK button in order to proceed and uninstall the device drivers. The entry for the uninstalled device should then disappear from the list in Device Manager.

A Disable option is available from the pop-up menu or the menu at the bottom of the General section of the Properties window. This option differs from uninstalling the drivers in that they remain on the disc and are ready for use. Windows will ignore them though, and the hardware becomes "invisible" to the system without the drivers installed. The relevant entry will remain in Device Manager, but with a little arrow on its icon to indicate that the device has been disabled. An Enable option is then available, so that the device can be reinstated again (Figure 3.19).

This facility is not designed solely as an aid to troubleshooting, but it is clearly useful to be able to temporarily disable a device that is suspected of causing problems. If the computer will boot perfectly well with the suspect device disabled, but not when it is enabled, it is certainly the source of the problem. If the problem persists when the suspect device is disabled, it is highly unlikely that it has anything to do with the boot failure. Note that it is not possible to select a category from the Device Manager list and then remove or disable it. Each entry has to be managed

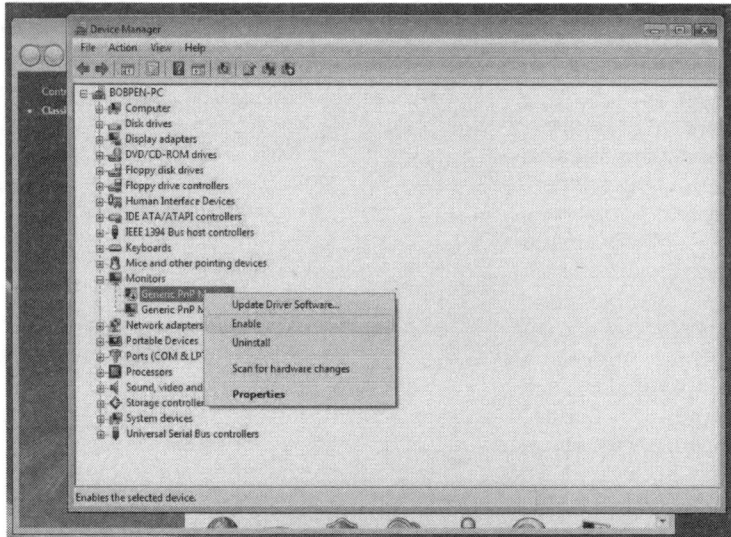

Fig.3.19 An Enable option permits the device to be reinstated

individually. A category will be removed if all the devices it contains are uninstalled.

Roll back

In addition to Uninstall and Disable options, Device Manager may also permit drivers to be rolled back. The Roll Back Driver feature is for use with recently installed device drivers that were supposed to give improved performance but actually make matters worse. This is unlikely to happen when using signed (Microsoft approved) drivers, but is quite likely to occur when testing beta versions. Unless you are suitable expert, using any sort of beta test software is not a good idea, and signed device drivers should always be used wherever possible.

If things do go badly awry with an updated driver, using the Roll Back Driver option is an easy way to remove the new drivers and reinstate the old ones. Obviously, this feature is only available where the original drivers have been updated, and an error message will appear if it is used with the original device drivers. It is otherwise just a matter of following the on-screen prompts until the roll back is complete.

Multiple drivers

Where (say) just one out of four drivers for a soundcard is not working properly, it is best to remove all the drivers and reinstall everything "from scratch". Note that it is not safe to equate each category in Device Manager with a single piece of hardware. For example, the category that has the entries for a soundcard might also contain entries for a modem. The entries in Device Manager usually make it clear which piece of hardware each one is related to, but if in doubt you can always right-click on an entry and select the Properties option.

Updating

Reinstalling drivers sometimes has the desired effect, but the problem is often due to a fault in the driver software. In some cases reinstallation seems to cure the problem, but before too long it returns again. In other instances the problem returns immediately when the drivers are reinstalled. If you have an Internet connection it is a good idea to check the manufacturer's web site to see if a more recent version of the driver software is available. There are usually frequent updates to the drivers for newer items of equipment.

In general, it is not a good idea to install an updated driver with the old version still in place, so use Device Manager to remove the original driver before installing the new one. One exception to this is where the updated driver is not actually a full set of driver software. Sometimes the new version uses some of the original files, while changing other files and (or) adding new ones. As always, read the installation instructions before installing the new software. This should state whether the original drivers should be left in place or removed. If it is does not, then the old drivers should be removed prior to installing the new ones. It might give other warnings, and it is often necessary to switch off anti-virus software before installing new drivers, for example.

The standard method of updating drivers is to use the Update Driver facility of Device Manager. This is straightforward in use, but many manufactures provide a Setup program with new drivers. This program is located using Windows Explorer, and then run by double-clicking its entry. Installation is then largely automatic, although there will be the usual licensing agreements to agree to. The new drivers will take effect as soon as the computer has been rebooted. Either method should work, but where a Setup program is included with the drivers, it is advisable to use it rather than try to install the drivers using Device

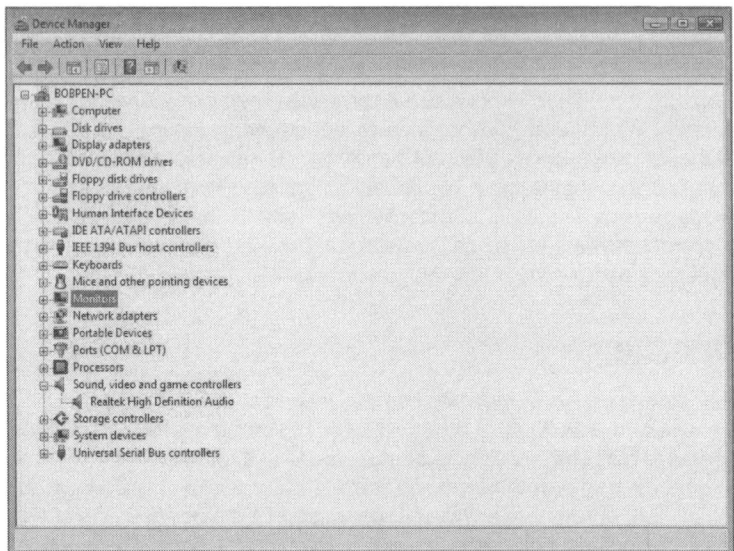

Fig.3.20 With the correct driver the soundcard works properly

Manager. In the case of the faulty soundcard I managed to find the proper driver software on the Internet. I ran the program, rebooted the PC, and the card then worked normally (Figure 3.20).

Hardware problems

If repeated reinstallation of the drivers fails to clear the yellow exclamation marks, and updated drivers do not help either, it is quite likely that the cause of the trouble is a hardware fault. In the case of an expansion card check that it is fitted in its expansion slot using the simple method outlined in chapter 2. If the PC can be booted in normal mode, use Device Manager to check the cause of the problem. Double-click on the entry for the troublesome device to bring up its Properties window. The program may be vague in its reporting of the fault, stating something along the lines that the device is not working properly, and that the hardware is faulty or the drivers are not installed.

Sometimes the reporting is more specific, perhaps stating that there is a hardware conflict. This means that the device needs to use resources of the computer that are already used by another piece of hardware. A problem of this type should not occur if the PC has been in use and working well for some time. It is more the type of thing that happens when new hardware is added to a PC, particularly if it is already fitted with some older expansion cards. A hardware conflict is not really a Windows problem, and it goes beyond the scope of this book.

Logging

If no problems can be found with the hardware, or sorting out the problems that are found makes no difference to the boot problems, it is time to look elsewhere for the fault. Newly installed software that makes a mess of a configuration file is probably the most common cause of Windows start-up problems. If the system refuses to boot just after some new software has been installed it is odds-on that the installation program has made a mistake somewhere in the process. There are two options in the Windows 9x start-up menu that help you to discover the root cause of the fault when the system refuses to boot. These are the logged start up and step by step confirmation modes. Windows XP and Vista offer a logged start up but no step by step confirmation mode is provided.

In the past, it was normal for PCs to display a long string of messages detailing what was happening during the boot process. These messages are not normally displayed on a modern PC unless it is booted in some sort of diagnostics mode. The basic function of the logged boot up is to write these messages to a file called Ntbtlog.txt that is placed in the Windows directory of the boot disc. This file can be read using any text editor or word processor. Note that this is different to the equivalent start up mode of Windows 9x where the log file was called Bootlog.txt and stored in the root folder of the boot drive. With Windows 9x the previous version of the file, if there is one, is saved as Bootlog.prv. There is no equivalent of this in Windows XP and Vista, so you must rename log files if you wish to avoid having them overwritten by any subsequent log files.

Apart from the fact that the log file is generated, Windows boots normally when the logged mode is selected. With Windows failing to boot properly, it is therefore necessary to boot in logged mode and let the boot process fail, reset the computer, restart it in Safe Mode, and then examine the contents of the log file. One of Window's built-in text editors can be used to examine the Ntbtlog file if your PC is not equipped with a word processor. From the Start menu choose Programs, Accessories and then Wordpad. This produces a simple but effective word processor, and the Ntbtlog file can be loaded by selecting File and Open. This produces the standard Windows file requester that can be directed to the Windows directory. Make sure that either text (txt) files or all files (*.*) is selected in the lower part of the window, or Ntbtlog.txt will be "invisible" to the file requester.

Once loaded, there is no difficulty in making a detailed examination of the file's contents. The list of messages is comprehensive and provides a full list of every action during boot-up. The file also shows whether each action was successful. This is just a small sample from a long Ntbtlog file:

Microsoft (R) Windows (R) Version 5.1 (Build 2600)

1 17 2002 23:42:37.500

Loaded driver \WINDOWS\system32\ntoskrnl.exe

Loaded driver \WINDOWS\system32\hal.dll

Loaded driver \WINDOWS\system32\KDCOM.DLL

Loaded driver \WINDOWS\system32\BOOTVID.dll

Loaded driver ACPI.sys

Loaded driver \WINDOWS\System32\DRIVERS\WMILIB.SYS

Loaded driver pci.sys

Loaded driver isapnp.sys

Loaded driver viaide.sys

Loaded driver \WINDOWS\System32\DRIVERS\PCIIDEX.SYS

Loaded driver MountMgr.sys

Loaded driver ftdisk.sys

Loaded driver dmload.sys

Loaded driver dmio.sys

Loaded driver PartMgr.sys

Loaded driver VolSnap.sys

Loaded driver atapi.sys

Loaded driver disk.sys

Loaded driver \WINDOWS\System32\DRIVERS\CLASSPNP.SYS

Loaded driver sr.sys

Loaded driver Fastfat.sys

Loaded driver KSecDD.sys

Loaded driver NDIS.sys

Loaded driver viaagp.sys

Loaded driver Mup.sys

Did not load driver Advanced Configuration and Power Interface (ACPI) PC

Did not load driver Audio Codecs

Did not load driver Legacy Audio Drivers

Did not load driver Media Control Devices

Did not load driver Legacy Video Capture Devices

Did not load driver Video Codecs

Did not load driver WAN Miniport (L2TP)

Did not load driver WAN Miniport (IP)

Did not load driver WAN Miniport (PPPOE)

As with all faultfinding, resist the temptation to jump to conclusions. In this short extract from the log file there are several lines that indicate something was not loaded. However, it is obvious that things did not come to an immediate halt because the boot process continued for hundreds more lines and processes. Most boot log files, whether for Windows 9x, XP, or Vista, seem to show a few failed processes that turn out to be of no consequence. With a Windows Vista upgrade it is very likely that there will be a large number of lines indicating that files were not loaded. Any "leftover" Windows XP files that no longer serve any purpose because they are incompatible with Windows Vista will not be loaded. Even where Windows Vista has been installed from scratch, it is possible that numerous files will not actually be loaded.

It is conceivable that an error early in the proceedings could result in failure later in the boot process, but it is towards the end of the boot log file that the cause of the problem is most likely to be found. Ideally, you should make a boot log file when the computer is functioning normally, and then save it on the disc under a new name. This file can then be compared with a new boot log file if boot problems should develop. This should reduce the risk of being misled by failed processes that are not completed during a normal boot into Windows. It is perhaps worth pointing out that unlike Windows 9x, Windows XP and Vista do not boot MS-DOS and then load Windows on top of MS-DOS. XP and Vista are both DOS-free and boot straight into Windows. Hence, the initial part of a Windows XP/Vista boot log looks very different to a Windows 9x type, with no sign of the usual MS-DOS start up files.

Error message

The cause of Windows stalling during start-up is something you will not necessarily have to strive to discover. More often than not Windows will halt with a message stating the reason for everything suddenly grinding to a halt. Sometimes the problem will be due to a missing file. In fact, it seems to be due to a damaged or missing file in most instances. A damaged file could be one that has become corrupted, or perhaps it has been overwritten by a rogue installer program. Some of the error messages are rather cryptic, but the Microsoft web site gives information on error codes that should help to clarify the likely cause of the problem. Using part of the error code in the search engine should be sufficient to produce some useful information on the problem.

If the problem occurs after a piece of software has just been uninstalled, it is likely that the uninstaller removed a file that is needed by another program. The easy solution is to boot in Safe Mode and reinstall the software, which should reinstate the file that Windows considers to be essential. Assuming that this is successful, you can either take the easy option and leave the reinstalled program in place, or try removing it again. The fact that the original removal of the program did not go entirely according to plan does not necessarily mean that a second attempt will also fail. On the other hand, it will not be a great surprise if it does fail.

It is worth making the point that installing and uninstalling software tends to be less troublesome if you always opt for the default directory rather than choosing another directory. I am not entirely sure why this should be, but it is probably due to minor errors in some installer and uninstaller programs. Anyway, unless there is a good reason to do otherwise, always settle for the default directory.

In the event of the boot process failing again, reinstalling the software once more should restore normal operation. You are not necessarily stuck with the program for life, and normal operation should be possible if the program is removed again and the contentious file is reinstated. The file causing the problem could be in the program's directory structure or in the Windows directory structure. Either way, using the file search function of Windows Explorer should soon locate it. Copy the file to a temporary directory and then uninstall the program.

If the file was copied from somewhere in the Windows directory structure, copy it back to that location. If it was it the program's own directory structure, the directory it came from might have been removed by the uninstaller. One approach to the problem is to remake part of the erased directory structure so that the file can be copied back to its original location. This might not be necessary though, and in most cases Windows will find the file if it is placed in the Windows directory structure where files of a similar type are located. In the case of a DLL file for example, Windows should find the file if it is copied to the Windows/System and Windows/System32 folders.

File hunt

In cases where reinstalling a recently uninstalled program is ineffective, or there is no recently uninstalled software to put back, reinstalling Windows is probably the best option. If Windows is reinstalled on top of the existing installation there should be no problems with your applications software. Any programs that are correctly installed with Windows should remain so after Windows itself has been reinstalled. This assumes that the existing Windows installation is not totally wrecked, and that it is repairable. Where large numbers of important files have been wiped out, there may be no option but to rescue as much of your data as possible and then reinstall everything from scratch.

Although one might think that reinstalling Windows would always cure any boot problems, it is only fair to point out that it is not a universal panacea. In a fair proportion of cases it will get things back into working order, but sometimes the problem with the old installation is carried through into the new one. When Windows is installed over an existing installation, some of the settings from the old installation are copied to the new one. This is necessary in order to integrate installed programs into the new Windows installation, but it provides a route for an existing problem to find its way into the new installation.

If no easy solution can be found to a Windows boot problem it is certainly worthwhile trying reinstallation before spending large amounts of time trying to precisely identify and cure the problem. Reinstalling Windows does not take all that long and there is a reasonable chance that it will get the operating system fully operational again. If the problem is due to a missing file, and it is a standard Windows file that has gone "absent

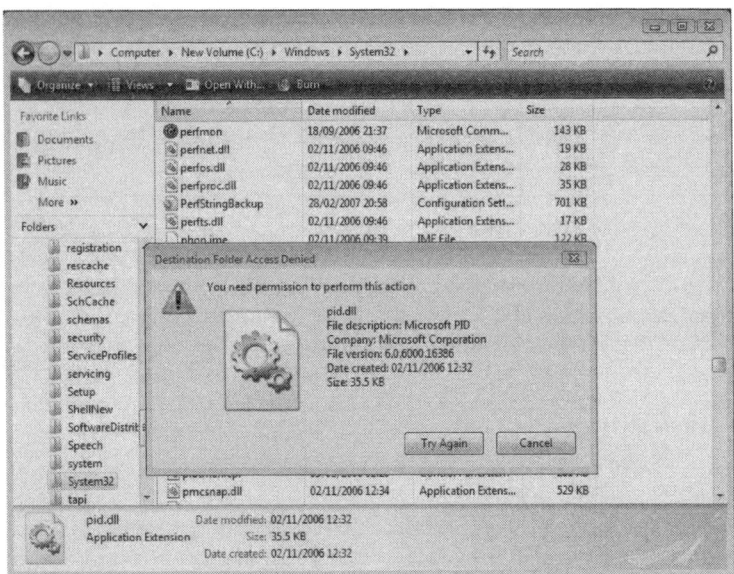

Fig.3.21 Vista blocks attempts to delete system files

without leave", reinstallation should get Windows running properly again. Similarly, if a standard Windows file has become corrupted, reinstalling Windows should overwrite the damage file with a sound version and cure the problem. Installing Windows "from scratch" and on top of an existing installation are both covered in chapter 6.

Problems with missing and corrupted files often involve dynamic link library files, or DLL files as they are usually termed. These files are easily spotted when browsing the hard disc as they all have a "dll" extension. Some users make a backup copy of all the DLL files on the hard disc so that any files of this type that are accidentally erased or overwritten by an earlier version can be easily replaced. Windows Vista does its best to protect system files, including DLL types. Try using Windows Explorer to locate a DLL file in the Windows/System 32 directory, and then delete it. You can try as often as you like, but Vista will block your attempts (Figure 3.21).

It is unlikely that any protection system will 100 percent effective while still permitting necessary changes to be made to the system. In addition, a hardware glitch could result in damage to any files. Consequently, it can still be worthwhile backing up DLL files. The subject of backing up DLL files is covered in chapter 5. There will be a vast number of DLL files on the backup disc or directory, but if the one you require is actually there it should not take too long to locate it using the Find Folders or Files facility in Windows Explorer. It can then be copied to the appropriate folder using Windows Explorer.

Windows Registry

The Windows Registry seems to be regarded by many as the place to go in order to cure any Windows problem, but matters are not as simple as that. Problems with Windows are not necessarily due to anything amiss in the Registry. If a hardware driver is not installed properly or is faulty, the Windows Registry is unlikely to provide an answer to the problem. Perhaps of greater importance, even where editing the Registry can clear a problem, unless great care is taken it is likely that the problem will be made worse rather than better. Making any changes to the registry has to be regarded as a high-risk activity.

Windows automatically produces back-up copies of the Registry and other system from time to time. It is possible to resort to one of these using the System Restore facility if the Registry becomes seriously damaged. Also, you can make your own back-up copies of the Registry files, which can be restored if you somehow manage to get the Registry files beyond redemption. If you are determined to go ahead and experiment with editing the Registry I would certainly recommend making back-up copies just in case things go seriously awry. Even if the Registry is well and truly backed up, it is still not a good idea to start making changes unless you are sure you know what you are doing. You can probably resort to a back-up copy if things go seriously awry, but realistically, unless you know what you are doing your chances of success when tinkering with the Registry are minimal.

What is it?

Probably most Windows users have heard of the Registry, but there are relatively few that know its exact nature and purpose. It is a database that contains all manner of Windows system settings. If you change settings via the Control Panel, you are actually making changes to the Windows Registry. The same is true when you install or remove software or hardware, or make practically any changes to the system. It is not just the Windows settings that are stored in the Registry, and it can be

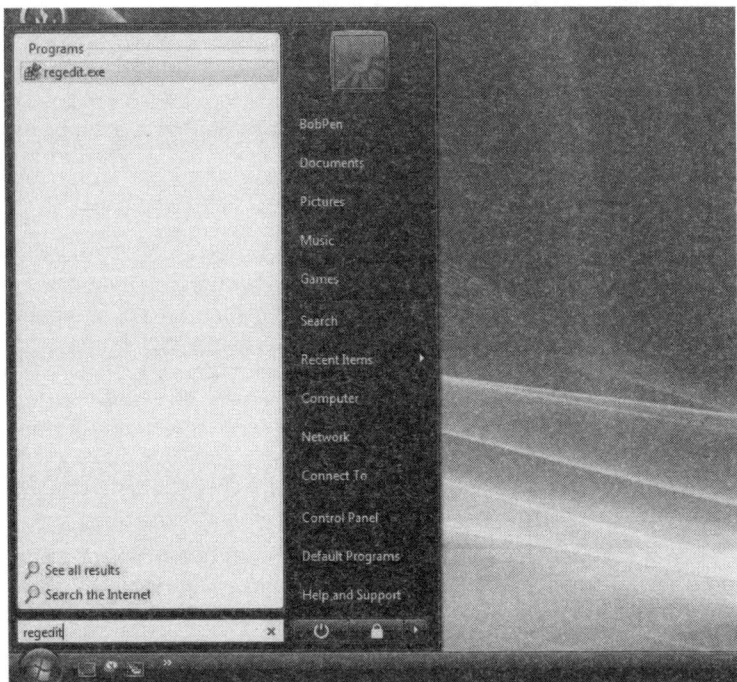

Fig.3.22 Enter "regedit" into the textbox

used to store configuration information for applications programs as well. The device drivers for items of hardware can also use the Registry. This factor probably increases the risk of the Registry being corrupted when software or hardware is installed or uninstalled. The Registry files can easily be damaged if the installer or uninstaller gets it slightly wrong.

Windows experts often edit the Registry as a means of customising their Windows installation. Obviously many aspects of Windows are easily changed via the standard routes, such as using the Control Panel to change things such as screen colours, resolution, etc. Hackers often prefer to go direct to the Registry because they can make some changes that are not possible via the approved channels. This is fine for those having the necessary expertise to make this type of change. Presumably, they also have the necessary expertise to repair any damage they cause. This type of thing it is definitely not to be recommended for occasional dabblers.

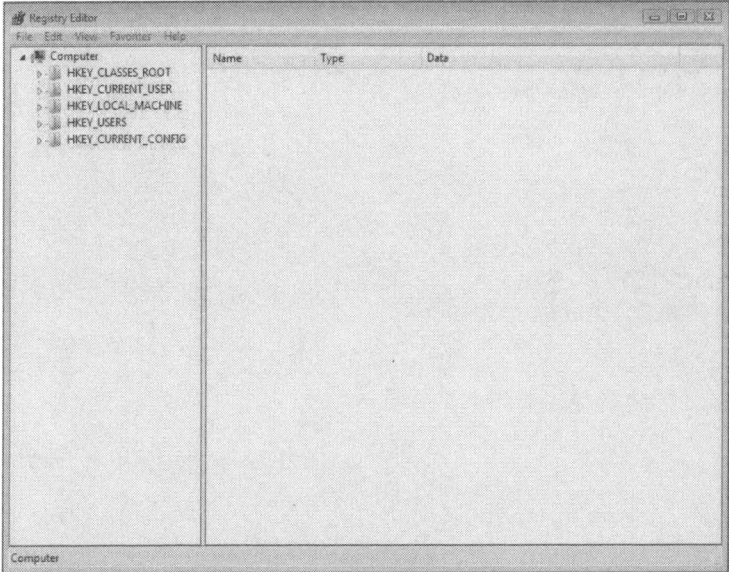

Fig.3.23 The initial screen of the Registry Editor

Editing

Many computer configuration files can be edited by simply loading them into a text editor or word processor and making the required changes. This method is not normally used with the Registry files, and instead they are edited via the special editing utility. This program is called Regedit, and it can be found in the Windows directory. One way to run Regedit is to go to the Start menu, type "regedit" in the text box at the bottom of the menu (Figure 3.22), and then press the Return (Enter) key. There is no need to include the path to the Regedit.exe file since Windows will know where to find it. Once launched, Regedit has the rather blank looking initial screen of Figure 3.23. Note that Regedit32, as used in some earlier versions of Windows, is not available in Windows XP or Vista. If you type "regedit32" into the Run textbox, Windows XP will actually run the standard Registry Editor program, and Windows Vista will treat "regedit32" as a normal search string.

The Windows Vista Registry should pose few problems if you are used to dealing with the Registry in previous versions of Windows. Both the Registry itself and the Registry Editor operate along broadly the same

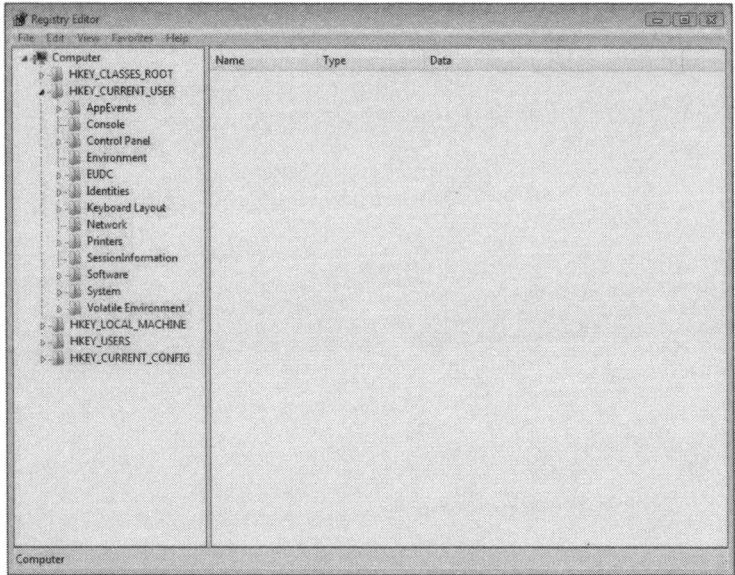

Fig.3.24 The keys on the left can be expanded to show their contents

lines as their predecessors. It will probably require some intense effort if you do not have any previous experience with the Registry. In operation, the Registry Editor is designed to be much like Windows Explorer. There are what appear to be files and folders, but you need to bear in mind the program is showing the contents of a database, and that it can not be used in exactly the same way as Windows Explorer. For example, the drag and drop approach does not work when using Registry Editor.

Double-clicking on one of the entries in the left-hand section of the screen expands it, as in Figure 3.24, to show what appear to be subfolders. In Windows Registry terminology the left-hand section of the screen shows keys, and double-clicking on one of these expands its entry to show the sub-keys. Left-clicking the little triangular button for an entry has the same effect. With subfolders, double-clicking on an entry will sometimes reveal further subfolders. Likewise, double-clicking on sub-keys will sometimes reveal a further layer of the key structure. Left-clicking the triangular button contracts its section of the key system.

Once the lowest level in the key structure has been reached, double-clicking on an entry produces something like the window of Figure 3.25.

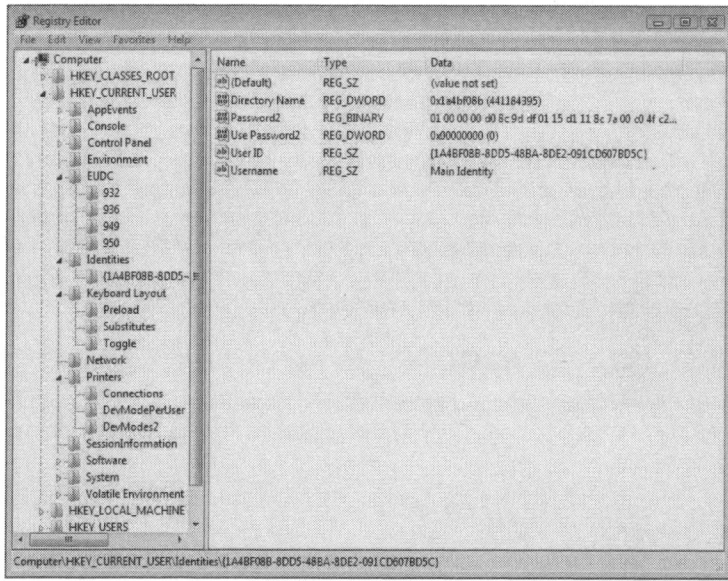

Fig.3.25 The right-hand panel shows details of the Registry entries selected on the left

Including the icons on the left, the right-hand section of the screen breaks down into three sections. The icon indicates the type of data stored in the key. An icon containing "ab" indicates that the key holds a string, which means that it contains letters and (or) numbers. An icon containing "011110" indicates that the key holds a numerical code, which is often in the form of a binary number and not an ordinary decimal type. The hexadecimal numbering system is also used, and numbers of this type are preceded by "Ox" to show that they are in this numbering system. This column also includes the name for each entry in the Registry, and the names usually give clues to the functions of the entries.

Next along from the icons is the Type column, and there are eight different types of data. REG_BINARY for example, is a binary value, and REG_DWORD is a double word, which is term used to describe a 32-bit value. The third column is the actual data stored in each value. You will notice that for many entries the Data column simply states "(value not set)". This means that not even default values have been assigned to these entries. However, should it become necessary to do so, values can be set for these parameters.

Navigation

You do not have to move around the Registry for long in order to realise that the number of values stored there is vast. I do not know how many values are to be found in an average Windows Registry, but it must be many thousands. There are five main Registry keys in the "root directory", which are known as hive keys incidentally. The Registry data is stored in several files that are sometimes referred to as hive files. It is obviously much easier to find the required value if you understand the significance of the hive keys, and know which one to search. These are the five hive keys and the types of value that each one contains:

HKEY_CLASSES_ROOT

All the file associations are stored within this key. This includes OLE information, shortcut data, and file associations for the recognised file types.

HKEY_CURRENT_USER

The desktop preferences are stored in this key. This mainly means parameters that are set via the Control Panel, but other data is stored here. Under the Software sub-key there is a further sub-key for each item of installed software, so there can be a vast number or entries here as well.

HKEY_LOCAL_MACHINE

Machine in a Windows context means the PC that it is running on. This hive key therefore contains data that is specific to the particular PC concerned. As one would expect, there is a Hardware sub-key here, but there are others such as a Network sub-key and a Security type. There is a Software sub-key here as well, but it is different to the one found under the HKEY_CURRENT_USER hive key. The information stored in this Software sub-key seems to be largely associated with hardware configuration and uninstalling the software, rather than things like screen colours.

HKEY_USERS

If the PC has more than one user, this hive key is used to store the preferences for each user. In most cases the users feature of Windows is not utilised, so the information here will simply duplicate that stored in the HKEY_CURRENT_USER hive key. Perhaps more accurately, HKEY_CURRENT USERS will duplicate the data stored in HKEY_USERS.

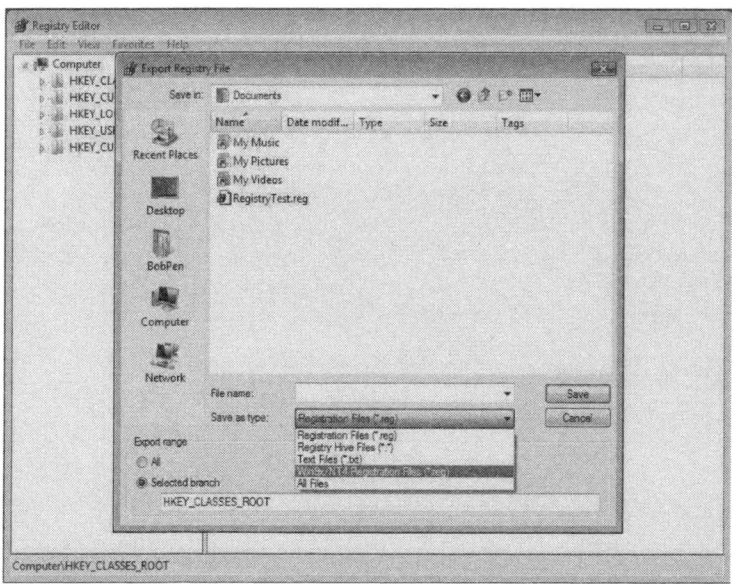

Fig.3.26 Several Registry file formats are available

HKEY_CURRENT_CONFIG

This key contains the current software and hardware configuration data. In the likely event that you are only using one configuration, it will contain the same data as HKEY_LOCAL_MACHINE.

Registry backup

It is a good idea to make a back-up copy of the Registry before undertaking any editing. One way of doing this is to use the System Restore facility to take a so-called snapshot of the system's state. If anything should go wrong, the Restore facility can be used to take the system back to this state, which should get it working again. Using the System Restore facility is covered in chapter 5. The Windows Vista Complete Backup and Restore utility can also be used to save and restore the full contents of the hard disc drive, including all system and configuration files and settings. This topic is also covered in chapter 5.

The Registry editor also has the ability to save and restore the Registry, or individual hives, via the Export and Import options in the File menu.

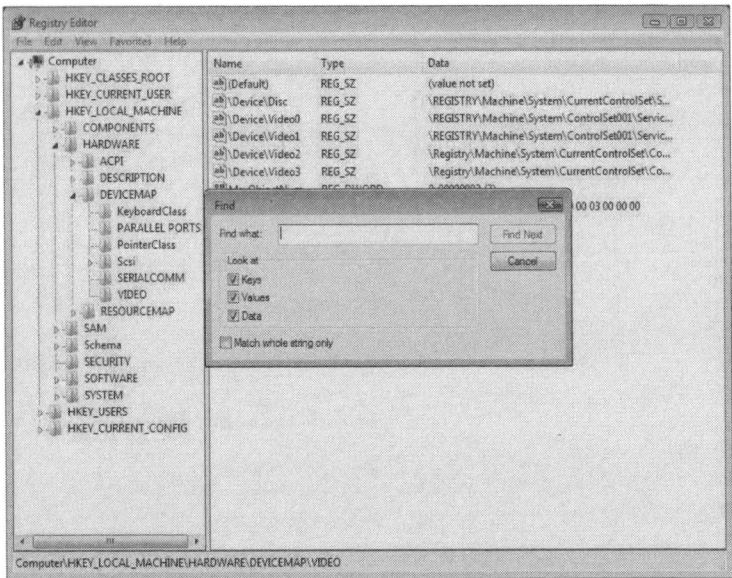

Fig.3.27 The Registry Editor has a search facility

The entire Registry can be exported by selecting the Computer entry in the left-hand section of the window prior to selecting the Export option. Individual hives can be exported by selecting the hive's entry prior to using the Export facility. There are several Registry file formats available from the file browser that appears when the Export command is selected (Figure 3.26).

The default "reg" format can be used for individual hives or the entire Registry. The "Registry hive files" option saves individual hives only, and an error message will be displayed if this format is used with the entire Registry selected. This is the format that is normally used for back-up purposes. The text option enables the Registry or an individual hive to be saved as a simple text file that can be viewed and edited using a word processor or text editor. Text files can not be imported though, and this is only indented as a means of viewing Registry files without using the Registry Editor. In theory, the Import feature enables all or part of the Registry to be restored from a back-up file. In practice, importing Registry files tends to be problematic. Consequently, it is often better to use System Restore to create a new restoration point. Microsoft recommends doing this before undertaking any editing of the Registry. This should

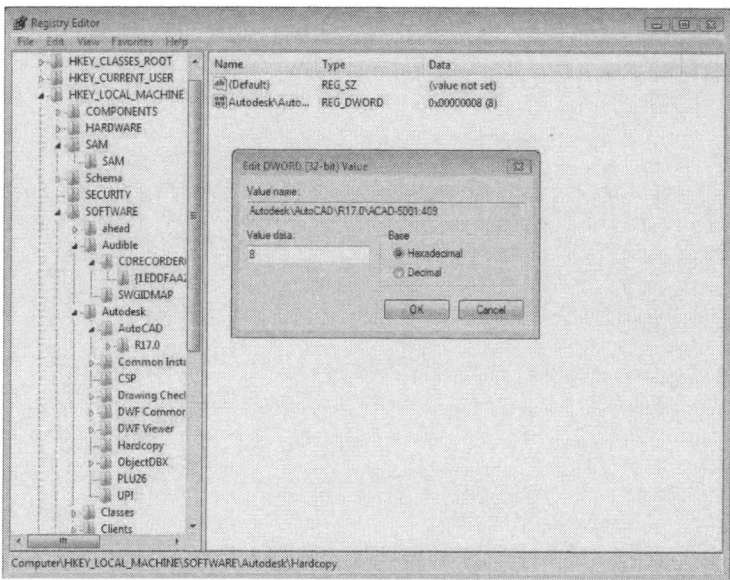

Fig.3.28 Data is edited via a small pop-up window

provide an easy way of restoring normal operation if the editing should happen to make a mess of the Registry.

Editing data

The first problem when editing a Registry value is actually finding it. Even if you know what you are looking for and roughly where to find it, searching through the numerous entries in the Registry can still be very time consuming. Fortunately, the Registry Editor has a Find facility that is similar to the Find Files and Folders facility of Windows Explorer. Selecting Find from the Edit menu brings up a Window like the one of Figure 3.27. Use the textbox to enter the text you wish to search for, and use the checkboxes to select the fields of the Registry you wish to search.

You can also opt for a whole string search. In other words, a match will only be produced if the full string in the Registry matches the one you have entered. If this option is not selected, a match will be produced if the string you entered matches part of an entry in the Registry. The whole string option can help to keep the number of matches to more

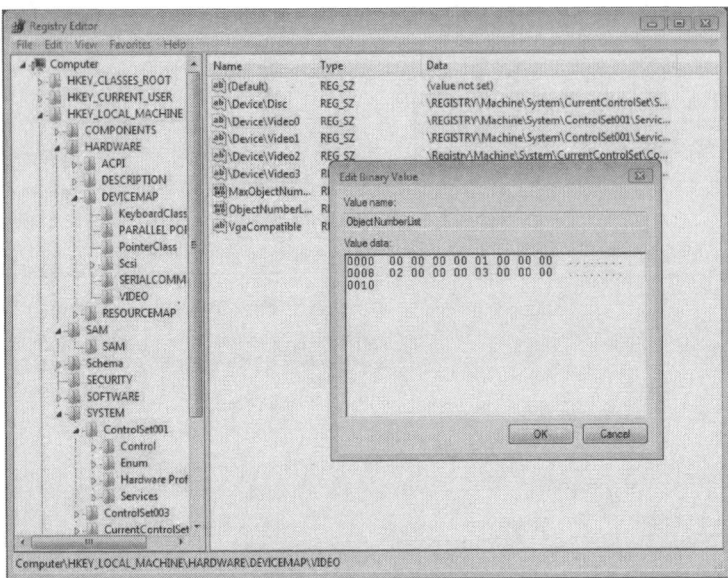

Fig.3.29 This is the editing window for binary data

manageable proportions, but you have to know precisely what you are looking for.

Press the Find Next button to search for the string. If a match is found, it will be shown highlighted in the main window of the Registry Editor. If this one is not the entry you are looking for, call up the Find facility again and operate the Find Next button, or just select the Find Next option from the Edit menu. Keep doing this until the required entry is located or the whole of the Registry has been searched. Note that the Computer entry should be selected prior to using the Find facility if you wish to search the entire registry. Select one hive key in order to search that hive for the specified string. This hive key and any sub-keys below it will be searched.

In order to edit a Registry entry, double-click on its icon in the right-hand panel to bring up the editing window, as in Figure 3.28. The data can then be edited using the textbox. The edit window varies slightly in appearance depending on type of data it contains. In this example it contains a double word, and the two radio buttons enable the value to be given in hexadecimal or decimal. Figure 3.29 shows the editing

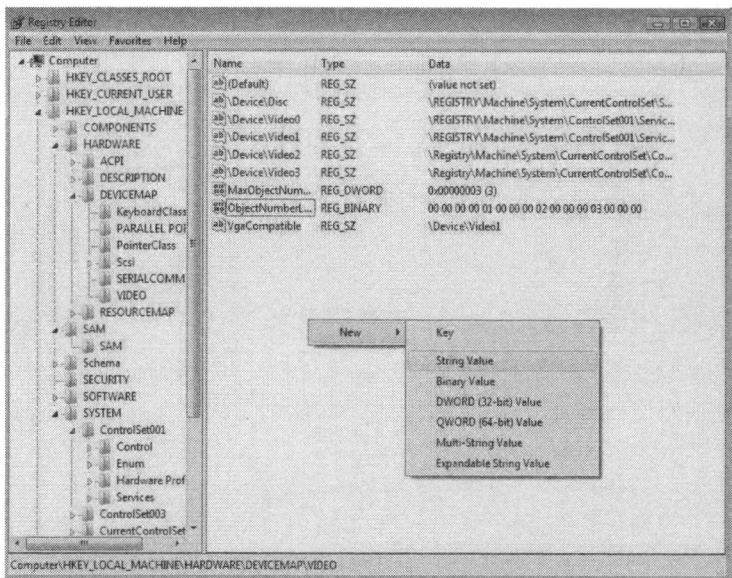

Fig.3.30 Use this menu to choose the required type of value

window for a binary value. Left-click the OK button when you have finished, or the Cancel button if you change your mind.

It is also possible to right-click on an entry and then use the pop-up menu to delete or rename it. A Modify option is also available from this menu, and it brings up the appropriate edit window. In order to add a new entry, right-click in an empty part of the right-hand panel to bring up the menu show in Figure 3.30. Then choose the required type of value (string, binary, etc.) from the submenu. The new entry will then appear in the right panel of the window, and it will be ready to have the name field edited. Then double-click on its icon and then edit its value in the normal way.

Clearly it is necessary to know exactly what you are doing before altering any registry entries. If you suspect an entry is giving problems it is not possible to remedy the problem by editing its data unless you know the correct data to use. Unless you have the necessary expertise it is better to alter the Registry only via indirect routes, such as installing or uninstalling software, using the Control Panel, etc.

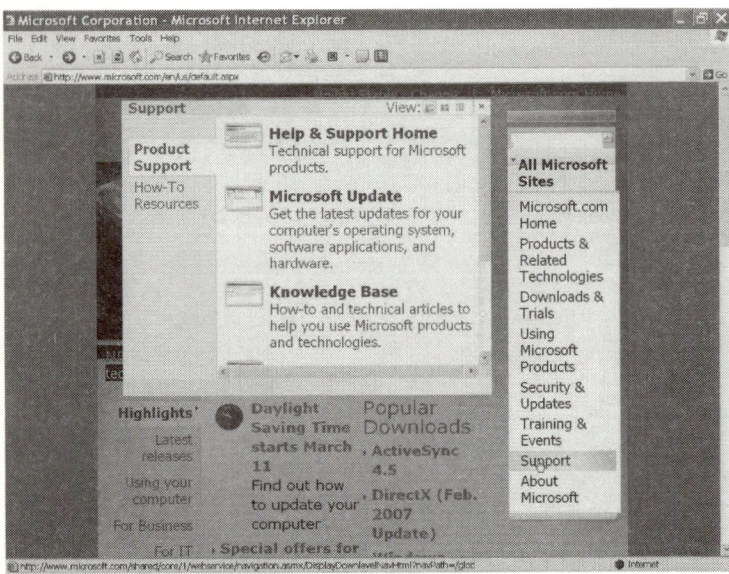

Fig.3.31 The Microsoft homepage

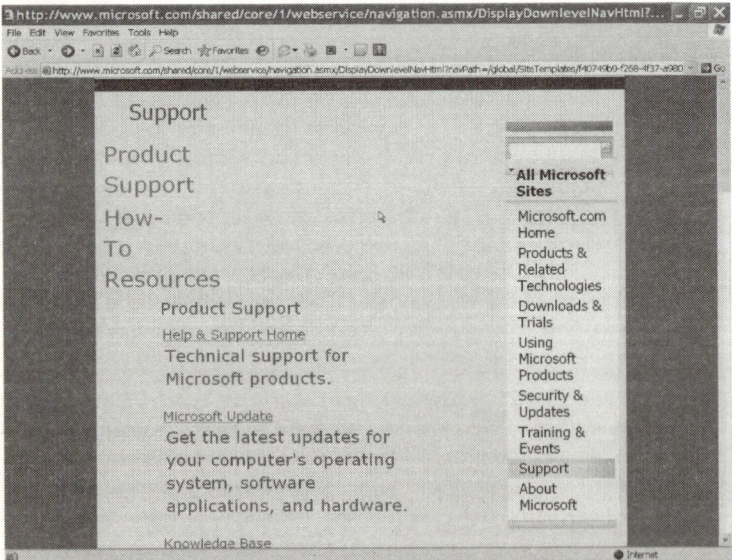

Fig.3.32 The Support section of the Microsoft site

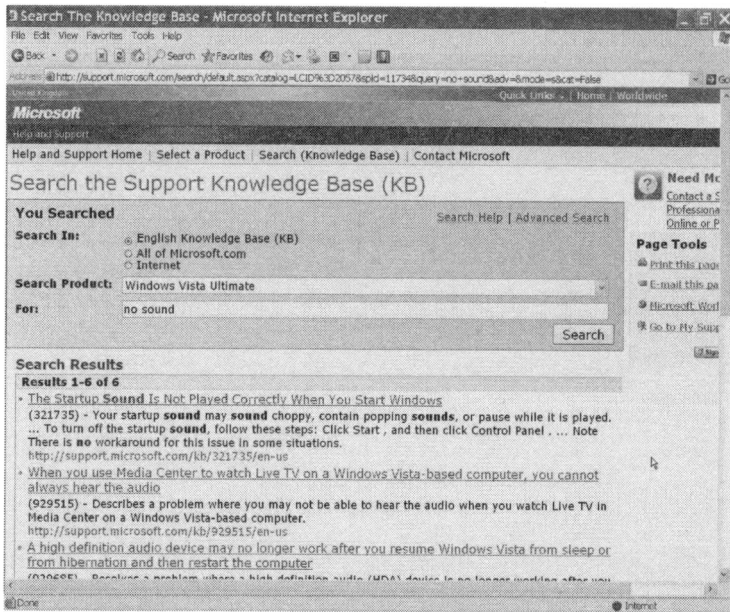

Fig.3.33 This page is effectively a search facility

Knowledge Base

In some circumstances there may be no option but to press on in an attempt to find a cure for the problem. With masses of important data on the hard disc and no means of backing it up, wiping the disc clean is not an option. The best course of action would be to have the computer fitted with some form of mass storage device so that the data could be backed up. Apart from leaving your reinstallation options open, this also guards against losing important data due to a hard disc failure. If you have a usable Internet connection and decide to press on rather than reinstall, it is worthwhile investigating the Microsoft Knowledge Base. There is actually a massive amount of help available at Microsoft's web site (www.microsoft.com), including articles for a large range of Microsoft products.

A good place to start is the Support section. This is accessed by a link in the homepage (Figure 3.31), which brings up a screen like the one in Figure 3.32. Scroll down the page to the Knowledge Base link, which produces the page of Figure 3.33. This is a search facility that can be

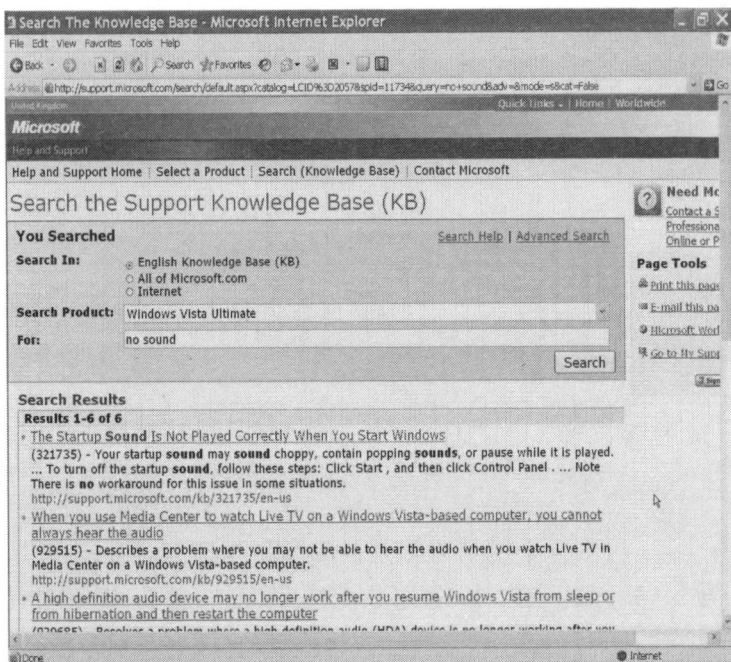

Fig.3.34 Using "no sound" as the search string produced six matches

used to hunt for information about a certain Microsoft product. The menu is used to select the product of interest, such as Windows Vista Ultimate. You then type a key word or words into the textbox.

As with any search engine, the obvious search words do not always provide the best results, so it might be necessary to have a rethink and try again. As an experiment I used "no sound" as the search string, and the Knowledge Base duly responded with six matches (Figure 3.34).

With perseverance, I would guess that practically any Windows problem could be solved using the information available from the Microsoft Knowledge Base. The only problem is that you will probably need a second PC to access the Internet while your faulty PC is being sorted out. Possibly, a friend can assist if you do not have a spare computer. Remember that much of the Windows Vista related material on the web site is also included in the Help system, and is available provided the computer can at least be booted in Safe Mode. Select Help and Support

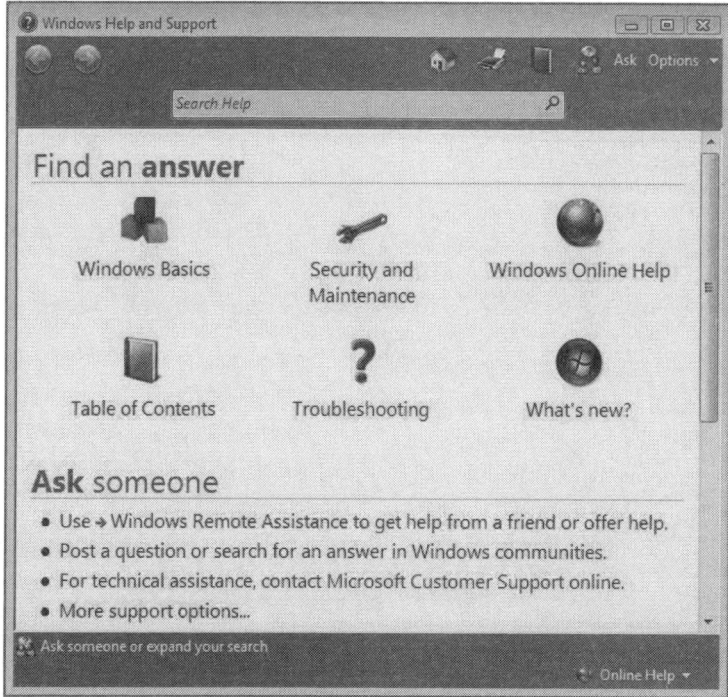

Fig.3.35 The initial window of the Vista Help system

from the Start menu to launch the Help system. This will produce a page like the one shown in Figure 3.35.

There is a search facility that helps the user to find information on specific topics. Type a search string into the textbox and then operate the magnifying glass button or press the Return (Enter) key. A list of search results is then displayed in the main panel of the window (Figure 3.36). Each result is a link, so left-clicking on one of the entries takes you to the appropriate page in the Help system. The Help system is rather like an on-disc web site, and you navigate around it in normal browser fashion.

Troubleshooter

In Windows XP there was a Troubleshoot button in a device's properties window, and operating it produced a Troubleshooter wizard for that

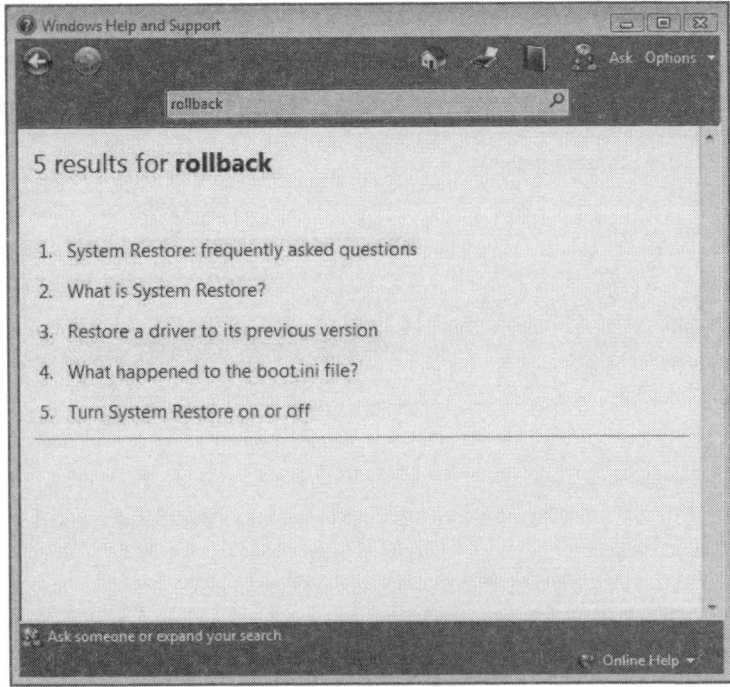

Fig.3.36 The main panel lists all the matches

particular type of hardware. This facility has not been included in Windows Vista, but there is a Troubleshooting option in the initial Help and Support window. Operating this link produces the window of Figure 3.37, where there are links to information on troubleshooting various types of problem such as connecting to the Internet, and networking difficulties.

Operating one of these links produces a list of common problems related to that topic (Figure 3.38), and left-clicking one of these links gives more specific information on that topic (Figure 3.39). In fact it is often necessary to work through further links in order to find the exact information you require, but this system will often locate something helpful.

Reinstallation

If the usual methods of fixing Windows fail to get results, realistically there are only two options available. One is to continue searching for

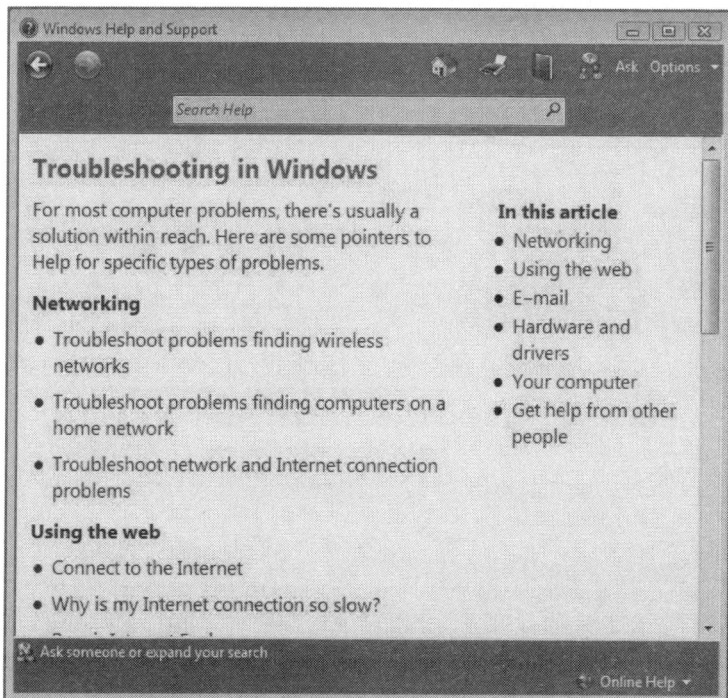

Fig.3.37 The initial window of the troubleshooting section

the cause of the problem, running diagnostic software, checking through configuration files, checking the hardware and drivers, or anything else you can think of. Option two is to reinstall Windows. Initially reinstall it on top of the existing version, which will leave your applications software properly installed and with luck will cure the problem. If that fails, any important data must be backed up to another hard disc or other mass storage device. The hard disc can then be wiped clean and Windows plus all the applications software and data must be reinstalled "from scratch".

This may seem like a defeatist attitude, but searching for the cause of an obscure fault in Windows can be very time consuming. A straightforward reinstallation is almost certain to be quicker, and even reinstalling Windows "from scratch" could be a quicker route to success. It is also

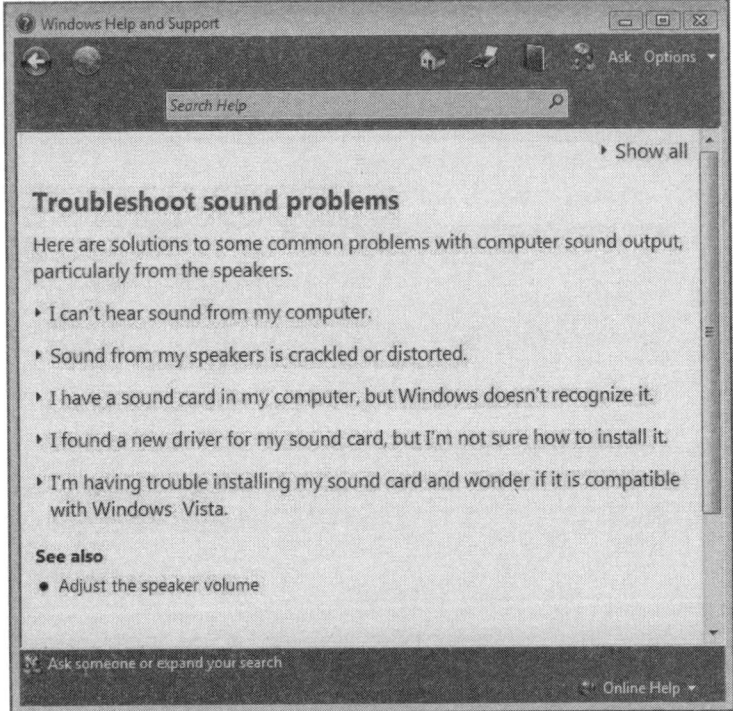

Fig.3.38 A list of common sound problems has been produced

worth bearing in mind that reinstalling everything has the beneficial effect of removing the numerous unnecessary files that tend to start cluttering the hard disc as a Windows installation grows older. This will often produce a significant reduction in the time it takes for the system to boot, for programs to load and the general speed of operation when hard disc accesses are involved.

Where there is no easy solution to a Windows problem, professional PC maintenance engineers tend to opt for the reinstallation option sooner rather than later. For those with less experience of these things it will probably be more of a last resort than a routine method of fixing and streamlining a damaged Windows installation. However, having reinstalled everything you will probably be quite happy that you did.

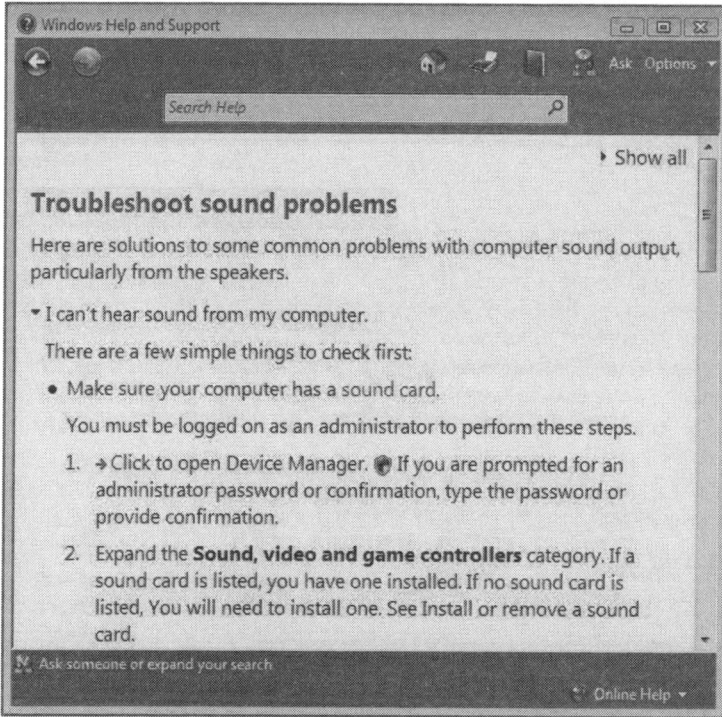

Fig.3.39 This window provides more detailed information

Recurring problems

If you are very unlucky, having reinstalled everything "from scratch" the problem will return. It is likely that the problem will keep reappearing if you keep reinstalling Windows. Where the problem is in some way hardware related, perhaps only happening when the soundcard is used, the most likely explanation is that one of the drivers or the hardware itself is faulty. It is more likely to be a driver problem than a fault in the hardware, so check with the technical support department of the hardware manufacturer to see if a later version of the driver software is available. These days most manufacturers have the latest drivers available on their web sites, where there may also be some troubleshooting hints, so the relevant web site should be the first port of call.

If everything works fine at first, but things go seriously wrong after a while or steadily worsen, the most likely culprit is an applications program. Finding the program that is causing the problem can be quite time consuming. If one program consistently goes "walkabout" and all the others work perfectly, it is virtually certain that the troublesome program is responsible for its own downfall. It is possible for one program to interfere with the system and cause problems with just one other program, but this is quite rare. Normally this occurs because installing one program results in a DLL file for a second program being overwritten with an older version of the file. Provided the problem is fixed by reinstating the newer version of the file there should be no further difficulties. If you simply keep reinstalling Windows and then install the applications in the same order, the problem will keep coming back. Installing the applications in reverse order should banish the problem, since the newer version of the DLL file will then replace the older version, rather than the other way round.

It is more common for the faulty software to damage the Windows installation, causing problems for itself and for other applications programs. The normal solution where recurring problems occur is to reinstall Windows plus one application. If that works all right for a while add a further application. If all is well add another application, and so on until a program is added and things start to go awry. It is then a reasonable assumption that the last program to be added is the one that is damaging the Windows installation.

Where to start

When a PC has problems booting into Windows Vista there are clearly a number of approaches that can be used in an attempt to sort things out. So where do you start? Where the computer will not even boot into Windows Vista in Safe Mode the options are relatively limited. Apart from reinstallation, there is little that can be done apart from booting from the Vista installation disc and using its troubleshooting facilities.

Fixing problems is generally easier if it is possible to boot into Safe Mode. The usual Windows facilities are then available if it is necessary to copy a file from the installation disc to the hard drive. Device Manager has some facilities unavailable in Safe Mode, but it is to a large extent usable. The built-in troubleshooting facilities are mostly operational in Safe Mode, and third party utilities should also work. Troublesome software and hardware can be installed or uninstalled, which will clear many boot-up problems.

It is best to resort to the System Restore facility where the problem proves to be less than straightforward to fix. By taking the computer back to an earlier configuration, most problems can be cured using this facility. The problem is likely to be a stubborn one if System Restore fails to find an answer. Reinstallation over the old system is well worth a try in these circumstances. Where that fails, the best option is probably to back up any unsaved data on the hard disc and then install Windows again from scratch.

Points to remember

If Windows fails to boot properly, do not be too eager to start fiddling with the system to find a cure. Try rebooting a few times to see if the problem clears itself.

If the computer fails during the POST (power-on self test) routine, it is not reaching the point where it starts to boot into Windows. The problem is then a hardware fault rather than something amiss with the Windows installation. There is probably a memory problem if the computer randomly boots or crashes at start-up.

Where the boot process halts very early it is likely that the boot files on the hard disc have been damaged. They can probably be repaired using the facilities available from the Vista installation disc (see chapter 2). The problem could also be a faulty hard disc.

It will be possible to boot in Safe Mode unless the Windows installation is badly damaged. Some basic checks can then be made, such as checking the hard disc, etc. Safe Mode has some limitations, but it is generally much better in this respect than its Windows 9x and XP equivalents.

Getting the computer to produce a boot log file can help to pinpoint the process that is causing the boot process to stall. However, boot logs can be very misleading and it is best not to jump to conclusions.

Device Manager can be used to check whether the hardware and the hardware drivers are functioning correctly, but remember that some hardware is not installed or operational in Safe Mode.

If a hardware driver is suspected of causing problems, use Device Manager to remove the existing driver before reinstallation. Also, check the hardware manufacturer's web site for an updated driver.

Windows will often give an error message that gives some clue to the nature of the problem. Information on a specific error message can be found on the Microsoft web site.

If a program has recently been uninstalled, reinstalling it will probably reinstate a damaged or missing file.

Windows includes a Registry Editor program, but only use this utility if you know what you are doing.

Reinstalling Windows over the existing installation will cure boot problems in a fair proportion of cases, but not all of them. Reinstalling Windows from scratch will cure boot problems unless the problem is not really Windows related. Recurring problems are due to a hardware fault or a bug in an applications program.

There are numerous Windows checking programs available, and these will often help to sort out boot problems, and more minor annoyances. Many will also help to keep Windows working efficiently.

Much Windows Vista troubleshooting information can be found at the Microsoft web site (www.microsoft.com), and some of this information is also included in the built-in Help system.

Windows Vista has a very useful System Restore facility that will usually cure boot problems. It effectively moves the Windows installation back to a time when the computer functioned properly.

Data rescue

Learning the hard way

A hard disc failure is potentially a major disaster for all those who use the PC, but if you use PCs for some years it is a failure you are almost certain to experience. A complete failure of the disc means that all the data it contains is lost. There are companies that offer a data recovery services, but there is no guarantee that the contents of the disc will be recoverable, and the cost of a recovery service is too high for many users anyway. As a minimum, any important data files should be backed up onto floppy discs, CDRs, DVDs, or any suitable media, so that they can be restored onto a new hard disc if the old unit fails. Ideally, the entire contents of the hard disc drive should be backed up using a program that enables it to be properly restored onto a new hard disc. This is very much quicker and easier than having to reinstall and configure the operating system, and then reinstall all the applications programs and data. Also, any customisation of the operating system or other software will be automatically restored. If you have heavily customised software, after reinstallation it can take a great deal time to get it set up to your satisfaction.

Having a back-up copy of the hard disc's contents is not only an insurance against a loss of valuable data if a hardware failure occurs. It can greatly simplify things if there is a major problem with the operating system. Provided the PC was fully operational when the back-up copy was made, resorting to the back-up will provide a fully functioning PC again. Full back-up software enables the system to be quickly restored to a previous and fully working configuration, but it in most cases it does so by installing the operating system from scratch and then reinstating program files, etc. Any data files produced since the back-up was taken will therefore be lost.

A full back-up is normally only undertaken every month or so, making it important to keep back-up copies of data files as they are produced. A lot of data is otherwise left at risk, especially as the time for the next back-up approaches. Provided data files are regularly saved to disc, there should be no difficulty in reinstating any missing data once a full back-up has been restored. The Windows Vista Backup utility installs the system from scratch and therefore loses any recently produced data. The System Restore facility operates in a different way, and it undoes changes to system and program files so that the system is effectively wound back to an earlier time. In this way the data files are left intact. Of course, System Restore is only usable if the file system is largely undamaged. Back-up software is still usable even if the contents of the hard disc have been completely erased.

When a major problem with the operating system occurs and some form of restoration option is available, it is almost certainly best to resort to this method sooner rather than later. There is little point in spending large amounts of time trying to repair a damaged installation if it can be replaced with a back-up copy quite quickly and easily. It is certainly worthwhile spending a small amount of time first to check for any minor problems that are easily sorted out. The back-up method is "using a sledgehammer to crack a nut" if the problem is something minor that is easily corrected. If a search for any obvious problems proves to be in vain, it is time to resort to the back-up software. The back-up program's manual should give detailed instructions on maintaining an up-to-date back-up and restoring the hard disc's contents.

The problem with the full back-up method is that it takes a fair amount of time to maintain an up to date copy of the hard disc. Also, it is only feasible if your PC is equipped with some form of mass storage device that can be used for back-up purposes, such as a CDR or DVD writer. It could otherwise require well in excess of a thousand floppy discs to do a full back-up of the hard drive! Even using some form of mass storage it can take a long while to back-up the gigabytes of programs and data stored on many modern hard disc drives. It can also require a substantial number of ZIP discs, CDRs, or whatever. The quickest and easiest way of providing a back-up is to opt for a second hard disc drive. Due to the current low cost of hard discs, this could well be the cheapest method as well.

Split discs

Many PC users now split their large hard drives into two logical drives, which usually become drives C: and D: as far as the operating system is concerned. Drive C: is then used in the normal way and drive D: is reserved for back-up purposes. This method is useless in the event that the hard drive develops a serious fault, because the main and back-up drives are the two halves of one physical drive. If one becomes faulty it is unlikely that the other will be usable either. The point of this system is that the back-up copy on drive D: is usable if there is a software problem rather than a fault in the hardware. Since most users have far more problems with the software than with hard disc faults, this method should get the user out of trouble more often than not.

Some users take a compromise approach and make a back-up copy of the hard disc when it contains a newly installed operating system having all the hardware properly integrated into the operating system and fully operational. Ideally the disc should also have the applications programs installed, and any customisation completed. Any important data is backed up separately as it is generated. If the operating system becomes seriously damaged it is then easy to resort to the backup which should be reasonably compact, but gives you a basic system that is fully customised and ready to use. Any essential data can also be restored, but there is no need to restore any data files that are no longer needed on the hard disc.

Clean copy

An advantage of this method is that it returns the PC to a "clean" copy of the operating system. Over a period of time most modern operating systems seem to become slightly "gummed up" with numerous files that no longer serve any purpose, and things can generally slow down. By returning to a fresh copy of the operating system you will probably free up some hard disc space and things might run slightly faster. By not bothering to restore any unimportant data files you free up further hard disc space.

If you lack a proper back-up copy of the hard disc and only have copies of the data files, all is not lost. In this situation you might prefer to put a fair amount of effort into fixing the damaged Windows installation rather than simply reinstalling everything. Even if you only use a few applications programs, reinstalling Windows and the applications software is likely to be pretty tedious and time consuming. If there are numerous programs to reinstall, the process is likely to be very tedious and time consuming.

Looking on the bright side, if everything does have to be restored from scratch you will have a "clean" copy of the operating system that should provide optimum performance. In fact many users habitually take the reinstallation route and consider any extra time and effort involved being well worthwhile.

The value of this approach depends on the amount of software you install and remove. It is probably doing things the hard way if you rarely or never make changes to the PC once it is set up to your satisfaction. It might be the only practical approach if you try every program you can lay your hands on.

I would not go as far as to advocate reinstalling everything at the first sign of trouble, but I would definitely advise against the opposite approach of always repairing the original set-up regardless of how long it takes. Apart from the fact this could be a very time consuming approach, an installation that has been patched up on numerous occasions, and perhaps had a number of programs added, upgraded, and removed over a period of time, is unlikely to provide peak performance. In fact, I have encountered several installations of this type that took an eternity to go through the boot-up sequence, in one case taking almost 10 minutes to complete the process! Once booted, PCs of this type seem to give the hard disc drive a "hammering" at every opportunity. This is the most common symptom of a system that is operating well below par.

Apart from making the computer slow and irksome in use, this type of thing increases the wear on the hard disc drive and presumably shortens its operating life. It should be possible to discover the sources of the problem and improve results. There are Windows "cleaner" programs that can help to streamline a Windows installation and remove clutter from the hard disc. However, reinstalling everything "from scratch" is the solution favoured by most when this situation arises. This should always ensure optimum performance and might be quicker anyway.

Windows on Windows

On the face of it there is no need to wipe the hard disc clean and undertake a complete reinstallation from the beginning. Simply reinstalling Windows over the old installation should restore normality. As with so many things in computing it is a case of yes and no. Yes, in some cases simply going through the Windows set-up routine will fix problems with the operating system and restore normal operation. Unfortunately, in other cases the problem will still exist once the reinstallation is complete. When Windows is installed on a hard disc, the Windows Setup program searches the disc for a previous installation and installed Windows application programs. Any installed software will be integrated with the new Windows installation, as may driver programs and other support files.

As a consequence, having reinstalled Windows it should not be necessary to reinstall the applications software as well. The down side is that any files giving problems with the old installation may be retained in the new one. Having reinstalled the operating system you could well find that it does not work any better than before. My experiences with Windows in general suggest that reinstalling Windows on top of the exiting installation probably has little more than a 50 percent chance of success. Possibly Windows Vista will achieve a higher success rate. As reinstallation is a reasonably quick and easy process it is probably worthwhile giving it a try before resorting to an installation "from scratch", but do not be surprised if it does not have the desired effect.

Do not be tempted to try upgrading to a newer version of Windows by installing it on top of a non-working version. People sometimes try this, working on the basis that the new version will have little dependency on the old one, and the problem with the old version will be "blown away" by the new version. In practice there is little likelihood of this happening. The Windows Setup program may detect that there is a problem and refuse to go ahead with the upgrade. If it does proceed, the most likely outcome is that the reinstallation will go very wrong somewhere along the line, and that it will never be completed. If you do manage to get the new version installed, it will probably have more problems than the old one.

Preliminaries

If you do decide to go ahead with reinstallation "from scratch", it is essential to back up any important data files first. If you are using heavily customised applications programs it is also a good idea to make copies of the configuration files so that the customisation files are easily reinstated. In fact, any files that are unique to your particular installation should be backed-up, including things like speech profiles of voice recognition programs. Some of your applications programs may have facilities for saving and reinstating customisation files. In other cases simply overwriting the default files with your customised versions will probably have the desired effect. However, there is no guarantee that this will work.

It is worth emphasising that backing-up important files should not be left until the PC gives problems. If there is a serious fault in the hard disc it may be impossible to recover any files that have not been backed up. Matters are less dire if the problem lies in the operating system rather than the disc itself, but it could still be difficult to make back-up copies of important files. With the computer not booting into the operating system properly you are unlikely to have proper access to all the drives and applications programs. Provided Safe Mode is functioning properly you can boot into a version of Windows, but one where drives other than the hard and floppy discs will not be fully functioning. In most cases the CD-ROM drive or drives can be used for read operations, but writing to the CD writers is unlikely to be possible. This severely limits your back-up options. There are ways of making a backup of a hard disc drive in an emergency, but this might involve buying some additional hardware. It is better to avoid getting into situations where drastic measures are needed in order to recover the situation.

Floppy discs

Floppy discs are suitable for back-up purposes where only a limited amount of data is involved. The upper limit depends on how many floppy discs you are prepared to use, a factor that is probably a reflection of how desperate you are! Backing up 30 megabytes of data onto about 20 or so floppy discs will be quite time consuming, but is still well within the bounds of reason. Backing up several hundred megabytes onto dozens of floppy discs is not a very practical proposition, and the discs could well cost more than some more convenient backup systems! In terms of megabytes per pound, floppy discs are not very competitive these days. Anyway, it is increasingly common for modern PCs to be supplied without a built-in floppy disc drive.

Where floppy discs are suitable, there is a potential problem in that some of the files you wish to copy may be too big to fit on a single floppy disc. The capacity of a high-density 3.5-inch floppy disc is 1.44 megabytes when the standard PC disc format is used. Things like DTP and graphics files can be substantially larger than this. The normal copying facilities of Windows Vista can not spread a large file across one or more discs. If you try to copy a file that is too large to fit onto the disc an error message to that effect will be produced. Fortunately, there are several Windows programs that can handle this problem. The later versions of the popular Winzip program for example, will compress and copy large files to several floppy discs if necessary. You can even copy a collection of files and save them as one large file spread across several discs.

Large scale

If floppy discs are not up to the task it is clearly necessary to resort to some form of mass storage device. It is highly unlikely that any installed device of this type will work in Safe Mode, apart from simple read-only

CD-ROM drives, and possibly DVD drives as well. These are of no use in the current context. It might be possible to get non-standard PC drives (Zip, etc.) to operate in MS-DOS. Where this is possible, the manufacturer's literature should give instructions for making an MS-DOS boot disc. However, booting from an MS-DOS floppy disc will not enable the hard disc drive to be read if it uses the NTFS filing system. The hard disc drive should be readable provided it uses the FAT or FAT32 filing system, but the Vista boot drive will be an NTFS type.

Second disc

If you have large amounts of data to back-up and no mass storage device, your choices are limited. One option is to simply keep trying to repair the Windows installation until you are successful. Any Windows installation should be repairable, and persistence should eventually pay off. You may get lucky and fix the problem fairly quickly, or a great deal of time could be involved in locating and removing the problem. The biggest drawback of this method is that you will still have no backup of the hard disc's contents, limiting your options if there are further problems with the Windows installation. Also, the contents of the disc will probably be lost forever if the drive becomes faulty.

Many users save data onto a hard disc thinking that their work is safe and secure, but this is definitely not the case. Having data on a hard disc is sometimes likened to hanging paper documents by a thin thread over an open fire. Modern hard drives are relatively reliable, but if used for long enough a hard disc drive will go wrong, and you will probably end up throwing away the drive together with all your hard work.

A better option is to add some form of mass storage device. An external Zip drive is not particularly expensive, and in an emergency it should work quite happily with the computer booted into MS-DOS. A few Zip discs can store several hundred megabytes of data, or even a few gigabytes, depending on the particular type of Zip disc in use. This should be sufficient to back-up any important data files, configuration files, etc. However, as pointed out previously, a hard disc will not be accessible from MS-DOS if it uses the NTFS file system, which could make it difficult to use a Zip drive in some circumstances. Note that any form of USB or SCSI storage device is unlikely to work with Windows in Safe mode or with MS/DOS. This is simply because the interface will not be recognised in Safe Mode or in MS-DOS, rendering the drive "invisible" to the operating system.

My preferred option is to add another hard disc drive. These days this probably represents the cheapest means of adding large amounts of extra storage capacity to a PC, and a hard disc also has the advantage of being very fast. Read and write speeds are measured in megabytes per second, unlike some other storage systems where it is specified as so many megabytes per minute. A further advantage of the hard disc approach is that the disc should work properly with Windows booted in Safe Mode. A hard disc drive is one of the standard PC drives, and as such it does not require any special drivers for basic operation. This makes life easier at the best of times, but greatly eases things when the Windows installation is damaged.

Adding a drive

Fitting a second hard disc drive obviously requires the lid or side panel of the PC to be removed, followed by some delving around inside the computer. It is not one of the more difficult upgrades, but unless you are reasonably practical it would be advisable to have the upgrade done professionally. Most shops that sell hard disc drives also offer an upgrade service, but it will almost certainly cost substantially more to have the drive fitted for you. However, this extra cost is preferable to damaging the PC and having to pay a hefty repair bill. Assuming you feel confident enough to go ahead with the upgrade yourself, the first task is to open the PC to determine the current configuration.

With older PCs the top and two sides of the case are in one piece, and are released by removing four or six screws at the rear of the unit. Be careful, because there will probably be other screws here that hold other things in place, such as the power supply unit. With the right screws removed, the outer casing should pull away upwards and rearwards, but it will probably take a certain amount of force to pull it free. More modern cases have removable side panels, and with most types these are again held in place by four or six screws at the rear of the unit. Both panels must be removed in order to give full access to the drive bays. If your PC has one of the more unusual case styles it will be necessary to carefully examine the exterior in order to "crack" it.

A modern PC has the hard disc interface on the motherboard rather than provided by an expansion card. In fact, there are two hard disc interfaces on the motherboard, or possibly four on a modern PC. These are known as IDE interfaces, and this simply stands for integrated drive electronics. In other words, most of the electronics for the hard disc drive controller is built into the drive itself. At one time the IDE interfaces were strictly for hard disc drives, but in a modern PC they can be used for other types of drive. These multipurpose interfaces are more accurately called EIDE interfaces, which stands for enhanced integrated drive electronics. In practice they are still often referred to as just plain IDE interfaces. Many types of drive can be used with an EIDE interface, including CD-ROM, Zip, and LS120 drives.

In a typical PC the hard disc drive is connected to IDE port 1 and the CD-ROM drive is wired to IDE port 2. However, each IDE interface supports up to two devices, so the hard disc and CD-ROM drive could be connected to IDE port 1 via a single cable. A more common configuration with modern PCs is to have the hard disc on one IDE interface, with a CD-ROM or DVD drive and a CD writer on the other interface. Provided your PC has no more than three internal drives, excluding any floppy drives, it should certainly be able to support another hard drive.

If you look at the cabling inside the PC you should find some wide cables, know as "ribbon" cables, which connect the drives to the motherboard. With luck, at least one of these cables will have an unused connector that can be used with the new drive. Note that any spare connector on the drive that connects to the floppy disc drive is of no use with a hard disc drive. The floppy variety uses a completely different interface having a smaller connector. A suitable power supply lead and connector is also needed. The connectors come in two sizes, which are a larger one for 5.25-inch drives and a smaller one for

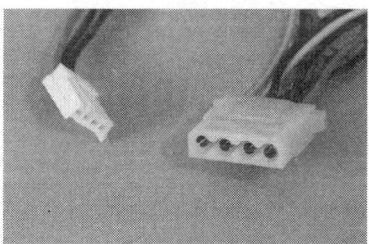

Fig.4.1 3.5-inch (left), and 5.25-inch (right) power connectors

the 3.5-inch variety (Figure 4.1). However, all the hard disc drives I have encountered use the larger connector regardless of whether they fit 3.5-inch or 5.25 in bays.

If you are out of luck, one or other of the required leads and connectors will not be present. If the hard disc and CD-ROM drive share an IDE interface, the other IDE interface will be available for the additional drive, but it will not be fitted with a cable. Another possibility is that the existing drives are connected to separate IDE interfaces using single cables rather than types having two connectors for drives. In either case a standard twin IDE data lead is needed in addition to the drive (Figure 4.2).

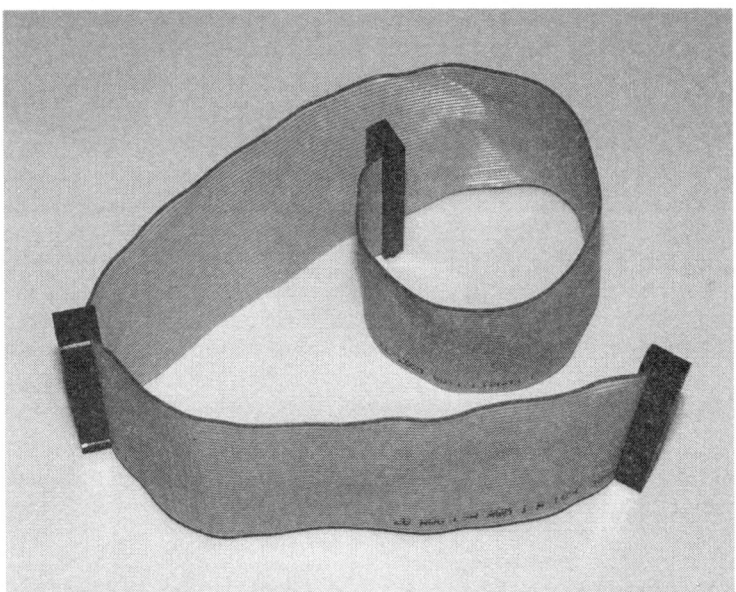

Fig.4.2 A standard twin IDE data lead

Hard drives are available in so called "bare" and "retail" or "boxed" versions. A bare drive may consist of nothing more than the drive itself. However, it will usually include an instruction manual and a set of fixing screws, but no data cable. Incidentally, if you find yourself with a hard drive but no matching manual, the web sites of most hard disc manufacturers include downloadable versions of the manuals for most of their hard disc units. Unless you are dealing with a very old or unusual drive, the information you require should be available on the manufacturer's web site.

The retail versions of hard drives normally include a cable in addition to a set of fixing screws and a more comprehensive manual. There may be other items such as a mounting cradle to permit a 3.5-inch drive to be used in a 5.25-inch drive bay. With modern drives there may well be two data cables included with the drive. One of these is a standard IDE cable that can be used with any IDE drive and any IDE interface. The other cable enables the drive to be used with a modern IDE interface that supports the UDMA66, and UDMA100, and UDMA133 standards. UDMA66/100/133 have the potential of faster data transfers than older standards such as the UDMA33 variety, but they can only be used if they are supported by the motherboard, the drive itself, and the correct cable is used. The instruction manual for your PC should state whether or not it supports anything beyond UDMA33.

If in doubt, the safe option is to use a standard IDE cable. This may provide something less than the ultimate in performance, but the disc should still work very well. It should certainly work well enough for making a backup of the main drive. Some advise against using a UDMA33 device together with a UDMA66/100/133 device and cable. It is generally considered safer to use a UDMA33 cable when using a UDMA66/100/133 device on the same interface as a UDMA33 drive. In my experience a UDMA66/100/133 cable works just as well in this situation, but either way the fast drive will be reduced to UDMA33 operation.

Rationalising

Of course, it is perfectly all right to have UDMA33 devices on one IDE interface and UDMA100/133 devices on the other. Rationalising things, this is probably the best solution. The new drive will presumably support UDMA66/100/133 operation, so you need to pair it with another UDMA66/100/133 drive in order to obtain optimum results. This normally means pairing it with the existing hard drive, because most CD-ROM drives only support UDMA33 operation. In theory there is some advantage in having devices on different IDE interfaces where it will be necessary to copy large amounts of data from one to the other. In practice this advantage might be outweighed if having the second drive on the other IDE interface downgrades it to UDMA33 operation. Anyway, in this situation I would pair the two hard drives on the first IDE interface.

In the unlikely event that the PC only supports UDMA33 operation, the new drive will also operate in this mode whichever IDE interface it is connected to. Where there is a spare channel available on the second IDE interface, this is the best place to install the new drive. This places it on a different interface to the main hard drive, which might help to speed up data transfers between the two. Any reasonably modern PC should have IDE interfaces that operate to at least the UDMA100 standard, and should therefore be capable of using a modern IDS hard disc drive at something close to its full potential.

Static

If you buy virtually any computer add-on to fit inside a PC it will be supplied in packaging plastered with dire warnings about the dangers of static electricity. Some of these are a bit "over the top", and suggest that going anywhere near the device without the protection of expensive anti-static equipment will result in it being instantly zapped. In reality the risks of static induced damage occurring are probably quite small. On the other hand, computer add-ons have yet to fall in price so far that they are in the "two a penny" category, and the risk of damage occurring is a real one.

The likelihood of damage can be reduced to insignificant proportions by observing a few simple rules. Rule number one is to leave the device in its packaging until it is time to install it. The plastic bags, foam lined boxes, etc., used for computer bits and pieces are not just for physical protection. They are designed to keep static electricity at bay. In some cases the packaging is designed to insulate the contents from high voltages. In others it is designed to conduct electricity so that no significant charge can build up between any two points in the device being protected. Any charges of this type will be almost instantly short-circuited by the conductive packaging.

Rule number two is to make sure that you are not charged with a high static voltage that could damage the device when you remove it from the packing. When working on computers do not wear clothes that are known to be good generators of static electricity. Manmade fibres are the most prolific static generators, but most modern clothes are usually made from natural fibres or a mixture of manmade and natural fibres, so this is not the major problem that it was at one time.

To make quite sure that both yourself and the device being installed are charge free, hold the device in its packing in one hand, and touch something that is earthed with the other hand. Any charge in you or the device should then leak away to earth. The metal case of the computer is a convenient earth point. With the cover or side panels removed there should be plenty of bare metal to touch. Touching the paintwork will not provide reliable earthing since most paints are excellent electrical insulators. Note that the computer must be plugged into the mains supply in order to use the mains earth connection, but it should not be switched on.

Rule number three is to keep the work area free of any large static charges. Any obvious sources of static charges should be removed from the vicinity of the computer. Television sets and computer monitors are good static generators, which means that the computer must be moved away from the monitor before you start work on it. This will normally be necessary anyway, because with the computer's base unit in its normal location it will probably be difficult to get proper access to the interior of the unit. It

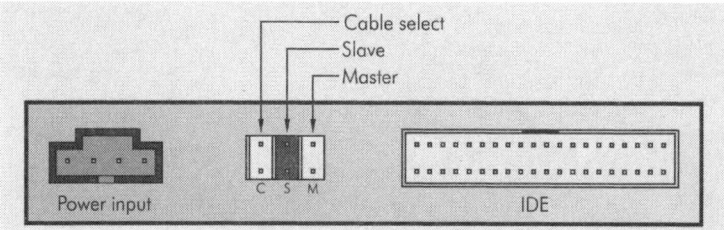

Fig.4.3 Typical layout for the rear of an IDE drive

needs to be placed on a table where there is good access to the interior and plenty of light so that you can see what you are doing. The table should preferably be one that it not precious, but if necessary the top can be protected with something like a generous quantity of old newspapers. It is a good idea to have the PC plugged into the mains supply but switched off at the mains socket. The earthed metal chassis of the computer will then tend to earth any static charges in its vicinity, preventing any dangerous charges from building up.

If you follow these simple rules it is very unlikely that the add-on device will be damaged by static charges. When dealing with hard disc drives it is as well to bear in mind that they are relatively delicate physically. Modern drives, although more intricate, are not as vulnerable as the early types. Even so, dropping a hard disc drive onto the floor is definitely not a good idea!

Jumpers

An IDE device has configuration jumpers that are used to set whether the unit will be used as the master or slave device on its IDE channel. Even if there is only one device on an IDE channel, that device must still be set as the master or slave unit. By convention, a single drive on an IDE channel is set as the master device. Therefore, if you are adding the new disc to an IDE channel that already has one device installed, the new drive must be set to operate as the slave device. If the new drive will be the sole device on its IDE channel, it must be set for master operation.

The rear of most CD-ROM drives and some IDE hard disc drives look something like Figure 4.3. The connector on the left is the power input and the one on the right is for the data cable. In between these are three pairs of terminals that can be bridged electrically by a tiny metal and plastic gadget called a jumper. A jumper can be seen in place in Figure

Fig.4.4 A jumper fitted to a drive

4.4. The "cable select" option is not used in a PC context, so only two pairs of contacts are relevant here. You simply place the jumper on the master or slave contacts, depending on which option you require. The configuration jumper should be supplied with the drive incidentally, and is normally set at the master option by default on a hard disc drive.

With hard disc drives matters are not always as simple as the arrangement shown in Figure 4.3. There is often an additional set of terminals, and these are used where the drive will be used as the only device on an IDE channel. Using this setting will allow a lone drive to be correctly identified and used by the PC. If the drive has these additional terminals (or they are fitted in place of the cable select pins), you must use them for a sole IDE drive. It is very unlikely that the drive will be picked up properly by the BIOS if the normal master setting is used. Getting it wrong is not likely to produce any damage, but the drive will be unusable until the mistake has been corrected. The manual supplied with the drive should give details of the configuration settings available.

If the new drive is used as the slave device on the primary IDE channel, the other hard drive will presumably be the master device on this channel. The existing drive will need its configuration setting altered if it is set to operate as the sole IDE device on its channel. The manual supplied with the PC should give details of the configuration settings. Alternatively, it should be possible to identify the drive from its markings, and it will almost certainly be possible to find its instruction manual on the Internet.

If there is no device on the secondary IDE channel, or only a single CD-ROM, and the motherboard only supports UDMA33 operation, it would probably be best to add the new drive on this channel. If a CD-ROM is present on this channel, adding the new drive as the secondary slave device is unlikely to require any configuration changes to the CD-ROM drive. If no device is already present, simply add the new drive as the master device or sole device, as appropriate. As pointed out previously, in theory data exchanges between the two hard discs will be quicker if they are on different IDE channels. Where possible, it is therefore better to arrange things this way when using UDMA33 IDE ports.

*Fig.4.5 The connections on the underside of the drive must not be
permitted to come into contact with the chassis, etc.*

It is definitely a good idea to check the configuration setting of the new
drive, and where necessary alter it, prior to fitting the drive in the case.
Once the drive is fitted inside the case it can be difficult to get at the
jumper and terminals, and it can be very difficult indeed to see what you
are doing when adjusting the jumper. Note that you do not have to look
at the jumpers on the existing drives to determine their master/slave
settings. The BIOS usually shows which drive is present on each IDE
channel during the startup routine.

Getting physical

It is not essential to install the new hard drive in the computer as a fixture.
You may prefer to simply connect the new drive to the data and power
cables, do the backup, reinstallation and restoration, and then disconnect
the drive again. It can then be stored safely away somewhere in case it
is needed at some later date. With the drive in storage rather than in use
it should not wear out, and should be ready for use if it is needed a few
years "down the line". I used this method successfully with a couple of
PCs for many years, although not strictly out of choice. If your PC has

one of the minimalist cases you may find that there are no spare bays for another hard disc drive. Note that it is possible to use a 3.5-inch drive in a 5.25-inch drive bay using an adaptor. This is just a metal cradle into which the drive is bolted, and the whole assembly then fits into the drive bay just like a 5.25-inch drive. This adaptor should be available from any large computer store. As pointed out previously, it is sometimes (but not always) included with boxed retail versions of hard disc drives.

When temporarily connecting a drive it is essential to make sure that no exposed connections on the unit come into electrical contact with the metal case, expansion cards, etc. Some drives are fully enclosed, but most have the underside of the circuit board exposed (Figure 4.5). Often the easiest way of keeping the drive safe is to place it on top of the computer with some newspaper to insulate the drive from the case. With a PC that has some form of tower case it is usually easier to work on the unit if it is placed on its side. The drive can then be placed on the side of the drive cage, again with newspaper being used to provide insulation.

Probably most users will wish to use the additional disc as a permanent feature. This is essential if you wish to use it to make frequent backups or you will be making backup copies of data files as they are generated. If you are using a drive bay that has no front opening, the new drive must be slid in from the rear. Any expansion cards that get in the way must be removed temporarily. Remove the screws that fix the cards to the rear of the chassis and it should then be possible to pull the cards free. The sockets on the drive are at the rear, so the other end is pushed into the rear of the drive bay. The manufacturer's name, etc., are marked on the top plate of the drive, so this side should be facing upward. In most cases the drive can be fully pushed into the bay, but it is sometimes necessary to ease it back slightly to get the mounting holes in the drive and the bay to match up properly.

In days gone by it was necessary to use plastic guide rails to mount the drives in the case, but most PCs made within the last eight years or more have drive bays that take the drives without the need for these rails. There are some exceptions, and these use an updated version of the guide rail system. With the old system there were two guide rails, and one was bolted on each side of the drive. The drive was then slid into place and the rails were bolted to the chassis. The new system has one guide rail per drive, and it usually just clips into place. One side of the drive is bolted to the chassis in the normal way, while the other simply clips into place. The point of this is that there is often limited access to one side of the drive bay. Using the clip-on rail on the appropriate side of the drive avoids the difficulty of fitting the mounting bolts on the awkward side. Your PC should have been supplied with one or two spare rails if it uses this type of drive mounting system

Four mounting bolts are normally supplied with the drive, and with the standard method of mounting these are used to secure the drive to the bay. If no fixing screws were supplied with the drive, the PC may have been supplied with some odds and ends of hardware. If so, there will probably be some suitable screws in amongst these. Failing that, you will have to by some metric M3 screws about 6 millimetres long. Note that the mounting screws must be quite short, and should not protrude more than a few millimetres into the drive. Longer mounting bolts could easily damage something inside the drive.

With a so-called "external" drive bay, it might be easier to insert the drive from the front. Where the interior of the computer is very crowded this can avoid having to remove expansion cards to get the drive in place. An external bay is really intended for use with a floppy drive, CD-ROM drive, or some other type where access is needed to the drive for changing discs. However, an external bay is perfectly suitable for a wholly internal drive such as a hard disc unit. The plastic cover at the very front of the bay can be carefully prised out using a flat-bladed screwdriver, and it might then be possible to slide the drive in through the front of the case. There will probably be a metal plate behind the plastic cover though. It may be possible to remove this by first removing two or three fixing screws, but in most cases the plate has to be repeatedly twisted backwards and forwards until the thin pieces of metal holding it in place fatigue and break. With the drive in place, the plastic cover plate can be clipped back into position.

Cabling

The ribbon cable used to provide the data connection has three identical connectors. There is no specific connector for the motherboard and each drive, but because the cable is quite short it will probably have to connect everything together in a particular way in order to reach everything. It should not take too long to fathom out the best way of using the cable. Things are much easier when the new hard drive is the sole device on an IDE channel. The cable should then connect the motherboard to the drive without difficulty.

The connectors must be fitted to the motherboard and drives the correct way round. In theory the connectors are polarised and can only be fitted the right way round. There is a protrusion on the lead's connectors and

Fig.4.6 Two polarised IDE connectors on a motherboard

a matching groove in the connectors on the motherboard and drives. Figure 4.6 shows the polarising keys in the two IDE connectors on a motherboard.

Unfortunately, some connectors, and mainly those on motherboards, are sometimes a bit too minimalist and are not properly polarised. In addition, some IDE connectors lack the polarising key. A search through the appropriate instruction manuals should show which is pin 1 on each connector. This information is often marked on the motherboard and the drives themselves. To make things easier, the ribbon cable has one red lead while the other 39 are grey. The convention is for the red lead to carry the pin 1 connection. Provided this lead is adjacent to pin 1 on the connector for the motherboard and both drives, everything will be connected together properly.

A spare power cable is needed for the new drive, and if there is a spare drive bay there should really be a spare power lead as well. However, it might be fitted with the smaller connector for 3.5-inch floppy drives, whereas it is the larger power connector that is required for hard disc drives, whether they are of the 3.5-inch or 5.25-inch variety. A large computer store should be able to provide a 3.5 to 5.25-inch power connector adaptor. If there is no spare power cable, a splitter adaptor is available. This provides two power connectors from a single power lead. Remove the power lead from the existing hard disc drive and connect it to the splitter. The two remaining connectors of the splitter are then connected to the hard disc drives. The power connectors are fully

Fig.4.7 Serial ATA ports are much smaller than the IDE variety

polarised and can only be connected the right way around. They are also quite stiff, and often need a certain amount of force in order to get them properly connected or disconnected again.

Serial ATA

Practically all new motherboard designs now include a relatively new type of disc interface called Serial ATA. This is essentially a serial version of the standard IDE disc interface, but with a maximum speed of 150 megabytes per second. It is sometimes referred to as an ATA 150 interface. Clearly a serial ATA interface is not much faster than a UDMA 133 IDE interface, and real-world hard disc drives do not really utilize the speed available from either type of interface. The real advantage of a serial ATA interface is that the cabling is much easier to deal with. Far fewer connecting wires are needed with a serial interface, and this is reflected in the size of the connectors on the motherboard. Figure 4.7 shows a group of four serial ATA ports on a motherboard. In order to give a sense of scale, Figure 4.8 shows a zoomed-out view that includes

Fig.4.8 Serial ATA ports (left), with floppy disc and IDE ports (right)

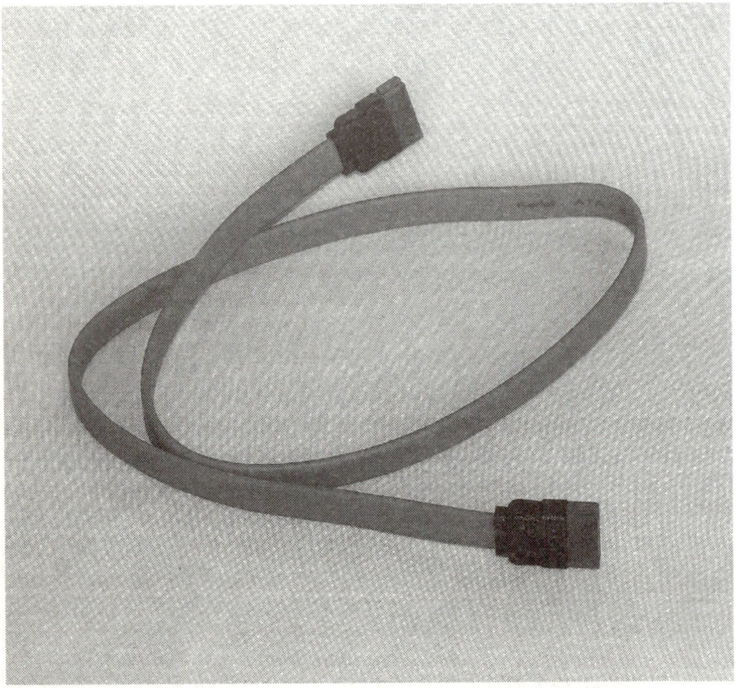

Fig.4.9 Serial ATA cables are much thinner than the IDE type

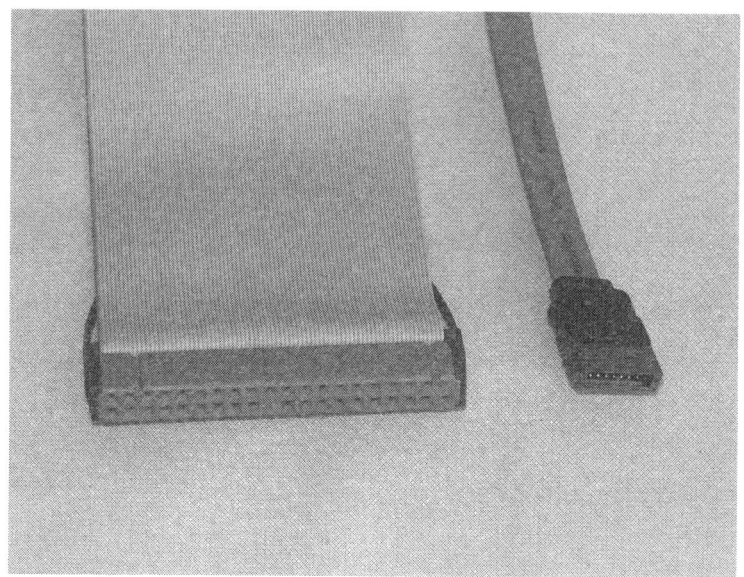

Fig.4.10 An IDE cable(left) and a Serial ATA cable (right)

a floppy disc port and a UDMA 133 type near the bottom left-hand corner. Perhaps of greater importance than the smaller size of the connectors, the serial cables can be much thinner.

A serial ATA data cable is shown in Figure 4.9, and Figure 4.10 shows both types of cable. A slight problem with the wide ribbon cables normally used for parallel disc interfaces is that they tend to hinder the flow of air inside the PC. This in turn tends to reduce the efficiency of the cooling system and raises the temperature inside the case. It is possible to obtain round versions of parallel IDE cables (Figure 4.11), but these are even less flexible than the type that uses ribbon cable, and can be awkward to use. Serial ATA cables are relatively flexible, easy to use, and do not significantly hinder the flow of air through the case. One relative weakness of the serial ATA approach is that each port can only be used with one drive, whereas each IDE port can be used with two drives. On the other hand, this removes the complication of master/ slave selection, since there are, in effect, only master devices with serial ATA interfaces. Motherboards mostly have plenty of serial ATA connectors to compensate for the restriction of one drive per serial ATA port.

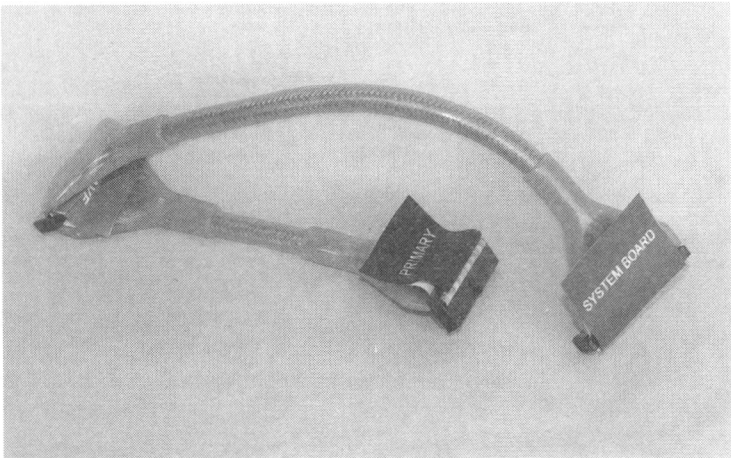

Fig.4.11 The "round" version of a dual IDE data cable

Serial ATA drives sometimes have standard 5.25-inch power connectors in addition to their own miniature type, but most only have the miniature power port. Unfortunately, PC power supplies often lack any spare serial ATA power connectors. Where a drive has a 5.25-inch power port, using it will probably be the best option. In most cases it will be necessary to power serial ATA drives from 5.25-inch power leads via an adaptor. The example shown in Figure 4.12 enables two serial ATA drives to be powered from a single 5.25-inch power lead. Serial ATA power leads are polarised and usually fit into place with a minimum of fuss.

BIOS Setup

Having physically installed the hard disc it will be necessary to go into the BIOS Setup program and set the appropriate parameters for the new disc. The BIOS is something that most PC users never need to get involved with, but for anyone undertaking PC upgrading it is likely that some involvement will be needed from time to time. It is certainly something that can not be avoided if you add a second hard disc drive. In days gone by it was necessary to have a utility program to make changes to the BIOS settings, but this program is built into a modern PC BIOS.

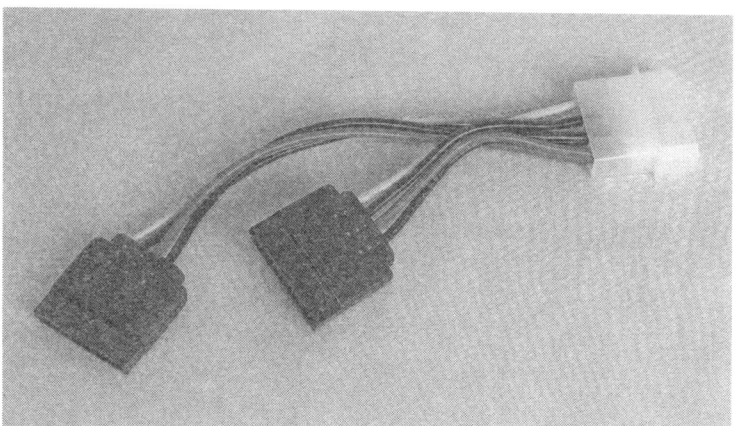

Fig.4.12 An adaptor to permit serial drives to be powered from an ordinary 5.25-inch power connector

A modern BIOS Setup program enables dozens of parameters to be controlled, many of which are highly technical. This tends to make the BIOS intimidating for newcomers and even to those who have some experience of dealing with PC technicalities. However, most of the BIOS settings are not the type of thing the user will need to bother with, and very few are relevant to the hard disc drives.

BIOS basics

Before looking at the BIOS Setup program it would perhaps be as well to consider the function of the BIOS. BIOS is a acronym and it stands for basic input/output system. Its primary function is to help the operating system handle the input and output devices, such as the drives, and ports, and also the memory circuits. It is a program that is stored in a ROM on the motherboard. These days the chip is usually quite small and sports a holographic label to prove that it is the genuine article (Figure 4.13). Because the BIOS program is in a ROM on the motherboard it can be run immediately at start-up without the need for any form of booting process. It is the BIOS that provides the test procedures when a PC is switched on, and the BIOS also starts the boot process.

The BIOS can provide software routines that help the operating system to utilise the hardware effectively, and it can also store information about the hardware for use by the operating system, and possibly other

Fig.4.13 A modern BIOS chip. This also contains the Setup program

software. It is this second role that makes it necessary to have the Setup program. The BIOS can actually detect much of the system hardware and store the relevant technical information in memory. Also, a modern BIOS is customised to suit the particular hardware it is dealing with, and the defaults should be sensible ones for the hardware on the motherboard. However, some parameters have to be set manually, such as the time and date, and the user may wish to override some of the default settings.

The Setup program enables the user to control the settings that the BIOS stores away in its CMOS memory. A back-up battery powers this memory when the PC is switched off, so its contents are available each time the PC is turned on. Once the correct parameters have been set it should not be necessary to change them unless the hardware is altered, such as a new hard disc drive being added or the existing hard disc being upgraded. In practice, the BIOS settings can sometimes be scrambled by a software or hardware glitch, although this is not a common problem with modern PCs.

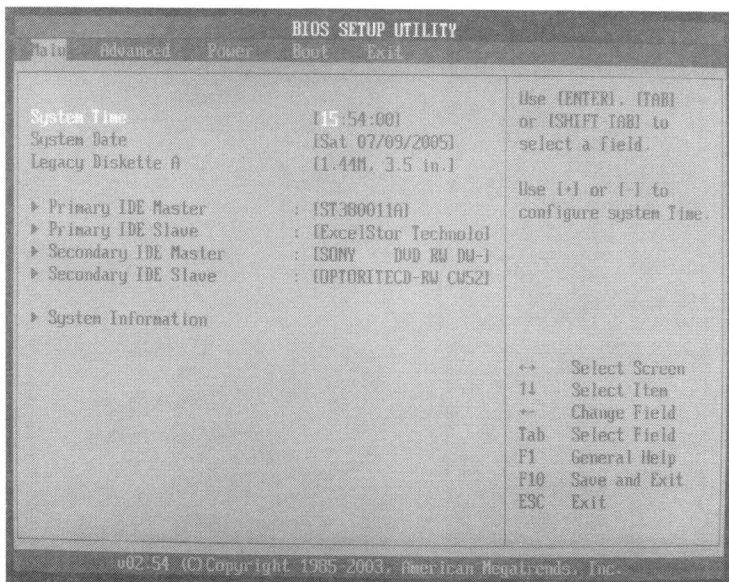

Fig.4.14 This AMI BIOS has five sections that are accessed via the
            tabs

Entry

In the past, there have been several common means of getting into the
BIOS Setup program, but with modern motherboards there is only one
method in common use. This is to press the Delete key at the appropriate
point during the initial testing phase just after switch-on. The BIOS will
display a message, usually in the bottom left-hand corner of the screen,
telling you to press the "Del" key to enter the Setup program. The
instruction manual should provide details if the motherboard you are
using has a different method of entering the Setup program. The most
common alternative is to press the "Escape" key rather than the "Del"
key, but numerous alternatives have been used over the years, and no
doubt some of these are still in use.

Every PC should be supplied with a manual that has a section dealing
with the BIOS. Actually a lot of PCs are supplied with a very simple
"Getting Started" style manual, but this is usually augmented by the
manufacturers' manuals for the main components. It is then the
motherboard manual that will deal with the BIOS. It is worth looking
through the BIOS section of the manual to before you actually go into

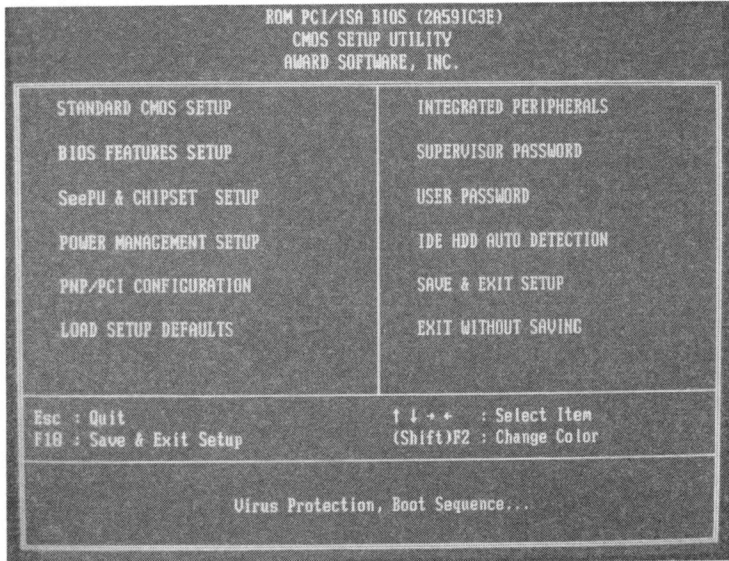

Fig.4.15 The initial screen of an Award BIOS Setup program

the BIOS program. This will give you an idea of how things work, but do not bother too much about the more obscure settings. In the current context it is only some of the Standard CMOS settings that are of interest.

Do not expect the manual to give detailed explanations of the various settings. Most motherboard instruction manuals assume the user is familiar with all the BIOS features, and there will be few detailed explanations. In fact, there will probably just be a list of the available options and no real explanations at all. This does not really matter, and you really only need to know how to get into the BIOS, make a few changes, save the changes, and exit the program.

There are several BIOS manufacturers and their BIOS Setup programs each work in a slightly different fashion. Award, Phoenix, and AMI are popular BIOS producers. At one time the AMI BIOS had a Setup program that would detect any reasonably standard mouse connected to the PC. With the aid of a mouse it offered a simple form of WIMP environment, although keyboard control was still available. This system seems to have been dropped, and a modern AMI BIOS uses a more conventional approach with tabs at the top of the screen providing access to the various

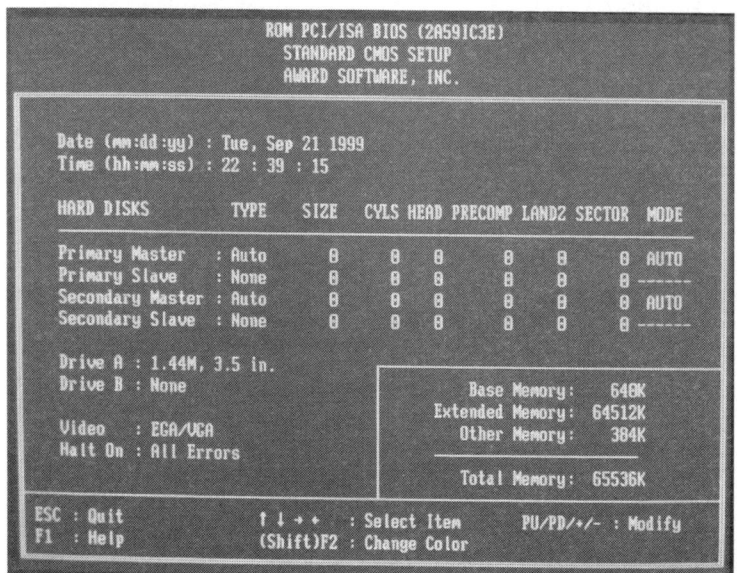

Fig.4.16 A typical Standard CMOS Setup screen

sections of the program (Figure 4.14). The required tab is selected via the keyboard and not using a mouse. The Award BIOS is probably the most common (Figure 4.15), and as far as I am aware it only uses keyboard control.

Apart from variations in the BIOS due to different manufacturers, the BIOS will vary slightly from one motherboard to another. This is simply due to the fact that features available on one motherboard may be absent or different on another motherboard. Also, the world of PCs in general is developing at an amazing rate, and this is reflected in frequent BIOS updates. Fortunately, the Standard CMOS section has not changed much over the years, so it should not differ significantly from the one described here unless you are dealing with a computer than falls into the "antique" category.

Standard CMOS

There are so many parameters that can be controlled via the BIOS Setup program that they are normally divided into half a dozen or more groups.

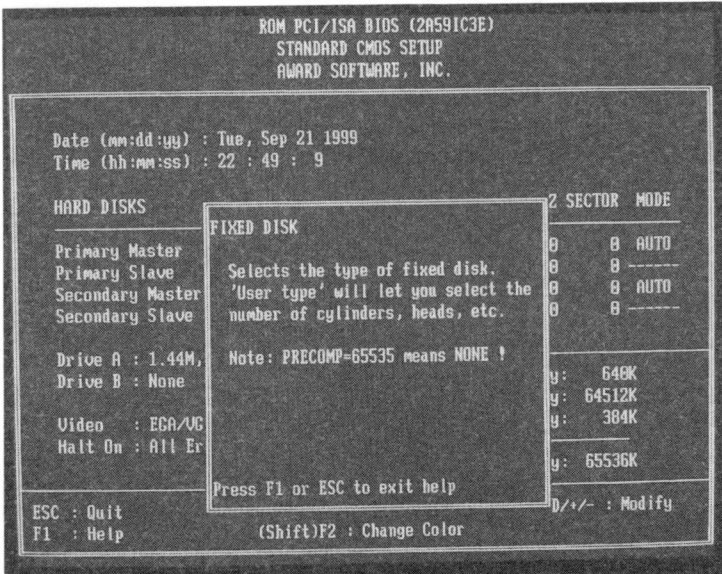

Fig.4.17 *Most Setup programs provide context sensitive help*

The most important of these is the "Standard CMOS Setup" (Figure 4.16), which is basically the same as the BIOS Setup in the original AT style PCs. The first parameters in the list are the time and date. These can usually be set via an operating system utility these days, but you can still alter them via the Setup program if you prefer. There are on-screen instructions that tell you how to alter and select options. One slight oddity to watch out for is that you often have to use the Page Up key to decrement values, and the Page Down key to increment them.

With virtually any modern BIOS a help screen can be brought up by pressing F1, and this will usually be context sensitive (Figure 4.17). In other words, if the cursor is in the section that deals with the hard drives, the help screen produced by pressing F1 will tell you about the hard disc parameters. It would be unreasonable to expect long explanations from a simple on-line help system, and a couple of brief and to the point sentences are all that will normally be provided.

Drive settings

The next section is the one we need, and it is used to set the operating parameters for the devices on the IDE ports. The hard disc is normally the master device on the primary IDE channel (IDE1), and the CD-ROM is usually the master device on the secondary IDE channel (IDE2). However, to avoid the need for a second data cable the CD-ROM drive is sometimes the slave device on the primary IDE interface. You might have fitted the new drive as any of the four available devices apart from the primary device on IDE1, which will be the original hard disc drive. If in doubt, this table should help you decide which device it is:

Channel/device	If the new drive is...
IDE1 secondary	on the same cable as the original hard drive
IDE2 primary	the sole device on the opposite channel to the original hard disc
IDE2 secondary	on the same cable as the CD-ROM drive (or other device such as a CD writer)

Having decided how the new drive fits into the overall scheme of things you can set the appropriate parameters. The drive should really be supplied with a manual that provides the correct BIOS settings, but it is usually possible to get by without it. One of the parameters is the hard disc's type number. In the early days there were about 40 standard types of hard disc drive, and a it was just a matter of selecting the appropriate type number for the drive in use. The BIOS would then supply the appropriate parameters for that drive. This system was unable to cope with the ever increasing range of drives available, and something more flexible therefore had to be devised. The original 40 plus preset drive settings are normally still available from a modern BIOS, but there is an additional option that enables the drive parameters to be specified by the user. This is the method used with all modern PCs and their high capacity hard disc drives, so choose the Custom setting and ignore the drive numbers.

The drive table parameters basically just tell the operating system the size of drive, and the way that the disc is organised. Although we refer to a hard disc as a singular disc, most of these units use both sides of two or more discs. Each side of the disc is divided into cylinders (tracks),

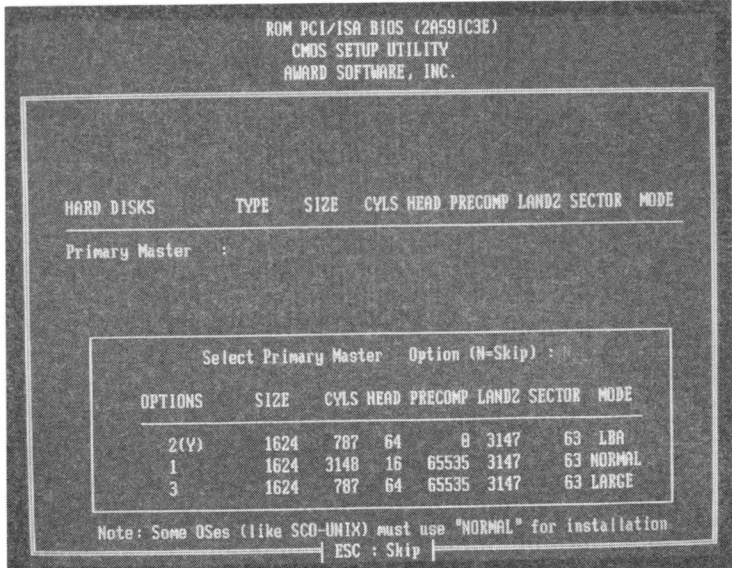

Fig.4.18 An IDE auto-detection screen

and each cylinder is subdivided into several sectors. There are usually other parameters that enable the operating system to use the disc quickly and efficiently. You do not really need to understand these parameters, and just have to make sure that the correct figures are placed into the drive table. As pointed out previously, the manual for the hard drive should provide the correct figures for the BIOS. If you do not have the manual, it can probably be downloaded from the disc manufacturer's web site.

Auto selection

If you do not have the manual or prefer to take an easier option, a modern BIOS makes life easy for you by offering an "Auto" option. If this is selected, the BIOS examines the hardware during the start-up routine and enters the correct figures automatically. This usually works very well, but with some drives it can take a while, which extends the boot-up time. If the PC has been set up with this option enabled, the drive table will be blank.

There is an alternative method of automatic detection that avoids the boot-up delay, and any reasonably modern BIOS should have this facility. If you go back to the initial menu you will find a section called something like "IDE HDD Auto Detection" (Figure 4.18), and this offers a similar auto-detection facility. When this option is selected the Setup program examines the hardware on each IDE channel, and offers suggested settings for each of the four possible IDE devices. If you accept the suggested settings for the hard disc drive (or drives) they will be entered into the CMOS RAM. There may actually be several alternatives offered per IDE device, but the default suggestion is almost invariably the correct one. If you do not know the correct settings for a drive, this facility should find them for you.

It is perhaps worth mentioning that with an IDE drive the figures in the drive table do not usually have to match the drive's physical characteristics. Indeed, they rarely if ever do so. The electronics in the drive enable it to mimic any valid physical arrangement that does not exceed the capacity of the drive. In practice it is advisable to use the figures recommended by the drive manufacturer, as these are tried and tested, and should guarantee perfect results. Other figures can sometimes give odd problems such as unreliable booting, although they are within the acceptable limits.

The last parameter for each IDE drive is usually something like Auto, Normal, LBA (large block addressing), and Large. Normal is for drives under 528MB, while LBA and Large are alternative modes for drives having a capacity of more than 528MB. Modern drives have capacities of well in excess of 528MB, and mostly require the LBA mode. The manual for the hard drive should give the correct setting, but everything should work fine with "Auto" selected.

It is increasingly common for modern motherboards to have four rather than two IDE interfaces. With a motherboard of this type it will usually be possible for the added hard disc drive to have its own IDE interface even if the PC is already fitted with something like one hard disc drive, a CD-ROM drive and a CD writer. Finding a spare IDE channel for the new drive should be that much easier, but in other respects things are essentially the same as when dealing with a twin IDE port motherboard. Motherboards that have more than two IDE ports usually have some form of RAID controller, and these provide clever facilities such as the ability to automatically back up data written to one drive on another drive. It is clearly worthwhile investigating any facilities of this type, which could clearly be more than a little useful in the current context.

Drive letters

Some users get confused because they think a hard drive that will be have more than one partition should have separate entries in the BIOS for each partition. This is not the case, and as far as the BIOS is concerned each physical hard disc is a single drive, and it has just one entry in the CMOS RAM table. The partitioning of hard discs is handled by the operating system, and so is the assignment of drive letters. The BIOS is only concerned with the physical characteristics of the drives, and not how data will be arranged and stored on the discs. There is usually no point in using more than one partition if you are adding a drive for back-up purposes. The only, and fairly obvious exception, is where the drive you are backing up has been partitioned to operate as two or more logical drives. It is then advisable to have the partitioning of the back-up drive match that of the main drive as closely as possible.

The other Standard CMOS settings are concerned with the floppy discs and the default display type, and should simply be left as they are. The same is true of the settings in the other pages of the BIOS Setup program. Do not be tempted to start playing around with these unless you know exactly what you are doing. Entering silly settings is unlikely to damage anything, but could well prevent the PC from operating properly. The BIOS will probably have options that enable the previous settings to be reinstated, or default settings to be used. These can be useful if you should accidentally scramble a few parameters.

Note though, that no settings are actually altered unless and until you select the Save Parameters and Exit option, and then answer Yes when asked to confirm this action. This is clearly the route you should take if everything has gone according to plan. Take the Exit Without Saving option if things have not gone well. Simply switching off the PC or pressing the reset button should have the same effect.

Strategies

With the early PC hard disc drives it was necessary to do low-level formatting of the drive before it could be partitioned and the high-level formatting could be undertaken. Modern hard drives are supplied with the low-level formatting already done. If there is a low-level formatting option in the BIOS Setup program, never use it on an IDE hard disc drive. Do not use any similar facility in any utility suites that you might have.

No low-level formatting is required, but with operating systems such as Windows XP, and Windows Vista the hard disc drive must be partitioned and high-level formatted before it can be used.

The best way to proceed with the data recovery depends on the condition of the Windows Vista installation. Your options are very limited if it is not even possible to boot in Safe Mode. Probably the only way of tackling the problem is to have the new drive set as the master on the primary IDE channel and the original hard disc on any available IDE channel. Windows Vista is then installed from scratch onto the new drive. It should then be possible to boot into the new installation and copy the files you need from the original hard disc. Any high capacity backup devices fitted to the computer should work properly with the new installation in place. It is then possible to copy the files to the new hard disc or the back-up devices.

Where it is possible to boot into Windows in Safe Mode an alternative strategy is available. The existing hard disc drive can be left as the boot drive and the second hard disc is then placed on any available IDE channel. With the computer booted in Safe Mode the required files on the main hard drive can then be copied to the second drive. Windows Vista can be installed from scratch onto the main drive, which will result in all the files on the main drive being erased. The rescued files on the second drive can then be copied back to the main drive. This is the best method to use if you do not wish to use the new drive as the main one. For example, if you obtain a cheap backup drive that has a much lower capacity than the main one, you will probably not wish to use the new drive as the main one. The second hard drive can be removed once the file recovery has been completed, but it is probably better to leave it in place as a back-up drive for important files.

Partitioning

The new drive can be partitioned from within Windows XP and then formatted using the FAT32 or NTFS file system. If you wish to use the FAT32 file system for some reason, Microsoft recommend partitioning and formatting drives larger than 32 gigabytes using Windows 9x rather than Windows XP or Vista. This is simply because Windows XP and Vista are not fully equipped to deal with the partitioning and formatting of large discs using this format. Partitioning and formatting using Windows 9x and Vista will be described here, starting with Windows 9x.

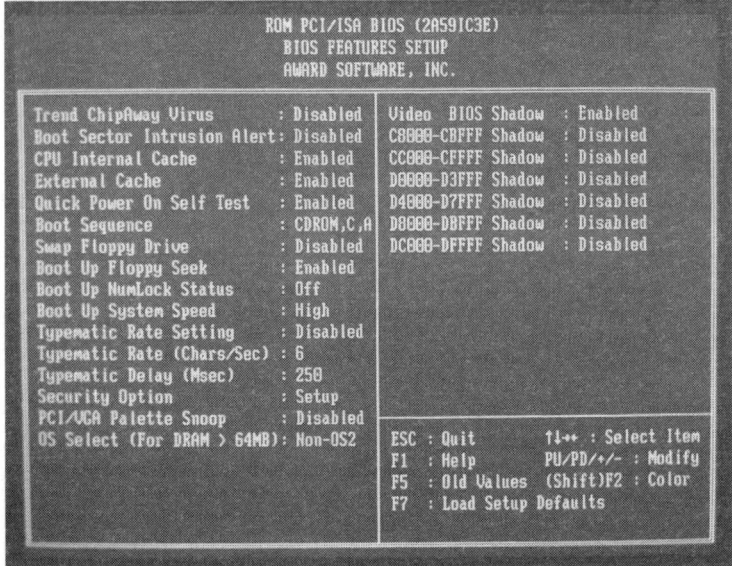

Fig.4.19 An example BIOS Features Setup screen. Amongst other things, this is used to set the required boot option

In order to partition and format the disc using Windows 9x it is not necessary to install Windows 9x onto the drive. All that is needed is a Startup disc, and one of these is normally produced as part of the Windows 9x installation process. If you do not have a Startup disc, one can be made using a system that runs Windows 9x. Start by going into the Windows Control Panel, and one route to this is to operate the Start button, and then select Settings and Control Panel. Once in the control panel double-click on the Add/Remove Programs icon, select Startup Disk, and finally operate the Create Disk button. Then follow the onscreen prompts. A blank 1.44 megabyte floppy disc is required. Note that you will be asked to insert the Windows 95/98/ME CD-ROM into the CD-ROM drive, because some of the files required are not normally stored on the hard disc. The method of making the disc is exactly the same for all three operating systems (95, 98, and ME) incidentally.

Having obtained the Startup disc, it should be used to boot the computer into the Windows 9x version of MS-DOS. It is probable that the BIOS will already be set to boot from the floppy disc drive, but if necessary you must use the BIOS Setup program to set the floppy drive as a boot device. There will be a page in the BIOS called something like BIOS Features

Setup (Figure 4.19), and this should enable various boot sequences to be chosen. Choose one that has the floppy disc (drive A:) as the first boot device, and hard drive C: as the second. Any subsequent boot options are irrelevant, since the PC will always boot from one or other of the first two options.

With the computer booted-up and running MS-DOS or the Windows 95/98/ME equivalent of MS-DOS, the new hard drive will not be accessible. Until it has been partitioned it will be largely "invisible" to the operating system. Note that a drive using the NTFS format will also be largely "invisible" to the system, so make sure that you process the right disc drive. Once the new drive is partitioned the operating system will be more willing to admit to its existence, but it will still be of no use until high-level formatting has been performed using the MS-DOS FORMAT program. However, you must first prepare the disc using the FDISK partitioning program. The Windows Startup disc contains copies of both FDISK and FORMAT, which are automatically placed on the disc for you when the Startup disc is created.

FDISK

FDISK is used to create one or more DOS partitions, and with discs of 2.1 gigabytes or less you may wish to have the whole of the disc as a single partition. Assuming the original hard disc has one partition, the new hard disc drive then becomes drive D:. By creating further partitions it can also operate as drive E:, drive F:, etc. The primary partition is normally the boot disc, and this is where the operating system would be installed. Obviously this does not apply to a second hard drive, and the primary partition is simply the first partition on the disc.

The MS/DOS and Windows 95 file systems set the 2.1-gigabyte partition limit. There is also an 8.4-gigabyte limit on the physical size of the drive. With Windows 98 or ME and any reasonably modern BIOS these limits do not apply, but you must use the FAT32 file system. To do this simply answer yes when FDISK is first run, and you are asked if you require support for large hard disc drives. Even if you do not wish to have a large disc organised as one large partition, it is still best to opt for large hard disc support. FAT32 utilises the available disc space more efficiently and reduces wastage. Note that if you only require a single partition you must still use the FDISK program to set up this single partition, and that the FORMAT program will not work on the hard drive until FDISK has created a DOS partition.

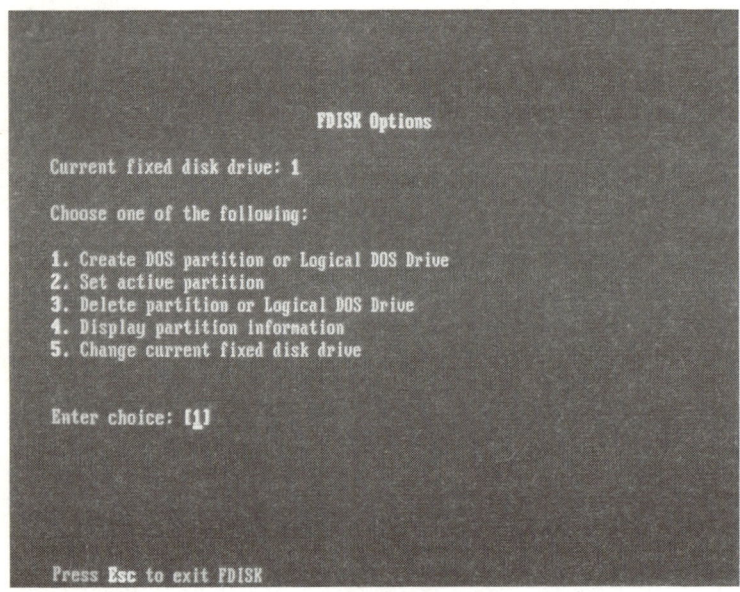

Fig.4.20 The main menu of the FDISK program

Some hard discs are supplied complete with partitioning software that will also format the disc and add the system files, which will be copied from the boot disc. Where a utility program of this type is available it might be better to use it instead of the FDISK and FORMAT programs. These MS-DOS programs are fairly straightforward in use, but using the software supplied with the drive will almost certainly be even easier. The only problem is that the software might be intended for use with drive C:, and might give problems if you try to use it with drive D:. The instructions supplied with the software should make it clear whether the software is suitable for use with a second hard disc drive. If the program insists on placing the system files on drive D:, this is not really a major problem. The system files will waste a small amount of disc space, but should not give any problems when the system is booted provided the boot options are set correctly in the BIOS. If in doubt, simply use FDISK and FORMAT.

Using FDISK

Once you are in FDISK there is a menu offering these five choices (see also Figure 4.20):

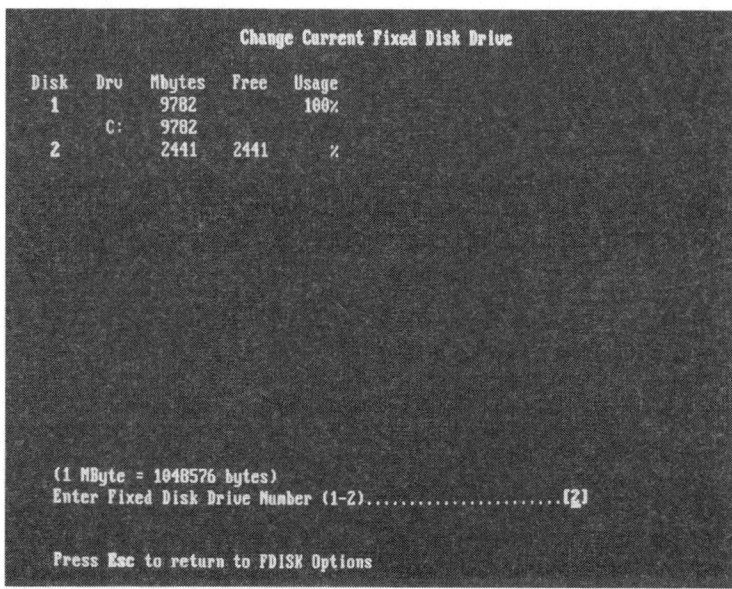

Fig.4.21 The partition information screen

1. Create DOS partition or logical DOS drive

2. Set the active partition

3. Delete partition or logical DOS drive

4. Display partition information

5. Change current fixed drive

Normally the first thing we need to do is create a DOS partition using option one, which is the default. However, in this case we are dealing with an additional hard drive, and we must first make sure that it is the one FDISK is dealing with. It is very important that you do not accidentally use FDISK with the wrong drive, since to do so would almost certainly remove all the data from the disc you are trying to back up! Select option 5, which should bring up a screen like that in Figure 4.21. The original hard disc unit is drive 1 and the new hard disc is drive 2. In this example drive 1 (C:) is the original drive of about 10 gigabytes in capacity, and drive 2 is the additional rescue drive having a capacity of about 2.4 gigabytes. Drive 2 will eventually be drive D:, but at this stage it has not yet been assigned a drive letter. If the current disc is drive 1, enter 2 for this parameter and press the Enter key to go back to the main screen.

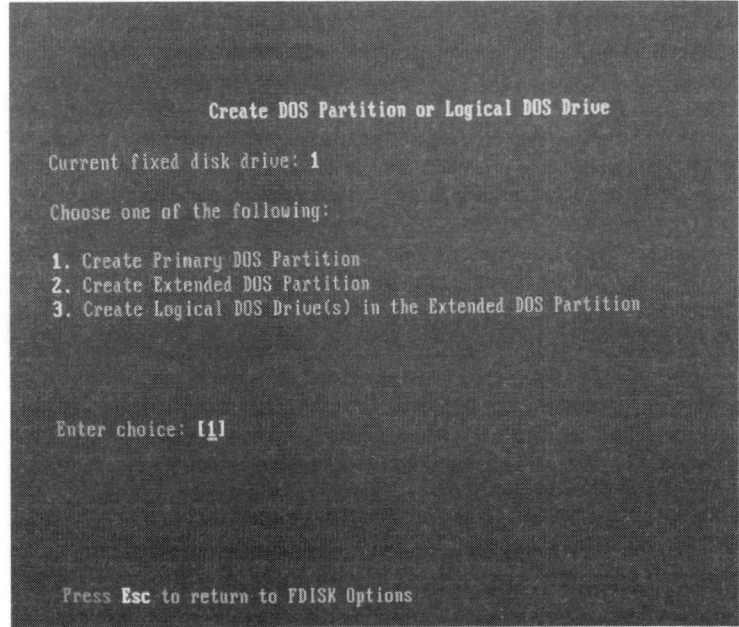

Fig.4.22 Creating a partition on a new hard disc

Once drive 2 has been set as the current drive it can be partitioned, and option 1 can be selected. This takes you into a further menu offering these three options (Figure 4.22):

1. Create primary DOS partition

2. Create extended DOS partition

3. Create logical DOS drive(s) in the extended DOS partition

It is a primary DOS partition that is required, so select option one, which should again be the default. After the disc has been given a quick test you will be asked if you wish to use the maximum space for the partition. If you answer yes, the whole disc, or as much of it as FDISK can handle, will be used for the partition. If you answer no, you will then have to specify the size of the primary partition in megabytes. After a further quick check of the disc the new partition will be created. Having created the partition, press the Escape key to return to the original menu (Figure 4.20). It is a good idea to select option four to check that the partition has been created successfully (Figure 4.23).

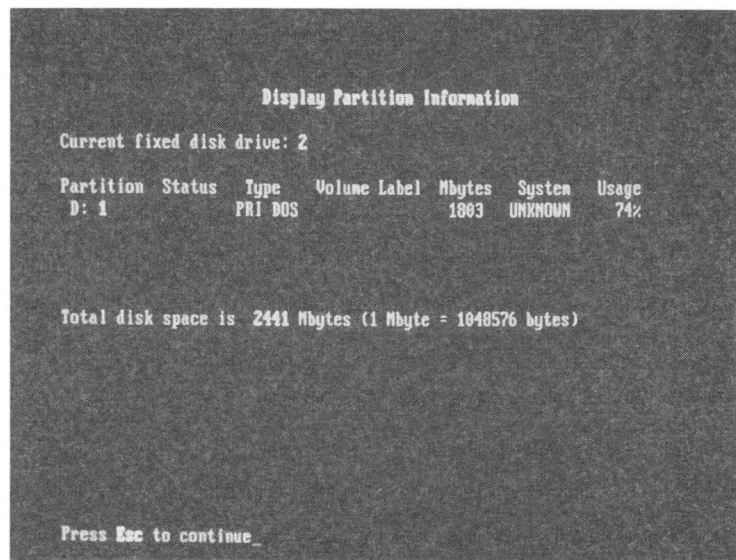

Fig.4.23 Checking that the new partition has been created

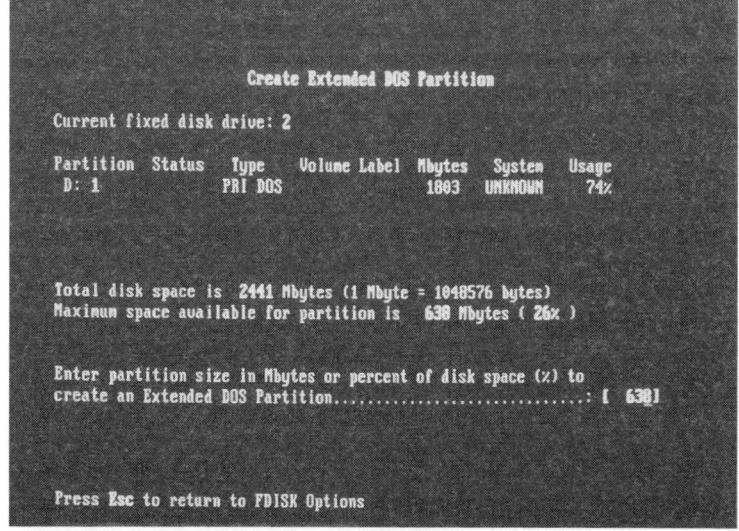

Fig.4.24 Unused space can be used for further partitions

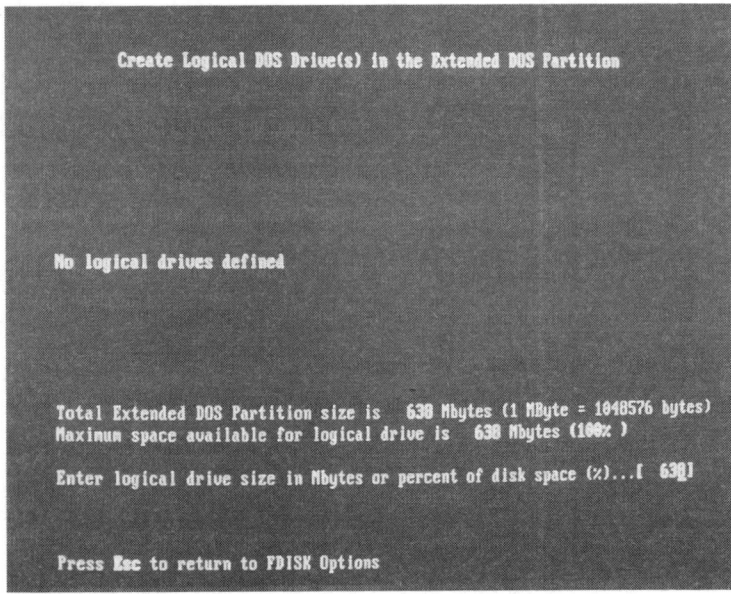

Fig.4.25 An extended partition must be given a drive letter

If a further partition is required select option one, and then option two, which is "Create extended DOS partition" (Figure 4.24). Enter the size of the partition you require and press the Return key to create the partition. Then press the Escape key, which will bring up a message saying "No logical drives defined" (Figure 4.25). In other words, you have created a partition, but as yet it does not have a drive letter. Assuming you require all the space in the partition to be one logical drive, simply press the Return key. This will make the partition drive E:, and a screen giving this information will appear (Figure 4.26). Press the Escape key to return to the main menu, and use option four to check that the partition has been created successfully.

It has been assumed here that the original hard disc has a single FAT32 partition. If it has more than one partition these will be drives C:, D:, etc., and the drive letter or letters for the additional drive will be moved up accordingly. For example, if the original disc is used as drives C: And D:, partitions of the new drive would become drives E:, F:, etc. These MS-DOS drive letters are not really of much importance once Windows Vista is in use, since it will assign its own drive letters.

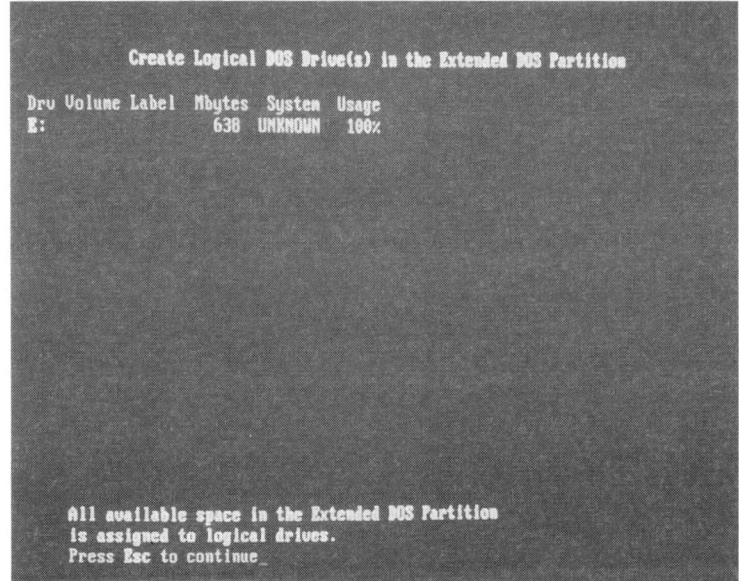

Fig.4.26 *This screen shows the drive letter for the new partition*

Formatting

Having created the partitions you require, the "FORMAT" command can
then be run. First you will have to press the Escape key twice to exit
FDISK, and then the computer must be rebooted so that the new partition
information takes effect. Make sure you format the correct disc, because
formatting a disc that is already in use will destroy any data it contains.
To format drive D: use this command:

format D:

This will bring up a warning to the effect that all data in drive D: will be
lost if you proceed with the format. As yet there is no data to lose, so
answer yes to proceed with the formatting. It might take several minutes
to complete the task, since there are a large number of tracks to be
processed and checked. If the hard disc has more than one partition
and is operating as drive D:, drive E:, etc., each partition must formatted
using a separate "FORMAT" command. To format drive F: for example,
this command would be used:

format F:

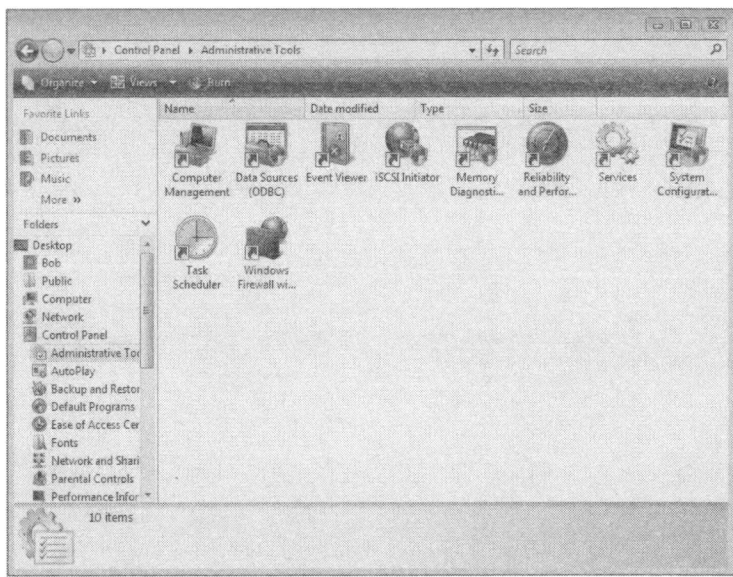

Fig.4.27 The Administrative Tools window

The new hard disc drive should then be fully operational, and it should appear in My Computer, etc., if you boot the computer in Safe Mode. The files you wish to rescue can then be copied to the new drive using Windows Explorer with Copy and Paste facilities. Windows Vista is then installed from scratch onto the original hard disc and the rescued files can then be copied back to this drive. As pointed out previously, it is not possible to install Windows Vista onto a hard disc drive that is formatted using FAT32, but a FAT32 hard disc drive will work fine as a simple data disc. Consequently, with this method it is necessary to back up the data files onto the new disc and reinstall Windows Vista on the old disc. Installing Vista on the new disc and then copying data onto it from the old disc is not an option.

Computer Management

Partitioning and formatting from within Windows Vista is achieved with the aid of the Computer Management utility, which is essentially the same as the equivalent function in Windows XP. This can be run by going to the Windows Control Panel and double-clicking the Administrative Tools

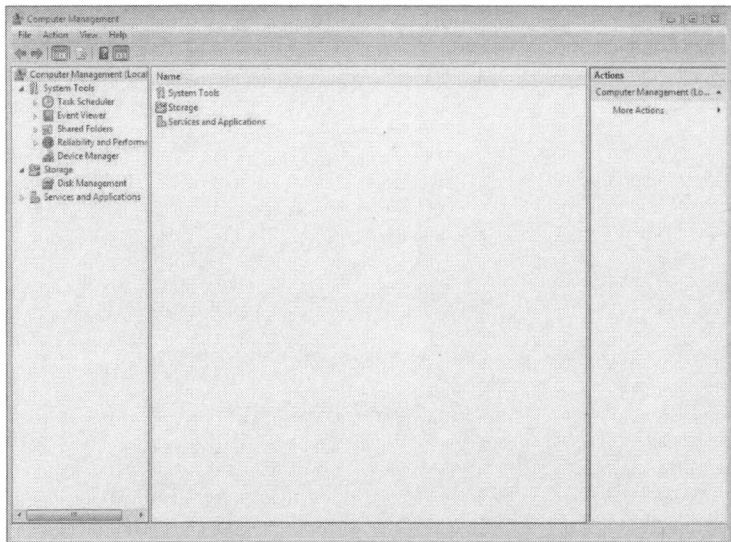

Fig.4.28 The Computer Management window gives access to several utilities

icon. This produces a window like the one of Figure 4.27, and double-clicking the Computer Management icon produces the new window of Figure 4.28. Several utilities are available from the Computer Management window, but the one required in this case is Disk Management. Left-clicking this entry in the left-hand panel changes the window to look something like Figure 4.29.

Details of the boot drive are given at the top of the right-hand panel, and in this example another disc is also listed. The second drive is actually a Compact Flash card in a USB card reader, but in Windows it is used as a removable FAT32 hard disc drive. The bottom section gives details of both drives, and the new back-up drive is Disk 0. In most cases the main (boot) drive will be Disk 0 and the new disk will be Disk 1, but there can be exceptions, as in this case, due to the way the disc interfaces are arranged.

The new drive is described as "Unallocated", which means that it is not partitioned or formatted at this stage. The black line to the right of the Disk 0 label and icon also indicates that it is not partitioned. To partition the disc, right-click on the black line and then select the New Simple Volume option from the popup menu. This launches the New Partition

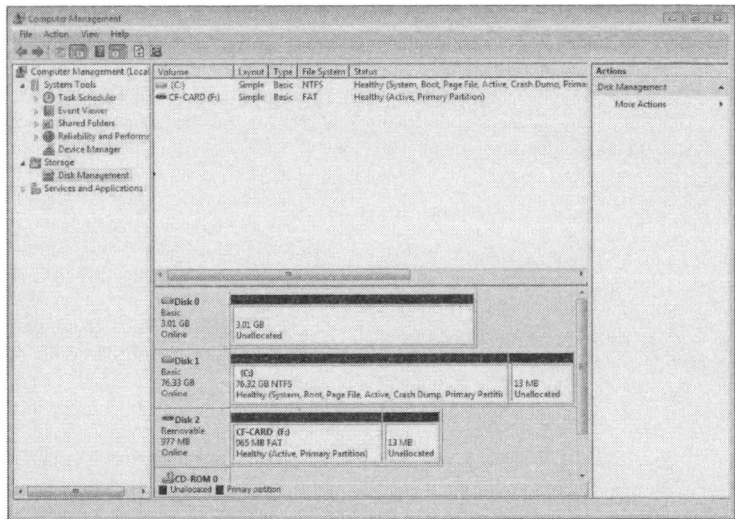

Fig.4.29 The Disk Management utility

Fig.4.30 The opening screen of the New Simple Volume Wizard

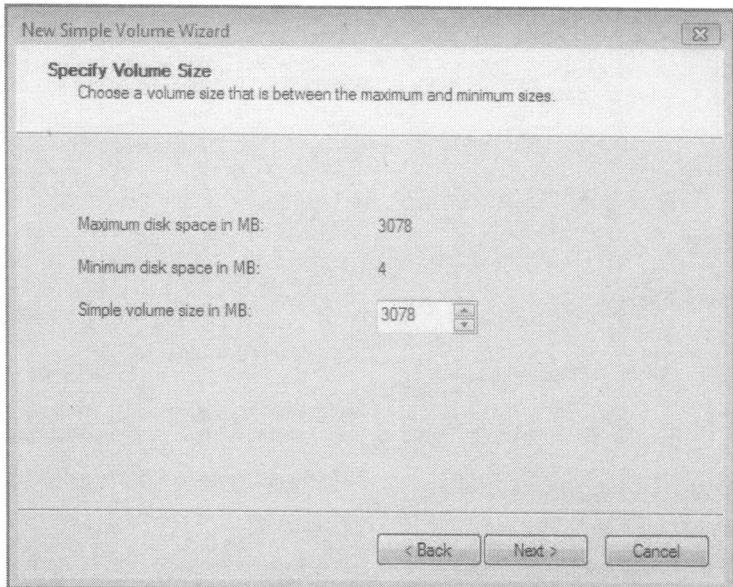

Fig.4.31 This window is used to set the partition size (in megabytes)

Simple Volume wizard (Figure 4.30). Windows Vista can handle sophisticated hard disc setups when suitable hardware is present, but for simple back-up purposes a basic disc is perfectly adequate.

The size of the partition is selected at the next window (Figure 4.31), and the maximum and minimum usable sizes are indicated. All the available disc space will be used by default, but a different size can be used by typing a value (in megabytes) into the textbox. It is probably best to simply have one large partition unless the disc has a very high capacity. You might then prefer to divide it into a few smaller and more manageable partitions. Operating the Next button brings up the window of Figure 4.32 where a drive letter is assigned to the new partition. Unless there is a good reason to do otherwise, simply accept the default drive letter.

At the next window (Figure 4.33) you have the choice of formatting the new partition or leaving it unformatted. Since the partition will not be usable until it is formatted, accept the formatting option. One of the menus offers a choice of FAT, FAT32, or NTFS formatting. Settle for the default option of NTFS formatting unless you need compatibility with another Windows operating system. Note that the Windows Vista version

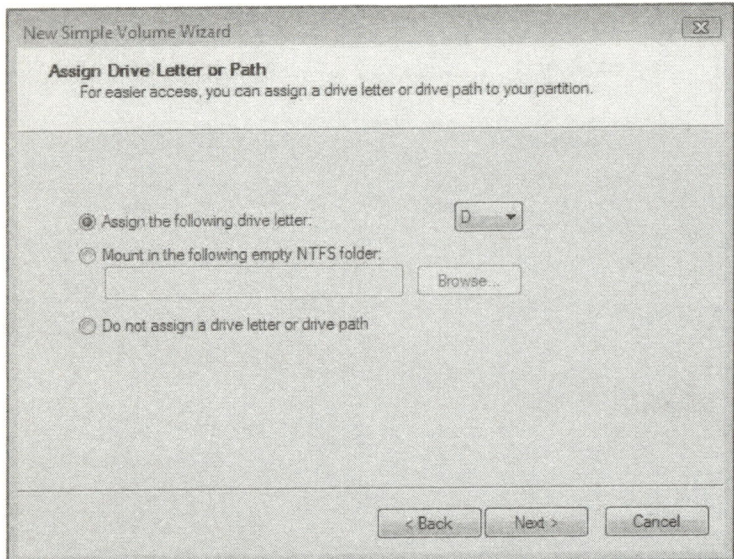

Fig.4.32 Here a drive letter is assigned to the new partition

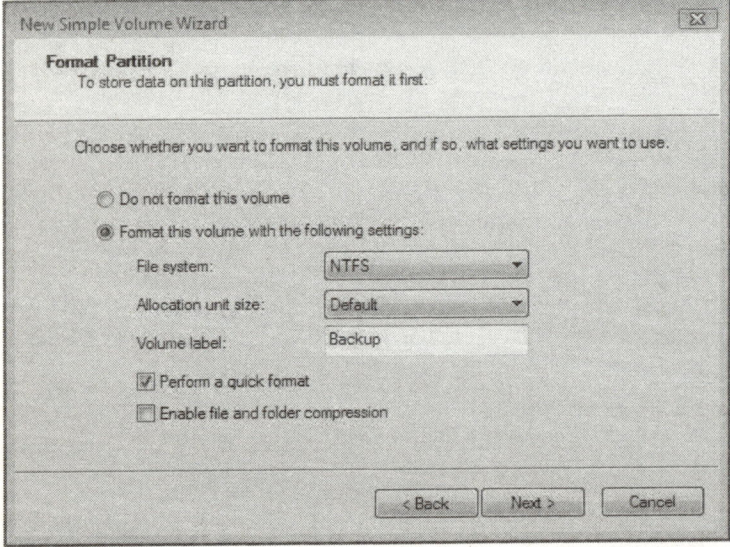

Fig.4.33 The partition can be formatted as a NTFS, FAT, or FAT32 type

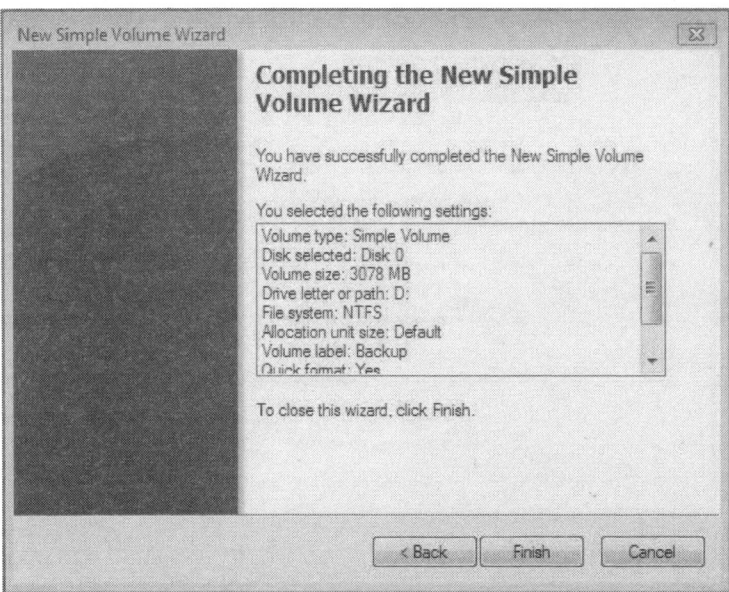

Fig.4.34 This window lists all the parameters that have been selected

of the FAT file system is not compatible with earlier versions of Windows. Settle for the default allocation unit size, which will be one that is appropriate for the partition size. A different name for the drive, such as "Backup", can be entered into the textbox if desired.

Tick the appropriate checkbox if the capacity of the disc is barely adequate to backup your files, and you wish to enable file and folder compression. The Quick Format option, as its name implies, performs the formatting more quickly than when using the standard type. The increased speed is obtained by not erasing any existing data on the disc. The formatting puts a new file table in place, but that is all. Normal formatting can be very time consuming when large discs are involved, so it is advisable to use the Quick Format option unless there is a good reason for not doing so. Left-click the Next button when you are satisfied with the settings.

The next window (Figure 4.34) lists all the parameters that have been selected, and provides an opportunity to change your mind or correct mistakes. If necessary, use the Back button to return to earlier windows and change some of the settings. Operate the Finish button if all the

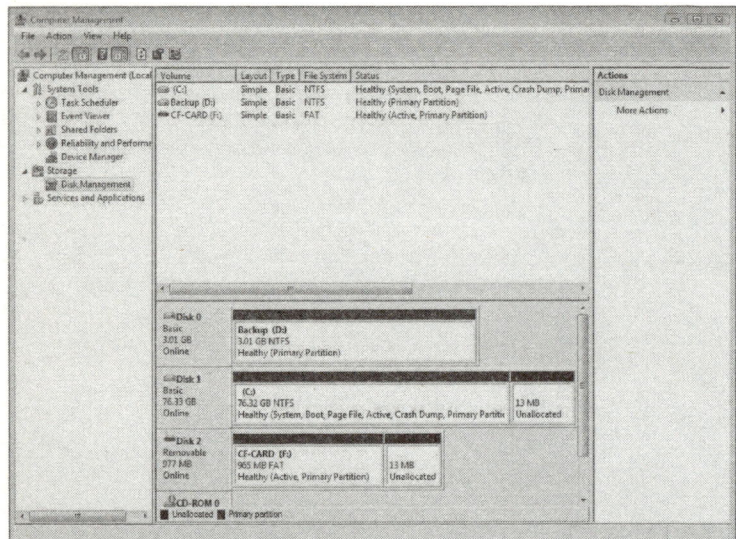

Fig.4.35 The Disk Management window shows the new partition

settings are correct. The partition will then be created, and it will appear as a blue line in the Disk Management window. It will then be formatted, and this may take half an hour or more for a large partition. The area below the blue line indicates how far the formatting process has progressed. Eventually the formatting will be completed, and the Disk Management window will show the new disc as containing a primary partition using the appropriate file system (Figure 4.35). Once the formatting has been completed, files on the main drive can be copied to the new partition using the Cut and Paste facilities of Windows Explorer.

If space has been left for a further partition on the disc, right-click on the black section of the line that represents the vacant disc space. Then select the New Simple Volume option from the pop-up menu, and go through the whole partitioning and formatting process again. A maximum of four primary partitions can be used on each physical disc.

Points to remember

Do not wait until things go wrong before backing up data. It should be possible to rescue your data if the operating system becomes seriously damaged, but it might be expensive to have it rescued from a faulty hard drive.

Data rescue services are available, but there is no guarantee that data will be retrievable from a damaged hard drive.

Not all back-up devices will work with Windows in Safe Mode or in MS-DOS. Lack of operation in either of these modes does not render a back-up device useless, but life is easier when using a more accommodating drive. An NTFS partition is "invisible" to the system if the computer is booted into MS-DOS.

If you find yourself with a Windows installation that seems to be impossible to repair, and no usable device to back-up masses of important data, there are three options. Carry on trying to repair Windows for as long as it takes, abandon your data and reinstall Windows from scratch, or add a suitable back-up device so that the data can be rescued prior to reinstalling Windows.

Another hard drive is the most practical option when disaster has struck and an emergency backup of data is required. These days a hard disc drive is a relatively cheap back-up option that will work in both Safe Mode and MS/DOS since it is a standard MS-DOS and Windows drive. Hard discs are also relatively fast in operation.

A modern PC can have at least four IDE drives (hard discs, CD-ROM drives, etc.) and will usually be able to accept an additional hard drive. If necessary, you can temporarily disconnect a CD-ROM drive to make way for the back-up drive.

If the PC will not even boot into Safe Mode, probably the best rescue method is to add a new hard drive as disc C: and have the original hard disc as drive D:. In other words, set the new drive as the primary master and the original drive as the primary slave. Install Windows Vista onto the new drive and then copy your data from the old drive.

A hard disc drive has to be partitioned and then high-level formatted before it is ready for use. This can be done using a Windows 9x Startup disc and the FDISK and FORMAT commands if a FAT32 disc is required. This is the best method for FAT32 discs having a capacity of 32 megabytes or more. FDISK must be used even if the disc will be organised as one large partition. No low-level formatting is required with a modern hard disc drive, since this formatting is done at the factory.

The Windows Vista Disk Management utility can be used to create partitions and format them using the FAT, FAT32, and NTFS file systems. However, this utility is only available if the computer can be booted into Windows Vista, either normally or in Safe Mode.

Proper back-up software can be used to back up your data, but Windows Explorer enables data to be easily copied from one drive to another. Complete directory structures can be copied using the Copy and Paste facilities and the usual dragging techniques.

Back up and restore

Back-up?

Using the methods outlined in the previous chapter it is possible to recover data from the hard disc when there is a serious problem with the operating system. Using a data recovery service it might even be possible to recover data from a faulty hard disc, albeit at a price. It is definitely advisable to avoid putting yourself into a situation where emergency measures have to be taken in order to avoid the loss of vital data, and this means backing up any important data. Of course, it you use a PC purely for pleasure and do not have any important data to back up, there will probably be little point in going to the trouble of backing up the hard disc. In the event of a serious problem everything can be reinstalled and there is no important data to lose.

These days most computer users are not dabblers, and their PCs are put to good uses. This means that important data is usually generated, and generated in large quantities. Whether it is family photographs from a digital camera, the company accounts, or your latest novel, most PCs contain data that is precious to the users. It makes sense to produce back-up copies of this data, even if it does involve a certain amount of time and expense.

Better save than sorry

If you are going to do the sensible thing and back-up important data it is not essential to use any back-up software. Having stored a file onto the hard disc using the SAVE function of the application software you can simply select SAVE AS and store it again on another drive, such as a ZIP drive or CD writer. This method enables data files to be restored to the hard disc using Windows Explorer if a major failure of some kind should occur, but it does not allow the operating system to be restored. Neither will it restore any of your applications software or any customisation of that software. If the hard disc has to be replaced or the operating system becomes seriously damaged, the operating system has to be reinstalled, the applications programs are then installed again, and finally the data files are restored.

This is not a particularly quick or neat way of doing things, but for most users it will get the PC fully operational again in a reasonable amount of time. It has the advantage that it requires a minimal amount of time to maintain the back-up copies, since only data files are being copied. As pointed out in previous chapters, it also gives you a "clean" copy of Windows that should operate quickly and efficiently. There are actually back-up programs that will automatically make copies of data files, but these are probably only a worthwhile proposition if you are producing large numbers of data files.

If you use applications that only generate small amounts of data, an ordinary floppy disc drive is adequate for making back-up copies as you generate them. Unfortunately, modern application programs tend to generate large amounts of data. With a relatively simple application such as word processing the amounts of data generated might be reasonably small, but software such as graphics and desktop publishing programs usually produce large amounts of data. The folder used to store the files for this book will probably contain something like 500 megabytes of data by the time the book is finished. Backing up data requires some form of mass storage device when large files or large amounts of small files are involved.

Back-up software

For anything beyond backing up data files it is best to resort to some sort of back-up program. With these it is possible to save selected directories or directory structures, or the entire contents of the hard disc drive. I think I am correct in stating that every version of Windows is supplied complete with a back-up program that has the imaginative name of Backup. Although basic compared to some programs of this type it does the job well enough for most users. Its lack of popularity possibly stems from the fact that the equivalent facility in Windows 3.1 was something less than user friendly, causing many users to look elsewhere for a back-up utility.

Perhaps the problem is simply that the Backup program is a part of Windows that has often been easy to overlook. Anyway, the standard Windows Vista version is more user-friendly and powerful than some of

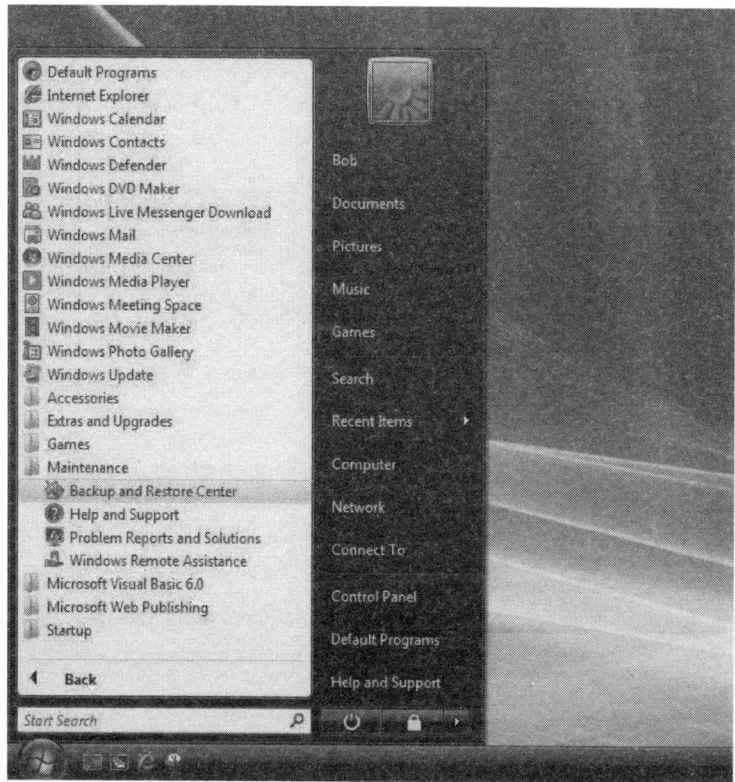

Fig.5.1   The Backup and Restore Center is accessed via the Start
menu

its predecessors. In the case of the more expensive versions of Vista
there are additional back-up facilities if you seek them out. Although the
mid-range and basic versions of Vista lack these additional back-up
features, including any form of complete backup facility, they still adequate
back-up facilities for most purposes. Keeping back-up copies of your
data files is certainly very easy with the standard Windows Vista Backup
and Restore utility.

Automatic back-up

An advantage of the standard back-up and restore feature of Windows
Vista is that it can be set to operate automatically, backing up your data

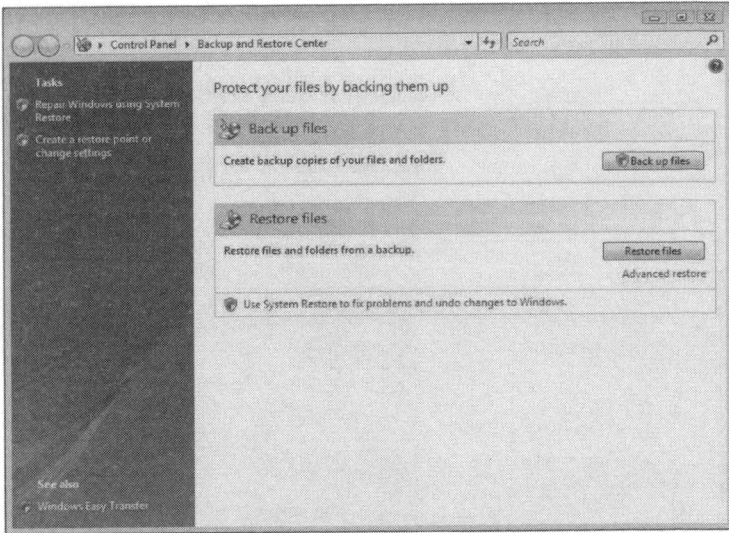

Fig.5.2   The initial windows of the Backup and Restore Center

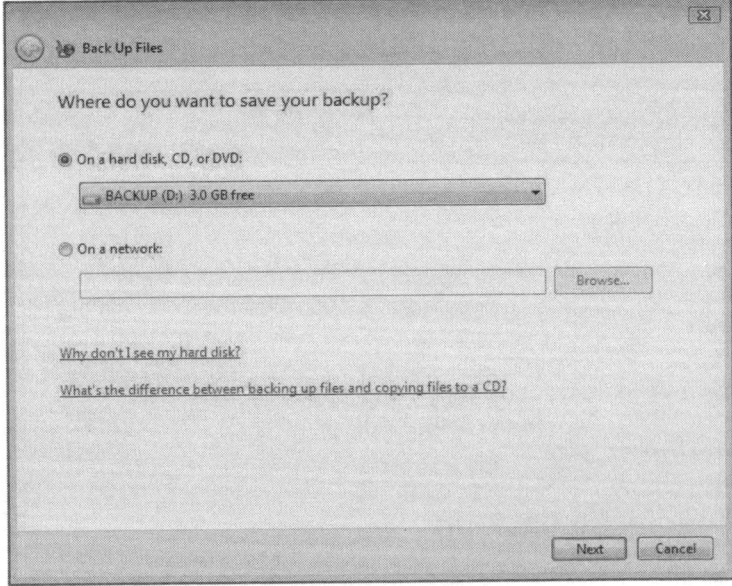

Fig.5.3   This window is effectively the first one of a wizard

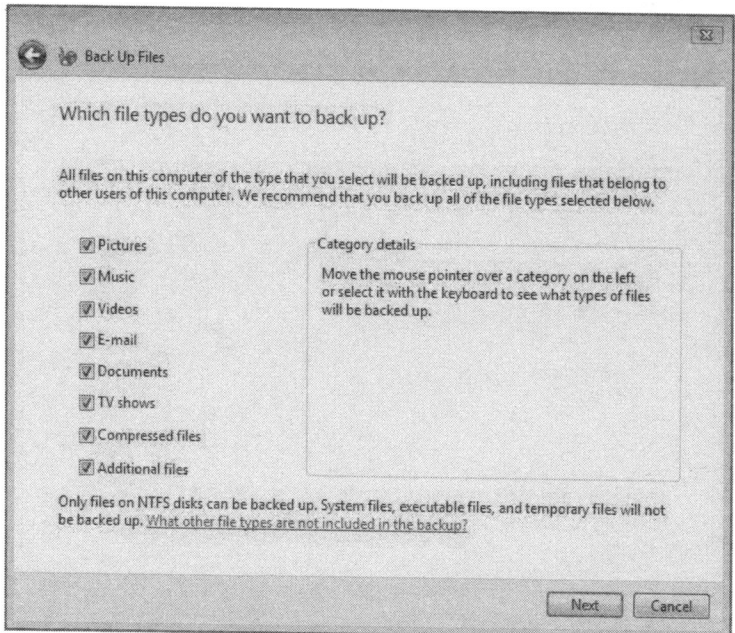

Fig.5.4 You can not select folders for inclusion in the backup, but you can choose general file types

once per week or every day. The Backup and Restore program is run by selecting Programs from the Start menu, followed by Maintenance, and then Backup and Restore Center (Figure 5.1). This launches a new window (Figure 5.2) that has buttons to select either the Backup facility or the Restore type. Of course, as yet there is no back-up to restore and it is the Backup button that is operated.

This launches another window (Figure 5.3), which is effectively a wizard that is used to select the correct back-up options. A disc drive will be used as the default back-up location, and it is possible to use a different drive by using the upper drop-down menu. Assuming the PC is on a network, it is possible to use a network location by selecting the lower radio button and then using the Browse function to locate and select the appropriate network folder or drive. For this example a small hard disc drive is being used as the back-up device.

At the next window (Figure 5.4) you use the checkboxes to select the types of data file that you wish to back up. This has to be regarded as a

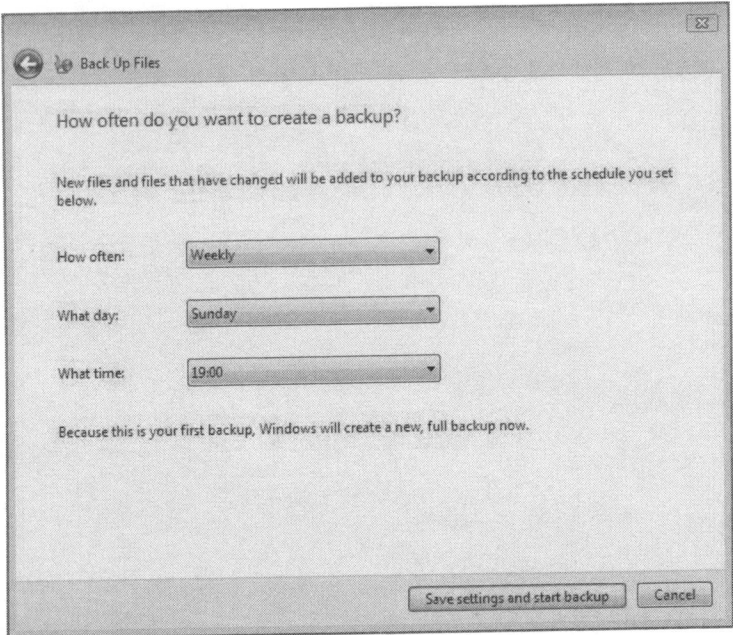

Fig.5.5 Choose the time, day, and frequency of automatic backups

weakness of the Vista Backup and Restore feature. It is very simple in that you simply tick the boxes for the types of data file you wish to back-up, or simply settle for the default arrangement and back-up all data files.

Unfortunately, this method is very limiting in that it is not possible to select folders that you wish to back-up. If you decide to include (say) music files, the program will back-up any music files that it finds on a hard disc drive. This could be the action you require, but there is no alternative if it would be better to back-up music files in certain folders while not bothering with those in others. You can sometimes find that the program finds huge quantities of files, many of which are not important enough to warrant inclusion in the back-up process.

Before starting the initial backup it is then just a matter of selecting the starting time and frequency of automatic backups (Figure 5.5). Choose the start time carefully, since the backup can not be started automatically unless the computer is switched on and running in Windows at the selected time. If you opt for a weekly backup, the day of the week and

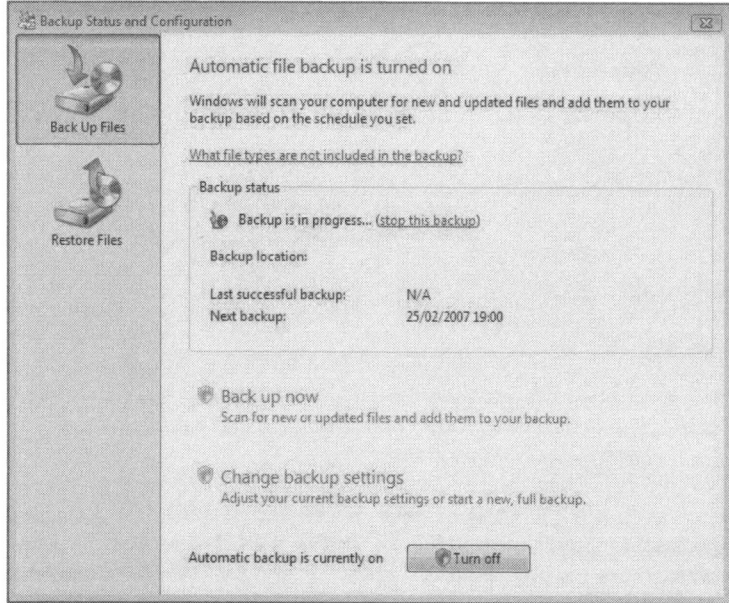

Fig.5.6 The backup has started

the start time must both be specified. Where the computer is used for work purposes, and it is used practically every day, it is important to opt for daily backups. Using a weekly backup runs the risk of losing practically a whole week's work. Bear in mind that removable discs can only be used for automatic backups if there is a suitable disc in the drive at the start time. Also, multi-disc sets can only be used if there will be someone present to undertake the disc changes.

The backup is then started by operating the large button near the bottom of the window. The original window then shows that the backup is in progress (Figure 5.6). A small window containing a bargraph will probably appear, and in standard Windows fashion this will show how things are progressing. This should eventually indicate that the process has been completed successfully (Figure 5.7). The progress window will look like Figure 5.8 (with a red bar instead of a green one) if an error occurs, such as the back-up drive having too little capacity.

You do not have to use the automatic back-up facility, and it is not switched on by default. It is easy to switch it off if you set up the computer to use

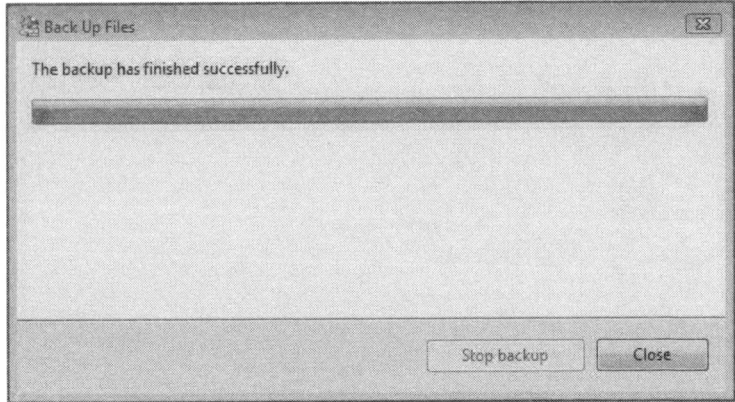

Fig.5.7 Eventually this window should indicate that the backup has
been completed successfully

this feature and then change your mind. Just go back to the Backup
and Restore Center and operate the Change settings link. This produces
a window like the one shown in Figure 5.9, and it is then just a matter of
operating the Turn Off button near the bottom of the screen. The Backup
Now facility can be used to manually start a backup at any time.

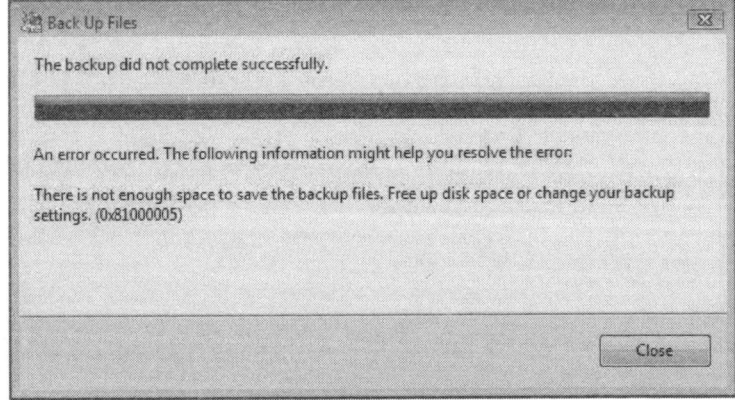

Fig.5.8 This window will appear if an error has occurred, such as there
being inadequate disc space available

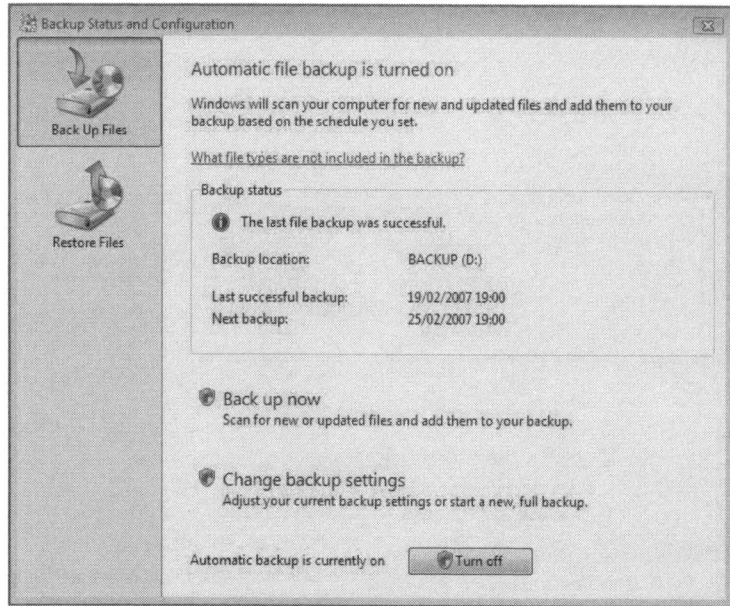

Fig.5.9 Automatic backups can be turned off

Restoring

If the worst should happen and it becomes necessary to restore lost files, the process is very straightforward. Launch the Backup and Restore Center and then operate the Restore Files button. This produces the new window of Figure 5.10, which is effectively the first section of a wizard that guides you through the restoration process. It gives the option of restoring files from the latest back-up archive or a previous one, and in most cases it is merely necessary to settle for the default setting. This will restore files from the latest back-up archive.

The next task is to select the files or folders to be restored (Figure 5.11). If you need to restore all the data files, or most of them, you can use the Select Folders button to launch the usual folder browser, and then use this to select the drive that was backed up. Similarly, you can use the Select Files button to launch the standard file browser and then select the files that are to be restored. Of course, selecting individual files is only possible in cases where a file has been damaged but is still on the

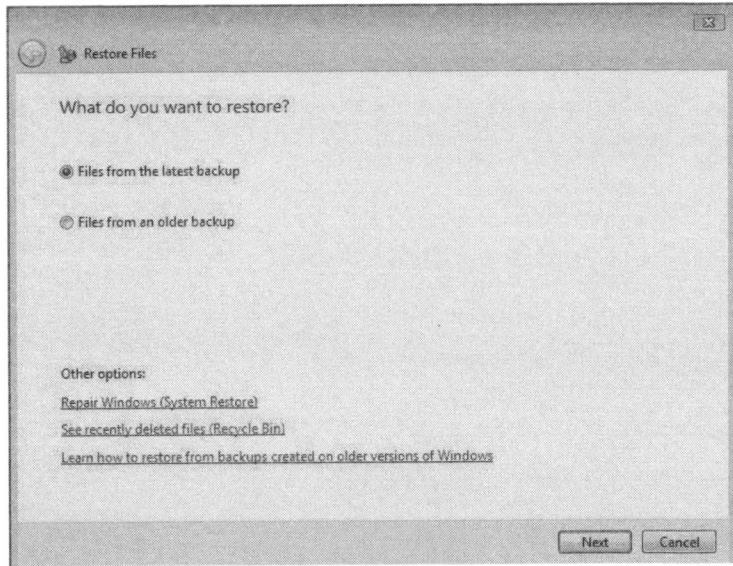

Fig.5.10 *The first screen of the restoration wizard*

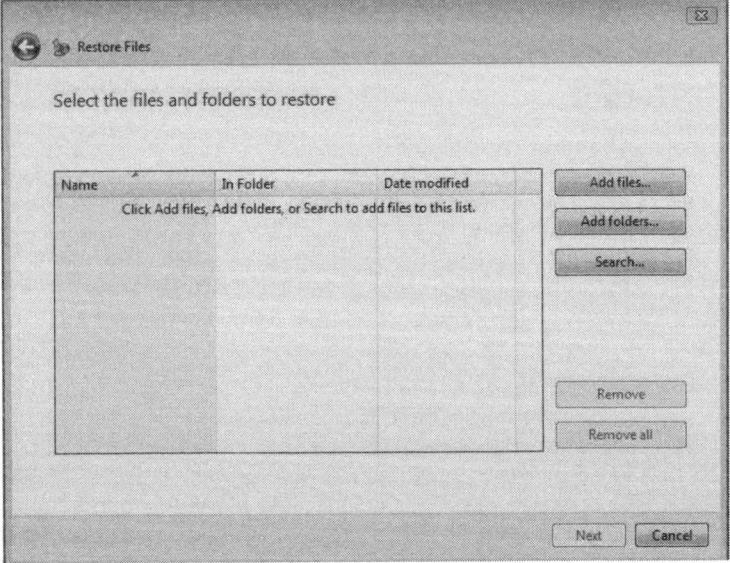

Fig.5.11 *Select the files or folders to be restored*

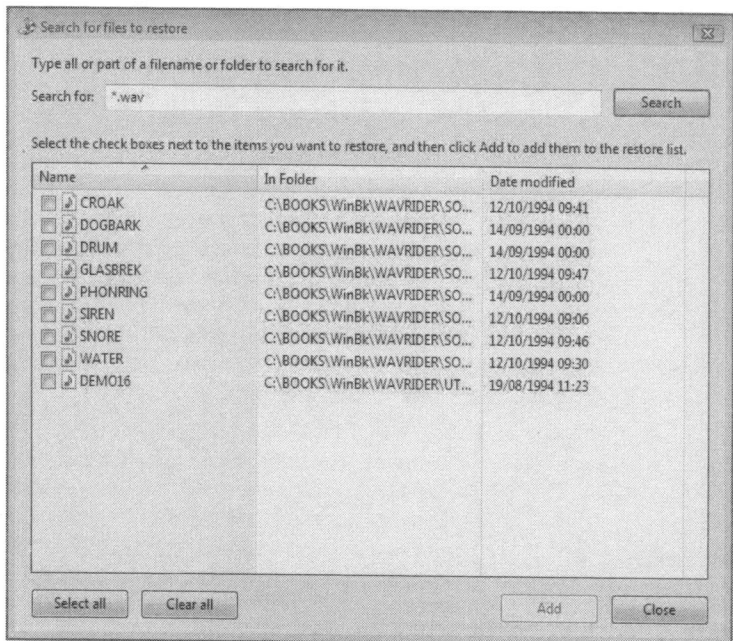

Fig.5.12 The result of a search for WAV music files

hard disc drive. It is then possible to use the Restore facility to replace the damaged file with the version stored in the back-up archive.

Using the Search facility it is possible to use the normal Windows search facilities to seek out individual files of types of file on the hard disc drive. In the example of Figure 5.12 I have used "*.wav" as the search string, and this has resulted in a number of sound files with a "wav" extension being located. In order to select files for restoration it is just a matter of ticking their checkboxes and operating the Add button. Although it is not possible to search the back-up archive for a file that you wish to restore, this system does provide a roundabout method of restoring a specific or files.

For this example I simply selected drive C (Figure 5.13) and then moved on to the next window (Figure 5.14). The files will be placed in their original location by default, but the lower radio button gives the option of restoring them to a specified location. In most cases you will probably need the files returned to their original locations on the hard disc drive.

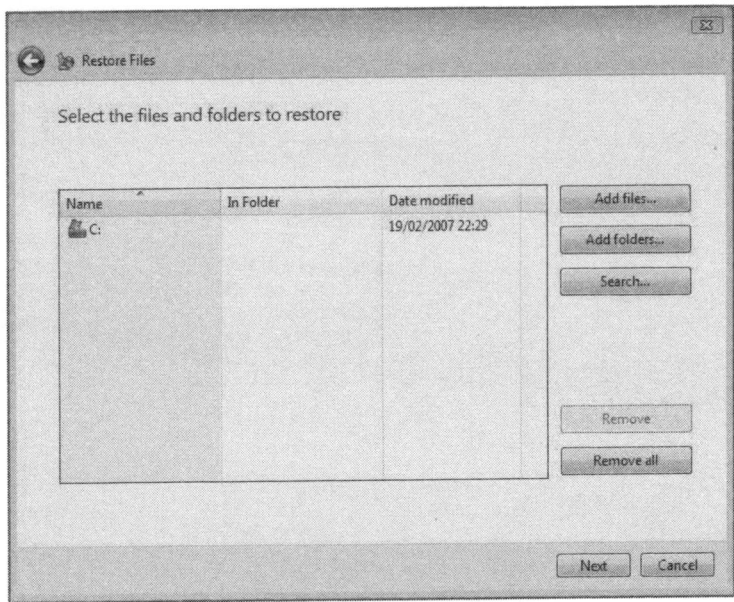

Fig.5.13 For this example drive C has been selected

However, this will result in any existing versions of the files being overwritten by the restored versions. A different location must be selected if you would prefer to restore files from the backup while leaving any existing files intact.

Having selected the required options it is then just a matter of operating the Start Restore button. The program will provide a warning if an existing file is about to be overwritten (Figure 5.15). You then have the option of going ahead and overwriting it or cancelling the restoration of that file. There is also the option of restoring the file and keeping the original. With this option the restored file has "(2)" added to the main part of the filename. For instance, music file called "piece45.mp3" would be renamed "piece45 (2).mp3".

Where a large number of existing files are being restored it is not very practical to go through this process for each file. Provided you require all duplicate files to be treated in the same fashion, it is just a matter of ticking the checkbox at the bottom of the window and then selecting the required action. Any further duplicate files that the program encounters

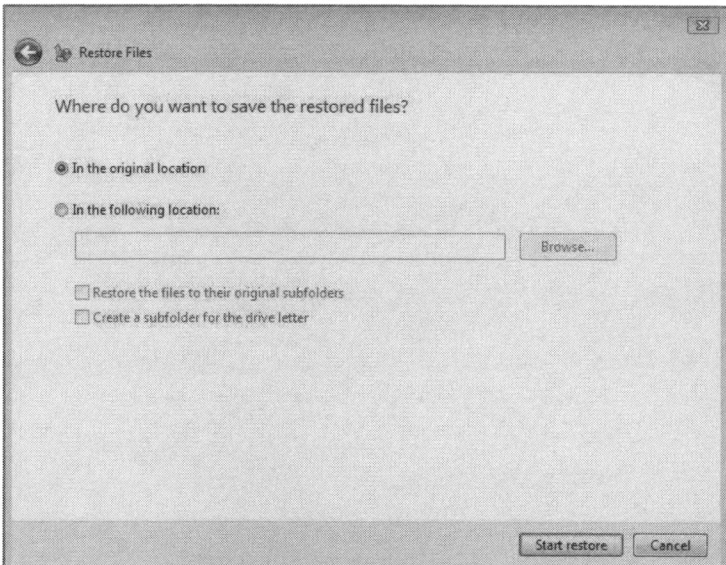

Fig.5.14 Files can be restored to a specified location

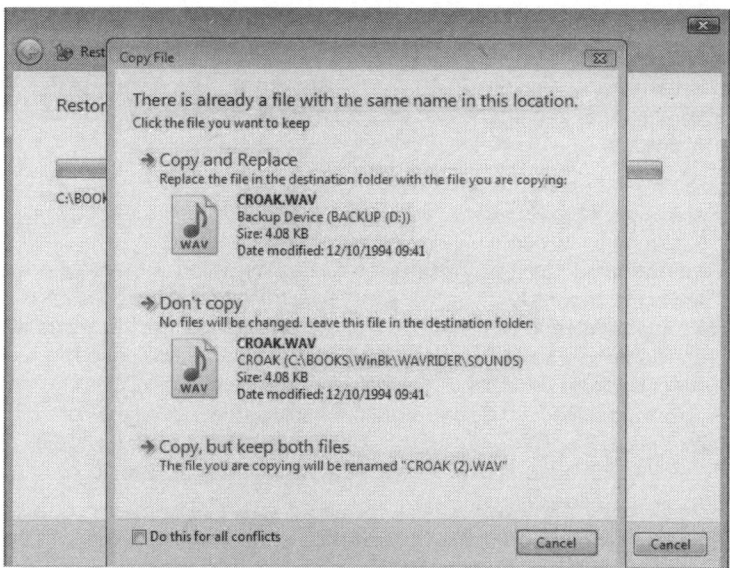

Fig.5.15 A warning is given if a file is about to be overwritten

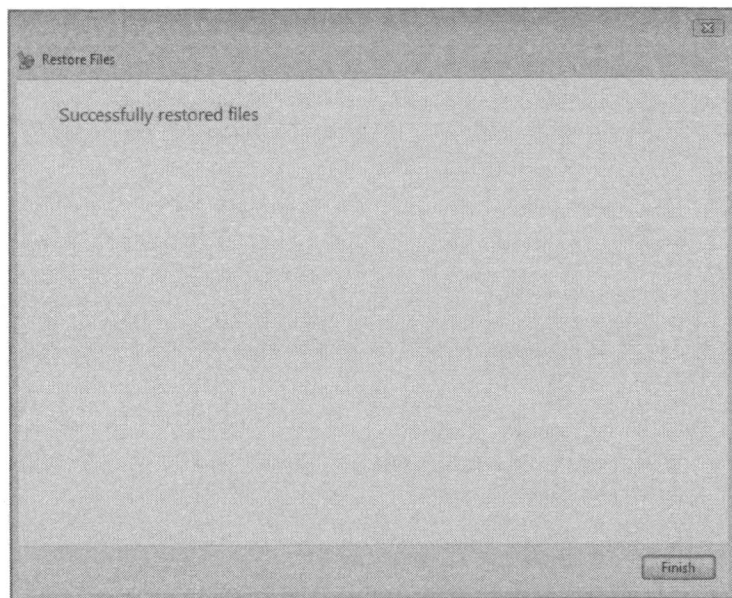

Fig.5.16 The restoration has been completed successfully

will then be automatically treated in the same way. The window of Figure 5.16 will appear when the file restoration process has been completed successfully.

System Restore

Windows Vista has a very useful rescue facility called System Restore. This is not a new feature, and it is essentially the same as the one featured in Windows ME and Windows XP. It has to be emphasised that this is not a conventional backup/restore program, and it can not be used to make a set of back-up discs for use in the event of a hard disc failure. System Restore uses the hard disc to store the back-up files, and if the hard disc fails, the back-up files are inaccessible. It only makes back-up copies of system and program files that are deleted or changed, and no back-up copies are made of most files.

System Restore is designed specifically to deal with problems in the operating system. The normal Backup and Restore programs are used

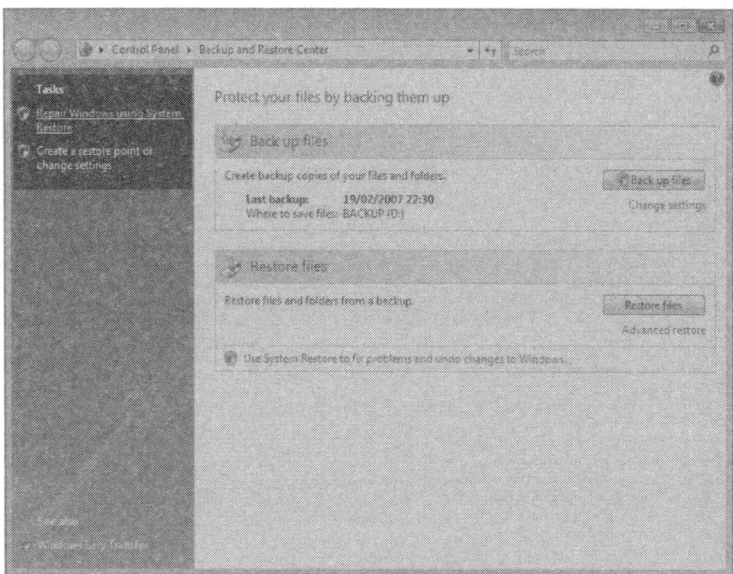

Fig.5.17 The links near the top left-hand corner of the window enable the System Restore feature to be accessed

to deal with hard disc failures. The purpose of System Restore is to take the system back to a previous configuration that worked. If there is a problem with the current configuration, taking the system back to a previous state should cure the problem. System or program files that have been deleted or changed since the restoration date are returned to their previous state, and any files that have been added are deleted. Strictly speaking, System Restore is a program that will work around operating system problems rather than fix them. It will often provide a quick fix, but you have to be careful not to reintroduce the problem.

The general idea is to periodically add new restoration points so that if something should subsequently go wrong with the operating system, it can be taken back to a recent restore point. Incidentally, Windows adds restoration points periodically, so it is not essential to routinely add your own. The main reason for adding your own restoration points is that there is increased likelihood of problems occurring.

The most common example of this is adding a restore point prior to installing new software. If anything should go horribly wrong during the installation process, going back to the restoration point should remove

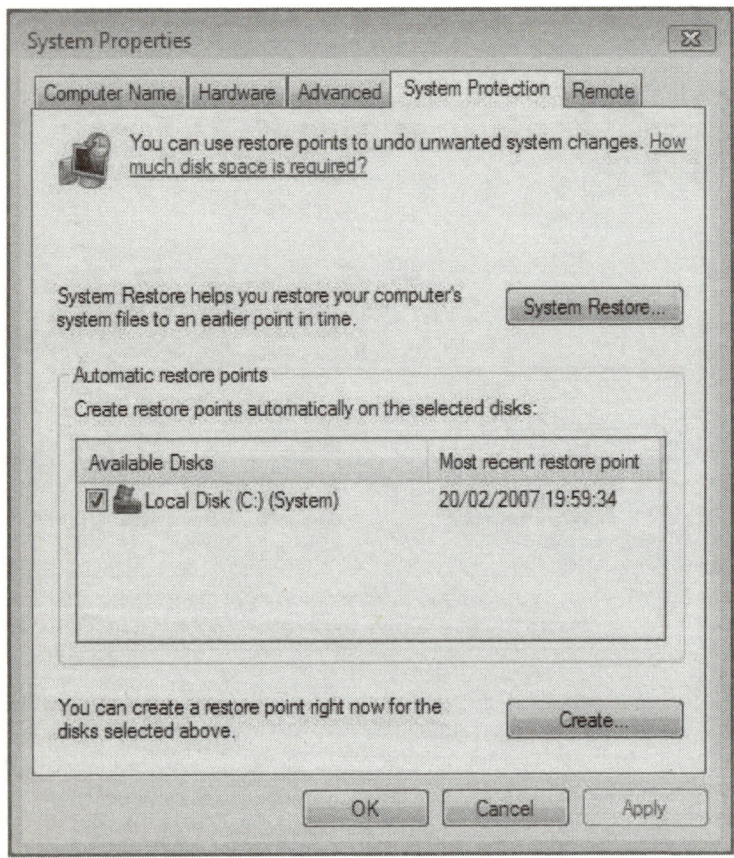

Fig.5.18 The System Protection section of the properties window

the rogue program and fix the problem with the operating system. You can then contact the software publisher to find a cure to the problem, and in the mean time your PC should still be functioning properly. It is also worth adding a restoration point prior to adding or removing new hardware. This provides a way back to normality if adding or removing the device drivers has dire consequences for the Windows installation.

When going back to a restoration point the program should remove any recently added programs, but it should leave recently produced data files intact. Of course, with any valuable data that has not been backed

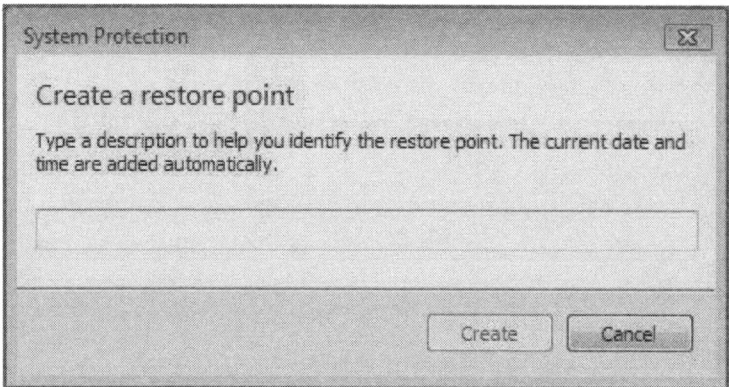

Fig.5.19 Add a meaninful name for the restoration point

up already, it would be prudent to make back-up copies before using System Restore, just in case things do not go according to plan. The program does itself does provide a way around this sort of problem in that it does permit a restoration to be undone. If a valuable data file should vanish "into thin air" it should be possible to return the PC to its original configuration, back-up the restored data, and then go back to the restoration point again. System Restore only backs up and restores system and program files, so it is unlikely to be responsible for data files going "absent without leave".

Create

With Windows Vista the System Restore program can be accessed by the two links near the top right-hand corner of the main Backup and Restore Center window (Figure 5.17). The lower link is used when creating a restoration point or making changes to the System Restore settings. Selecting this option launches the System Properties window and automatically selects the System Protection section (Figure 5.18). In the unlikely event that there is more than one disc that can have a restoration point, the appropriate disc must be selected from the list in the window's main panel.

A restoration point is generated by operating the Create button near the bottom of the screen and then typing a description for the restoration point into the textbox that appears (Figure 5.19). It is helpful if the name

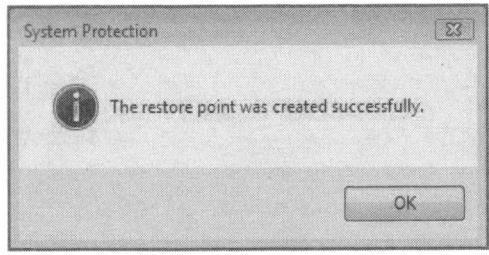

Fig.5.20 The new restoration point has been created

is something meaningful. For example, if the restoration point is added prior to installing a word processor, it could be called something like "preword". There is no need to include a date, because the program automatically records the date and time for you. Operate the Create button to go ahead and create the new restoration point. There will probably be a few seconds of frantic disc activity followed by the message of Figure 5.20, confirming that the task has been completed successfully.

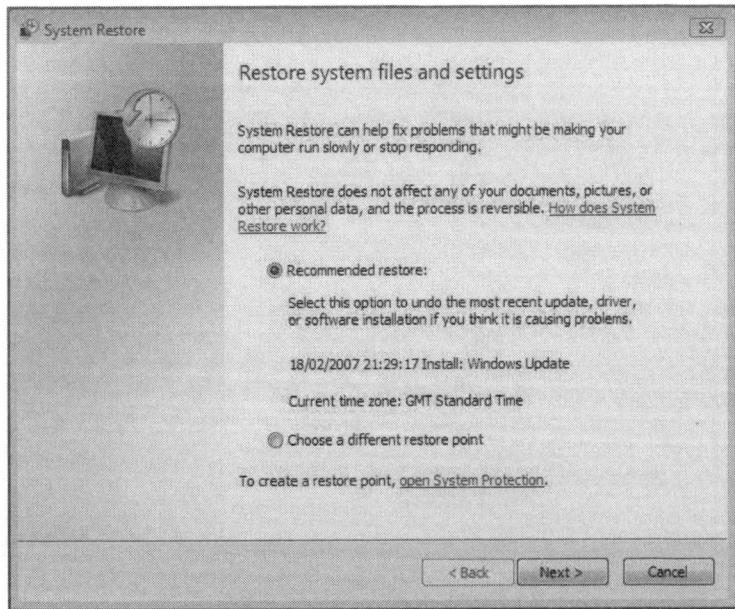

Fig.5.21 The initial window when using the System Restore program to go back to an earlier restoration point

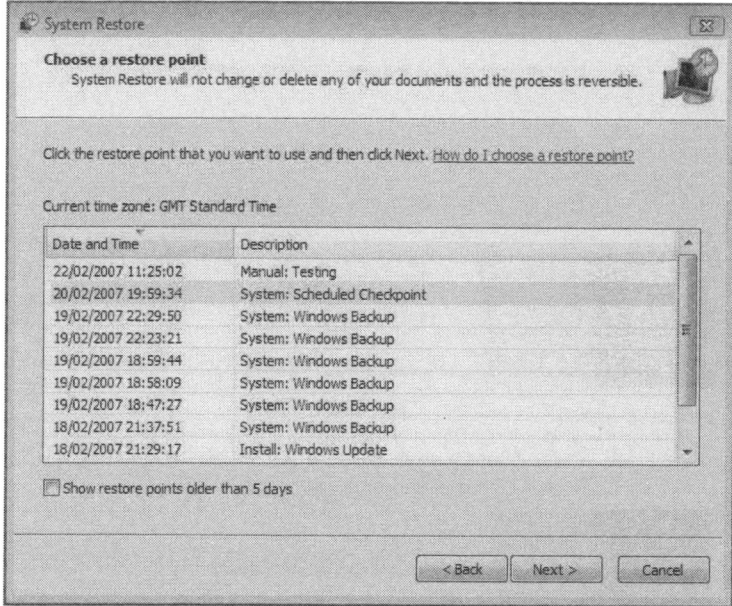

Fig.5.22 *The available restoration points are listed in this window*

It takes me back

In order to restore the system to its state at an earlier time it is necessary to run the System Restore program. This can be launched using the link in the Backup and Restore Center, or the System Restore button in the System Properties window. Either way, the initial window of the System Restore program (Figure 5.21) should appear. By default the program will select a restoration point for you. This will probably be a very recent one, and will not necessarily be one that is suitable. The lower radio button gives the option of choosing the restoration point yourself, and for the sake of this example we will assume that this method is used.

Operating the Next button moves things on to a list of the available restoration points (Figure 5.22). The list indicates whether each point was produced manually or automatically by the system. The name is included for points that have been produced manually, with the creation date and time being included for all the restoration points. Left-click the appropriate entry in the list and then operate the Next button.

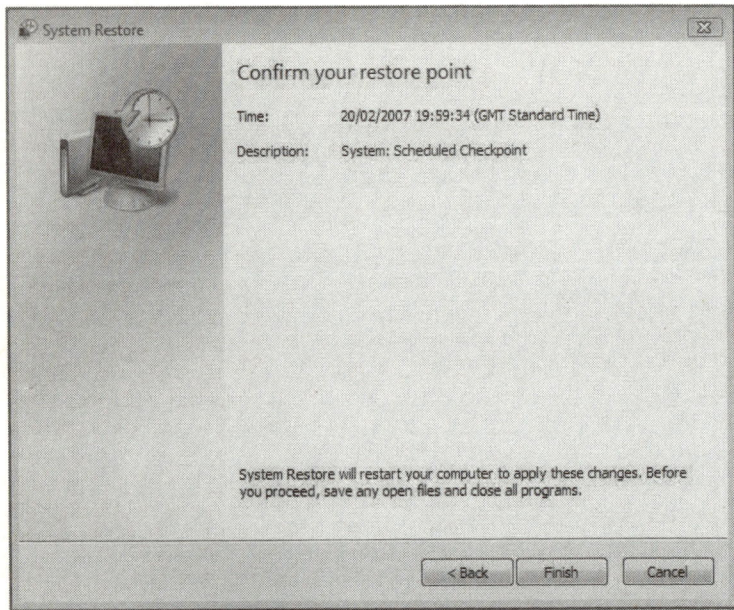

Fig.5.23 You must confirm that you wish to proceed

You are then asked to confirm that you wish to proceed using the selected restoration point (Figure 5.23). There are also some warning messages. You should heed these, and where appropriate, save your data and close any programs that are running before proceeding. Operating the Finish button produces a further warning message (Figure 5.24). This is basically just warning you not to interrupt the restoration process, which

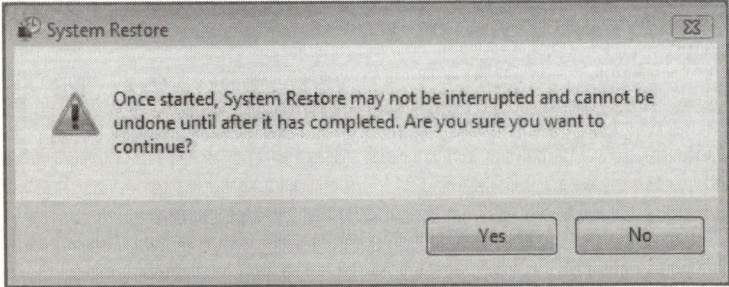

Fig.5.24 Once started, the process must not be interrupted

can not be undone until it has been completed. In other words, once you operate the Yes button you are committed to going through with the process, but you can revert to the original settings once the restoration has been completed.

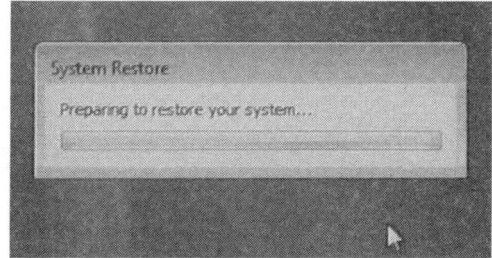

Fig.5.25 A bargraph shows how things are progressing

If you are satisfied that the correct restore point has been selected and that everything is ready, operate the Yes button and the program will begin the restoration process. A small window will then appear (Figure 5.25), indicating that the restoration process is under way. Various information screens will then appear, such as the example shown in Figure

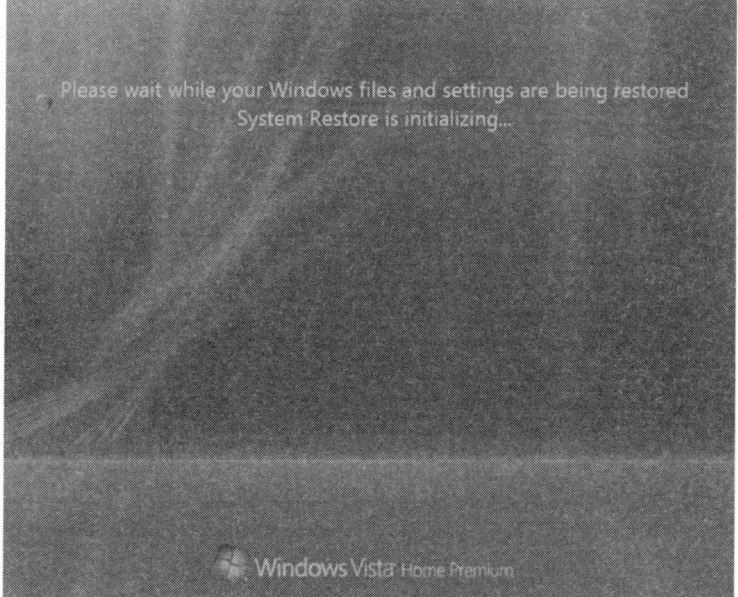

Fig.5.26 Information screens appear during the restoration process

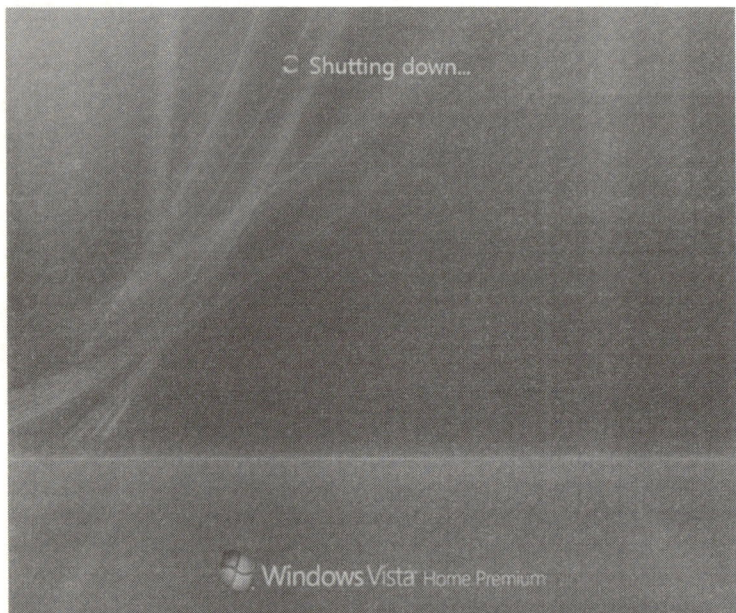

Fig.5.27 The process has been completed, and the PC will shut down

5.26. Eventually the one of Figure 5.27 will appear, and the computer will shut down Windows Vista and reboot the computer. After the normal rebooting routine you should end up back in Windows Vista with a message like the one of Figure 5.28, indicating that the restoration process has been completed successfully. It is only fair to point out that System

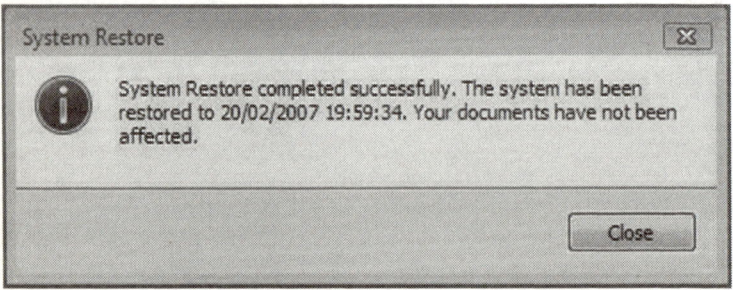

Fig.5.28 Back in Vista, this message confirms that all is well

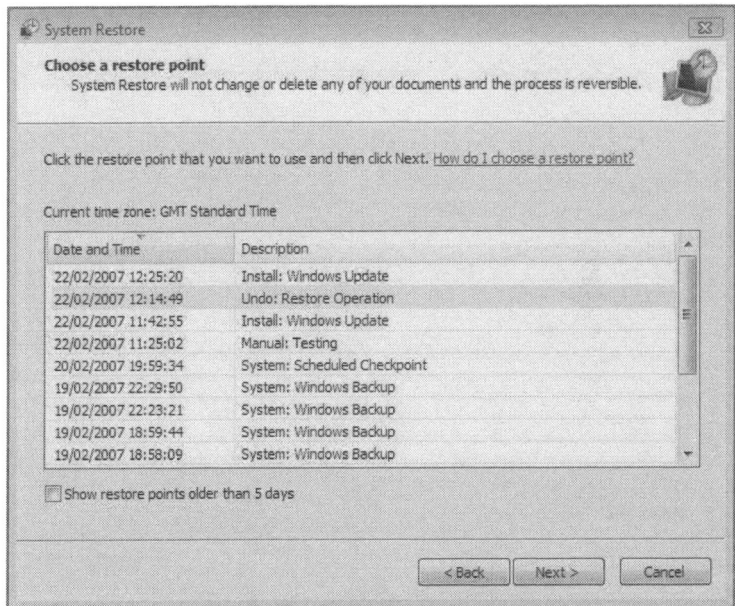

Fig.5.29 If necessary, the restoration can be undone

Restore is not infallible, and that it will not always manage to take the system back to its earlier state. It will usually manage to do so, but there will be an information screen giving details of the problem if the required restoration point is unavailable for some reason. When this occurs there is the possibility that the problem is blocking all the listed restoration points, but it will probably be worth trying one or two others to see if these give better results.

Undo

It is possible to undo a restoration once the System Restore facility has been used. There is obviously no point in doing so if the problem has been cured by taking the system back to an earlier state, but you might prefer to undo the process if it has not cured the problem or has actually made things worse. The first step is to run the System Restore program, and then opt to select your own restoration point. The list of available points should include one that will permit the restoration process to be undone, as in the example of figure 5.29. It is then just a matter of going

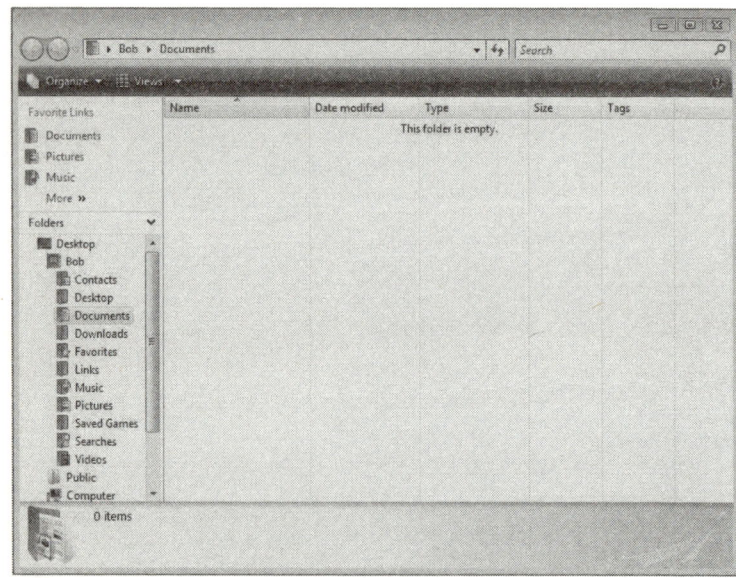

Fig.5.30 The Vista version of Windows Explorer

through the undo process, which is the same as the one used to go back to the restoration point. At the end of this process the system should have been returned to its original state.

The System Restore utility is a very worthwhile facility that can often cure problems that would otherwise be difficult to fix. The similar feature in Windows ME and XP has often proved to be very useful as a quick solution to a system that refuses to operate properly. It seems reasonable to assume that the Windows Vista version will be at least as effective. No system restoration program will ever be infallible though. As pointed out previously, some problems can prevent the System Restore program from returning the computer to an earlier configuration. In addition, there is no guarantee that returning to a restore point will cure every problem. It is probably not a good idea to use the System Restore program as a first resort if there is a problem with the operating system, but it is certainly worth a try where the problem has no simple solution. It will often have the desired effect.

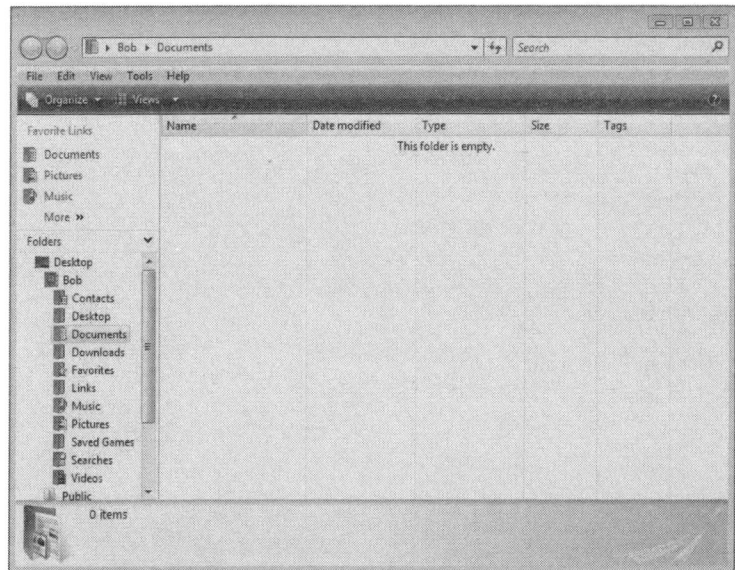

Fig.5.31 The traditional Windows Explorer menu bar can be used if preferred

System files

If Windows becomes troublesome due to a missing or damaged system file, life is a lot easier if you have a back-up copy of the file in question. One of the main causes of problems are DLL (dynamic link library) files, which are used extensively by Windows and applications programs. DLL files provide program code for frequently performed functions, such as displaying menus and dialogue boxes. Some are supplied as part of the Windows operating system, while others are loaded onto the hard disc when applications programs are installed.

Reinstalling a standard DLL file from the Windows installation disc should not be difficult, but one installed by an application program could be more difficult to replace. Firstly, you might not know which program supplied the file. The second problem is that searching the relevant CD-ROM for the file might not be successful. Files are often stored on installation discs in some form of compressed or archived form, making it difficult to locate and extract the one you require.

The DLL files are likely to be liberally spread across the hard disc, but using Windows Explorer it is easy to locate all of these files and copy

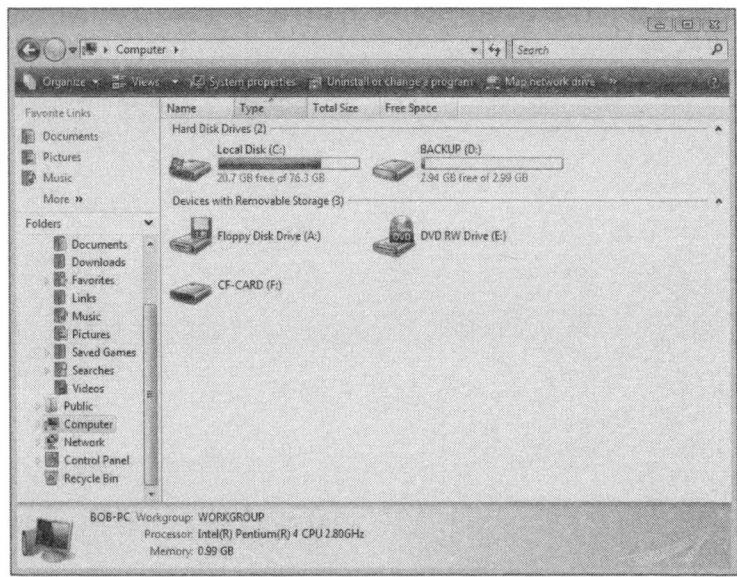

Fig.5.32 Use the program to display the installed disc drives

them to a mass storage device such as a CD or DVD writer. The amount of storage space required will vary considerably from one Windows installation to another, and the more applications that are installed the more DLL files there will be. Backing up the DLL files on one of my PCs required some 500 megabytes or so of storage space, which is probably quite typical. Since the DLL backup is intended for use when the system becomes damaged, rather than for use in the event of a hard disc failure, many users simply copy the files to a folder on the hard disc.

In order to copy the DLL files, launch Windows Explorer, which looks a little different to its predecessors in Windows XP, ME, etc. (Figure 5.30). If preferred, the traditional Windows Explorer menu bar can be added (Figure 5.31) by going to the Organise menu and selecting Layout, followed by Menu Bar from the submenu. The same menu options are used if you need to switch the menu bar off again. For the sake of this example we will assume that the new menu system is used.

The first task is to select the boot disc, which is the one that should contain all the dll files. Operate the Computer link in the left-hand column, which should produce icons for all the installed disc drives in the main

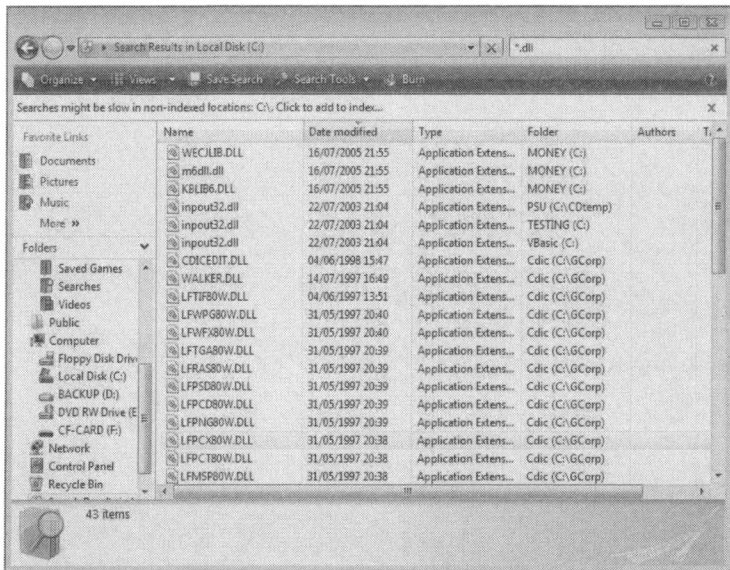

Fig.5.33 A number of DLL files are soon located

panel (Figure 3.32). Double-click the icon for the boot drive to select it. The boot drive will normally be drive C. Next enter "*.dll" in the Search textbox near the top right-hand corner of the window. The "*" character in the filename tells the search program to accept anything as the main part of the filename. Any file that has a "DLL" extension will therefore produce a match. By default the search routine will look for matches in any folders or subfolders, so it will locate all the DLL files on the boot drive. This will probably take more than a few seconds, since there will be tens of thousands of files on the boot drive. The search bar near the top of the window acts as a bargraph that shows how things are progressing, and the matching files are listed in the main panel (Figure 5.33).

Matches

Eventually the searching will be completed, with the number of matches found and the total size of all the files being indicated at the bottom of the list (Figure 5.34). I am not exaggerating when I say that there will probably be a few thousand files listed! In this example the PC has a typical hardware specification and a variety of application programs

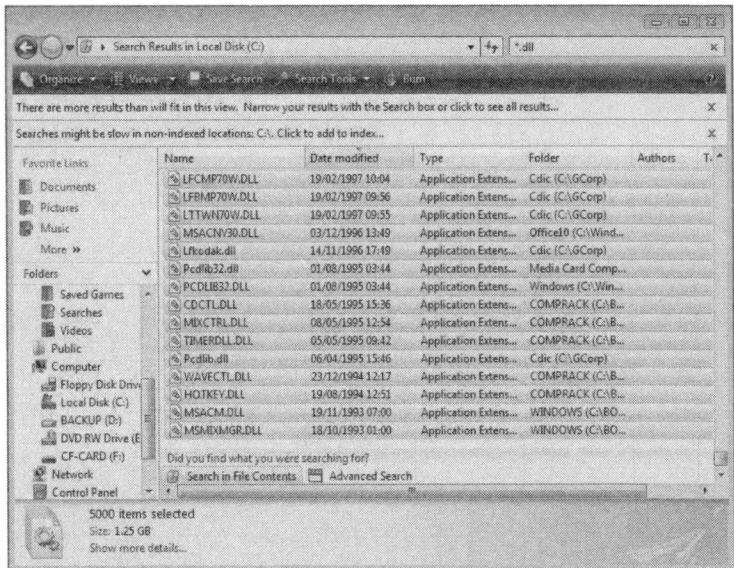

*Fig.5.34 The process has been finished, and some 5000 DLL files
have been found on drive C*

installed. The search found some 5000 files having a "DLL" extension,
with a total file size of 1.25 gigabytes! This total was undoubtedly boosted
by the remnants of an old Windows installation on the hard disc drive,
but there are typically around 3000 to 4000 DLL files. It is important to
note the total size of all the files, since the back-up medium must be
capable of handling this much data. There will probably be too much for
a single CDR disc, but some form of DVD or a back-up hard disc drive
should be sufficient. In this example the files will be copied to a backup
hard disc drive.

Despite the large number of files, copying them is very easy. Highlight
all the files by going to the Organize menu and choosing the Select All
option (Figure 5.35). Then go to the Organize menu again and select
Copy. The DLL files can then be Pasted to back-up folder on the hard
drive, a CD-R, or whatever, using Windows Explorer. In Figure 5.36 the
files have been copied successfully to a folder on the back-up drive.

If the files are to be stored on something like Zip discs or CDRs that can
not store all the files on a single disc, the copying process becomes

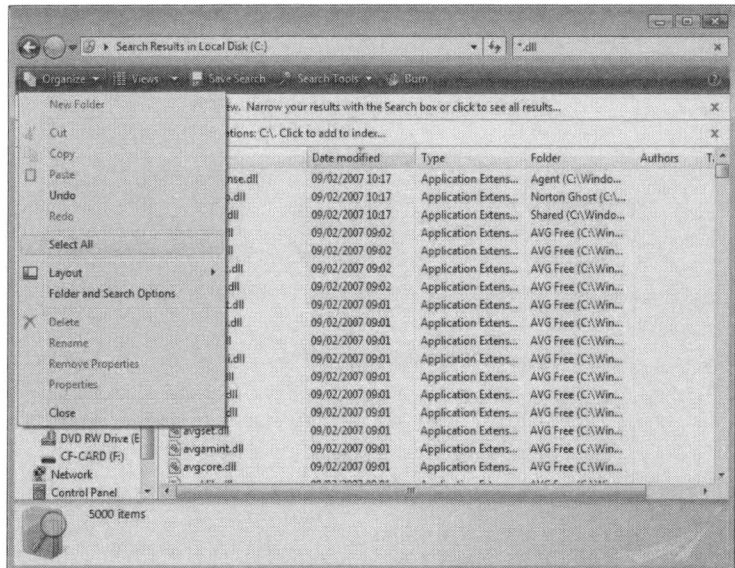

Fig.5.35 Choose Select All from the Organize menu

more difficult. Batches of files must be highlighted manually and copied to the back-up discs, being careful not to have any batch larger than the storage capacity of the disc.

It is possible that during the copying process you will be asked whether or not to replace a file that has already been copied, with another file of the same name (Figure 5.37). This conflict occurs when there are two files having the same name on the hard disc drive, but they are in different folders. There is no conflict on the boot drive, but there is when you try to copy the files to the same folder. The rule here is to not replace a newer file with an older version, so check the dates of the two files and proceed accordingly. The safest option is to copy both files. In order to avoid filename conflicts, the second file will have "(2)" added to the main part of the filename.

Obviously it could be very time consuming to manually search the back-up disc or discs for a specific DLL file that you need. The quick way is the use the Search facility of Windows Explorer to locate the file. This can search through thousands of files and locate the one you require in a few seconds. Having found the required file, the Copy and Paste

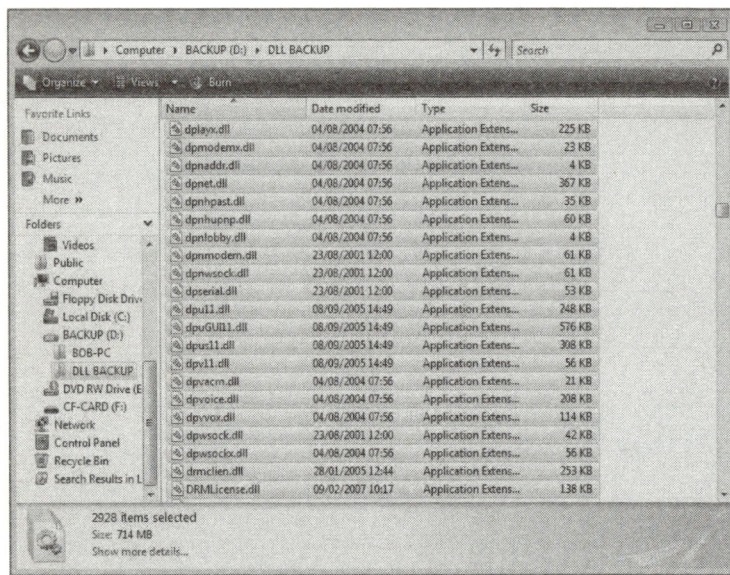

Fig.5.36 The files have been copied to the back-up drive

facilities of Windows Explorer can be used to copy it to the appropriate folder on the hard disc.

Complete version

The more upmarket versions of Windows Vista have a more sophisticated version of the Backup and Restore Center, which can handle a complete backup of the computer. In other words, rather than just backing up data of various types, it can back up the entire contents of the boot drive, and other drives if required. A backup of this type is normally stored on some form of external storage, such as a USB hard disc drive or a set or writable DVD discs.

Even if the boot drive is completely destroyed, it is then relatively easy to get the PC back to its previous state. With the damaged hard disc drive replaced, the back-up disc or discs are used to reinstall Windows. However, the backup will actually do rather more than reinstall Windows. Its real effect is to take the computer back to its state when the backup was made. All the installed data and programs, plus all the settings of

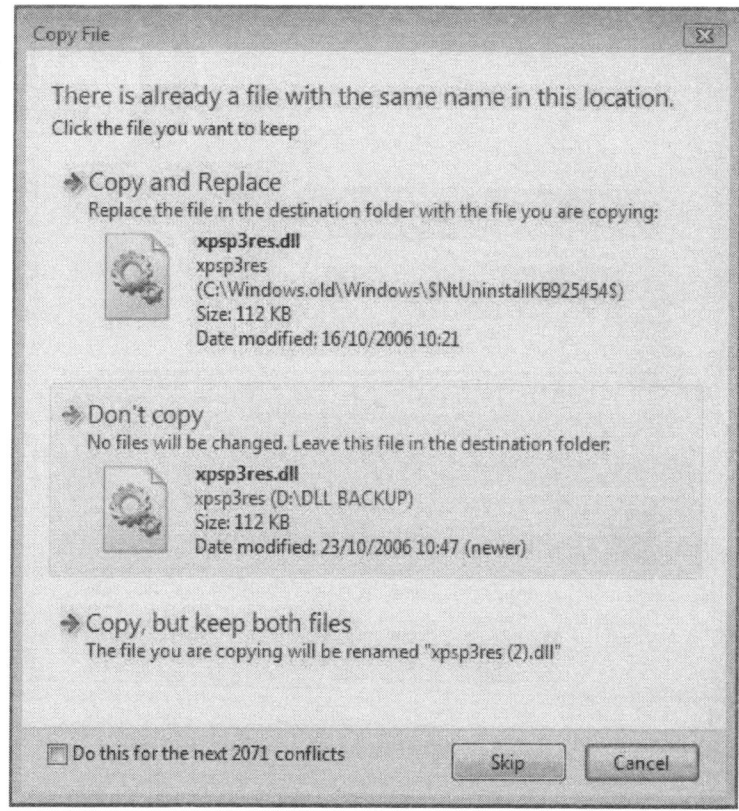

Fig.5.37 Two files of the same name are being copied

the computer and software at that time, will be included in the installation when the backup is restored.

Unfortunately, making a backup of this type tends to be quite time consuming, since the hard disc drives of most PCs contain huge amounts of data. In order to back-up the complete system you therefore need something like a high capacity external hard disc drive or a DVD writer and plenty of writable DVDs. It is not the type of thing that most people would undertake every day, or even on a weekly basis. This type of backup is normally made once per month, or even once every few months.

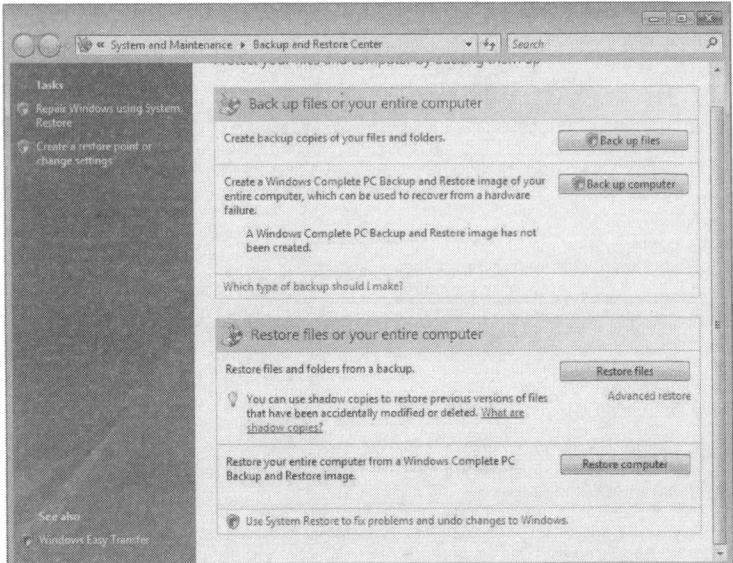

Fig.5.38 The more advanced version of the Backup and Restore Center

Recent data

Because a full backup is only made infrequently, it is important to keep a separate backup of any important data. This data can either be saved to a back-up device as and when it is generated, or it can be backed up using the appropriate section of the Backup and Restore Center. Like the full backup, it should be stored somewhere other than on the computer's hard disc drive. If the hard disc drive becomes faulty, you then have a copy of the full system plus any data made after the complete backup.

Things can be restored to normality by replacing the hard disc drive, restoring the complete backup, and then restoring the recently produced data. While this process might not be particularly quick, it is certainly much faster than reinstalling everything from scratch, making adjustments to various settings, and then copying data backups onto the hard drive. Unfortunately, this approach is not possible with some versions of Windows Vista, including both of the Home versions (Home Premium and Home Basic). It is included in the Business and Ultimate versions. Of course, there are third-party programs that provide essentially the

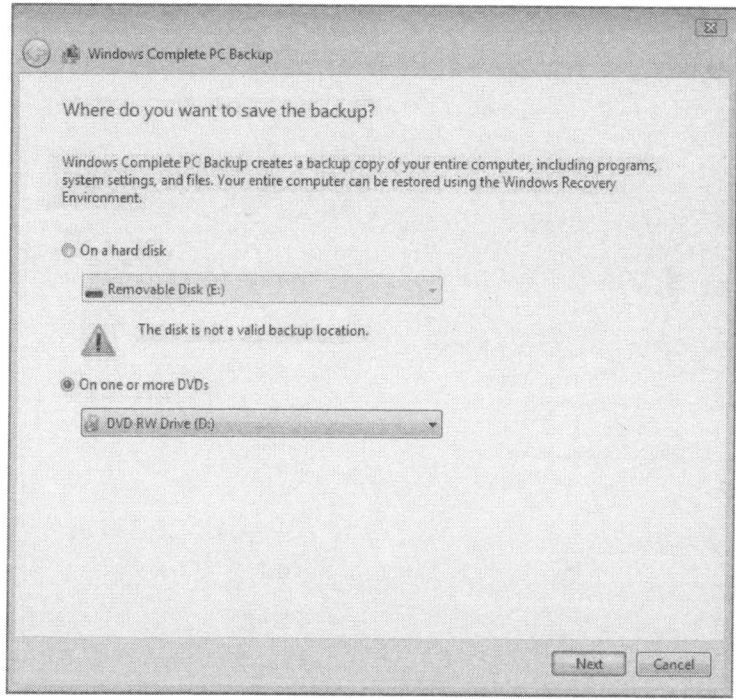

Fig.5.39 Use this window to select the back-up drive

same features as Vista's Complete Backup and Restore function, and it is probably worth investing in one of these if you own Vista Home Premium or Home Basic.

Complete backup

If you are running a version of Windows Vista that includes the complete version of the back-up feature, the Backup and Restore Center will look like Figure 5.38, with an extra back-up option. Start a complete backup by operating the "Back up computer" button. This produces a window where you choose the disc drive that will be used to store the backup (Figure 5.39). By default, a hard disc drive other than the boot drive will be selected. In this example the selected hard disc drive is actually a Compact Flash card in a card reader, and its capacity is too low to act as

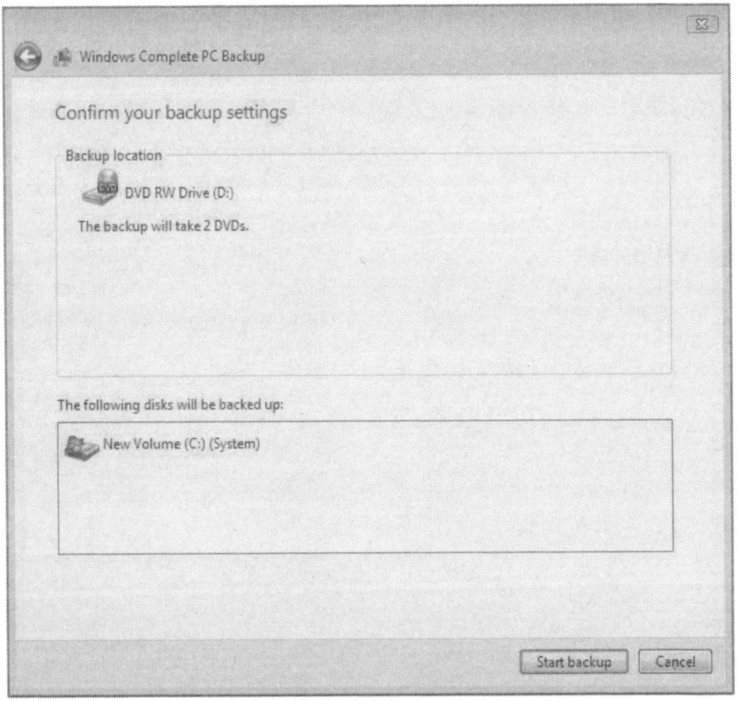

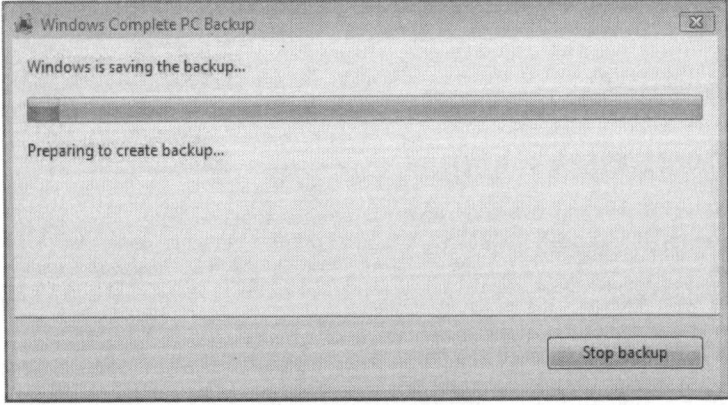

Fig.5.40 Here you confirm your choice of back-up drive

Fig.5.41 The usual bargraph shows how things are progressing

the back-up drive. I therefore opted to use the DVD writer plus a few writable DVD discs.

At the next window (Figure 5.40) you are asked to confirm your choice. Where the back-up drive is a DVD type, you are given an estimate of the number of discs that will be required. This is just an estimate though, and the actual number of discs needed could be slightly lower or higher. The bottom section of the window indicates the drive that will be copied during the back-up process, and by default this will be the boot drive,

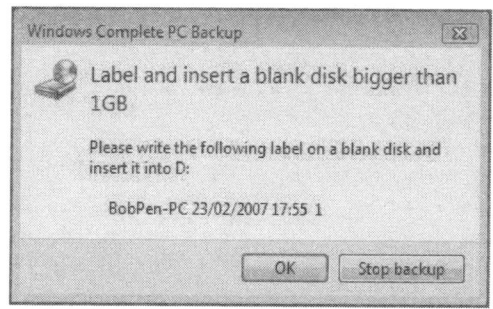

Fig.5.42 If prompted, insert a disc into the back-up drive

Operating the "Start backup" button produces the small window of Figure 5.41, which has the usual bargraph to show how things are progressing. If you are using some form of removable storage such as writable DVDs, you will be prompted to insert a disc into the appropriate drive (Figure 5.42). In the case of a DVD disc you might be asked if you would like to format it (Figure 5.43). You must operate the Format button in order to go ahead with the backup. Where the backup is being stored on a multi-disc set, at the appropriate times you will be prompted to remove the DVD and

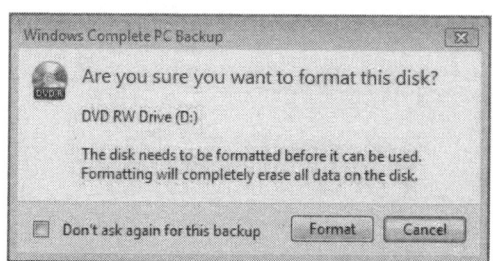

Fig.5.43 It might be necessary to format the disc

replace it with blank DVD. Eventually you should get the window of Figure 5.44, indicating that the backup has been completed successfully.

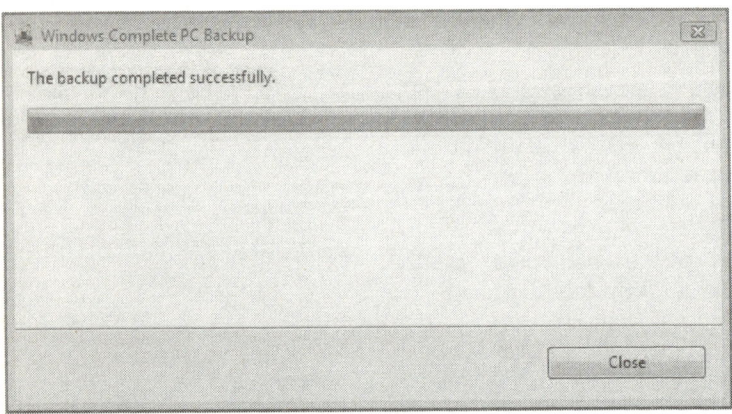

Fig.5.44 The backup has been completed successfully

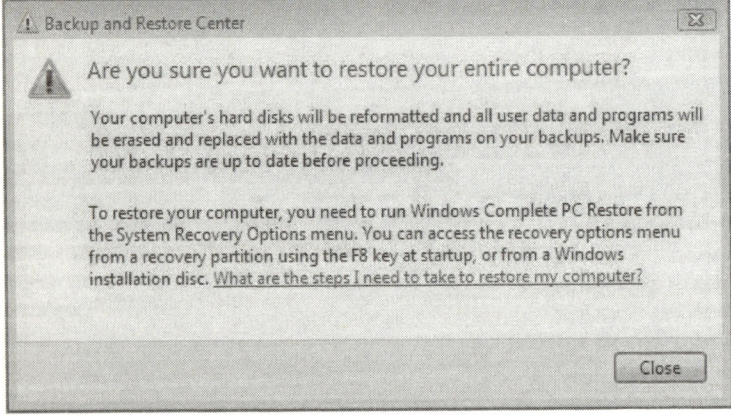

Fig.5.45 You can not restore a backup from within Windows Vista

Complete restore

On the face of it, you can restore a complete backup by going to the Backup and Restore Center and operating the "Restore computer" button. This will actually produce the message of Figure 5.45, which explains that the computer must be booted from the Windows Vista installation disc in order to perform a complete restoration. It has to be borne in

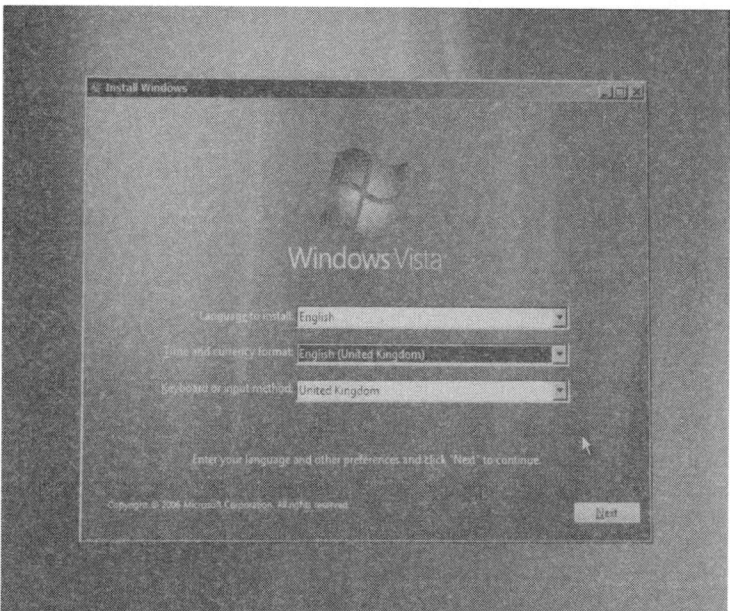

Fig.5.46 Select the appropriate language

mind here that the boot drive will often be new (and blank) when restoring a full backup. Consequently, there will be no existing Windows installation that can be used to boot the PC. Alternatively, there will be a Windows installation on the hard disc drive, but it will be damaged to the point where it is not in a bootable state. The only practical way of handling things is to boot the PC from a bootable DVD and then use its facilities to control the restoration process.

You might find that the PC will boot from the Windows Vista installation DVD without any user-input, but it will probably be necessary to press any key on the keyboard when a prompt to this effect appears on the screen. This prompt usually appears at the bottom of the screen, almost as soon as the computer has completed its initial checks. It will then take a while for the boot routine on the DVD to go through some checks and copy files into memory.

Eventually the window of Figure 5.46 will appear on the screen. Normally this screen is used to ensure that Vista is installed with the correct language settings, but this does not apply when restoring a Vista

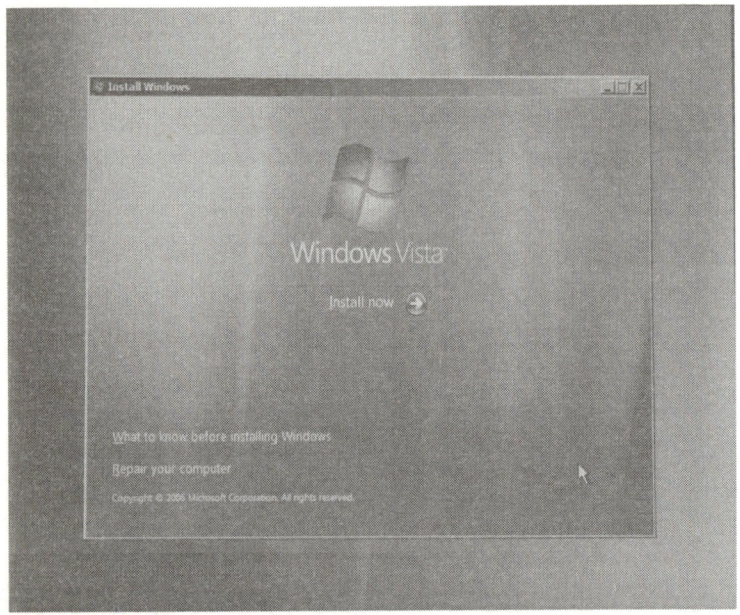

Fig.5.47 Choose the "Repair your computer" link

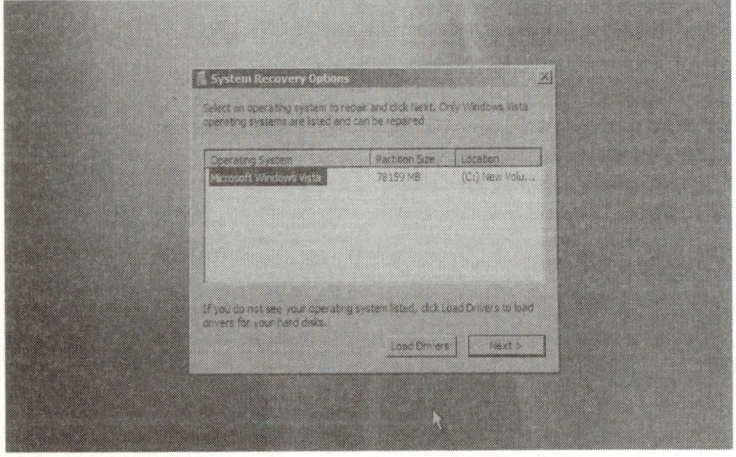

Fig.5.48 Select the operating system you wish to repair

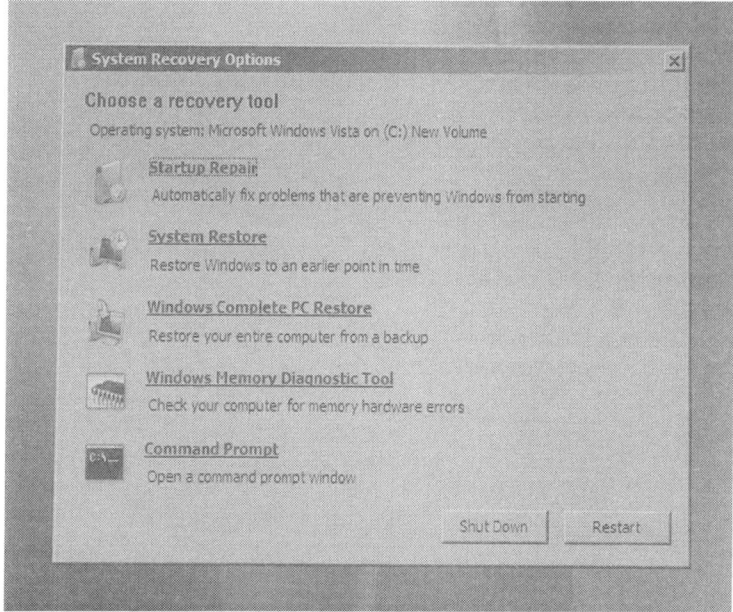

Fig.5.49 Here the "Windows complete PC restore" option is selected

installation. The restored installation will use the same language settings, etc., as the original. However, you still need to use the right language settings at this window, so that subsequent screens in the restoration process use the correct language.

At the next window (Figure 5.47) it is the "Repair your computer" link that must be used. If a window like the one shown in Figure 5.48 appears, select the operating system that you wish to repair. Unless you are using some form of multi-boot system there will only be one operating system listed. A number of options are available at the next window (Figure 5.49), which is really just a simple menu. In this case it is the "Windows complete PC restore" option that is selected. The warning message of Figure 5.50 will appear if you are using a backup that is stored on DVDs. The Vista installation DVD must be removed from the drive and the first of the back-up discs is used in its place. You can then try again, and the back-up process should get under way properly this time.

At the window of Figure 5.51 you are asked to confirm that the back-up copy that is about to be restored is the right one. Assuming it is, operate

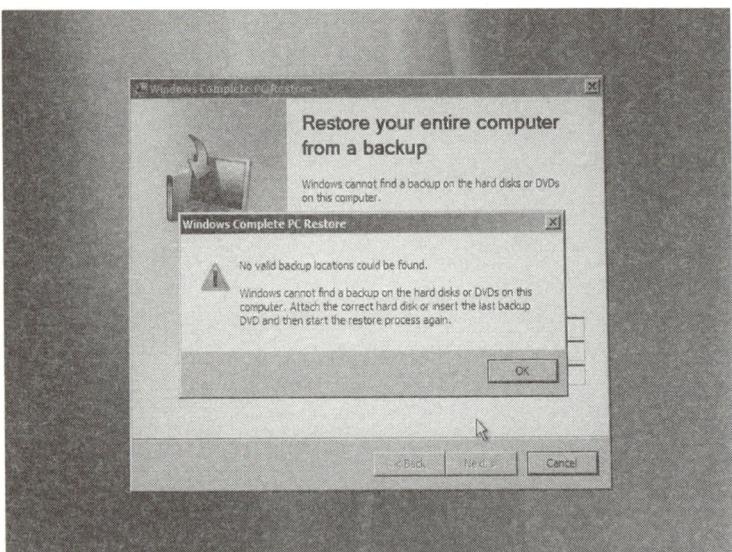

Fig.5.50 *This message indicates that a blank DVD must be inserted into the DVD writer*

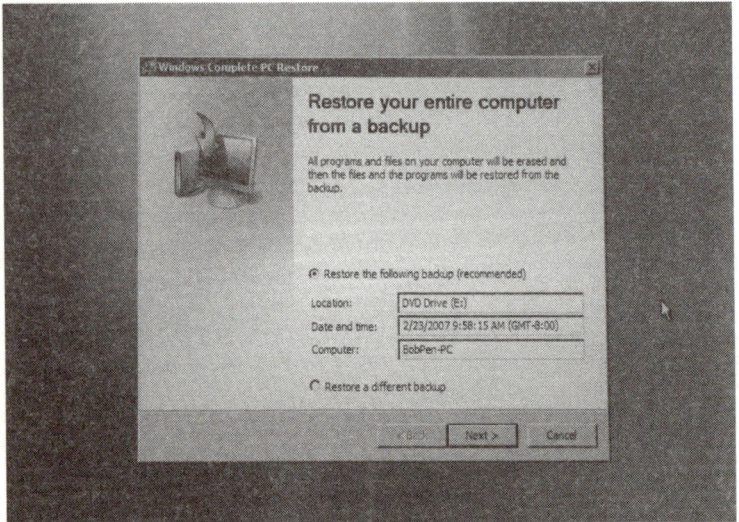

Fig.5.51 *Confirm that the right backup has been selected*

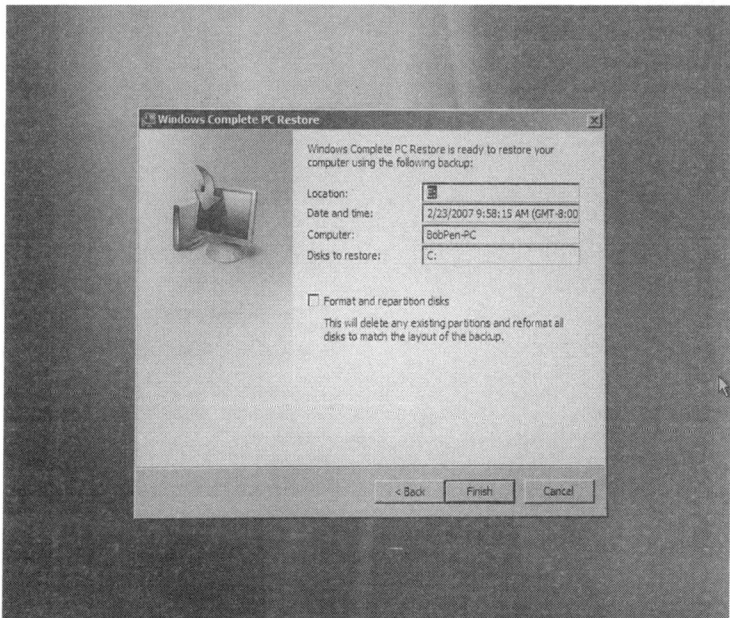

Fig.5.52 There is the option of repartitioning and formatting the drive

the Next button, which moves things on to the window of Figure 5.52. This has a checkbox that gives the option of treating the boot drive as though it is blank. In other words, it will be repartitioned and formatted before the backup is restored. This option must be used if the backup is being restored to a drive that is indeed completely blank, or if it is not an NTFS type. It must also be used if there is a possibility that there is a problem with the existing partitioning and formatting. For this example the backup was being restored to a hard disc that was properly partitioned and formatted, so I left the checkbox empty.

The restoration process is then fully automatic, with no further user-input being required. There is the usual status screen that shows how things are progressing (Figure 5.53). Eventually the computer will reboot, and if everything has gone according to plan it will then go into a Windows Vista installation that is identical to the one stored on the back-up disc or discs. In this example everything worked correctly, and the computer did correctly boot into Vista (Figure 5.54). It is then just a matter of restoring any data files that were backed up after the full backup was made, and the computer should then be ready to use again.

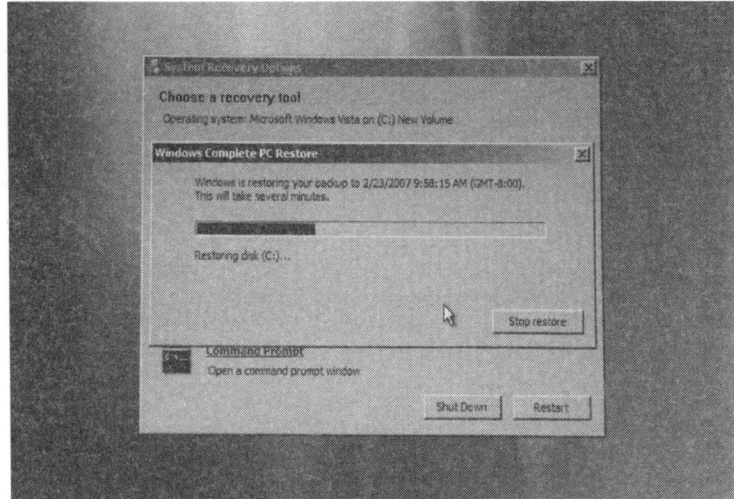

Fig.5.53 Once again, a bargraph shows how things are progressing

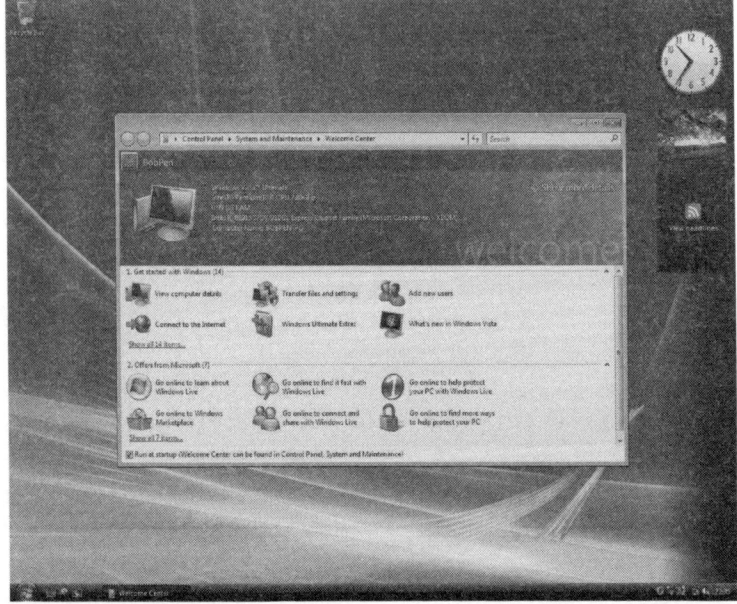

Fig.5.54 The restored PC has booted into Vista without any problems

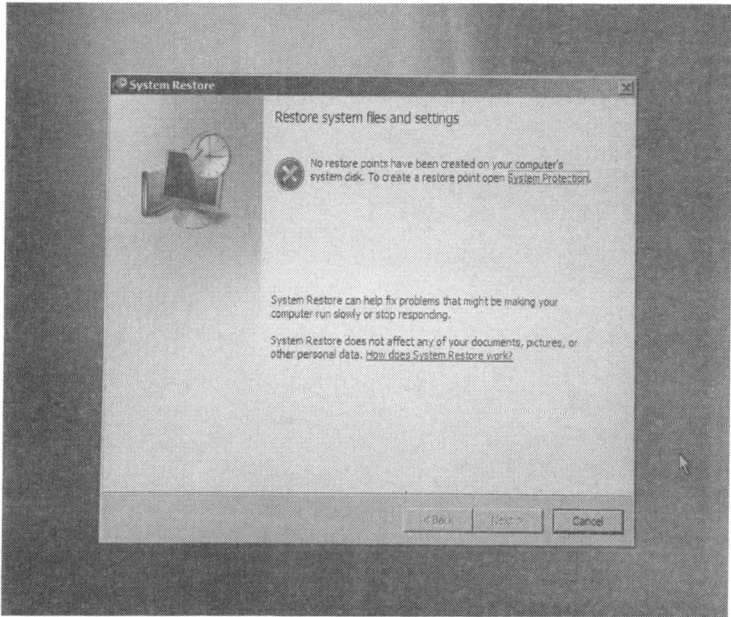

Fig.5.55 In this case, no viable restoration point could be found

System Restore 2

There is a potential snag when using the System Restore feature from within Windows Vista. This is simply that it is only possible to use System Restore in this way if it is possible to boot into Windows. It is impossible to use this method when there is a problem that is preventing the computer from booting into Windows. However, it is possible to use the System Restore feature via the installation DVD, and this method does not require the system on the hard disc drive to be in a bootable state. You boot using the installation DVD, and then proceed in the same manner as when undertaking a complete restoration from a backup source.

Eventually you arrive at the menu of Figure 5.49, but here the System Restore option is selected. It will not necessarily be possible to use the System Restore feature. Its viability depends on the amount of damage done to the system, and the availability of valid system restoration data. If you are unlucky, a message such as the one shown in Figure 5.55 will be displayed, and this probably means that the only practical way of

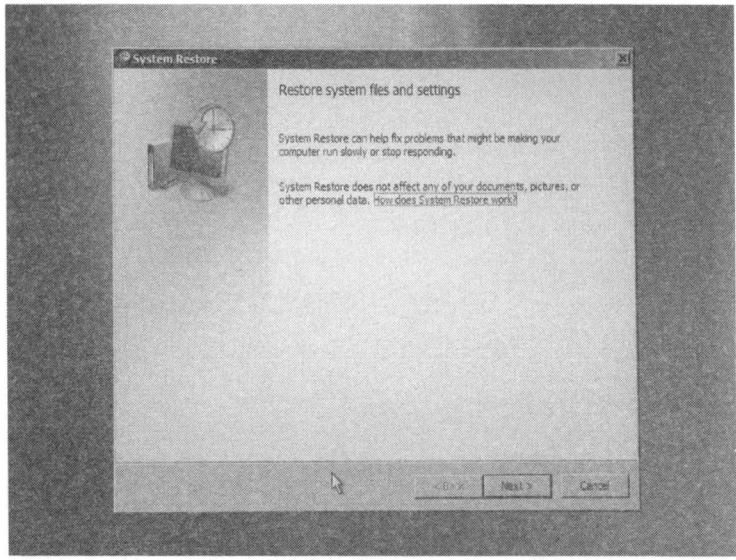

Fig.5.56 Here the System Restore feature can be used

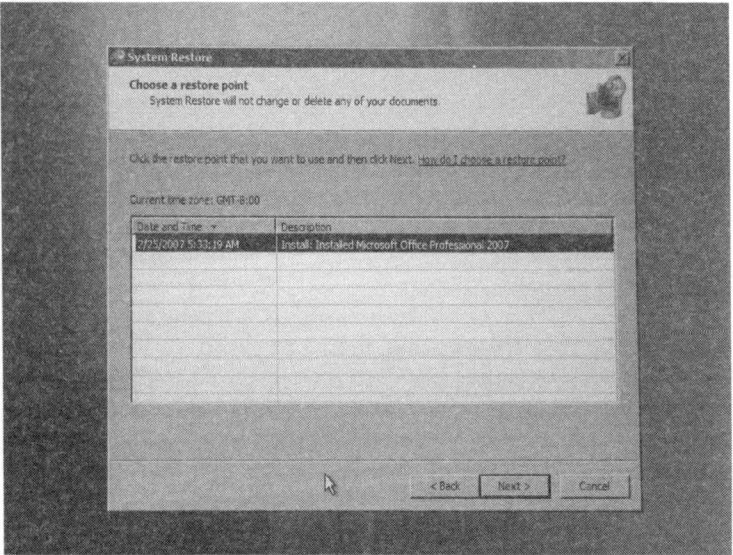

Fig.5.57 In this example only one restoration point is available

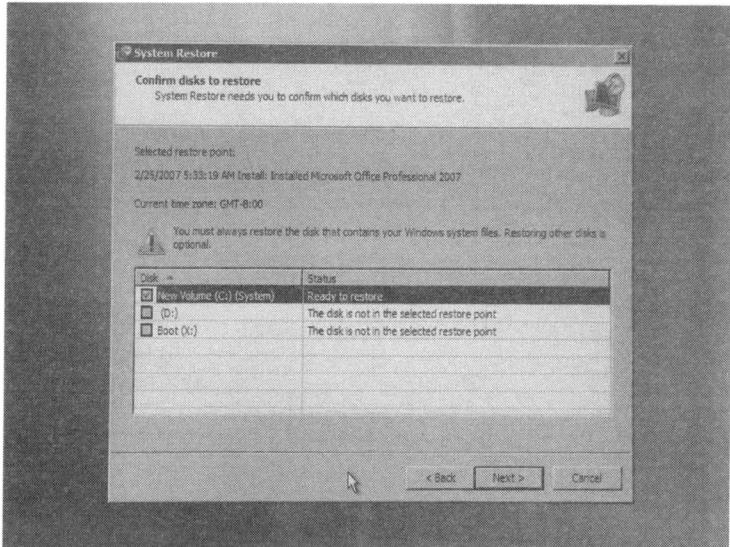

Fig.5.58 If necessary, select the disc or discs to be included

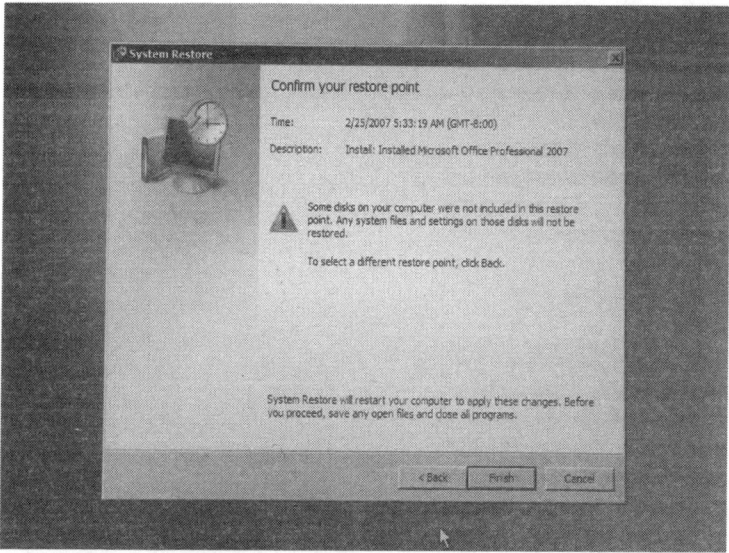

Fig.5.59 Confirm the selected restoration point

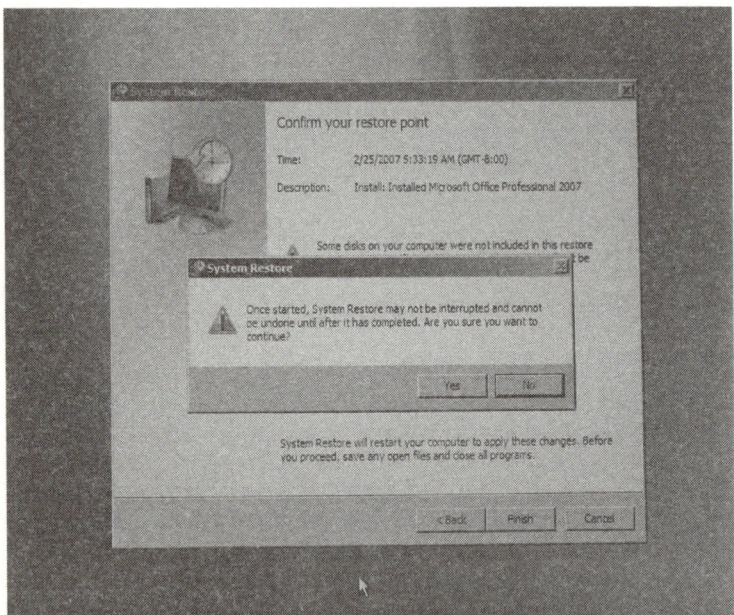

Fig.5.60 The restoration process should not be interrupted

resolving the problem is to rescue as much data as possible and then reinstall Windows from scratch.

In most cases it will be possible to use the System Restore feature, and the information window of Figure 5.56 will be displayed. The next window (Figure 5.57) lists the available restoration points. In this example the Windows installation is almost new and there is only one restoration point available, but there will usually be a long list of accessible points. Choose one from a time when you are sure that the computer was functioning perfectly, and then operate the Next button.

Matters are complicated slightly in this example because the computer has three hard disc drives. The window of Figure 5.58 enables the appropriate disc or discs to be selected, and in this case there is only one drive (C) that is covered by the System Restore feature. Accordingly, this drive was selected and the Next button was operated. The window of Figure 5.59 asks you to confirm the restoration point, by operating the Finish button. Doing so produces the warning message of Figure 5.60, which simply informs you that the restoration should not be interrupted once it has been started.

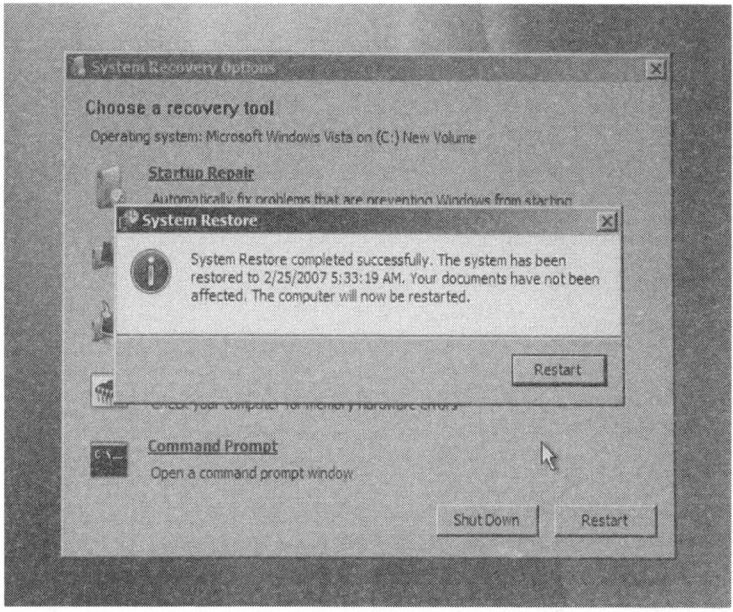

Fig.5.61 The restoration process has been completed successfully

Operating the Yes button results in the System Restoration starting in earnest, and it is carried out automatically. Provided all goes well, the message of Figure 5.61 will eventually appear, indicating that the restoration process has been completed successfully. It is then just a matter of left-clicking the Restart button and waiting to see if the computer will boot into Windows. In this case it did so, and the small message window of Figure 5.62 confirmed that the system had been taken back to the selected restoration point.

Of course, there is no guarantee that using

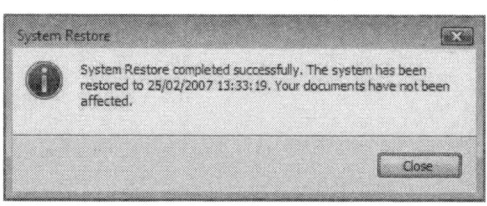

Fig.5.62 The computer booted correctly at the restoration point

the System Restore feature via the installation DVD will get the system running properly again. The fact that the computer will not boot into

Windows suggests that the damage to the system could be quite severe, which in turn indicates that the chances of System Restore curing the problem are relatively low. Looking on the bright side, if it will actually take the system back to an earlier state, it is quite likely that it will indeed cure the problem.

Points to remember

Backing up data and (or) system information to another drive is the only way to guard against a hard disc failure. Backing up system information to the main hard drive is sufficient to guard against problems with the operating system.

Floppy discs are inadequate to cope with the large amounts of data produced by many modern applications. A DVD writer, CD writer, Zip drive, additional hard disc, or some other form of mass storage device is required. A mass storage device is also required in order to make a full backup of the main hard disc drive. Note that the Windows Vista back-up programs are not compatible with all types of storage device. DVD writers and most types of hard disc drive are supported.

It is only necessary to save important data and configuration files, but it is much quicker to get things back to normal if you make a full backup of the hard drive.

Plenty of third party back-up software is available, but the Windows Vista Complete Backup and Restore utility is adequate for most purposes. Combined with an additional hard disc drive or DVD writer, this provides a fast and cost effective method of providing a full system backup.

The Complete Backup and Restore facility is not available in some versions of Vista, including both of the Home versions. It is available in the Business and Ultimate versions. Note that it is only usable for a full backup and restore. It can not be used to restore selected files.

The normal Windows Vista back-up feature can be used to backup selected types of data file (music, documents, etc.). Regularly backing up the full contents of a hard disc is relatively time consuming. A more practical approach is to make full backups relatively infrequently, with data being backed up very frequently. This makes it easy to get the PC running again if there is a catastrophic failure, but it ensures that only minimal amounts of data can be lost. The data backup facility is available in all versions of Windows Vista.

Windows Vista has a System Restore program that can be used to take the system back to the way it was at some previous time. Using System Restore to take the system back a day or two will usually remedy boot problems, etc. Any data files generated since the restoration point will not be erased. The System Restore facility can be accessed by booting from the Vista installation disc.

It is worthwhile making a back-up copy of all the DLL files on the hard disc. In the event of a DLL file becoming deleted or overwritten by an older version, the original is then easily found and reinstated. It is not necessary to have a back-up device for the DLL files. Storing them in a folder on the hard disc is perfectly all right.

Reinstallation

Clean sweep

Things have gone badly, attempts to fix the Windows installation have failed, System Restore does not get things working again, and there is no backup of the complete system. You therefore decide it is time to install Windows Vista from scratch. Alternatively, the system may be working, but with numerous programs having been installed and uninstalled, it is running in a very hesitant fashion. Attempts to "tune" the system have proved to be ineffective, so you decide that it is time to start again with a fresh installation of Vista. Either way, having decided to install Windows and your applications from scratch, and having also done any necessary backing up of data files, etc., how do you start the reinstallation process?

Before you start, it is worthwhile considering the alternative option. Unless you have definitely decided that it is time to "sweep away the cobwebs" and start from scratch, I would certainly recommend trying to fix Windows by reinstalling it on top of the broken version. If this fails to cure the problem, then it is time to install Windows from scratch. The advantage of reinstallation on top of the old Windows installation is that the programs should remain usable with the new version. This will not happen if there is massive damage to the original installation, but in most cases all the programs will work fine with the refreshed version of Windows. Unfortunately, the problems with the original installation might be carried forward into the new one, and it could still be necessary to install Windows from scratch. A great deal of time can be saved if reinstallation on the old copy of Windows works, so it is well worth trying this method.

The process is very similar whether the operating system is installed from scratch or on top of an existing Windows installation. If Windows Vista is already on the hard disc it will be detected by the Setup program, which can then reinstall Windows Vista on top of the existing installation. Note that the versions of Windows Vista supplied with some PCs do not have the standard installation disc. The methods described here are

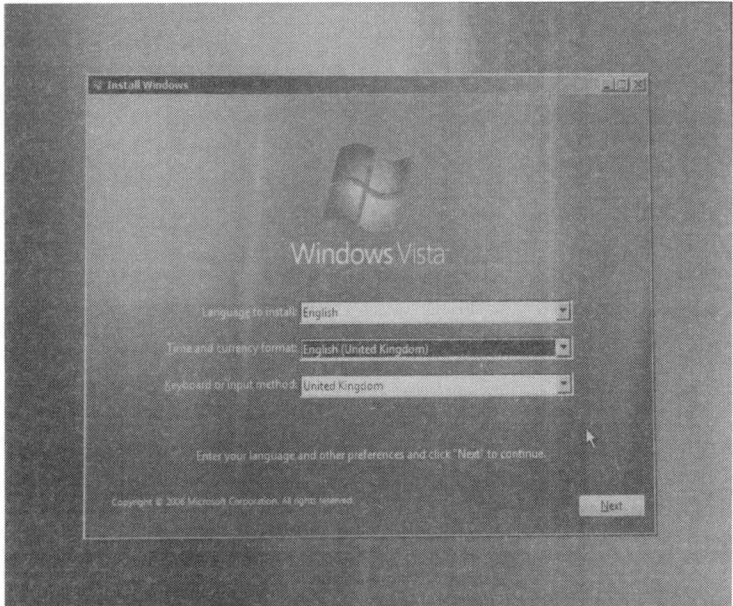

Fig.6.1 Use this window to select the correct language settings

only applicable if you have the standard Windows Vista installation disc. If your PC was not supplied with a standard installation disc it probably came complete with a recovery disc that makes it easy to return to a basic Windows installation. With a PC of this type you should consult the instruction manual, and this should give concise information about reinstalling Windows. In most cases it is essentially just a matter of booting from a DVD and letting the recovery program get on with reinstallation.

Booting from DVD

Whether reinstalling on top of the current installation or reinstalling Windows Vista from scratch, the first step is to boot from the installation DVD. The BIOS must be set to boot from the DVD drive before it tries to boot from the hard disc. It is unlikely that the computer will attempt to boot from the DVD drive if the priorities are the other way around, and it will certainly not do so unless the DVD is set as one of the boot devices. If all is well, a message will appear on the screen indicating that any key must be operated in order to boot from the DVD drive. This message

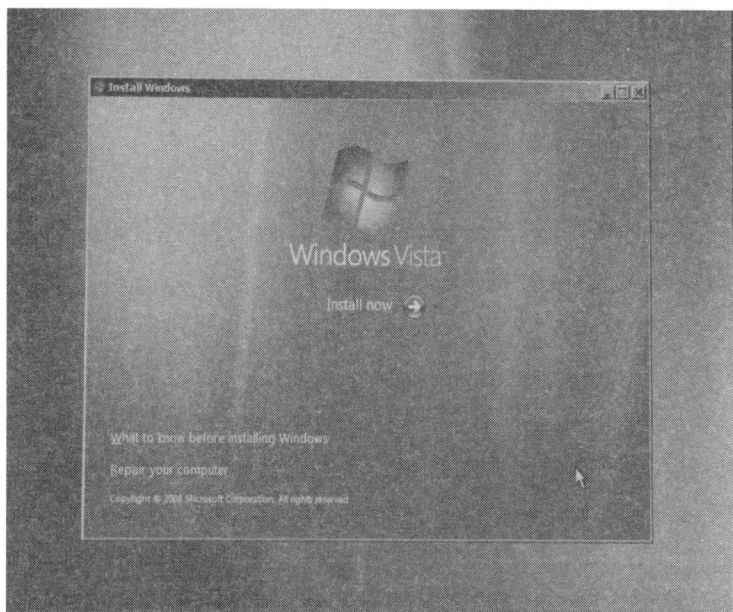

Fig.6.2 Select the Install Now option

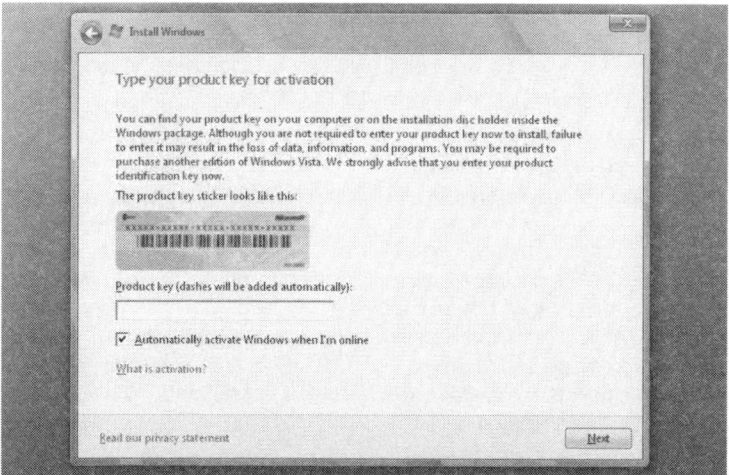

Fig.6.3 It is advisable to take this opportunity of entering your product code

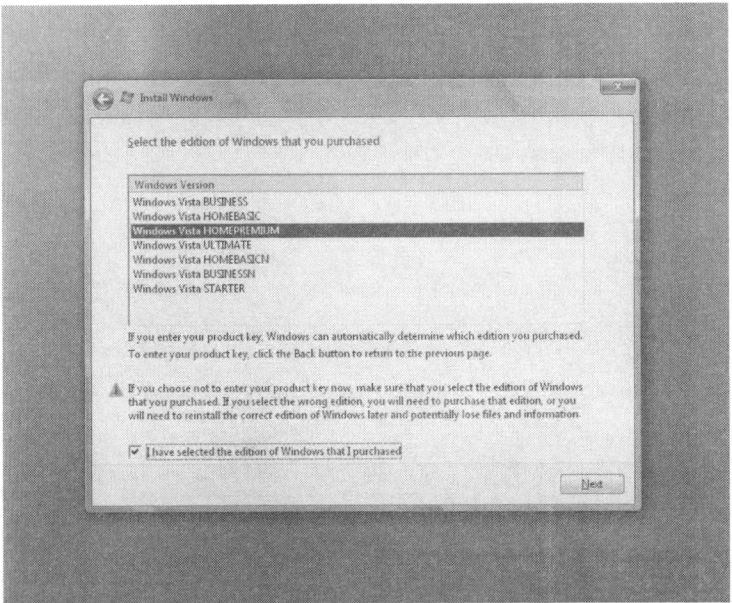

*Fig.6.4 Be careful to select the version of Vista that you have
purchased*

appears quite briefly, so be ready to press one of the keys. The computer
will try to boot from the hard disc if you "miss the boat". It will then be
necessary to restart the computer and try again.

After various files have been loaded from the DVD, things should come
to a halt with the screen of Figure 6.1. Here you use the three menus to
set the installation language, the time and currency format, and the
keyboard language or type. For a UK user these are normally set at
English, English (United Kingdom), and United Kingdom respectively.
Operating the Next button moves things on to the screen of Figure 6.2,
where the "Install now" option should be selected. At the following screen
(Figure 6.3) you have the option of entering your product key. It is not
essential to do so at this stage, but it is definitely a good idea to do so.
With a reinstallation it is also a good idea to opt for automatic activation
by leaving the checkbox ticked.

If a screen like the one in Figure 6.4 appears, use the list to select the
version of Vista that you have purchased, and then tick the checkbox.
The Next screen (Figure 6.5) is the usual licence agreement, and you

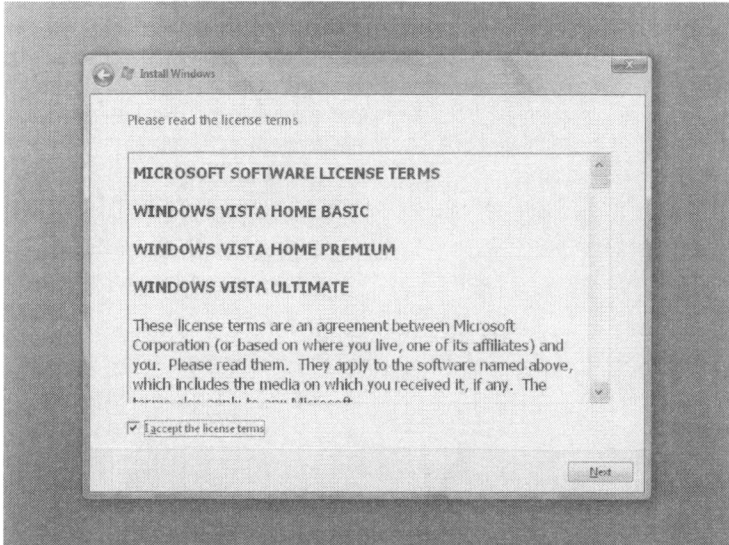

Fig.6.5 You must agree to the terms in order to proceed

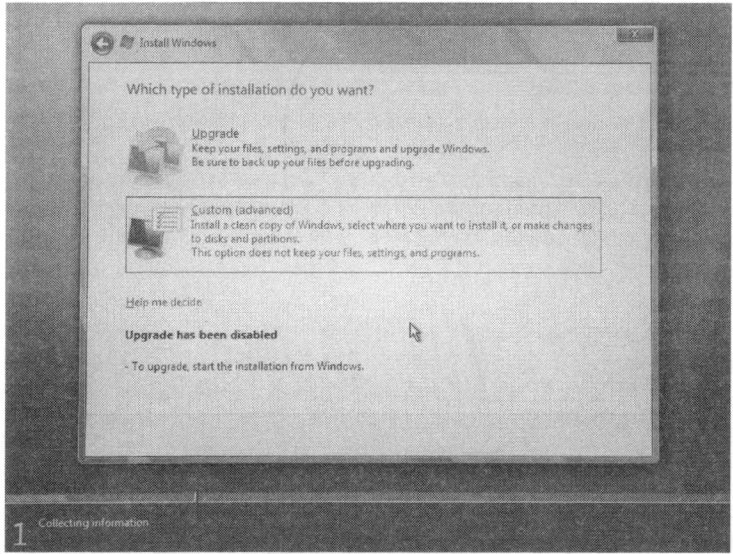

Fig.6.6 Choose the Custom (advanced) option at this window

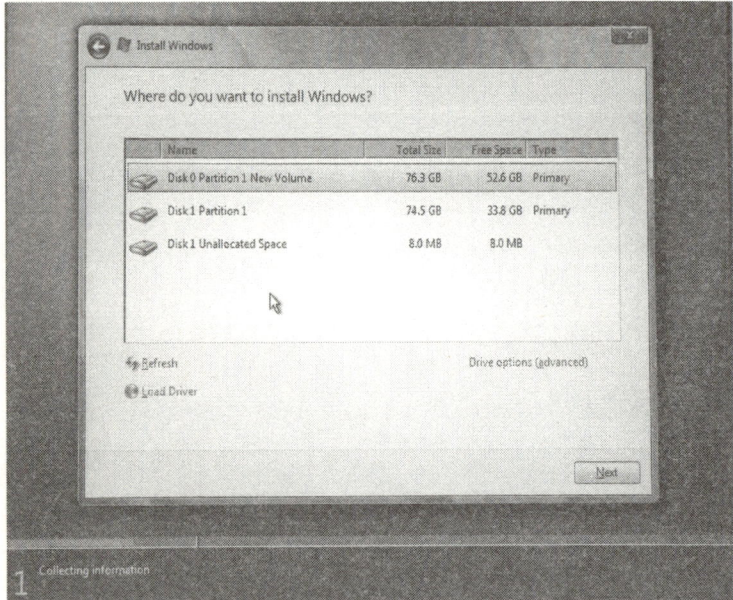

Fig.6.7 Select the drive that will be used for the installation

have to tick the checkbox in order to agree with the licensing terms. Note that Windows Vista can not be installed unless you do agree to the licensing conditions. At the next screen (Figure 6.6) you supposedly have the choice of upgrading an existing Windows installation or installing a fresh one, but the upgrade option is unlikely to be active. This does not matter, because it is the "Custom (advanced)" option that is required in this case.

The available disc drives are listed at the next screen (Figure 6.7), where you select the drive that will be used for the Windows Vista installation. In this example it will be installed on Disk 0 Partition 1, but there is an obvious problem in that the original installation is still present here. One option is to go ahead and install the fresh copy of Vista on this partition, but this will produce the warning message of Figure 6.8. This explains that the files associated with the existing Windows installation will be moved to a folder called Windows.old, but the old version of Windows and the installed programs will not be usable.

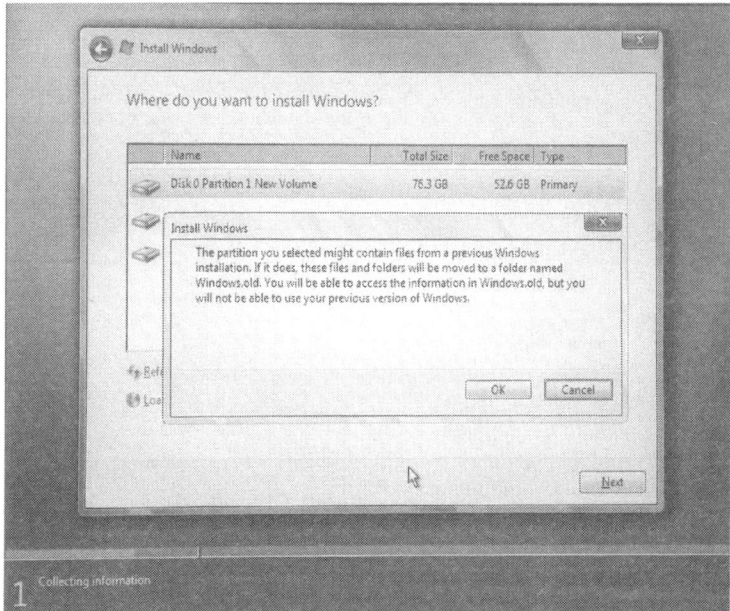

Fig.6.8 The old installation will be saved, but will not be used

You might prefer to do things this way provided the hard disc drive is large enough to take the old files and the new installation. Unwanted files can be deleted once the new installation is in place and fully operational. However, this approach is not really taking advantage of the "clean sweep" provided by a fresh installation on a blank partition. It is certainly not a good way of handling matters in cases where the old Windows installation is believed to carry a virus or other form of infection. In a situation of this type it is necessary to rescue as much of your data as possible and then wipe the partition before reinstalling Windows.

Formatting

The Vista installation program includes a facility for formatting partitions, making it easy to wipe the boot partition of all existing files and folders. These facilities are accessed by operating the "Drive options (advanced)" link, which changes the screen to look like Figure 6.9. Where appropriate, make sure that the correct drive/partition is selected in the upper panel, and then operate the Format button in the lower section of the screen.

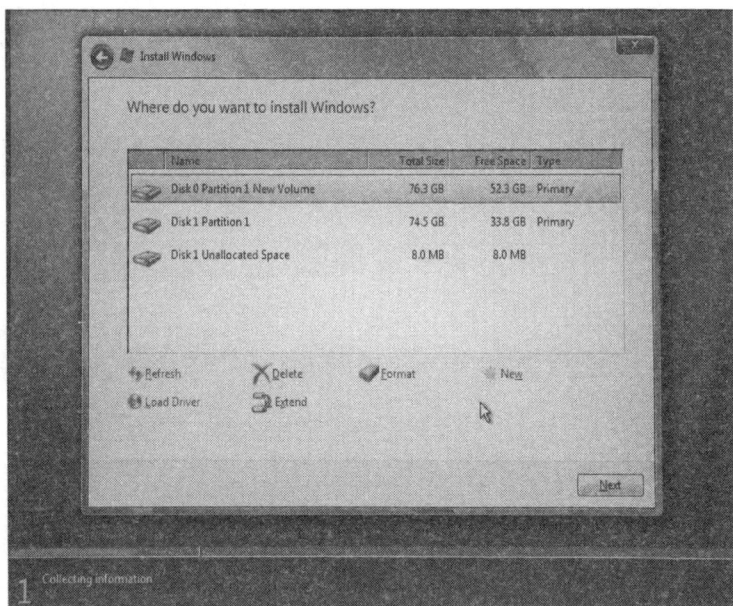

Fig.6.9 The advanced drive options have been activated

This will produce a warning message (Figure 6.10), which explains that all the files in the partition will be deleted when it is partitioned. This is, of course, exactly what is required in this case, but bear in mind that any data on the partition that has not been backed up will almost certainly be lost for ever once the formatting has started.

Operate the Next button once the partition has been formatted, and the installation of Windows Vista will then commence. The screen will change to show a list of tasks, and each one will be ticked as it is completed (Figure 6.11). Installation of a modern operating system takes a fair amount of time, so be prepared to wait several minutes while various tasks are performed. The computer will be restarted at least once during installation, and it is important that it is allowed to boot from the hard disc drive when this happens. Do not get it to boot from the installation DVD, or you will just end up going through the same steps over and over again with installation never being completed. The message of Figure 6.12 will be displayed if the computer reboots correctly from the hard disc drive.

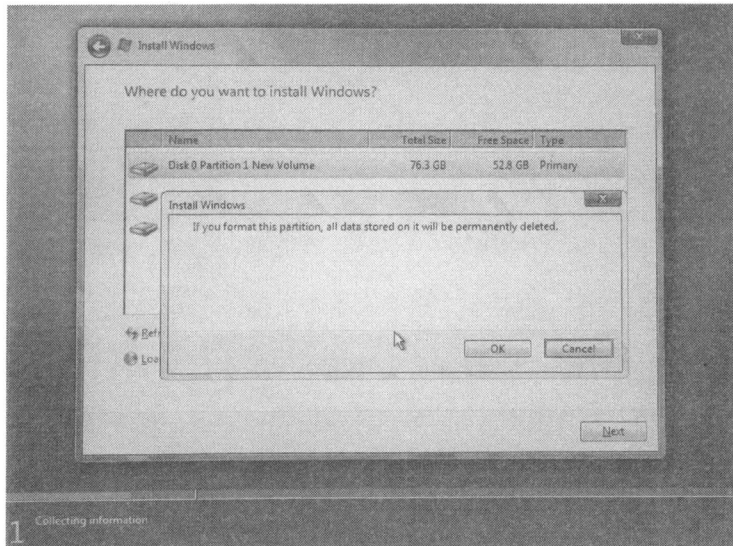

Fig.6.10 All the files on the drive will be deleted if it is formatted

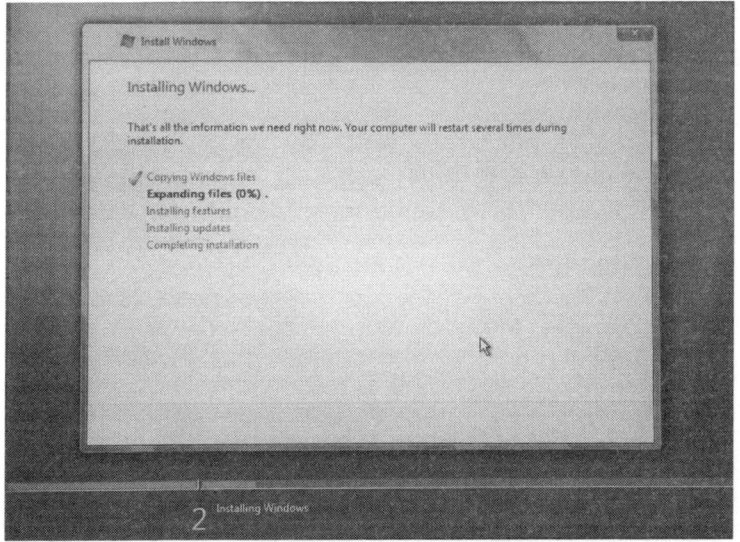

Fig.6.11 Each stage of installation is ticked as it is completed

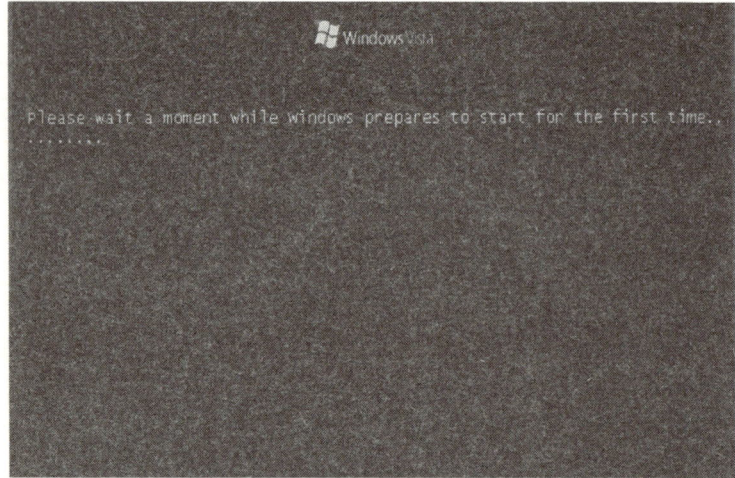

Fig.6.12 The computer will reboot at least once

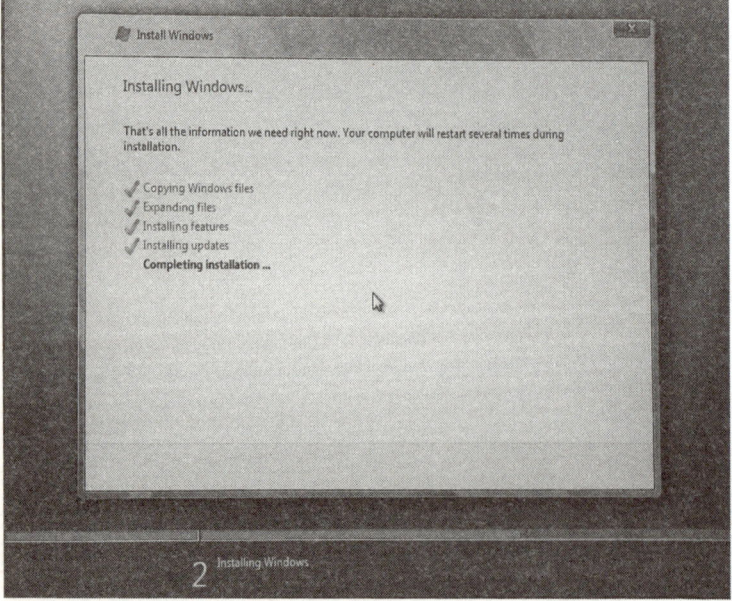

Fig.6.13 Installation has resumed and is nearing completion

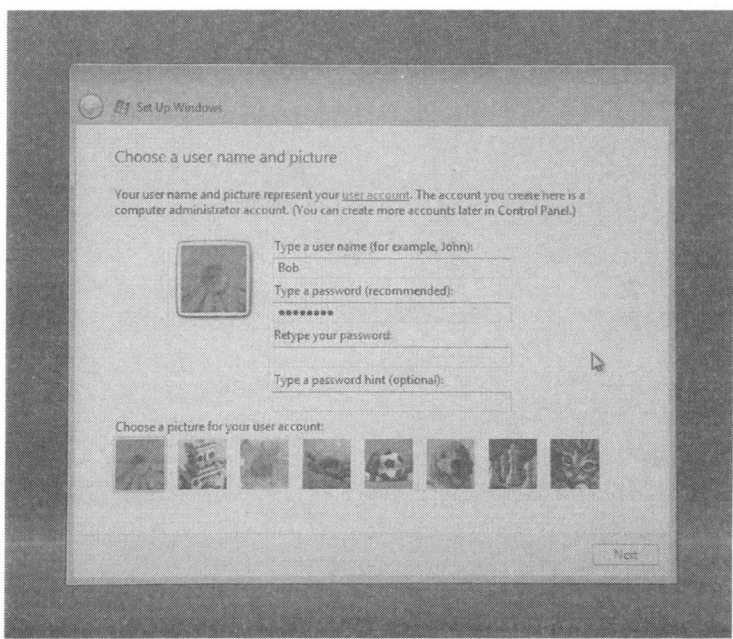

Fig.6.14 Supply a name for your account

The screen of Figure 6.13 will appear once the computer has rebooted, and the final stages of installation will then be completed. Although the installation process is largely automatic, it is still necessary for the user to enter some simple information. When the screen of Figure 6.14 appears, you have to select a picture to represent your account, and supply a name for your account.

It is not essential to use password protection, but it is probably best to do so. As usual, you will have to enter your choice of password into one textbox and then confirm that it is correct by entering it again in another textbox. An optional hint can be entered in another textbox, and the hint should be something that will help you to remember the password if you should happen to forget it. Bear in mind that you will be locked out of your account if you forget your password and do not manage to remember it.

The next screen (Figure 6.15) is used to enter a name for the computer, or the default name can be used. Do not confuse the account name and

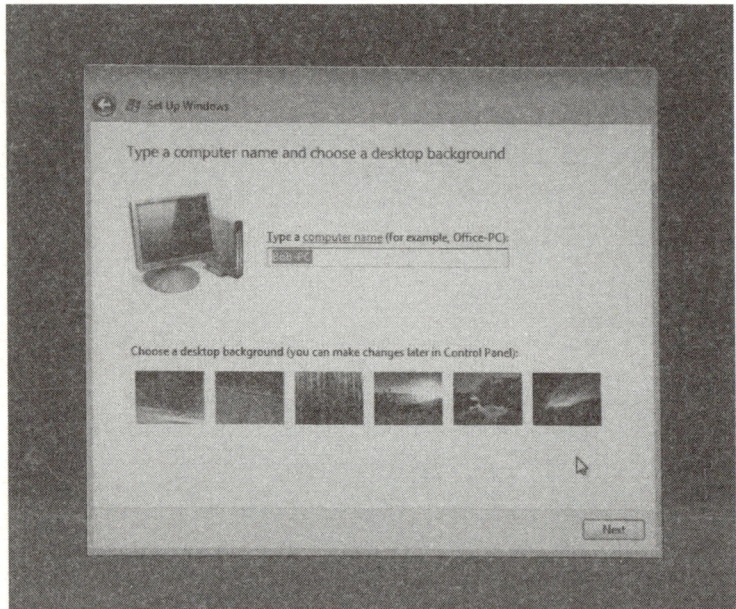

Fig.6.15 A network name for the computer is entered here

the computer name. The name for the computer is the one that will be used to identify it if the computer is connected to a network. This name must therefore be different to the names used for any other computers on the network. It does not matter too much what name is used if the computer will not be used as part of a network. The account name given at the previous screen is the one used for your account on the computer. Other accounts can be added once Vista is installed and running properly, but this is not mandatory. The general idea is to have a different account for each user, so there is usually no point in having more than one account if there is only one user.

This screen is also used to select a background design for the Windows desktop. The first design in the row of thumbnail images will be used if you do not select one. Of course, the desktop's background is easily changed to just about anything you like once Vista has been installed, so it does not matter too much which design is chosen at this stage. There are three options at the following screen (Figure 6.16), which is where you select to have recommended updates installed, important updates, or neither at this stage. It is probably best to opt for at least

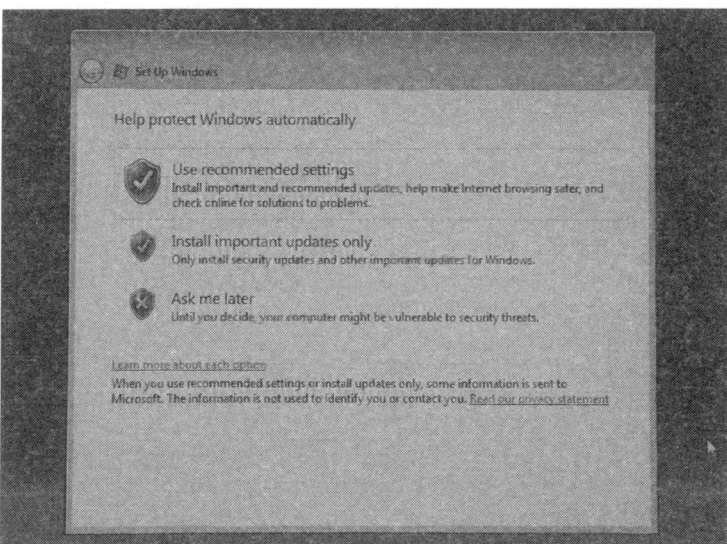

Fig.6.16 The screen is used to control automatic updates

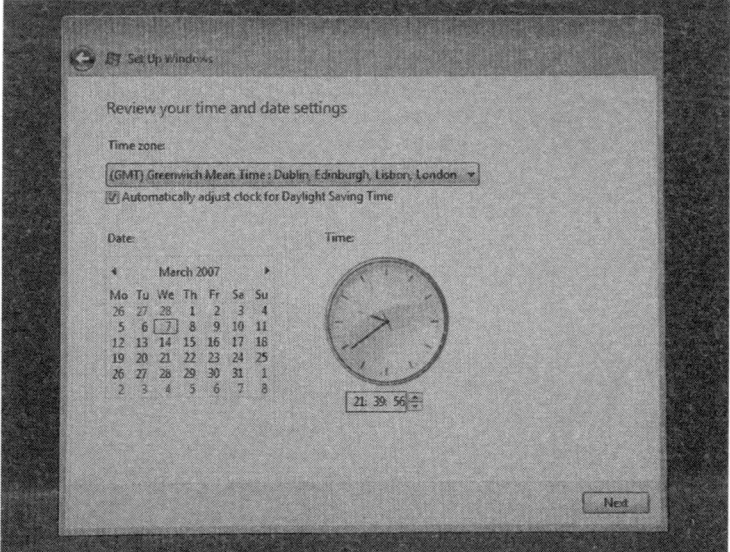

Fig.6.17 Set the correct time, date, and time zone

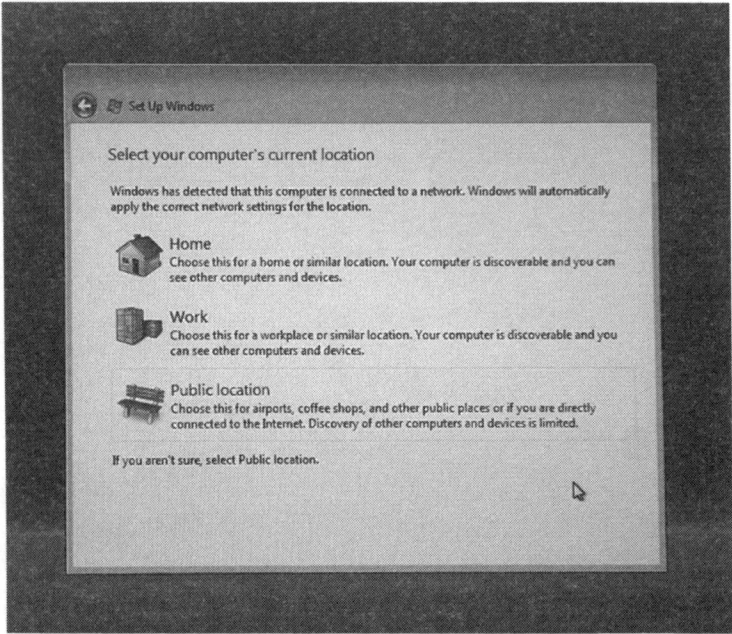

Fig.6.18 Choose whether the PC will be used at a home, work, or public location

important updates to be installed, but the automatic update settings can be altered once Vista is installed, so there is no need to make a final decision at this stage.

The next screen allows the time, date, and time zone to be altered, if necessary. The existing settings will probably be correct, but this screen provides an opportunity to check that the time setting is accurate, and to make any necessary adjustments. Tick the checkbox if you wish to have Vista automatically adjust the system clock for daylight saving. Things then move on to the screen of Figure 6.18 where you select Home, Business, or Public Location, depending on where the computer will mainly be used.

This completes the setting up procedure, which will be confirmed by the screen of Figure 6.19. Operating the Start button results in a series of information screens appearing, such as the example of Figure 6.20, while the installation is finalised. The usual log-on screen (Figure 6.21) will then appear if you opted to use a password. Log-on in the usual way,

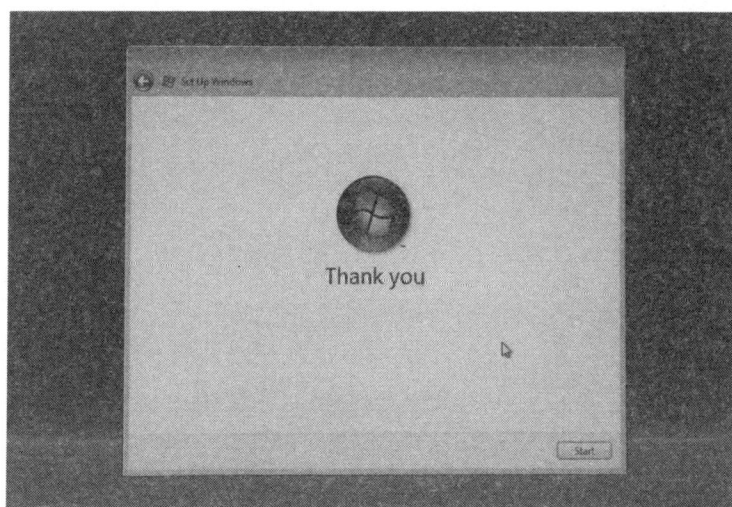

Fig.6.19 This screen indicates that the setting up has been completed successfully

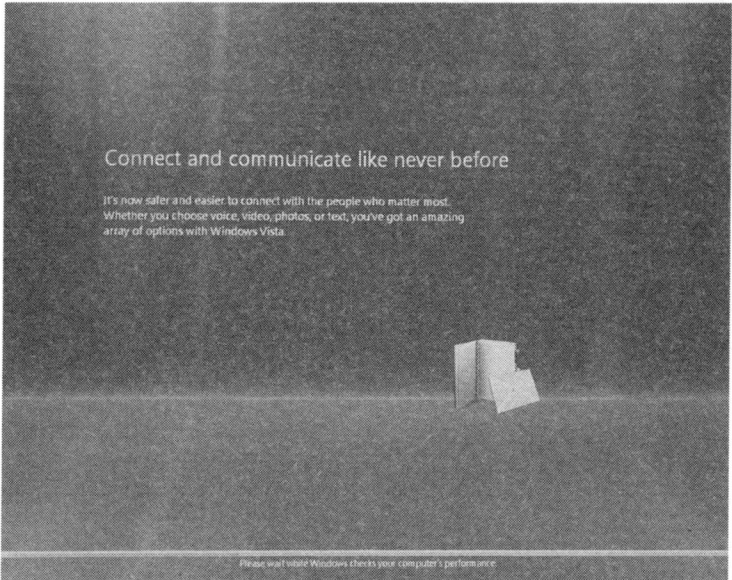

Fig.6.20 This is one of a series of information screens

Fig.6.21 Log on to the system in the usual way

and the Windows Vista desktop (Figure 6.22) should then be obtained. The desktop will appear straight away if no password was entered during the setting up procedure. Of course, it is just the bare desktop that is obtained when Vista is reinstalled from scratch. In order to get things back into full working order it is necessary to reinstall all the application software, reinstate any customisation of the Windows environment, restore your data files, etc.

Video settings

The resolution and colour depth of the video system is usually set at something fairly basic when Windows XP and earlier versions of Windows are installed. You then have to go to the Control Panel to set the required resolution and maximum number of colours. In most cases this is not possible because only a generic video driver is installed. The range of resolutions provided by a driver of this type tends to be a bit limited, as does its performance. In order to get the video system working properly

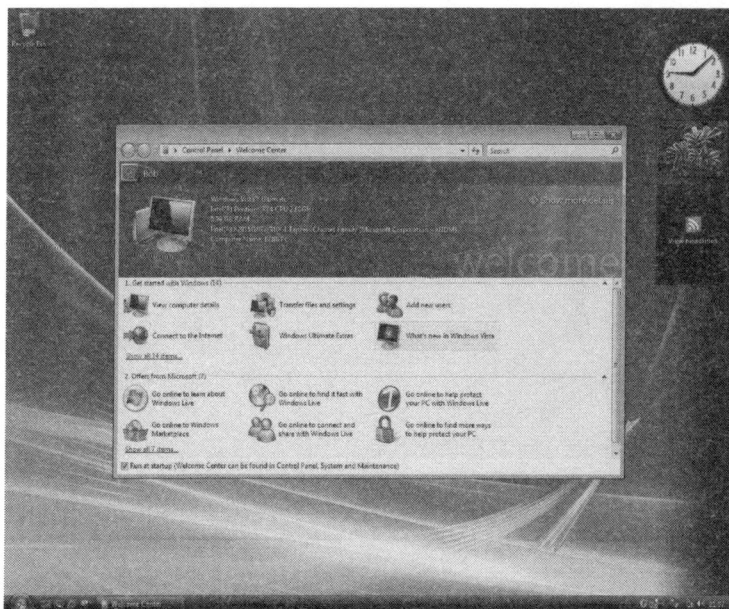

Fig.6.22 The computer has booted into the new Vista installation

it is therefore necessary to install the correct video driver software first, and then set the required parameters.

Essentially the same routine might be needed in order to get the video system working properly once Windows Vista has been installed. This will not necessarily be the case though. In this example the most up-to-date video driver was installed during the installation process, and the resolution was set at the optimum level for the flat screen LCD monitor. Presumably the monitor is a Plug-N-Play type, and the installation program set the resolution at the native level of the monitor.

Of course, Vista will not always be able to locate and install the optimum video driver. Its chances of success are quite good if you are using a video card that is a year or two old, but are rather less good if your PC is fitted with the latest card that has only just been released. Another point to bear in mind is that the installation program can not mind-read. It will apply settings which are likely to be the ones that most users will require, but it will not necessarily use the ones that you deem to be the most suitable. If you prefer something less than the highest available resolution

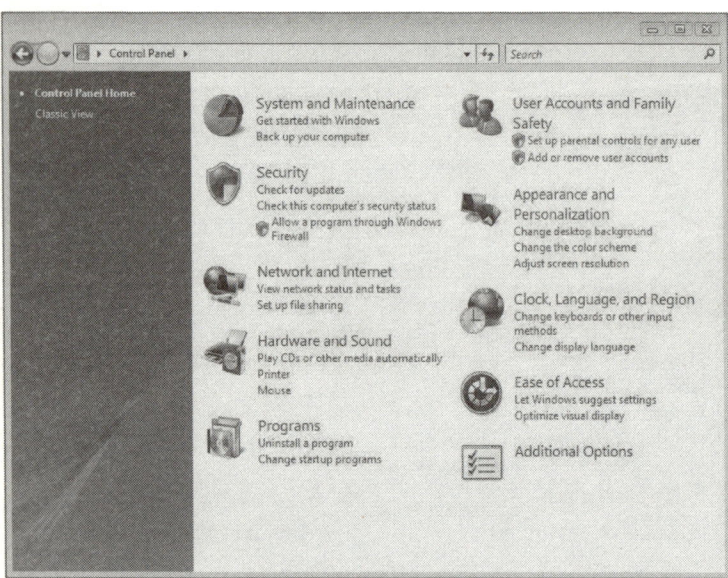

Fig.6.23 The Windows Control Panel (standard view)

so that the screen is easier to read, you will probably have to set the required resolution manually.

In order to adjust the video settings it is first a matter of going to the Start menu and launching the Windows Control Panel. With the Control Panel in the standard (Home) view (Figure 6.23), left-click the "Adjust screen resolution" link, which is in the "Appearance and Personalization" section. This produces the window of Figure 6.24 where the screen resolution can be adjusted via the slider control.

The colour depth is set via the "Colors" drop-down menu, but there will probably be just two options here. These will be 16-bit and 32-bit, with the latter probably being used by default. Using the 16-bit option gives over 65,000 colours, and this is adequate for most purposes. The 16-bit option is less demanding on the hardware, so it can be advantageous to use it if the computer has a relatively small amount of memory and (or) a processor that is not particularly fast.

The refresh rate of the screen is not usually too important with LCD monitors, but it is important to use the highest possible rate with CRT monitors. Using a low refresh frequency tends to give noticeable screen

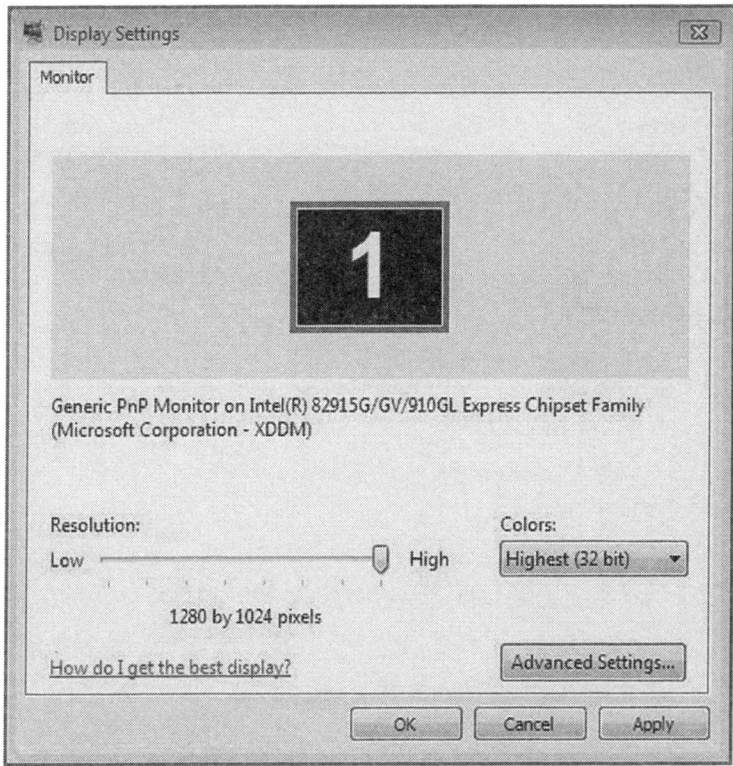

Fig.6.24 Use the slider control to set the screen resolution

flicker with CRT monitors. The refresh frequency can be adjusted by operating the Advanced Settings button, which produces a new window (Figure 6.25). This will probably show the Adapter section by default, but in this case it is the section under the Monitor tab (Figure 6.26) that is required. The pop-down menu should offer a few options at higher frequencies than the current setting, and it is a matter of using trial and error to find the optimum setting. This is the highest setting that enables the monitor to produce a proper picture.

The small window of Figure 6.27 appears when a new setting is selected and the Apply button is operated. At least, it will do so provided the monitor is capable of supporting the selected refresh frequency. If this window does appear, and a stable picture is obtained, operate the Yes

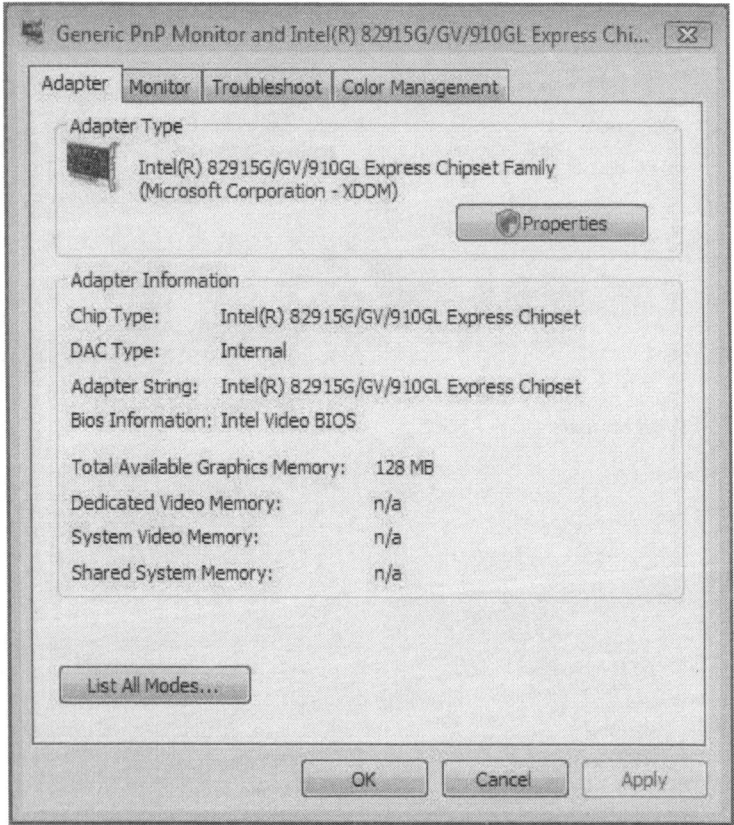

*Fig.6.25   The Adapter section of the window will probably appear by
default*

button. If not, the original refresh rate will be restored after six seconds,
and you will not be stuck with an unusable video system. You can then
try again using a lower refresh frequency. Note that the maximum scan
rate for a CRT monitor generally reduces as the screen resolution is
increased. Consequently, the higher the screen resolution used, the
lower the scan rate that will have to be set.

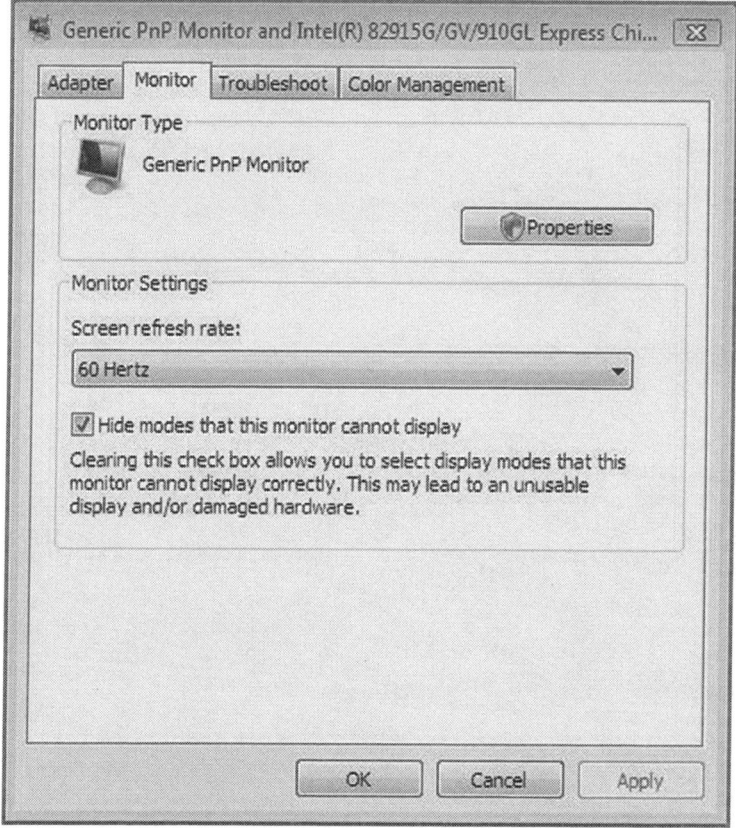

Fig.6.26 The menu offers a range of refresh frequencies

Video driver

The video system will not provide optimum results unless the driver software is the proper type for the video card, and it is the most up-to-date version of the software. If your PC or video card was supplied complete with video driver software for Vista, this can be installed in accordance with the manufacturer's instructions. It is possible that this software will be older than the version already installed, but you will then get an onscreen message to that effect and the installation will not go ahead.

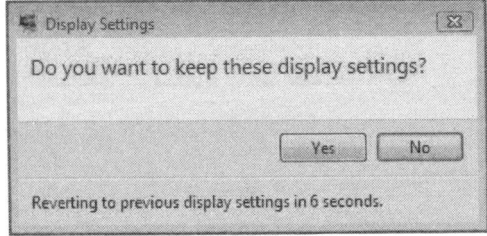

Although Windows has facilities for installing driver software, these are not necessarily used when installing device drivers. In fact it seems to be quite normal for hardware manufacturers to "do

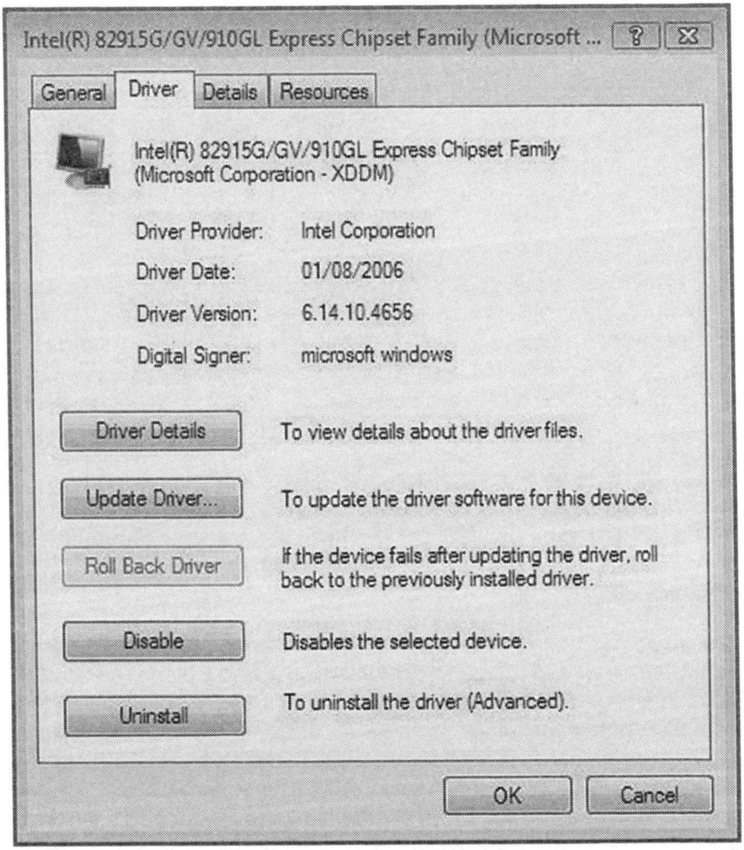

Fig.6.27 Operate the Yes button if this window is visible

Fig.6.28 Operate the Update Driver button

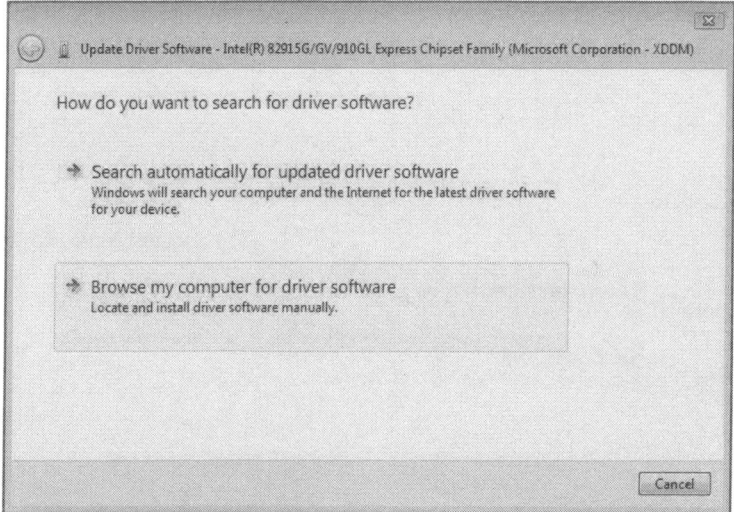

Fig.6.29 Just the computer or the computer and the Internet can be searched for more up-to-date drivers

their own thing" in this respect. Therefore, whenever you install hardware drivers, read the manufacturer's installation instructions and follow them "to the letter". There is no point in trying to install drivers through the official Windows route when the driver software is designed for some other method. The most common installation method these days is to run a Setup program that installs the driver software automatically, or in a largely automatic fashion. It is then just a matter of restarting the computer to make the changes take effect, and the hardware is then ready for use.

Updating

It is advisable to check that the video driver software you are using is the latest version, and one way of doing this is to go to the manufacturer's web site yourself to check for updates. The alternative is to let Windows do the searching for you. This is done by going into Device Manager and finding the entry for the piece of hardware that you would like to update. Double-click the entry to launch its properties window, or right-click its entry and choose Properties from the pop-up menu. Select the driver section of the properties window (Figure 6.28) and then operate the Update Driver button.

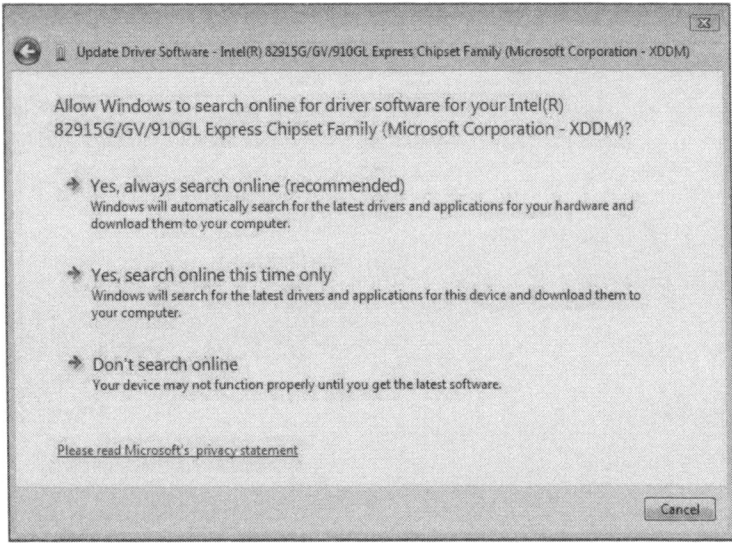

Fig.6.30 The choices here govern future searches for drivers

A new window will then appear on the screen (Figure 6.29), and this offers the choice of having Windows search the computer and the Internet for a newer driver, or just the computer. In this case it is the Internet that we wish to search for a new driver, so it is the upper link that is activated. The window then changes to the one shown in Figure 6.30, where three options are offered. These are to always search online, to only search online on this occasion, or to not search online at all. Either of the first two options will suffice in this case.

There will then be a delay while the search is made. You will be asked if you wish to go ahead and install the newer driver if something suitable is found. It is then just a matter of going ahead with the usual installation process, which is unlikely to require any input from the user. In this example a more up-to-date driver was not available, as explained by the information window of Figure 6.31.

Correct channels

The installation CDs supplied with most hardware includes a Setup program. However, in some cases the disc contains device drivers but it does not include a program to install the drivers. The same is true of

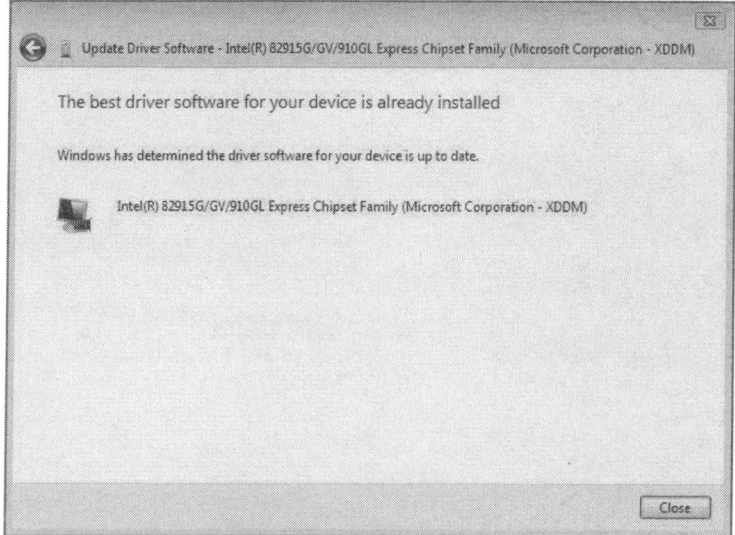

Fig.6.31 In this case no more recent driver was found

driver software obtained via the Internet. Where the instruction manual gives installation instructions, or the installation method is described in a Read.me file, always follow the supplied instructions. Using the wrong installation method could result in serious damage to the operating system, making it impossible to boot into Windows.

With some low-cost hardware you are simply left to your own devices. One way of tackling the installation of hardware of this type is to launch Vista's version of the Add Hardware Wizard. Go to the Control Panel, if necessary set the Control Panel to the Classic View, and then double-click the Add Hardware Wizard icon. This launches the first window of the Add Hardware Wizard (Figure 6.32).

Heed the warning notice about using the manufacturer's installation program wherever possible. Check the installation CD to ensure that it does not contain an Install or Setup program. Where the driver software was downloaded from a web site, check the site carefully for installation instructions, and also look through the downloaded files for a Read.me or other text file that might contain installation advice, or a Setup program.

If you are sure that there is no installation program, operate the Next button to move the wizard on to the next stage Figure 6.33. The Add Hardware Wizard uses the normal technique of providing information

Fig.6.32 The first window of the Add Hardware wizard

screens and offering various options. This window gives the option of installing the device manually or having Windows try to detect it. There is no harm in trying the detection method, but it is likely Windows is incapable of detecting the hardware if it has not done so already. If you opt for automatic detection it is likely that you will still end up taking the manual route. Anyway, for this example I tried automatic detection, which, as expected, failed to find the new hardware (Figure 6.34).

Operate the Next button in order to proceed with manual installation. This produces a window like the one of Figure 6.35. This gives a list of hardware types, and you must select the correct category for the device you are trying to install. Moving on to the next window (Figure 6.36) gives a list of manufacturers in the left-hand section, and devices for the selected manufacturer in the right-hand section. Obviously you should select the appropriate entry for your device if it is listed, but this is unlikely.

It is normally necessary to operate the Have Disk button, which brings up a window like the one of Figure 6.37. Either type the path to the disc and folder containing the device drivers, or use the Browse option to locate the drivers. Having pointed Windows to the drivers, operate the

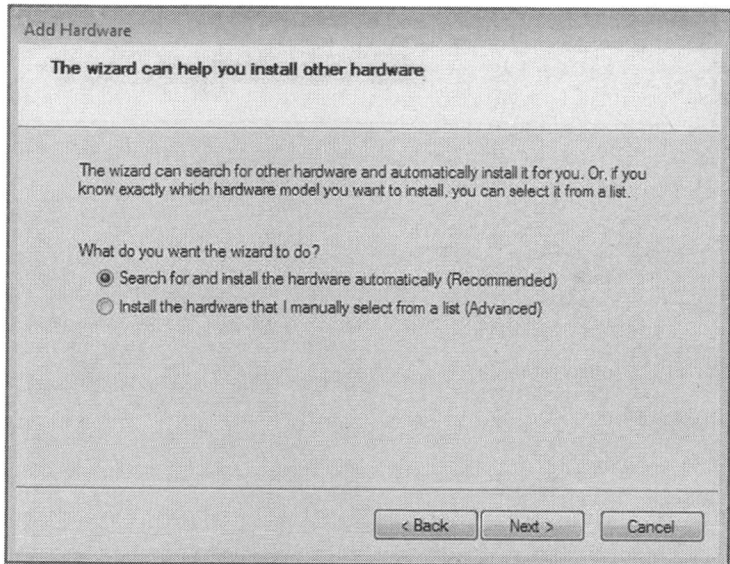

Fig.6.33 The driver can be installed manually or automatically

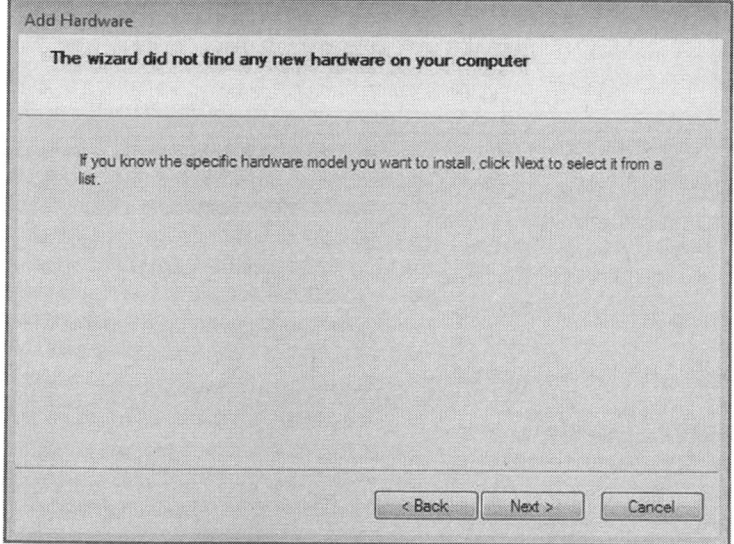

Fig.6.34 Automatic detection was not successful this time

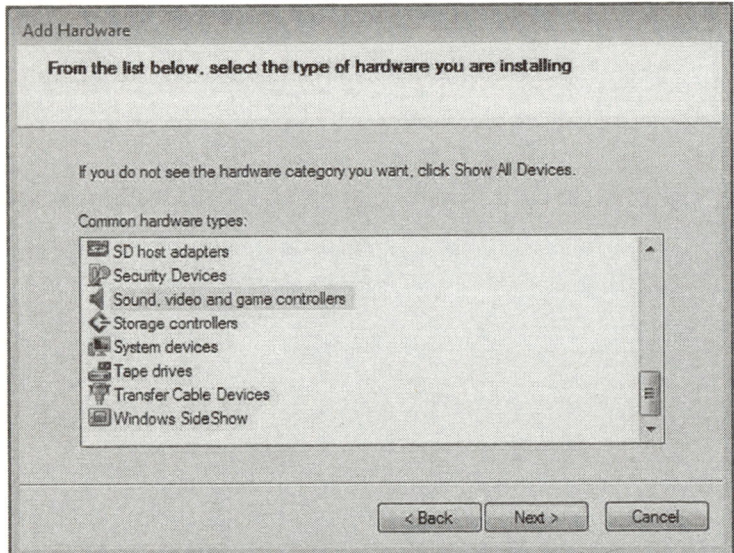

Fig.6.35 Choose the appropriate type of hardware

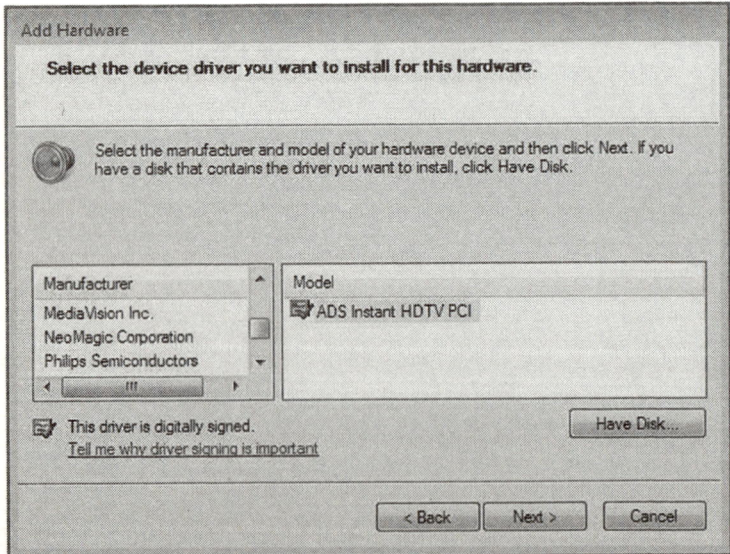

Fig.6.36 If it is listed, choose the device you are trying to install

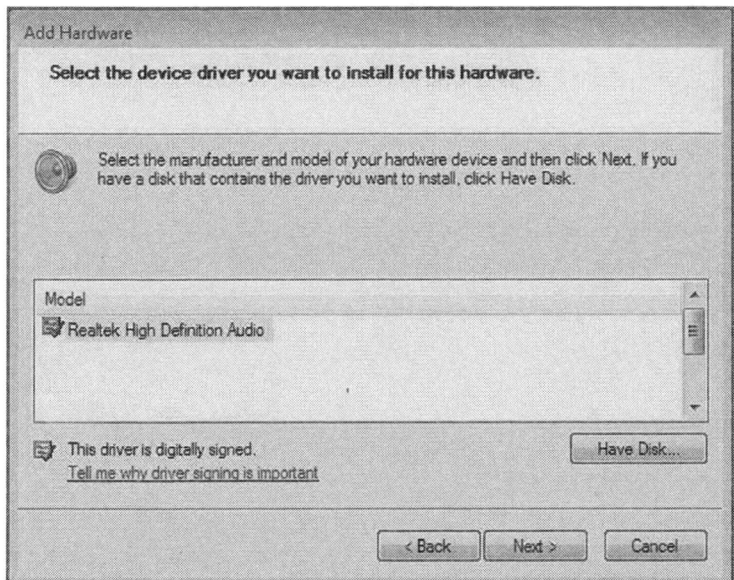

Fig.6.37 Operate the Have Disk buttonn and locate the driver files

Next button. You are then asked to confirm that the specified driver software should be installed (Figure 6.38), and the installation will then go ahead (Figure 6.39). It will probably be necessary to restart the computer in order to complete the installation of the new driver software.

Driver upgrade?

In many cases the problem is not that Vista has failed to find the hardware. The problem is that it has found and identified the hardware, but it can not find a suitable driver. There will be an entry for the hardware in Device Manager when this occurs, but there will also be a yellow exclamation mark against the entry (Figure 6.40). The General section of the device's properties window will explain that the driver software is not installed and that it is not working.

Although there is no matching driver software installed, the Update Driver button in the Driver section of the properties window will be active (Figure 6.41). It is therefore possible to update the non-existent driver using the normal procedure. Make sure that the driver software is available on

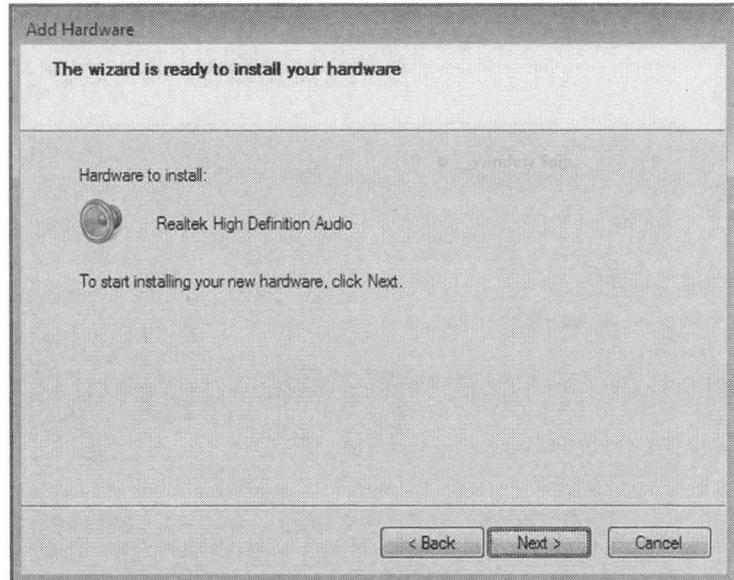

Fig.6.38 Confirm that you wish to install the driver software

one of the computer's drives so that update facility can find it when it goes through its search routine. The device in this example is a soundcard which came complete with a driver installation program. Running this program (Figure 6.42) and restarting the computer removed the exclamation mark in Device Manager and put the soundcard into full working order (Figure 6.43).

User accounts

One user account is produced as part of the installation process, but any further accounts have to be added once Vista has been installed and is working properly. The first step in adding a new account is to go to the Control Panel and double-click the User Accounts icon. This launches a window like the one in Figure 6.44. Then left-click the "Manage another account" link, and in the new version of the window (Figure 6.45) left-click the "Create a new account" link. This switches the window to the one shown in Figure 6.46. Type a suitable name for the account into the textbox.

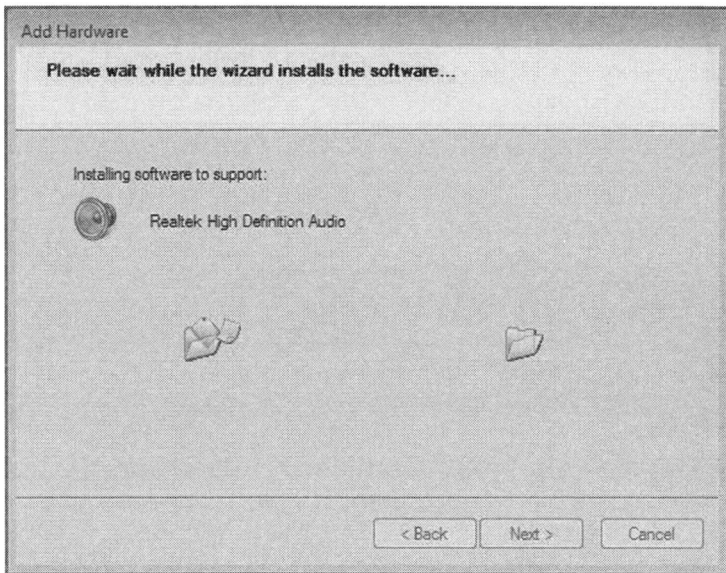

Fig.6.39 The installation is under way

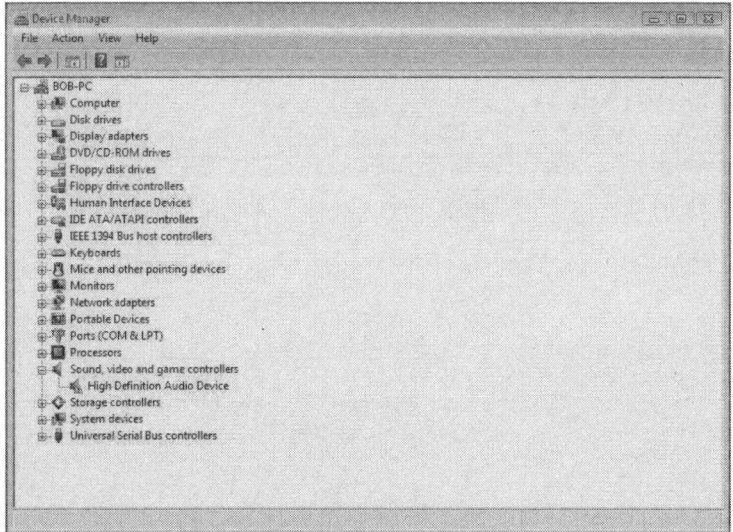

Fig.6.40 There is a problem with the soundcard

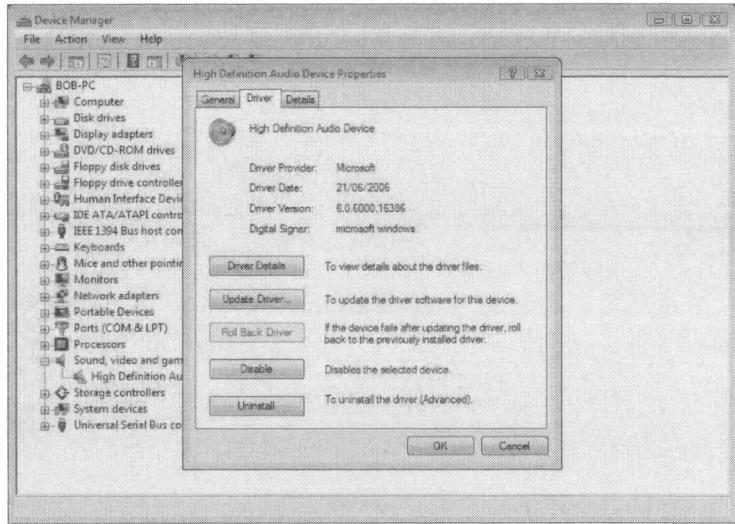

Fig.6.41 Operate the Update Driver button

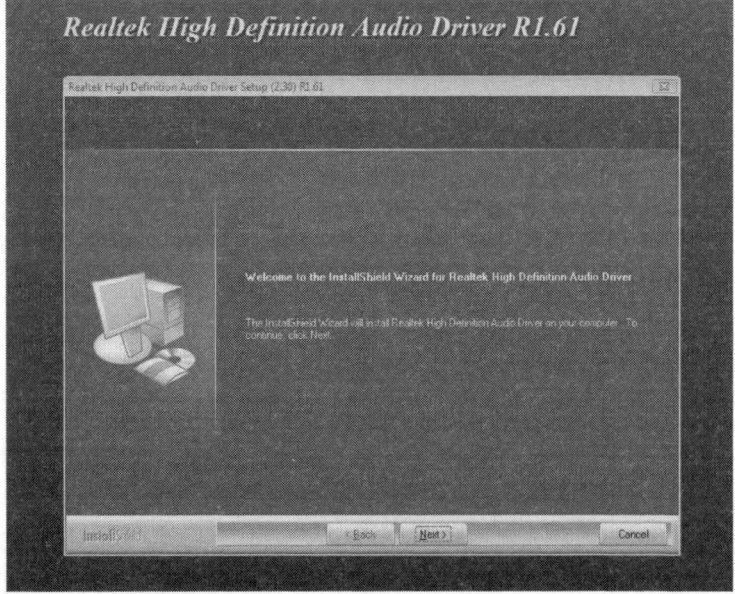

Fig.6.42 There was a driver installation program for the soundcard

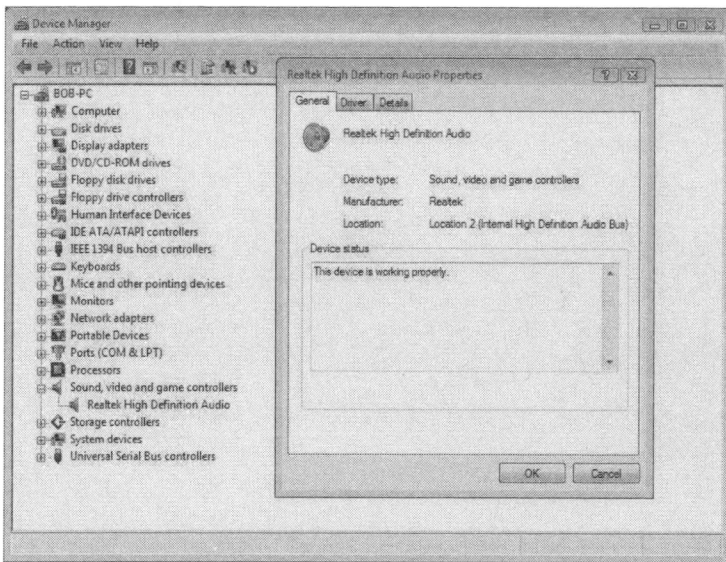

Fig.6.43 The soundcard driver software has been installed

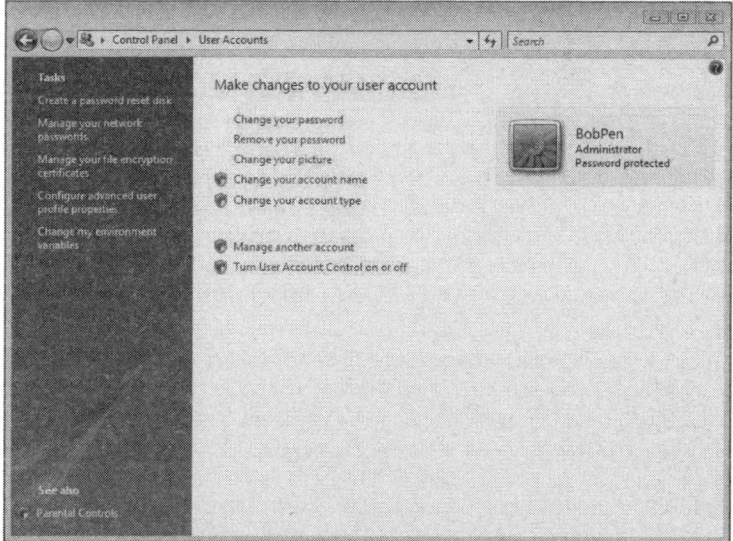

Fig.6.44 The User Accounts window

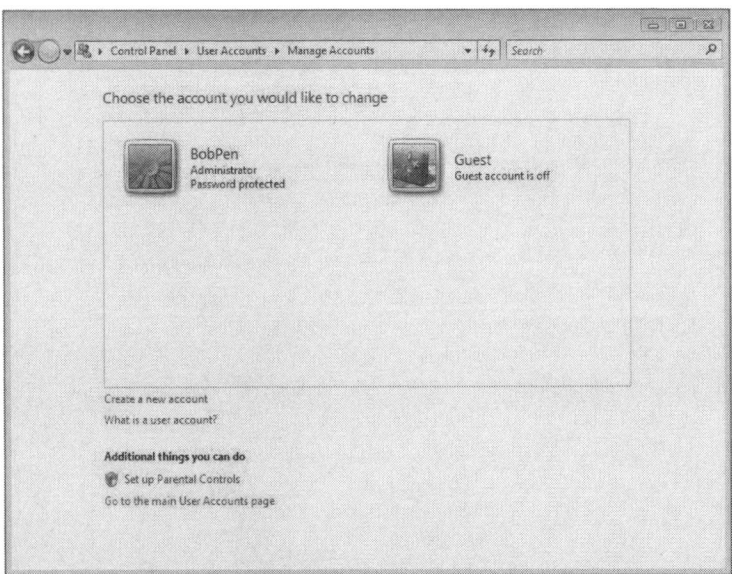

Fig.6.45 Left-click the "Create new account" link

The type of account is selected using the two radio buttons. An administrator account provides freedom to make changes to the system, but these abilities are not needed for day to day use of the computer. A standard user account, or limited account as it used to be termed, is generally considered to be the better choice for normal use, since its restrictions reduce the risk of the system being accidentally damaged. Note that you might not be able to install programs when using a limited account. Also, some programs produced prior to Windows 2000 and XP might not be usable with a limited account. Consequently, there is no alternative to an administrator account if maximum flexibility is required.

Having selected the type of account using the radio buttons, operate the Create Account button. The original User Accounts window then returns, but it should now contain the newly created account (Figure 6.47). There are other facilities in the User Accounts window that enable the log-on and log-off settings to be altered. By default, the Welcome screen is shown at startup, and you simply have to left-click the entry for the new account in order to use that account. Note that the new account will start with a largely blank desktop. Each account has its own desktop and other settings, so each account can be customised with the best

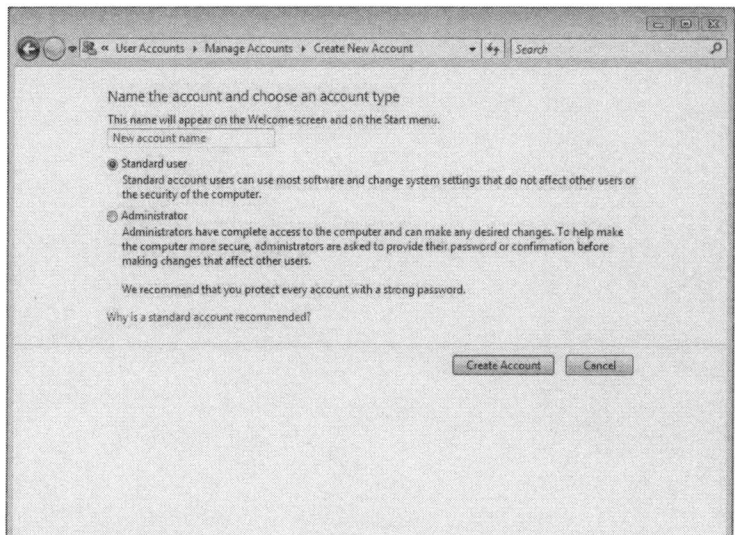

Fig.6.46 Type a name for the account into the textbox

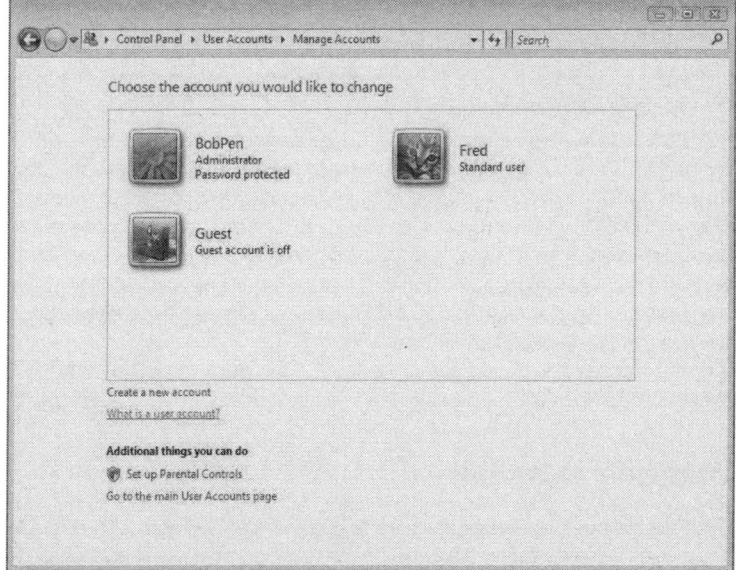

Fig.6.47 The new account has been created

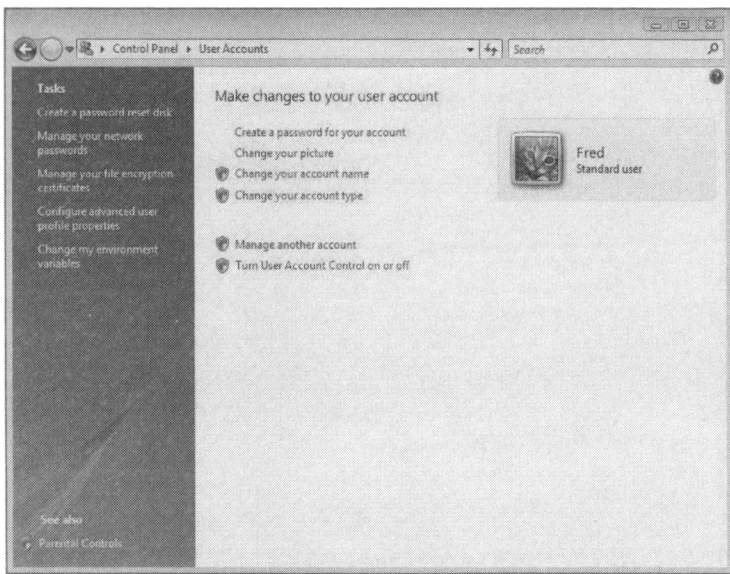

Fig.6.48 Left-click the "Create a password for your account" link

settings for its particular user. Of course, if software is installed using an option that makes it available to all users, then it will be available via all newly created accounts.

Accounts are not password protected by default. To add a password, log on to the relevant account, and then go to the User Accounts window (Figure 6.48). Next, left-click the "Create password for your account" link. At the next window (Figure 6.49) the password is typed into the top two textboxes, and a hint is entered into the other textbox. The hint is something that will jog your memory if you should happen to forget the password. Next operate the Create Password button, which takes things back to the User Accounts window (Figure 6.50), which should now show that the account is password protected. This completes the process, and the password will be needed the next time you login to that account.

Upgrade reinstall

As pointed out previously, it is generally worthwhile trying to reinstall Vista over the existing version before resorting to the "belt and braces" approach of reinstalling it from scratch. Reinstalling Vista over the existing

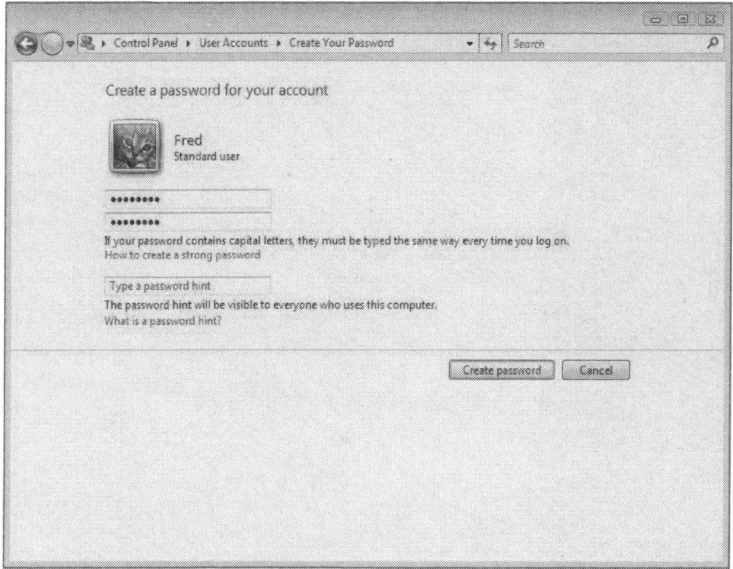

Fig.6.49 Enter the new password twice. The password hint is optional

version, provided it works, largely avoids the need to reinstate any customisation used in the original installation. With luck, you can just reinstall Windows Vista and then carry on using it as if nothing had happened. Of course, if the original problem was due to a virus or other form of malicious software, this must be dealt with before reinstalling Vista. Otherwise you will have a new and working copy of Windows that will soon run into problems again.

There is no provision as such for reinstalling Windows Vista over an existing installation. However, this is effectively what happens if the installation DVD is used to upgrade the existing Windows installation. Of course, no upgrade is actually taking place, since the upgraded version of Windows is the same as the original one. It simply has the effect of refreshing the existing installation, and (hopefully) repairing any damaged files or replacing any that are missing.

Note that even this method of reinstallation will probably require a certain amount of setting up, such as the reinstallation of non-standard drivers. Note also, that it is not possible to upgrade when running the computer in Safe Mode. It is necessary to start in Normal Mode, and have the

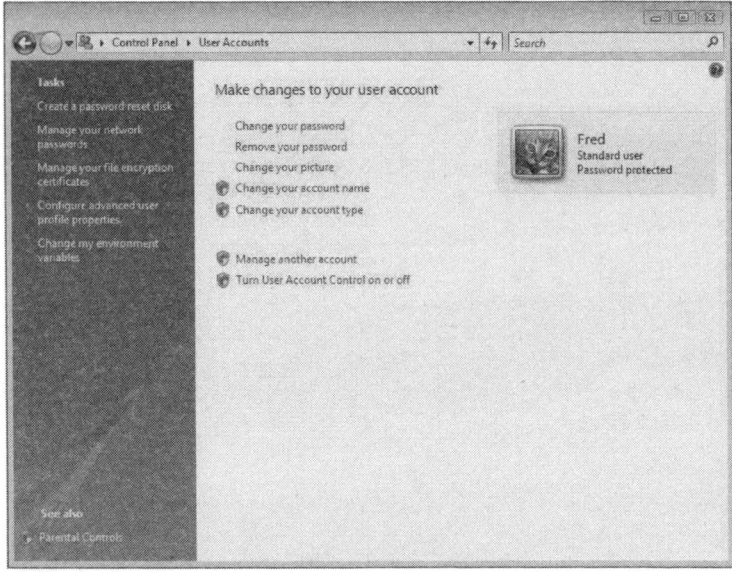

Fig.6.50 The account is now password protected

computer to some extent operational in this mode. The upgrade program must have at least a semi-viable installation to work with, and reinstalling Windows over an existing version is never likely to be successful where major damage to the operating system has occurred.

Points to remember

PCs that are supplied with Windows Vista preinstalled are not necessarily supplied with a normal Windows installation disc. Windows then has to be installed in accordance with the computer manufacturer's instructions. The exact method of reinstallation varies somewhat from one manufacturer to another.

Installing Windows Vista on top of an existing version might cure problems with the operating system, but it is not guaranteed to do so. Installing Windows Vista "from scratch", with all the previous files removed from the hard disc should effect a cure to any Windows problems. If it does not, the computer probably has a hardware fault.

When reinstalling Windows Vista from scratch it is necessary to reformat the hard disc, which can be done as part of the reinstallation process. This clears away any trace of the original installation, but all data will also be removed from the partition. Therefore, make sure that any important data is reliably backed up prior to installing Windows Vista from scratch. Data should not be lost when reinstalling Windows XP on top of the existing version, but it is a good idea to back up any important data in case there are problems.

The reinstallation process is largely automatic, but the user has to provide some basic information. The Setup program installs the Windows files and sets up the essential hardware.

Once Windows Vista has been reinstalled, some further work is usually required in order to get all the hardware properly installed. The screen resolution and colour depth might need adjustment. Some hardware has its own installation routines and does not go through the normal Windows routes. In fact, most hardware is now installed in this way. Always install hardware in accordance with the manufacturer's instructions.

Install the device drivers for system hardware on the motherboard first, followed by the video drivers, and then any other drivers that are needed.

6   Reinstallation

Do not install applications software until all the hardware is installed and working properly.

Any user accounts and passwords are lost when Windows Vista is installed from scratch. These can be rebuilt by going to the User Accounts window, which is accessed via the Control Panel.

It is possible to reinstalled Vista over an existing installation, provided the existing installation is not too seriously damaged. This will leave your original data, settings, and programs fully operational, and much as they were before the problem was encountered. This type of reinstallation is achieved by "upgrading" the existing installation.

Index